LANDSCAPE PLANTS FOR WESTERN REGIONS

An illustrated guide to plants for water conservation

by Bob Perry

To Russell Beatty
A good friend
Bob Perry

Published by
Land Design Publishing
Claremont, California, 91711

First Published 1992

LIBRARY OF CONGRESS CATALOGING-IN-PUBLICATION DATA

Perry, Robert C.

Bibliography: p. 305   Index: p. 311

1. Landscape Architecture—Western North America—Landscape Design. 2. Landscape Architecture in Water Conservation—Western North America—Water Conservation. 3. Botany—Ecology—Arid Regions Flora. 4. Plants—Cultivated—Western North America—Native Plants for Cultivation. 5. Plants—Ornamental—Western North America. 6. Gardening—Western North America—Landscape Gardening

Library of Congress Catalog No. 92-073474
Trade edition: ISBN 0-9605988-3-9
Text edition: ISBN 0-9605988-4-7

Printed by Dai Nippon Printing Company, Ltd., Hong Kong
Graphic Assistance: Geographics, Riverside, California

Contents

Foreword

I am pleased to have the opportunity to express these ideas on landscaping in a book. These ideas reflect some 20 years of study and observation in the field of landscape architecture. During this time, I have been principally interested in the study of landscape plants and how they can be used in our quest to develop a successful urban environment. This book emphasizes plants that are especially suited to dry climate regions with the belief that they can help in our efforts to conserve our resources, particularly water and energy. While there are many plants that can be grown in the richly varied regions of the West, plants that have naturally evolved and adapted to Mediterranean and arid climate regions are particularly appropriate. My desire is to describe and illustrate them in a manner that enables us to understand them more fully. Hopefully, this will help assist us in our efforts to improve the sustainability of our ornamental landscapes and to contribute to our appreciation of our natural environment.

This book has come about as a result of a long sequence of events. In the early stages when studying landscape architecture in college, I acquired a number of skills and ideas that emphasized what I call the traditional aspects and values of landscaping, namely, the development of spaces for people to live, work, and play within. Much of this effort was directed toward using plants for their visual character—their forms, colors, textures, and patterns. My goal was to achieve a landscape that had strong visual composition and seemed to address the specific needs and concerns of my client.

After I became involved in teaching, I began to study native plants of California. On field trips or family outings into natural landscapes, I felt particularly uneasy when someone would want to know the name of a plant they were seeing. This provided the impetus to develop an interest in expanding my knowledge of plants. Here was another area of challenge. I began this effort by doing some plant community studies in my planting design classes at Cal Poly, Pomona. Students and I would go out and select different sites to collect plant samples and then obtained reference material that helped identify these plants and explain their ecology. It was not long before I could see that my theory of planting design needed to embody an awareness of the natural landscape and the ecological relationships that sustain native plant species and communities.

In the early stages of this effort, I made the simple observation that much of California had a dry climate and that many native plants were adapted to drought. This, in combination with the 1974-77 drought cycle, led me to want to advocate the concept of water conservation. After several years of study, I was able to write a book that presented a number of plants that could be used in landscapes to reduce our water use. This was a good effort. One of the best decisions I made was to include as many color photographs as I could. I reasoned that most people needed some type of visual reference to help attract them and convince them that water conserving landscapes would look good. Pictures help us to shape and visualize our ideas in many ways.

Since the completion of **Trees and Shrubs for Dry California Landscapes** in 1980, I have pursued the study of landscape plants with renewed interest and rigor. I felt obligated to really know my stuff. I wanted to have so much information on plants that I could answer any question regarding their needs and tolerances, and could give the best advice on the ecological guidelines that influence our use of them. So, I collected better reference materials, made more field observations, and started to travel to other parts of the world in an effort to see some of our ornamental plants growing in their natural environments. I am far more attracted to this form of study and learning than to doing field tests and controlled research on a more focussed level. What I wanted was an overview—to see general patterns of plants at first, then specific details next.

This book is the product of my efforts. There are so many things I want to say regarding my observations and discoveries that it has become difficult to sort everything out. However, I am pleased with much of the material here. The photographs are improved, and the increased information on plant habitats is exciting. I have tried to bring greater attention to organizing plants in groupings that are similar to natural plant communities. In this process, my ethics have deepened towards plants and environment. I see the need more than ever to regard plants as living organisms that are not simply commodities to be used as clothing around our homes and buildings. I can see the need to respect the limits to all resources we use in developing and maintaining our landscapes—and to abandon habits of excessive consumption and waste. In particular, I see that our urban landscapes must contribute to overall environmental well-being on planet Earth.

To this end, landscapes must be planned and maintained in greater likeness to the principles and processes of natural environments. This will lead to landscapes that are more viable and require less use of resources. I believe in order to achieve these landscapes there will be a new balance among our values and attitudes that is deeper and wiser. Everyone wins. Landscapes will function in greater harmony, and people and the environment at large will be both enriched. The visual and aesthetic expression of these values will carry an even greater level of quality and cultural meaning than ever before.

Along the way in preparing this book, I discovered the value of many people and can see how much enrichment has been added to my thoughts, ideas, and information. I am inspired by many people, Scott Wilson, Jim Degen, Fred Lang, Lili Singer, and Randy Baldwin who embody a knowledge of plants and an attitude toward the challenge of landscaping that brings meaning to my efforts. Several people are close colleagues and friends who are mentors by their own method of living and working. Rod Tapp, Gordon Bradley, Francis Dean, Bob Clapper, Ken Nakaba, Jeff Olson, and Russell Beatty quickly come to mind. I have had the marvelous fortune to have been assisted by many fine people, including Verna Jigour, Karen Adams, Robert Black, Gerald Taylor, and Carrie Pryor. And, I have had the ongoing support and love from my family. My parents have always encouraged my goals and have provided generous support in meeting many of the costs of this venture. My wife, Faith, is my biggest fan. I express my deepest appreciation for her confidence and support throughout this effort and for her strong emphasis on family values and needs.

Section 1 Issues and Goals

Introduction:

When I first became involved in landscape architecture, I was quickly overwhelmed by two issues. First, how was I to learn to do good design? Second, how was I to learn so many plants? These were very early impressions and they seemed overwhelming and insurmountable. In retrospect, I was fortunate to see only two issues. Now when I stop to consider this beginning, I smile at the simplicity. Today, I tend to be overwhelmed by many more issues: how is it possible to design urban landscapes that are sustainable, functional, aesthetic, affordable, and socially and environmentally correct? I have discovered that the challenge and fulfillment of landscaping has become as far reaching as I have the ability to make it.

Like many people in this field, I have been working to understand this challenge and find a basis for my ideas and attitudes. In this effort, I have made a number of discoveries that are reflected in this book. Some come from specific areas of study, others come from experience and observation. For instance, the study of ecology describes a number of principles and concepts that are essential to landscaping. Ecology clarifies the need to have urban landscapes function and be managed in greater likeness to natural environments. This approach will contribute to the conservation and preservation of all resources—a very necessary goal to be pursued in all areas of human endeavor.

Landscaping is also a very human activity. We pursue it with the intent of making our places of home and work complete. In one regard, landscapes serve our health and safety. This includes actions such as stabilizing slopes, reducing fire risk, mitigating air pollution, and improving microclimates. In another area, landscapes help address our restorative needs through recreation, open space, and connection with natural environments. And, our landscapes very often convey values and attitudes of success, image, and aesthetics. A highly ornamental and well maintained landscape has become the standard goal in many urban areas. As a result, many people see this visual character as being one of the principal purposes of urban landscapes.

This section presents a series of thoughts regarding the changing nature of landscaping and our need to keep redefining our goals and knowledge. Many of these thoughts address environmental issues and encourage us to pursue the goal of sustainability by improving our ability to protect and conserve the natural environment and its resources.

The Pursuit of Landscaping:

I remember a simple survey done in the early 1970's that concluded that people involved in landscaping were essentially happy and satisfied with their work—that much of our purpose was to do good for people and the environment. Landscaping involved being outside and working with plants. Landscaping involved setting your imagination loose to create exciting gardens for people. These are still very satisfying reasons for many people to be in this field. However, many changes have occurred since this survey. The scope and emphasis of landscaping has become more complex.

In the last twenty years alone, landscaping has evolved from a casual and loosely defined practice to become an expected and even mandated commitment for all parts of our communities. Initially, landscaping was done by the individual and typically reflected the images and values they were familiar with: green and colorful. With time, the practice of landscaping started to make greater sense on a neighborhood and community scale, particularly with ongoing population growth and urbanization.

In response to this growth, a whole landscape industry has emerged to provide education, planning, design, construction, manufacturing, and maintenance services. Additionally, laws and ordinances at many levels of government have been developed that provide landscape guidelines and standards. We have become very prepared to do the business of

Landscaping combines art and science in addressing cultural, environmental, and economic goals.

landscaping in a very serious way. Landscapes are not simply an add-on, rather they are an integral part of achieving quality in our communities.

Today, landscaping is consistently planned for and implemented; it challenges all of our imagination and knowledge. With this commitment to landscaping, one of our most common goals, as well as successes, has been to make landscapes affordable and available to everyone. The benefit of landscapes, from parks and open spaces to personal gardens, is directed to all people. As such, landscapes address a diverse mixture of environmental, cultural, and economic goals.

From an environmental perspective, many people bring interest and concern regarding stewardship of the environment, including the conservation of resources, into the process of landscaping. With the passage of time, we are able to see these interests and concerns with greater clarity. One of the emerging concerns pertains to the concept of sustainability. We use many resources in the process of building and maintaining our landscapes. Understanding the value of these resources and their limits is highly important. Increasingly, we need to find ways to achieve successful landscapes with fewer resources. If we pause to look at the population growth in dry climate regions and observe some of the current landscaping practices, perhaps we can discover areas for change in the future.

Transformation and Resource Consumption:

The process of population growth and urbanization brings many changes to the land. In some areas, these changes have started with agriculture that is later replaced by urban communities needing more space for housing and industry. Much of this change has led to the complete transformation of the land and its natural landscape. With this transformation, native plants are destroyed and wildlife displaced;

In many dry climate regions of the West, natural landscapes have been removed for agricultural and urban uses on a remarkable scale.

many streams are channelized, and the land itself is reshaped to accommodate buildings and roads. We are mainly interested in the land itself, and we seldom fully understand or value the natural processes and features that we are altering and removing.

In many areas, this transformation is occurring on a vast scale. Many acres of land are developed each year to accommodate this growth. As a result, we must find an abundance of resources and use them to build our communities and landscapes. In dry climate regions of the West, we see a particular need to provide water to our new landscapes.

But, water isn't the only issue. Soils are amended with fertilizers, gypsum, and nitrogen stabilized sawdust. Virtually every square foot of the landscape is graded to improve drainage. Irrigation systems are installed that provide head-to-head overlapping coverage to assure that there are no dry spots. All of these activities, from supplying water, to manufacturing and installing drainage pipes, irrigation systems, and fertilizer involve the use of energy. These initial actions are completed in preparation for the planting of trees, shrubs, and ground covers. In the end, we have assembled an entire landscape.

Currently, this activity often reflects a very strong mandate for handsome visual character as quickly as possible. There is urgency to use fast growing plants, to provide lots of color, and to achieve an immediate finished appearance. In many cases, this results in the use of an abundance of turfgrass, and various shrubs and trees that are most highly appreciated for their visual appeal.

The demand placed upon resources doesn't stop with the construction of landscapes. Rather, we are at the beginning of a long term commitment to provide additional management and support to these landscapes for many years. There needs to be a careful accounting of resource use that is associated with both the construction as well as projections of long term maintenance.

Environmental Success of Ornamental Landscapes:

For many years we have been relatively uninhibited by the costs or availability of resources in pursuing our landscape goals. Instead, we have been preoccupied with providing these resources and services in a timely and convenient way. The challenge has often been seen as overcoming the deficiencies and conditions of the site. Soils are poor, summers are dry, water and plants are needed. Today, it is possible to see that the most difficult site can be transformed into a rich and lush landscape if we are willing to invest the resources to build and maintain it.

However, are we really succeeding in achieving some of our most basic landscaping and environmental goals? We need to assess this immediate success within a longer timeframe and from a broader perspective. There is not only the loss of the original landscape and its benefits, but we are now developing many types of landscapes that are successful only as long as we provide ongoing support from the use of water, energy, fertilizer, and labor. How much support is needed? How much is appropriate?

From one view, we can see that most ornamental landscapes in dry climate regions rely almost entirely upon a constant subsidy of water, energy, fertilizer, and maintenance. Such landscapes will quickly decline without this continual support. When we add up the amount of water, energy, fertilizer, and time we invest in landscapes over a 15 or 20 year period, we can see several significant economic and environmental costs. And, as our population increases, we are more rapidly seeing the limits to our resources and their ever increasing costs.

From another view, our landscapes are typically believed to be beneficial to people and the environment. This is a common and widespread belief that arises when we observe the landscape's visual appeal, feel the shade, and enjoy the sense of living plants around us. Landscapes that embody qualities such as these are often cited as a balance to various

 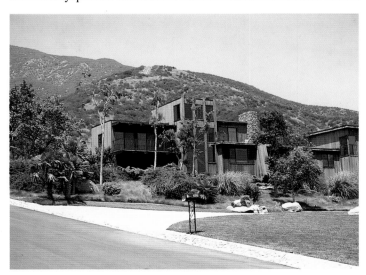

Ornamental landscapes in dry climate regions depend heavily upon water and energy resources, especially if they do not fit regional and local microclimates.

The urban environment is not complete without the development of ornamental landscapes including parks, street trees, and individual gardens.

ills and conflicts that are associated with urban life. Plants produce oxygen, store carbon, provide shade, filter air pollution, and even provide food and shelter to a wide variety of wildlife. From this view, we have largely assumed ornamental landscapes to be of positive contribution to the environment and have been slow to measure many of the environmental costs that are required to build and maintain them.

Recent case studies and research projects are beginning to challenge many of our assumptions and beliefs. In many instances, it can be demonstrated that our ornamental landscapes actually lead to a net depletion of resources from the environment, and contribute significantly to air, soil, and water pollution, as well as to the landfill space problems in many states. For example, just our use of fossil fuels alone, for operating our equipment, pumping water, synthesizing fertilizer, and hauling landscape clippings to landfills, consumes more oxygen from the atmosphere than our built landscapes can produce. This same consumption of fossil fuels also releases more carbon into the atmosphere than these landscapes can absorb. Chemical fertilizers, herbicides, and pesticides are widely used and are highly problematic on the basis of long term water and soil pollution. Additionally, a vast amount of greenwaste is generated from our landscape clippings that currently amounts to more than 30% of the landfill waste that comes from our residential communities.

These studies further reveal how many areas of landscaping result in wasteful consumption, resource shortages, and increasing economic costs. Vast amounts of resources are being used with little sign of constraint. With increasing frequency, a variety of resources are becoming limited in supply; in other cases, costs from unwise and inefficient practices are reaching new thresholds. From both an environmental and economic perspective, when ornamental landscapes require excessive amounts of energy, water, labor, and other resources, sustainability is diminished and ultimately, many of the goals and benefits of landscaping are not met.

Reducing the Costs, Improving the Benefits of Landscapes:
Based upon this discussion, a number of goals and actions in landscaping must be refined. Efforts must be made to understand the environmental costs and benefits of landscapes with greater accuracy and over longer periods of time. We must understand the significance of the natural environment that we have removed, and be capable of planning and managing a new urban environment that can be sustained on fewer resources. These issues need to be worked with at many scales, from the individual property to the entire community.

Several approaches can be used to improve the environmental benefits from our ornamental landscapes. One approach is to emphasize the idea of efficiency. We want to use our resources for the highest and best purposes, and to do so without waste. We should make sure to emphasize actions that lead to benefits such as microclimate and air pollution mitigation, fire safety, and recreational activities. Attention is brought to landscapes that provide the greatest benefit to the most people. In this process, efficiency also addresses the issue of waste. At every step, we should carefully manage the use of our resources to avoid wasteful practices that lead to excessive use of energy, water, and labor. Waste of resources is often one of the first areas to assess.

A broader foundation to improving ornamental landscapes can be found by studying the character and function of natural landscapes with respect to ecological principles and relationships. Natural landscapes demonstrate a high level of sustainability and can serve as a model to shape our ornamental landscapes. The sustainability in natural landscapes is highly efficient because all parts of the environment are intricately connected and work together as ecosystems. Additionally, these ecosystems have evolved over time to fit regional and local conditions, resulting in many different adaptations and relationships. Furthermore, even within the many different types of ecosystems that exist, the inherent use of energy and materials is done with an efficiency

Grading, soil amending, irrigation, and planting efforts are vigorously pursued in order to achieve ornamental landscapes.

Once a landscape is designed and installed, attention must be given to the long term management efforts. Virtually all ornamental landscapes quickly lose their value and character without proper maintenance activities.

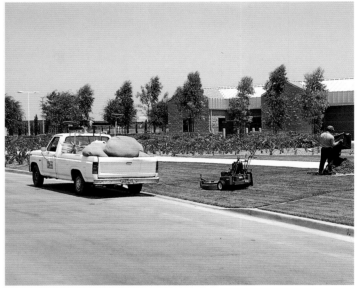

Landscape management efforts in ornamental landscapes must help to schedule and supervise regular maintenance practices including watering, mowing, pruning, trimming, fertilizing, weeding, and trash removal.

Greenwaste from the maintenance of ornamental landscapes currently comprises more than 30% of the solid waste that is produced in many communities. Much of this material is disposed in landfill dumps.

Planning decisions influence large scale land use patterns and development policies to work with the regional climate, topography, and natural ecosystems.

that is characterized by a high degree of recycling and reuse. But, natural landscapes go beyond concepts of efficiency. They have the marvelous capacity to adapt and to sustain a great diversity of life. A fuller understanding of the sustainability of natural landscapes can help us appreciate the value of the landscape that is being transformed for urban uses. It also helps us to understand our ultimate dependency upon the environment for our own survival.

With these ideas in mind, ornamental landscapes must increasingly be pursued with greater emphasis being placed upon the principles provided by natural environments. Landscapes should be viewed as whole systems and not be approached as assemblages of different plants. Landscapes need to be planned to fit within regional and local conditions in order to reduce the need to subsidize them with such a heavy reliance upon resources. Landscapes must be designed and managed upon natural adaptations and associations of plants and be given time to evolve, adapt, and become as much a whole system as is possible within the urban setting. These concepts can help reduce the costs and improve the benefits of ornamental landscapes.

In order to pursue these ideas, planning, design, and management efforts must be integrated. All three areas must work together on similar principles to produce landscapes that are not only efficient, but also recognize that we are working for the collective benefit of people and environment—and that true benefit can only occur when both are sustained.

Planning:

Planning is a process that helps us to establish our broad goals and policies regarding landscapes. Planning addresses these issues from a broad viewpoint and on a long term basis. Cultural, economic, and environmental goals must be identified, integrated, and given priorities; standards and guidelines can also be prepared for more specific actions. As population growth continues, these efforts need to reflect an ever expand-

ing agenda of needs and concerns with strong effort made to understand the limits placed on future choices.

At a large scale, we can assess how far a community can integrate and interact with the natural environment. It is at this scale of study that we are in a good position from which to choose how we are going to treat the topography of the land; the occurrence of watersheds, rivers, and streams; and to reflect the regional climate, vegetation, and wildlife patterns. Land use decisions regarding open space and recreation, circulation, housing, and development standards must be made. In some situations, there might be a lot of conflict with the natural systems of the land. But no doubt, communities and environments are partners in the greater scope of things, and this fitting together is necessary for both to succeed.

Planning also helps us to look at our many goals and policies with the future in mind. Policies regarding reclaimed water, groundwater basins, waste management, regional composting, urban forests, habitat protection, and species diversity must be addressed from a long range perspective. This effort helps us to identify basic limits and principles to guide our decisions. From an environmental perspective, it has always been difficult to understand the significance of the many resources we consume during our use of the land. The relative abundance and low cost of resources has helped to allay our concerns. Until recently, we have seldom looked for or assessed the extenuating impacts of taking vast amounts of resources such as water and energy from other regions. Concepts of responsible consumption, recycling, and reusing resources become more evident from the long term point of view. What good does it do to sustain ourselves at home, while overdrafting resources and causing loss elsewhere? Eventually, these resources will fail, and the losses will be accounted for, even at home.

Ecological principles can help us in the process of planning and in addressing broad goals and policies on a long term basis. One of the

Use of reclaimed water for landscaping and composting and reuse of landscape greenwaste need community level planning and action.

Planning goals, policies, and standards can help preserve riparian areas and influence the long term urban forest character.

most fundamental principles explains how highly interconnected everything is on this planet. At all scales of study, from regional to specific sites, we can see that the climate, land, plants, and animals are fitted together. This high level of integration is always at work and is always evolving. It has taken centuries of time to achieve the specific types of plants and animals on this planet and they are all heavily dependent upon many specific relationships that are all unified and working together. As a result, the success of all of the parts is dependent upon the success of the whole.

Since the beginning of this planet, these ecological principles and relationships have evolved in concert together and provide the foundation for everything to exist. If we disrespect these ecological relationships, we will slowly disassemble them and the life that is supported. If we continue this process at a large enough scale and for a long enough period of time, we can destroy the basis of life on a regional and global basis. We are currently seeing enough of this destruction to become concerned about the ongoing sustainability of our actions. Planning must help to consider the whole foundation and outcome of ornamental landscapes.

Planning can help tip the balance of many development decisions in favor of the environment and for our long term benefit. This can begin with a number of issues that apply at a regional scale. For instance, in dry climate regions decisions can reflect the scarcity of water and the abundance of sunlight and warm weather. This can be done in part through development patterns that address the orientation of buildings for microclimate benefit and with respect for fire hazard in transition areas. Urban landscapes can be planned to provide large scale open spaces, often with the intent to protect and preserve significant ecological features such as stream corridors and sites with high levels of biodiversity. Public lands can be landscaped with greater emphasis on the indigenous plant life and to work as a fabric to keep as much of the natural ecology intact as possible.

Perhaps one of the most important areas that planning can address pertains to education. It is relatively straightforward to see how influential education is. As we become more aware of these emerging issues, such as sustainability, it is important that we all participate in many types of educational experiences. This approach to understanding and integrating environmental considerations into cultural and economic goals can be our best long term strategy. Education can range from hands-on planting programs and school science projects to developing community preserves around sensitive ecological areas and botanic gardens and arboreta that people can visit and directly experience.

Design:

The decisions and choices made at the planning level will determine to a large extent the potential sustainability of urban landscapes. Good planning can provide a sound framework for design and management actions that further the goals of sustainability in landscaping.

Design involves a decision making process very much like planning. A clear set of goals and objectives needs to be identified, and a series of steps must be followed in order to make some very specific decisions. Design often occurs at a smaller scale than planning, usually a specific site, and is better suited to address the specific nature of sun, soils, plants, water, visual character, and aesthetics. All parts of this process, from goals to planting decisions, should reflect a number of basic environmental considerations.

Design decisions can emphasize conservation of water and energy in many ways. Plant species can be selected for their inherent compatibility with both regional and site specific conditions. These plants can be organized into groupings that are similar to natural plant communities leading to improved efficiency in water and soil management. Planting areas can be located and proportioned in size to achieve a functional and aesthetic balance between areas of trees and shrubs, turfgrass,

Educational programs and demonstration gardens inform people of conservation goals and techniques.

Photos by Tom Ash.

Design efforts can organize the landscape into planting zones for different needs and activities. In this process, various types of spaces can be created; water conservation, plant groupings, species diversity, wildlife value, seasonal character, and regional suitability concepts can be emphasized in many creative ways.

Design concepts can help reduce resource consumption by using plants to create microclimates that provide shade on buildings and outdoor spaces. This can reduce the energy that is used for summer cooling and include suitable groupings of plants that have lower supplemental water and fertilizing needs.

Irrigation systems can be designed that apply water with greater efficiency; composting and use of edible plants can conserve water and increase landscape productivity.

walkways, patios, and decking. Plant groupings can be located in suitable microclimate areas that are beneficial to the plants and that can lead to mitigation of sunlight and wind conditions on buildings. Effective placement of plants can help reduce the energy we use in heating and cooling our buildings and in creating pleasant outdoor spaces in Mediterranean and arid regions.

Landscapes can become more productive in a number of ways. Species can be selected for their edible fruits, as well as for wildlife benefit. Community gardens are a highly productive form of landscape that bring many people together where they become involved in growing plants. Parks and open spaces can be planned to use larger plant types that lead to increased levels of vegetative biomass for carbon storage and oxygen production. Park areas are often suited for species diversity and the use of native species that have been removed in other areas.

Landscapes often can be sustained with fewer resources through a number of design actions. The use of efficient irrigation systems can lead to significant water savings by limiting overspray and by placing water closer to the rootzone. Some areas can be graded to receive runoff from irrigation and rainfall to help infiltrate water that can sustain larger trees and their increased levels of biomass. In many situations, the landscape can be designed to be covered with organic mulches that help suppress weeds, reduce soil erosion, and retain soil moisture. This mulch can slowly decompose and improve the nutrient levels in the soil, thereby reducing the need for fertilizers.

Currently, we frequently select plants that are not highly adapted to dry climate regions and need regular care and attention to perform well. We also rely heavily upon irrigation systems and intensive maintenance to make everything work. This situation is aggravated when we mix plants into groups that have different cultural preferences and needs. Performance among plants is inconsistent, and by necessity most plants become subjected to the same maintenance routine. Over the years, this approach has led to standardized lists of plants that have proven to do well with simple maintenance and watering practices. Today, we rely more on plants for their tolerances than we do to select and organize them according to their preferences and compatibilities.

Management of Landscapes:
Good landscape planning and design seldom occurs without a strong understanding of landscape management schedules and maintenance practices. Management schedules the activities and resources that help keep the landscape viable and functioning.

In practice, the actual point of resource conservation occurs in the area of managing landscape maintenance activities. A very good example of this applies to our irrigation habits. Currently, we are overwatering many of our urban landscapes. All too often this overwatering is excessive and leads to many plant diseases and other management problems. In addressing this excessive water use, it is a widespread observation that the greatest area of savings can come through proper scheduling and attention to the repair and adjustment of irrigation systems. In these situations, improving irrigation scheduling and maintenance can save more water than making radical changes to the plants we are currently using. Recent developments in measuring evapotranspiration loss in dry climate areas are helping us to identify the amounts of water to provide to our landscapes on a daily, weekly, and seasonal basis.

Another basic management concept pertains to the growing and resting cycle of plants. Plants that are adapted to Mediterranean and arid climates have evolved with strong correlation to the availability of water. As a result, many of these plants have active growing and flowering cycles in late winter and spring, and become less active from summer through fall as water supplies fail. The year around irrigation of these plants, particularly during the summer, leads to excessive growth and soil and water-related disease problems.

Soil and weed management can also reflect the inherent adaptations of Mediterranean and arid climate type plants. Many plants that are adapted to dry summers fall prey to diseases associated with summer watering. Warm, moist soil leads to very active decomposition of organic matter that is fully capable of attacking the roots and living tissue of plants. Many western natives cannot survive this condition easily. The most visible case in point are native oaks. However, it is true of many other natives as well. It has been noted that young plants are often quite vigorous and have a greater capacity to resist pest and disease problems. Older plants, or ones that are stressed by drought and injury, are less capable of resisting some of these types of problems.

Weed abatement and natural soil development can begin with the use of organic mulches. This material can retard weed growth, reduce the loss

of moisture from exposed soils by evaporation, and keep the root zone of many plants cooler. These mulches slowly decompose and release nutrients into the soil and only require periodic replenishment.

Looking to the Future:
Future ornamental landscapes should be planned, designed, and managed to provide a greater number of benefits, from microclimate improvement to air pollution mitigation and wildlife support. Additionally, landscapes must become more efficient regarding the use of energy, water, and labor. On first consideration, these observations suggest a straightforward appeal for improving the costs and benefits of landscapes. We want to achieve our urban landscape goals with improved levels of efficiency. We want to preserve a little more of nature. We want to save water, control maintenance costs, reduce trash, and economize wherever possible. With this approach, the use of plants and other resources in our landscapes can be planned more carefully using budgets and management techniques.

On further consideration, we are also being challenged to rethink our cultural perceptions and attitudes. Many of our current attitudes and values encourage us to value resources such as land, water, and plants as simple commodities. Our concern for resources is directed to obtaining and using them—not where they come from, or what happens after their use. Often, there is little respect for the inherent qualities of every living thing, or for the ecological relationships that enables all life to successfully survive. The need for ornamental landscapes will not diminish. Western regions are among the fastest growing areas within the United States, with the population increase in California alone averaging more than 750,000 people each year from 1980-1990. This trend is expected to continue. However, the combination of increasing costs, resource shortages, and greater environmental awareness is leading us to reassess our landscaping efforts.

Attitudes and values that do not regard the fundamental limits of resources and that cannot appreciate the need for the whole ecology of our environment will eventually lead to failure. When landscapes continue to require excessive amounts of resources, supplies diminish, costs increase, and ultimately, the goals of sustainability are lost. Maintaining the ecology of our environment is the key to success, not maintaining ornamental landscapes at the expense of this ecology. Using this value as a foundation, conservation and efficiency can be achieved with greater success. Planning, design, and management that reflects these ideas can lead to greater sustainability in landscaping.

Ornamental landscapes can be planned, designed, and managed with increased levels of efficiency and productivity.

Section 2 Regional Characteristics

Introduction:

A sustainable condition within an ornamental landscape begins with a strong relationship to the nature of its region. In looking at western states we observe splendid diversity and regional variation in terms of climate conditions and physical habitat characteristics. Climates range from cool and wet in the Pacific Northwest to arid and dry in the southwestern deserts. Habitats range from coastal edges and bluffs to foothills, valleys, and mountains. Additionally, there are long distances between southern and northern regions; elevations range from below sea level to over 14,000 feet, and soils vary from deep valley loams to clayey marine sediments.

These many climate and habitat variations provide important parameters to guide many of our landscape decisions. By understanding factors such as seasonal rainfall, temperatures, evapotranspiration stress, and soil characteristics, we are able to select plants and develop landscapes that are appropriate to specific locations. In this effort, it is helpful to develop a basic understanding of climate and habitat characteristics at both a regional and a local scale. This section provides a summary of regional characteristics in areas that experience dry climate conditions. Maps have been prepared to illustrate a number of regions along with summaries of information to help explain their differences.

Landscape Regions:

Landscape regions can be defined on the basis of large scale climate and habitat features. Climate is the result of large scale movements of air across land and water surfaces. We most frequently describe climate in terms of temperature, rainfall, humidity, and wind. These aspects of climate are always changing in a cyclical manner: daily, seasonally, annually, and longer. At a minimum, it is desirable to understand the temperature extremes, rainfall amounts, and wind conditions on a seasonal and annual basis for each region. In dry climate regions, we have developed a special interest in the calculation of regional and local evapotranspiration stress. Evapotranspiration is a term that describes the amount of moisture that can be lost from the evaporation of surface soil moisture and from the cooling transpiration processes of plants. This moisture loss is highly dependent upon such conditions as wind, humidity, temperature, daylight length, and moisture availability. This issue is discussed in greater detail on page 29.

We can expand our understanding of landscape regions by studying other habitat characteristics such as topography, geology, soils, and the occurrence of water bodies. Topography that is comprised of foothills and valleys will change air currents, influence the movement of precipitation, and modify the intensity of sunlight. Latitude north or south of the equator has major bearing upon temperature and precipitation and the length of growing seasons throughout the year. Regional geology underlying topography is also an important basis for the development of soils. Rainfall occurs in greater amounts at higher elevations, on ocean facing slopes, and in northern latitudes. Evapotranspiration stress increases in areas that have longer warm seasons, more equatorial latitudes, and are further from ocean influences. Daytime temperatures are cooler at higher elevations. Nighttime temperatures are also cooler at higher elevations, but where topography permits, cool air drains from high elevations into valley floors. During winter months, cold downslope air brings frost to valleys in all regions whether coastal, inland, or desert. All of these factors help us to distinguish landscape regions and provide us with a framework for selecting landscape plants.

When we turn our attention more directly to areas of the West that have dry climate conditions, it is possible to see a number of significant differences that help us to identify different types of dry regions. From a large view, these dry regions are dominated by two basic types of climates. One type of climate is Mediterranean, the other is arid or desert. These climates are shaped by the interaction of maritime influences

Mediterranean climates throughout California exist as a result of the occurrence of the Pacific Ocean.

occurring within the Pacific Ocean and the gulfs of California and Mexico with influences stemming from the large land masses of the continent. Climates that are dominated by ocean bodies typically have moderate temperatures and higher levels of moisture; Mediterranean climates distinctly reflect this ocean influence. Climates that are shaped within continental regions are colder and can be quite dry. Arid climates throughout the Southwest are strongly dominated by continental influences that result in very low amounts of rainfall and colder temperatures at higher elevations.

Mediterranean Climates and Regions:

Much of California, from the San Francisco Bay area south to San Diego, experiences a Mediterranean type of climate. Generally, this climate provides moist and cool winters, warm and dry summers. Rainfall typically occurs during the late fall through early spring but often is erratic and unpredictable in occurrence. This is complicated by the recurrence of drought cycles that can last for many years in a row. In normal years, winter rainfall typically ranges from 10-25 inches; the summer dry season often extends from May until November. This climate is also described by climate experts as being humid subtropical as a result of the moisture in the air and the infrequent occurrence of heavy winter frost. Conditions adjacent to the coast are distinctly mild and absent of frost. The ocean influence dominates the climate 80-90% of the time, resulting in morning fog, daily afternoon winds, and lower maximum temperatures. The frost map on page 18 illustrates the influence of the ocean and the mean annual frequency of winter frost among various landscape regions.

Upon closer study, this Mediterranean climate isn't the same everywhere. A great deal of variation exists within this climate as a result of

Arid regions in the Southwest are dominated by climate stemming from continental land masses and separation from coastal influences.

However, not all desert regions are alike. Significant differences exist as a result of temperature extremes and the season of precipitation. Communities such as Palmdale and Victorville, occuring within high desert regions of the Mojave, experience long, cold winters with regular frost. Rainfall can be as little as 2-4 inches and occurs only during the winter months. This combination of conditions make the high desert region one of the most difficult planting areas in the West. Lower Colorado desert regions from Palm Springs to Blythe and near to Phoenix seldom have frost but have higher summer temperatures that last for longer periods of time. The Arizona Upland desert around Tucson experiences both heat and cold but not to the same extreme levels as the high and low deserts. This is an intermediate region that has two seasons of rainfall, winter and summer. The summer rains are the result of storms that develop within the Gulf of California. This rainfall pattern leads to two growing cycles among many native desert plants.

Helpful References:

Barbour, Michael G., and Jack Major, ed. Terrestrial Vegetation of California. New York: John Wiley & Sons, 1977.

Brown, David E., ed. "Biotic Communities of the American Southwest—United States and Mexico." Desert Plants. Volume 4, Numbers 1-4. University of Arizona, 1982.

Critchfield, William B. Profiles of California Vegetation. USDA Forest Service Research Paper psw-76. Forest Service. U.S. Department of Agriculture. Berkeley, 1971.

Hogen, Elizabeth L., ed. Sunset Western Garden Book. Menlo Park, California: Lane Publishing Co., 1988.

Holland V. L., and David J. Keil. California Vegetation. San Luis Obispo, California: El Corral Publications, California Polytechnic State University, 1989.

Kahrl, William L., ed. The California Water Atlas. Governor's Office of Planning and Research in cooperation with the California Department of Water Resources. Sacramento: the State of California, 1979.

Kuchler, A. W. The Map of the Natural Vegetation of California. Lawrence, Kansas: University of Kansas, 1977.

Munz, Philip A. A Flora of Southern California. Berkeley: University of California Press, 1974.

Pacific Gas and Electric Company. Generalized Plant Climate Map of California. San Francisco: Pacific Gas and Electric Company, 1989.

the diverse California topography and changes in latitude from northern to southern regions. Foothills, mountains, and valleys influence temperature, sunlight, and rainfall patterns tremendously from area to area.

Northern coastal regions near San Francisco are influenced to a greater extent by the cooler and more moist maritime climate of the Pacific Northwest. In contrast, as we travel south through Los Angeles to San Diego, we find an increasingly dry and more subtropical and arid climate. Winter storms are typically stronger in northern areas and become weaker as they move south. The rainfall map on page 19 shows the relative abundance of moisture that occurs in northern regions and at higher elevations in contrast to southern regions and inland deserts. The evapotranspiration map on page 31 illustrates the significant increase in potential moisture loss from the landscape due to warmer and drier conditions in southwestern areas. Additionally, when we travel inland from the coast, we encounter a number of foothills, mountains, and valleys that cause many areas to have more winter frost and higher average summer temperatures. Inland regions are increasingly cooler in the winter, drier and warmer in the summer. In the parts of southern California that are further from the coast and closer to the deserts, the climate can be dominated by air from continental land masses by as much as 85% of the time.

Arid Climates and Regions:
The Mediterranean climate largely stops in California along the western slopes of the Sierra Nevada, and along the San Gabriel, San Bernardino, San Gorgonio, San Jacinto, and Palomar mountains. In these mountain ranges, elevations above 5,000 feet often experience snow during the winter and become more of a temperate climate with distinct winter seasons that are colder and more moist. These tall ranges do not permit much winter moisture from maritime sources to reach past their slopes to areas that are further inland to the east. This situation leads to the development of several desert regions throughout the Southwest. These include the Mojave, Lower Colorado, and Arizona Upland deserts. The climate of these regions ranges from cool arid to arid subtropical. Rainfall is extremely scarce. By one definition, a desert is a region where annual rainfall is less than 10 inches. At the same time, the higher temperatures and low humidity lead to very high moisture loss from soil, water bodies, and plants.

All desert areas are greatly influenced by intense sunlight, wind, and aridity that combine to create a year around drying influence on plants.

The rainfall map on page 19 / The evapotranspiration map on page 31

Map of Landscape Regions (Right)

The study of climate and habitat characteristics in parts of the West helps us to recognize a number of landscape regions. These regions are highly varied in size and shape and reflect significant differences in moisture, temperature, topography, and soils. From this view we can see that many major urban areas have developed within regions having dry climates and scarce water resources, particularly in the Southwest.

The environmental diversity and complexity of western regions provides many exciting opportunities regarding the variety of plants we can use in ornamental landscapes. In addition, when we look at these broad regions at a smaller scale, we discover many other important microclimate and habitat conditions that are important for landscape consideration. As a result, we find that a tremendous variety of plants will thrive and grow within very short distances of each other due to the diversity and complexity of local conditions.

We have also discovered that many of the dry climate regions can sustain even greater landscape diversity if we provide supplemental water. In an effort to help manage the use of water and other resources, the regional maps on the following pages help us see the underlying characteristics and conditions on a broad scale. This can help us plan and design landscapes that have greater compatibility with regional conditions.

The regions on this map reflect unique combinations of temperatures, soils, rainfall, evapotranspiration stress, and natural vegetation. Detailed descriptions of many of these regions occur on the following pages.

Map of Landscape Regions

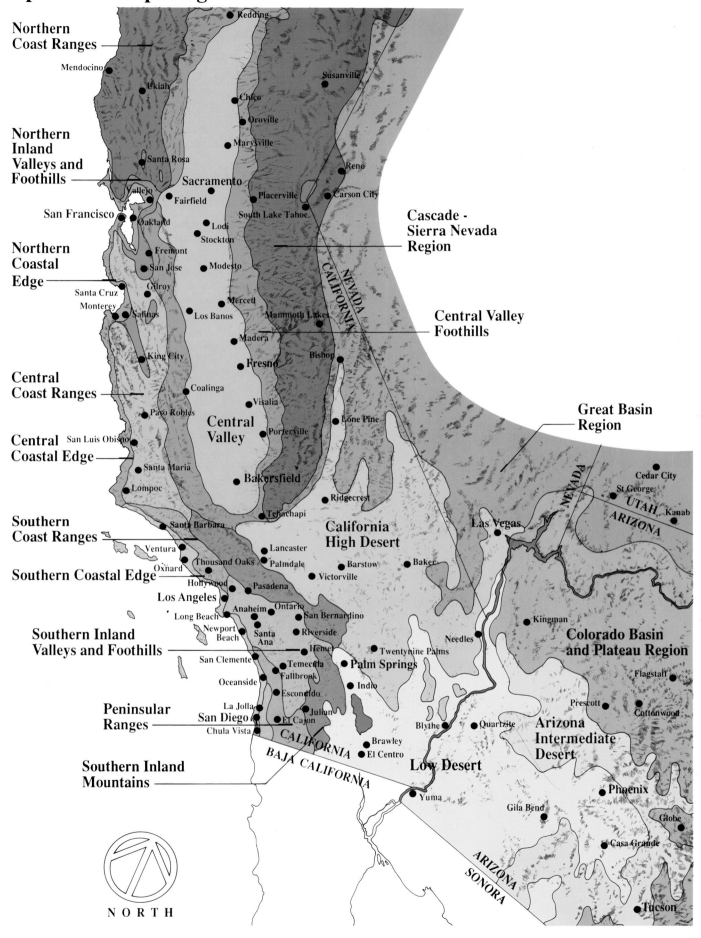

Northern Coast Ranges

Northern Inland Valleys and Foothills

Northern Coastal Edge

Central Coast Ranges

Central Coastal Edge

Southern Coast Ranges

Southern Coastal Edge

Southern Inland Valleys and Foothills

Peninsular Ranges

Southern Inland Mountains

Cascade - Sierra Nevada Region

Central Valley Foothills

Great Basin Region

Colorado Basin and Plateau Region

Arizona Intermediate Desert

Central Valley

California High Desert

Low Desert

Redding
Mendocino
Ukiah
Chico
Oroville
Susanville
Marysville
Santa Rosa
Reno
Vallejo
Sacramento
Fairfield
Placerville
Carson City
San Francisco
Oakland
Lodi
Stockton
South Lake Tahoe
Fremont
San Jose
Modesto
Gilroy
Merced
Santa Cruz
Monterey
Salinas
Los Banos
Mammoth Lakes
Madera
King City
Bishop
Fresno
Coalinga
Visalia
Paso Robles
Lone Pine
San Luis Obispo
Porterville
Santa Maria
Lompoc
Bakersfield
Ridgecrest
Tehachapi
Santa Barbara
Ventura
Lancaster
Thousand Oaks
Palmdale
Oxnard
Barstow
Baker
Hollywood
Victorville
Pasadena
Los Angeles
Anaheim
Ontario
Long Beach
San Bernardino
Newport Beach
Santa Ana
Riverside
Hemet
San Clemente
Temecula
Twentynine Palms
Fallbrook
Palm Springs
Oceanside
Indio
Escondido
La Jolla
Julian
San Diego
El Cajon
Chula Vista
Blythe
Brawley
El Centro
Yuma
Las Vegas
Cedar City
St George
Kanab
Kingman
Flagstaff
Prescott
Cottonwood
Needles
Quartzite
Phoenix
Gila Bend
Globe
Casa Grande
Tucson

CALIFORNIA
NEVADA
UTAH
ARIZONA
BAJA CALIFORNIA
SONORA

NORTH

Frost Map for Landscape Regions

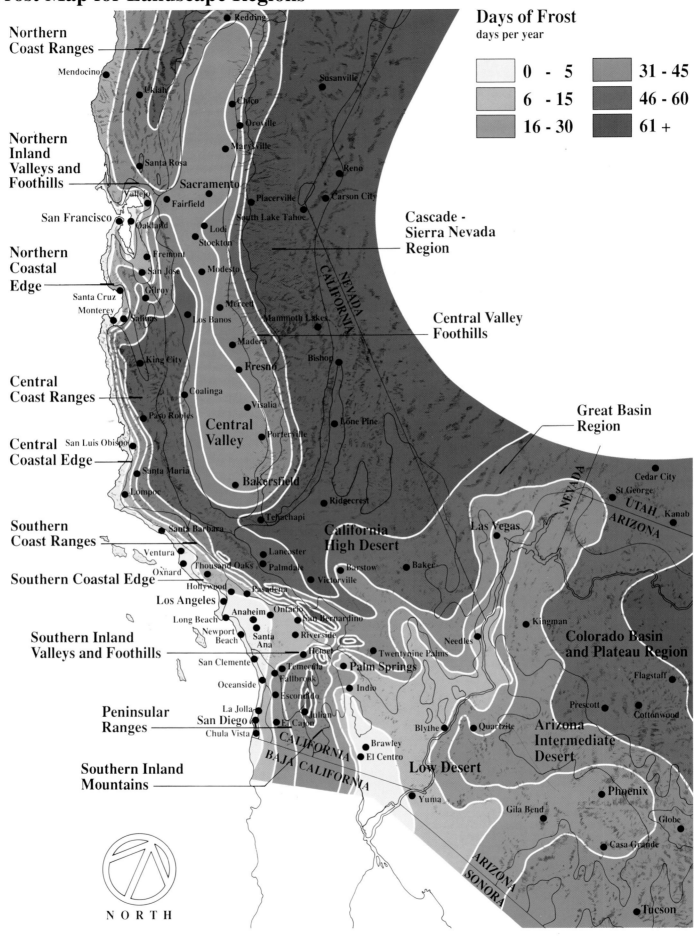

Days of Frost
days per year

0 - 5	31 - 45
6 - 15	46 - 60
16 - 30	61 +

Northern Coast Ranges

Northern Inland Valleys and Foothills

Northern Coastal Edge

Central Coast Ranges

Central Coastal Edge

Southern Coast Ranges

Southern Coastal Edge

Southern Inland Valleys and Foothills

Peninsular Ranges

Southern Inland Mountains

Cascade - Sierra Nevada Region

Central Valley Foothills

Great Basin Region

Mendocino · Redding · Ukiah · Chico · Oroville · Marysville · Santa Rosa · Vallejo · Fairfield · Sacramento · Placerville · Susanville · Reno · Carson City · San Francisco · Oakland · Lodi · Stockton · South Lake Tahoe · Fremont · San Jose · Modesto · Gilroy · Santa Cruz · Monterey · Merced · Salinas · Los Banos · Mammoth Lakes · Madera · King City · Fresno · Bishop · Coalinga · Visalia · Lone Pine · Payo Robles · Central Valley · Porterville · San Luis Obispo · Santa Maria · Bakersfield · Lompoc · Ridgecrest · Tehachapi · Santa Barbara · California High Desert · Las Vegas · Cedar City · St George · Kanab · Lancaster · Palmdale · Barstow · Baker · Ventura · Thousand Oaks · Oxnard · Victorville · Hollywood · Pasadena · Los Angeles · Anaheim · Ontario · San Bernardino · Kingman · Long Beach · Newport Beach · Santa Ana · Riverside · Needles · Colorado Basin and Plateau Region · Hemet · Twentynine Palms · San Clemente · Temecula · Palm Springs · Flagstaff · Oceanside · Fallbrook · Indio · Escondido · Prescott · Cottonwood · La Jolla · Julian · San Diego · El Cajon · Chula Vista · Blythe · Quartzite · Arizona Intermediate Desert · Brawley · El Centro · Low Desert · Globe · Yuma · Gila Bend · Phoenix · Casa Grande · Tucson

NEVADA · CALIFORNIA · UTAH · ARIZONA · BAJA CALIFORNIA · SONORA

NORTH

Rainfall Map for Landscape Regions

Precipitation
inches per year

- 0 - 10
- 11 - 20
- 21 - 60
- 61 +

Northern Coast Ranges

Northern Inland Valleys and Foothills

Northern Coastal Edge

Central Coast Ranges

Central Coastal Edge

Southern Coast Ranges

Southern Coastal Edge

Southern Inland Valleys and Foothills

Peninsular Ranges

Southern Inland Mountains

Cascade - Sierra Nevada Region

Central Valley Foothills

Great Basin Region

Redding
Mendocino
Ukiah
Susanville
Chico
Oroville
Marysville
Reno
Santa Rosa
Sacramento
Placerville
Carson City
Vallejo
Fairfield
South Lake Tahoe
San Francisco
Oakland
Lodi
Stockton
Fremont
San Jose
Modesto
Gilroy
Santa Cruz
Monterey
Merced
Salinas
Los Banos
Mammoth Lakes
Madera
Bishop
King City
Fresno
Coalinga
Visalia
Lone Pine
Paso Robles
Central Valley
Porterville
San Luis Obispo
Santa Maria
Bakersfield
Lompoc
Ridgecrest
Tehachapi
California High Desert
Las Vegas
Cedar City
St George
UTAH
Kanab
NEVADA
ARIZONA
Santa Barbara
Ventura
Lancaster
Barstow
Baker
Oxnard
Thousand Oaks
Palmdale
Victorville
Hollywood
Pasadena
Los Angeles
Anaheim
Ontario
Kingman
Long Beach
San Bernardino
Newport Beach
Santa Ana
Riverside
Needles
Colorado Basin and Plateau Region
San Clemente
Hemet
Twentynine Palms
Flagstaff
Temecula
Palm Springs
Oceanside
Fallbrook
Indio
Prescott
Escondido
Cottonwood
La Jolla
San Diego
Julian
El Cajon
Blythe
Quartzite
Arizona Intermediate Desert
Chula Vista
CALIFORNIA
BAJA CALIFORNIA
Brawley
El Centro
Low Desert
Yuma
Gila Bend
Phoenix
Globe
Casa Grande
ARIZONA
SONORA
Tucson

NEVADA
CALIFORNIA

NORTH

Coastal Regions:

Northern to Southern Coastal Regions:
The climate of the California coast from Crescent City to San Francisco is quite similar to the Pacific Northwest maritime climate. Winters provide greater than 35 inches of rainfall and are largely frost free; summers are cool, foggy, with normal highs of 65°F. Monthly rainfall typically exceeds evapotranspiration stress for 8-10 months of the year.

Around the San Francisco Bay region, the climate begins to develop more characteristic Mediterranean patterns. There are cool, moist winters and long, dry periods in summer. However, there are areas of marked temperature and moisture variation throughout this region. The coastal edge is cool, foggy, and exposed to daily winds. Winter rainfall ranges 15-20 inches; summers are dry but cooled and moistened by fog. The coastal edge presents landscaping challenges due to its soils, wind, and fog. Larger plants can be shaped by persistent winds and damaged by salt spray. Adapted landscape species include Monterey cypress, Australian tea tree, drooping melaleuca, pink melaleuca, and myoporum.

Cities and communities located around San Pablo and San Francisco bays are largely sheltered from the harsh coastline exposure. These communities are situated on topography that includes flat baylands as well as rolling foothills. While the climate of this area is dominated by maritime conditions, air currents, water bodies, and topography produce many seasonal and annual variations in microclimate. There are warm and mild microclimate conditions with southerly exposures that sustain plants adapted to subtropical type climates such as bougainvillea, as well as cooler and moister areas that sustain plants such as New Zealand Christmas tree, New Zealand tea tree, and Monterey cypress and Monterey pine.

Generally, rainfall is greatest around San Rafael, averaging 37 inches. It quickly decreases to 21-23 inches in San Francisco, Berkeley, and Oakland, and even lower to 14-15 inches in Palo Alto and San Jose. Annual evapotranspiration loss from landscapes ranges 30-35 inches in San Rafael, San Francisco, and Berkeley and increases to 40-45 inches of loss in Oakland, Palo Alto, and San Jose. These records reveal the warmer and drier climate conditions of the communities that are further away from the mouth of the San Francisco Bay. When compared on a monthly basis, evapotranspiration exceeds rainfall from April to October in most areas of the Bay area communities.

Central coastal communities including San Luis Obispo and Santa Maria have mild winter temperatures and annual rainfall ranging between 13-18 inches. Evapotranspiration stress averages 41-43 inches. On the average, these coastal areas experience a climate that is similar to parts of the Bay Area.

Southern coastal regions experience a stronger Mediterranean climate pattern with lower winter rainfall and greater seasonal drought. These characteristics become quite distinct near Santa Barbara and increase further south to San Diego, the coastal climate has warmer summer temperatures that increase evapotranspiration stress. Santa Barbara receives an average of 17-18 inches of rain each year, Santa Monica 13-14 inches, Laguna Beach 12-13 inches, and San Diego 10-11 inches. Annual evapotranspiration ranges from 40 inches in Santa Barbara to 44 inches in San Diego. Winter rains are increasingly erratic and unpredictable. This situation, in combination with high evapotranspiration loss, leads to virtual year around moisture stress on landscape plants. Even winter irrigation is necessary to offset evapotranspiration stress in some ornamental landscapes.

Frosts in southern coastal regions are quite rare but temperatures to 24°F have been recorded. A great variety of frost sensitive plants are grown in these regions ranging from bougainvillea, sea lavender, and lantana to hardy Mediterranean plants including Australian tea tree, eucalyptus, and olive trees.

Soils in coastal areas are often medium to fine textured clays near the surface and calcareous and shale-type below. These calcareous shale-types are of marine origin and are often exposed by wave action along coastal bluffs. These marine soils are low in iron and often have a high pH. Coastal valleys around Salinas, Santa Maria, and Ventura and other low lying plains often have fine textured loams and clays that have been deposited from higher elevations. These soils are slightly acid and relatively high in fertility and well suited to plant growth.

The San Diego coastline.

Natural vegetation from the San Francisco Bay Area to San Diego is dominated by the coastal strand, coastal sage scrub, and chaparral plant communities. These communities reflect the relatively dry conditions and presence of salt spray, daily breezes, and summertime fog. In northern coastal areas where coastal foothills extend very close to the Pacific Ocean, there are occurrences of broadleaf evergreen forests and redwood forests that reflect increased levels of moisture.

Coastal Regions Climate

Key Northern Cities and Communities with Coastal Climates:
San Francisco, San Rafael, Richmond, Berkeley, Oakland, San Mateo, Pacifica, Aptos, Monterey, Pacific Grove, Santa Cruz, Carmel

Climate Characteristics:
Average Annual Rainfall: **20-30 inches**
April-October Rainfall: **3-5 inches**
Annual Evapotranspiration: **30-35 inches**
April-October Evapotranspiration: **25-28 inches**
Average Length of Growing Season: **300-325 days**
Average Number of Yearly Frosts below 32°F: **1-2 days**
Record Low Temperature Range: **22-27°F**
Average High Temperature Range: **57-77°F**

Key Southern Cities and Communities with Coastal Climates:
Santa Barbara, Ventura, Santa Monica, Manhattan Beach, Redondo Beach, Long Beach, Huntington Beach, Newport Beach, Laguna Beach, San Clemente, Oceanside, La Jolla, San Diego

Climate Characteristics:
Average Annual Rainfall: **10-14 inches**
April-October Rainfall: **2 inches**
Annual Evapotranspiration: **40-45 inches**
April-October Evapotranspiration: **25-30 inches**
Average Length of Growing Season: **330 days +**
Average Number of Yearly Frosts below 32°F: **1-3 days**
Record Low Temperature Range: **24-29°F**
Average High Temperature Range: **65-77°F**

Inland Regions

Northern to Southern Inland Valleys and Foothills:
Inland valley and foothill landscapes throughout California often reflect less and less dominance by maritime climate conditions. Salt air is absent, fog occurs less frequently, and daily onshore winds are diminished. The combination of distance from the ocean and the higher elevations of the coast ranges combine to reduce winter moisture and to increase summer drought stress.

The coastal climate in northern California begins to transition into warmer and drier inland areas throughout the foothills around the Bay Area including Berkeley, Oakland, and Palo Alto, and in foothills and valleys inland from Santa Cruz and Monterey. These areas are often dominated by ocean breezes, but experience greater heat and cold. These foothill locations are relatively frost free; adjacent valleys experience several days of frost most years.

Communities that have developed with more foothill separation from the ocean such as Santa Rosa, Napa, and Concord can receive 25-30 inches of winter rain, but also have 45 inches and more each year of evapotranspiration stress. Most of this evapotranspiration occurs from spring through fall; averaging 36 inches of moisture loss from April through October. Supplemental irrigation for ornamental landscapes easily extends 8-10 months of the year. The natural vegetation of these northern inland valley and foothill regions is comprised of grassland, chaparral, and evergreen forest plant communities. Protected canyon habitats and seasonal streams sustain dense forest and riparian communities.

A wide range of plants from Mediterranean and warm maritime climates are ideally suited to these northern valleys and foothills. Some highly popular native species include madrone, coast live oak, manzanita, and wild lilac species. Many plants from Mediterranean climates include deodar cedar, atlas cedar, strawberry tree, sweet bay, rockrose, and lavender species. A great variety of other ornamental plants can grow in this region, especially in foothill and microclimate areas where there is little frost.

Valley communities that are located far from the coastline such as Hollister and King City receive as little as 10-15 inches of rainfall, while potential moisture loss from irrigated landscapes can be 45-50 inches annually. King City also experiences an average of 51 days of frost each year which further reflects the combination of low elevations and inland location.

Inland valley and foothill regions are far more extensive throughout southern California. They are also among the most heavily populated areas within the state. The climate of these southern inland areas is significantly warmer and drier than those found in northern California. Cities located at the base of inland mountains including Pasadena and Glendora receive up to 20 inches and more of rainfall with evapotranspiration stress being measured at 52 inches per year. Other cities that are located further inland such as Elsinore, Riverside, and San Bernardino receive approximately 10-15 inches of annual rainfall while experiencing more than 55 inches of evapotranspiration stress. Many ornamental landscapes are provided with year around supplemental irrigation to offset moisture loss. The natural vegetation of this region was heavily dominated by sage scrub and chaparral plant communities. Seasonal washes and streams supported local stands of riparian vegetation. Much of this natural landscape has been removed through urbanization.

A highly diverse range of plants can be grown within southern inland valley and foothill regions. Frosts are seldom and the availability of supplemental water has been made available to sustain both exotic and native species. Milder locations have been highly successful for subtropical plants as well as for citrus, grapes, and avocados; truck crops including asparagus, strawberries, and tomatoes have been grown for many years in fertile valley soils. Landscapes designed for water conservation find many successful choices in Australian and Mediterranean species including eucalyptus, acacia, olive, oak, and deodar cedar. Many California native species can be grown, however, popular species including manzanita, wild lilac, and Oregon grape benefit from microclimates that provide some shade from intense heat and sun.

The city of Claremont, located within an inland region in southern California.

Inland Regions Climate

Key Northern Cities and Communities with Inland Climates:
Santa Rosa, Napa, Concord, Berkeley Hills, Pleasanton, Oakland Hills, Palo Alto, Hayward, San Jose, Hollister, Salinas, King City

Climate Characteristics:
Average Annual Rainfall: **15-20 inches**
April-October Rainfall: **2-4 inches**
Annual Evapotranspiration: **40-45 inches**
April-October Evapotranspiration: **34-38 inches**
Average Length of Growing Season: **300 days +**
Average Number of Yearly Frosts below 32°F: **10-20 days**
Record Low Temperature Range: **15-21°F**
Average High Temperature Range: **57-82°F**

Key Southern Cities and Communities with Inland Climates:
Thousand Oaks, San Fernando, Pasadena, Glendora, Riverside, San Bernardino, Corona, Elsinore

Climate Characteristics:
Average Annual Rainfall: **10-20 inches**
April-October Rainfall: **1-3 inches**
Annual Evapotranspiration: **50-55 inches**
April-October Evapotranspiration: **39-43 inches**
Average Length of Growing Season: **330 days +**
Average Number of Yearly Frosts below 32°F: **13-14 days**
Record Low Temperature Range: **22-27°F**
Average High Temperature Range: **66-94°F**

Central Valley and Foothill Regions

Central Valley and Foothill Regions:
The great Central Valley of California is a remarkable region. This broad valley runs for more than 500 miles from north to south and ranges 30 to 70 miles in width; it comprises more than 18,000 square miles. The northern portion is called the Sacramento Valley, and the southern end, the San Joaquin Valley.

Elevations range from sea level to 500 feet. The northern end is narrower and characterized by elevated terraces; the southern end is characterized by large, broad basins. Many of the soils have been formed through centuries of erosion of the surrounding highlands. In northern and central portions, these soils are extremely deep and fertile. In drier more southerly locations, there are some deep sands as well as hardpan conditions.

The Mediterranean climate brings 18-25 inches of rain to northern valley cities such as Sacramento and Chico, and as little as 5-8 inches in the south near Bakersfield. Summers are long, warm, and dry. Evapotranspiration stress ranges from 49-50 inches in northern areas, 55 inches and more from Visalia to Bakersfield. Winters are cool and have many days of overcast, foggy conditions. The average frost free season varies from 230 days in the north to as much as 350 days in the south. The limiting factor to most plant growth is water availability, not cool temperatures. Supplemental irrigation for many ornamental landscapes is frequently needed from April through October.

The natural vegetation of the Central Valley is mainly grassland and oaks. Most grasses are species that were introduced in the 1800's in support of the cattle grazing industry. Native bunch grasses are largely gone. Valley oaks are one of the dominant trees of the lower basins and valleys. Toward the foothill edges the blue oak is commonly found. In areas along seasonal streams there are riparian communities comprised of willows and cottonwood poplars.

The Central Valley is one of the most productive agricultural regions in the world. This is largely due to the excellent climate, soils, and availability of sub-surface and imported water. Temperatures in parts of this valley are cool enough during the winter to provide necessary chilling degree days to sustain many types of stonecrop tree fruits. In warmer parts of the San Joaquin Valley, citrus, kiwi, grapes, and cotton are produced. Walnuts, almonds, figs, and olives can be grown in both reaches of the valley.

A wide variety of ornamental plants grow throughout the valley region. Plants such as deodar cedar, stone pine, valley oak, and Italian cypress often grow to monumental sizes. The combination of heat, water, and soils leads to good growth for most ornamentals. Plants from temperate type climates such as silk tree, mulberry, and Canadian redbud experience a good balance between winter dormancy and extended summer growth. Plant groups that are not well suited to the Central Valley include subtropical types, subject to winter frost damage, as well as most desert species that reject the relatively humid air, rich soils, and supplemental water. California native plants from cool, coastal climate areas will perform best when they are located in spaces that provide shade and protection from extreme heat and cold.

The Central Valley is circled by foothills in all areas except the Sacramento delta region that extends into the San Francisco Bay. These foothills begin to create microclimate variations, particularly at elevations above 2,000 feet, and in canyons and along seasonal water courses. The east facing foothills of the coast ranges are often the driest areas throughout the valley, particularly in southern stretches from Coalinga to Maricopa. Northern foothill communities such as Redding experience an average of 41 inches of annual rainfall and 49 inches of evapotranspiration stress. This area also has an average of 20 days of frost each year which is relatively few when compared to other foothill communities.

Most communities occur in the western foothills of the Sierra Nevada mountain range. These communities are relatively small in population and have been developed in microclimate locations along rivers, in valleys, and along major highway routes into recreation areas. Many are located at elevations that experience periodic snow during the winter months but also have warm and dry summers. Most of the communities benefit from a naturally rich forest landscape that creates

Central Valley and Foothill region.

a highly pleasing sense of character. Colorful natives include the western redbud and California buckeye. Temperate plants such as honey locust are highly adapted to these foothills, but often escape and are not desirable. Many types of wild lilac, manzanita, and hardy Mediterranean species are popular in ornamental gardens.

Central Valley and Foothill Regions Climate

Key Cities and Communities in the Central Valley Region:
Red Bluff, Chico, Marysville, Sacramento, Stockton, Modesto, Merced, Los Banos, Fresno, Visalia, Bakersfield

Climate Characteristics:
Average Annual Rainfall: **5-25 inches**
April-October Rainfall: **2-4 inches**
Annual Evapotranspiration: **49-55 inches**
April-October Evapotranspiration: **42-48 inches**
Average Length of Growing Season: **230-350 days**
Average Number of Yearly Frosts below 32°F: **20-40 days**
Record Low Temperature Range: **22-27°F**
Average High Temperature Range: **55-95°F**

Key Communities in the Central Valley Foothills:
Redding, Oroville, Auburn, Placerville, Jackson, Oakhurst

Climate Characteristics:
Average Annual Rainfall: **30-40 inches, some as snow**
April-October Rainfall: **7-8 inches**
Annual Evapotranspiration: **48-51 inches**
April-October Evapotranspiration: **40-43 inches**
Average Length of Growing Season: **330 days +**
Average Number of Yearly Frosts below 32°F: **15-20 days**
Record Low Temperature Range: **8-20°F**
Average High Temperature Range: **50-93°F**

Desert Regions

Desert Regions:
The climate throughout much of the Southwest is arid and dry. Rainfall is often less than 10 inches per year while potential evapotranspiration loss can range from 60 to 90 inches due to extreme heat and aridity. These conditions apply over a very wide area and shape a complex desert environment. However, this environment can be divided into several parts. Variations in temperature, frost, rainfall, and soils form differing regions referred to as the high, intermediate, and low deserts.

The deserts of the Southwest have high mountains surrounding them to the West. These mountains prevent most Pacific maritime moisture from reaching these areas. Additionally, continental air currents, temperature regimes, and rainfall patterns provide very little moisture and maintain long periods of heat and drought. However, southern locations can benefit from summer storms that track northward through the Gulf of California. These fairly reliable summer rains stimulate second growing seasons for some native plants.

In terms of ornamental landscaping, rainfall in desert regions is very limited, highly erratic, and too unreliable for landscape use. Rainfalls in winter months often are gentle and drop moisture more slowly; summer storms are typically intense, localized, and are very limited in coverage. The low amounts of rainfall, compounded by very high levels of aridity, temperature, and wind frequency combine to cause very high levels of evapotranspiration stress for ornamental plants. As a result, most ornamental landscapes require year around irrigation.

Developing microclimate spaces that provide shelter from extreme heat, aridity, and wind is highly important for many ornamental species. Microclimates that reduce heat and sun stress can sustain a long growing season that can become almost year around for many ornamentals as long as water is provided. Landscape water use can be managed carefully through reference to climate data that measures evapotranspiration stress.

Desert soils also challenge landscaping. These soils are not highly suited to sustain exotic species. One very common occurrence is that of dissolved salts that create alkaline or saline conditions. Alkalinity is often found in basin areas where sodium and calcium salts have precipitated out of evaporated runoff water.

Many types of desert soils are sandy and contain little organic matter. Sandy soils drain very fast and have little water holding capacity. These soils can require weekly, and even daily, irrigation to sustain ornamental landscapes. Sandy soils benefit from additions of organic matter to help retain moisture and improve effectiveness of drip and trickle irrigation systems. While parts of Palm Springs and Palm Desert are developed on deep sandy soils, other locations have fine textured soils that can cement together to form a hard pan that is called caliche. These soils create very difficult problems in the preparation of planting areas, particularly in terms of their poor drainage. These soils need to be wetted very slowly in order to have moisture penetration.

Experience in desert regions indicates that an average of 2-3 years of careful irrigation and maintenance is needed to successfully establish plants, even when using species that are native to arid climates and habitats. Hardy exotic species such as Afghan pine, eucalyptus, oleander, and the like will always be highly dependent upon a regular supply of supplemental water. Careful water management is the key to conservation. Accurate application of irrigation water to meet local evapotranspiration loss can help achieve efficient use.

It is significant to note that many desert native trees are found growing along washes and have an ability to develop long root systems to tap deep ground moisture. Trees that grow to larger sizes and in greater numbers indicate greater amounts of available moisture. These species also shed their leaves to become deciduous under drought stress and during winter months. Some species have even developed photosynthetic bark that is capable of performing the functions of foliage.

High, Intermediate, and Low Desert Regions:
The high desert regions of the Southwest are most commonly defined by the limits of the Mojave Desert in California, southern Nevada, and northern to central Arizona. Major centers occurring in this region include, Palmdale, Lancaster, Victorville, Barstow, Twentynine Palms, and Las Vegas. Rainfall is very scant, averaging about 4-8 inches yearly, and occurs mainly in winter. Summer high temperatures

Palmdale, located within a high desert region.

Desert Regions Climate

Key Cities and Communities in High Desert Regions:
Palmdale, Lancaster, Victorville, Barstow, Apple Valley, Twentynine Palms

Climate Characteristics:
Average Annual Rainfall: **4-8 inches**
April-October Rainfall: **1-3 inches**
Annual Evapotranspiration: **65-84 inches**
April-October Evapotranspiration: **43-66 inches**
Average Length of Growing Season: **250-300 days**
Average Number of Yearly Frosts below 32°F: **60-80 days**
Record Low Temperature Range: **-4-6°F**
Average High Temperature Range: **60-100°F**

Key Cities and Communities in Intermediate Desert Regions:
Tucson, Carefree

Climate Characteristics:
Average Annual Rainfall: **8-12 inches**
April-October Rainfall: **10 inches**
Annual Evapotranspiration: **74 inches**
April-October Evapotranspiration: **60 inches**
Average Length of Growing Season: **300 days +**
Average Number of Yearly Frosts below 32°F: **40 days**
Record Low Temperature Range: **3°F**
Average High Temperature Range: **61-95°F**

Principal Cities and Communities in Low Desert Regions:
Palm Desert, Palm Springs, Desert Hot Springs, Coachella, Indio, Blythe, El Centro, Needles, Phoenix

Climate Characteristics:
Average Annual Rainfall: **3-8 inches**
April-October Rainfall: **1-4 inches**
Annual Evapotranspiration: **70-90 inches**
April-October Evapotranspiration: **56-70 inches**
Average Length of Growing Season: **330 days +**
Average Number of Yearly Frosts below 32°F: **4-15 days**
Record Low Temperature Range: **13-17°F**
Average High Temperature Range: **70-109°F**

Desert Regions

average from the high 80's to the low 100's °F; annual evapotranspiration stress ranges 65-84 inches per year. Wind and aridity are ferocious. The combination of extreme heat, drought, and cold winters makes the high desert one of the most difficult regions to landscape.

High desert regions are characterized by flat expansive topography that is periodically interrupted by foothills and rocky peaks. These foothills and peaks create local microclimates and soil conditions that help to sustain succulent plants in rocky terrain, and wash-type flora in runoff areas. Rainfall is rarely sufficiently abundant to uniformly wet all areas, instead water flows in torrents across flat areas into gullies and seasonal stream channels. Even when these stream channels are not visually prominent, they can be identified by the scrub plantings that inhabit them.

The natural vegetation is Mojave desertscrub and is adapted to survive extreme drying as well as low temperatures. Frost is a common occurrence, to about 80 days per year, and single digit temperatures have been recorded. Some of the best known species common to the Mojave include creosote, Joshua trees, burrobrush, and saltbush.

The intermediate desert region is most distinctly recognized in Arizona. It occurs at transitional elevations between high, cool plateaus and the lower elevations of the warmer deserts. These areas are still very arid but do not experience the extremes of heat and cold that characterize other desert regions. Portions of Tucson and areas north of Phoenix fall within the intermediate desert region. Phoenix, in particular, is located in a transition zone between low and intermediate deserts. Average summer high temperatures reach 105°F near Phoenix, 95°F in Tucson. Average high temperature in the low desert regions around Palm Springs is 109°F. The difference in these high temperatures is quite significant in terms of the types of exotic plants that can survive in these three communities.

An intermediate desert region around Tucson.

Intermediate desert regions receive 8-12 inches of rain each year with much of this falling in the hot summer months. Annual evapotranspiration rates are among the highest in the West, averaging about 74 inches; frost occurs on an average of 40 days per year and extreme low, single digit temperatures have been recorded. Monthly mean high temperatures range from the low 60's to the mid 90's °F.

The natural vegetation of these areas is highly variable Sonoran desertscrub. Areas to the south of the Phoenix urban area are included within this zone and support a saltbush type vegetation. In contrast, at higher elevations outside Phoenix, the vegetation is a richer form of Sonoran desertscrub that contains a greater diversity of plants including palo verde and cactus vegetation and the very distinctive saguaro. This type of natural landscape is very characteristic around Tucson. Other natives common to this vegetation include ironwood, chuparosa, and creosote. In a relatively short distance from Phoenix to the west, we can see the intermediate desert climate transition to lower elevations that experience warmer summers, milder winters, and receive less rainfall. These are the conditions of the low desert.

Low desert regions include Palm Springs and the Coachella Valley in California as well as extending into the Imperial Valley and to Blythe and Needles. Much of this region exists within an arid subtropical climate zone. This zone extends southward from Palm Springs to the Gulf of California and eastward towards Phoenix and Tucson in Arizona. Rainfall in low deserts is erratic and can occur in both winter and summer months, ranging between 2-8 inches per year. Rainfall is higher in the Arizona portions of this zone with most additional moisture coming in the summer months. Low deserts in California can experience 5-7 days of frost each year with low temperatures ranging 17-23°F. The number of frosts increase in regions to the east, reaching 20 days of frost in the Phoenix area and up to 40 days in Tucson.

Annual evapotranspiration stress is quite uniform throughout and ranges to above 70 inches. Soils are often very sandy, deep, lightly calcareous, with little water holding capacity. Deep irrigation is applied on weekly basis.

The natural vegetation of these low desert areas includes Chihuahuan desertscrub as well as heat-adapted species found in the cooler deserts. Common plants include creosote, chuparosa, and ocotillo. The presence of significant summer rains in the eastward reaches can cause native plantings there to have summer and winter growth periods.

Palm Springs, located within a low desert region.

Section 3 Plants and Environment

Introduction:

The topic of plants and environment can be explored in many ways. In an effort to increase our basis for urban landscaping, I have found a number of principles and concepts stemming from the study of ecology and natural environments that deserve greater attention.

In natural environments, the study of ecology brings attention to the many relationships that exist between plants and animals and the physical environment, including climate and habitat conditions. We can determine which plants tolerate cold, need shade, or grow in areas of ample moisture. We can also determine how various plants have developed these adaptations.

It is necessary to develop an understanding of many ecological relationships and their significance to assist our efforts in developing successful landscapes. In many instances, the study of ecology helps clarify the processes and adaptations of plants to various environmental conditions. This begins with a basic understanding of needs and tolerances of such conditions as temperature, moisture, sunlight, soil nutrients, and growing season.

This section provides a brief introduction to several ecological concepts and insights that can help us in planning and designing landscapes. On one hand, these concepts and insights help to describe how everything fits together to function as a whole ecosystem. On the other hand, we can learn more about individual plants and their adaptations in order to assist us in designing new landscapes that work in greater likeness to the natural model.

Ecosystem Concepts:

Let me begin by making the observation that individual plants, as well as plant communities, are highly adapted to the environments in which they have evolved. They have had many years in which to develop their growth processes and physical form in response to specific climate and habitat conditions.

This success of native species and natural landscapes is a result of the complex process of evolution. Because of this, when we look at natural landscapes we see a remarkable fitting of flora and fauna with climate and habitat. We know that the nature around us is suited to the sun, temperature, light, soil, and water. It is also a sustainable process—one that has ecological relationships that enable it to achieve remarkable levels of diversity and the capacity to adapt and survive on the resources within the system. As such, natural landscapes are a marvelous synthesis of many varying factors and conditions. And, this synthesis is not a static phenomenon; it is always changing and adapting.

There is an important principle at work within these relationships. All relationships, from the availability of water and nutrients to growth and death, are connected to everything else and collectively work as a whole system. This is a remarkable situation—there is need to value and understand the natural environment for its significance as a whole entity. It is perhaps the most basic idea to draw into our planning and design efforts. We must make efforts to visualize the landscape as a whole system, and not an assemblage of individual plants or separated environmental conditions.

By studying ecological relationships, we can observe how all parts of these natural landscapes are woven together. It is this awareness that everything is connected and works as a whole system that causes us to stop and appreciate the complex phenomenon of landscapes. We do not see plants or any part as a separate component. No plant or animal would exist without everything else being there.

We can look at a native oak as an example. The structure and function of this tree reflects an entire ecosystem from soil nutrients and moisture to sunlight and topography. During its evolution, associated species of squirrels and birds have come to depend upon it for food and shelter that are necessary for their survival. At the same time, they often bury acorns

Understanding both natural and ornamental landscapes as a whole system is fundamental to many planning and design decisions.

in places where new trees become established. The shade and leaf litter produced by such a tree provides microclimate conditions and a source of nutrients for understory plants. This increased diversity of plants provides additional sources of food, shelter, and habitat for animal and plant survival. In one respect, the community is often most viable when the range of diversity is the greatest. Additionally, the loss or change of one part of this community will affect all other parts. This last point helps us to realize the need to relate to plants as members of communities, not as individual species. It is important to plan urban landscapes in ways that reflect this level of interdependence and association. Currently, it is a very common tendency to study plants according to their individual merits and to overlook the goal of community.

These ecological principles and concepts provide us with important perspectives regarding ornamental landscapes. We can attain higher levels of environmental benefit and sustainability when we develop landscapes that are similar to this natural model. Where possible, landscapes must become planned as communities and be managed in ways that permit more of their natural level of diversity and functioning to occur. This is not an easy goal to attain; it is one that we are still endeavoring to understand beyond these simple explanations. In an effort to further our understanding of this goal, a number of aspects regarding plants and environment can be summarized. This summary begins with climate and habitat observations and extends into plant adaptations.

This natural landscape including western sycamore, coast live oak, toyon, and sugar bush illustrate the integrated development of species and communities.

Climate and Habitat:

One of the most fundamental relationships that exists between plants and their environment pertains to climate cycles. Daily, seasonal, and annual cycles establish short and long term rhythms of plant growth and rest. For example, plants that have evolved and adapted to Mediterranean climates are most active and productive from mid-winter through late spring. This is in coincidence with moisture from rain, mild temperatures, and increasing day length. Many of these species will enter a period of relative inactivity or dormancy in summer through fall as moisture runs out and summer temperatures reach their highest level. Plants that grow within desert regions are also most active when moisture is available. Greatest activity occurs in high desert regions for several months between late winter and early spring, following the winter rains. In intermediate and low desert regions, there are often two growing seasons. One season occurs as a result of winter rains, the other from summer thundershowers from subtropical storms. When moisture runs out, these plants also rapidly become dormant and resort to other mechanisms to survive the lack of moisture.

It is also significant to note that the potential growing season in Mediterranean and arid regions is dominated by the availability of water rather than the frequency of low temperatures. The growing season of a region is typically determined by the number of days that occur between the last frost in the winter until the first frost in the fall. Conceivably, this is the period of time that plants could grow if all other conditions are also suited to growth. Since the occurrence of frost is relatively infrequent in many dry climate areas of the West, the availability of moisture is the principal limiting factor that restricts annual plant growth.

In contrast to these natural conditions, the management of ornamental landscapes has often resulted in the year around supply of moisture to landscape plants. This practice has helped to sustain many exotic species in good appearance with almost continual growth for most of the year. It is important to understand that all plants are adapted to cycles of growth and rest. Providing year around moisture to stimulate continual growth is not desirable. Plants that are adapted to Mediterranean and arid climates in particular are adversely affected by extended growing cycles caused by extended irrigation practices. Many of these plants respond with faster growth and larger sizes, but they soon become over extended as well as more susceptible to disease problems. These plants do best with a short to moderate length growing cycle with long periods of relatively low activity.

Temperature and Moisture:

In studying climate and plant relationships on a more specific level, we have come to learn that the occurrence of cold temperatures is a particularly significant factor affecting the growth and survival of plants. One of the most frequently asked questions in ornamental landscaping is regarding the amount of seasonal frost and extreme low temperatures various plants can tolerate. This is such a critical condition affecting plant survival that many efforts have been made to record and map cold temperature zones for all parts of the world and including the West. Temperatures below 32°F can cause moisture in plant leaves and stems to freeze and rupture plant cells. Temperatures that stay below freezing for extended periods of time are particularly harmful to plants native to subtropical and tropical climates, especially if they have been stimulated to produce new growth through late summer into fall. It is also widely noted that freezing temperatures also can damage plants that are native to coastal regions in Mediterranean type climates of Europe, Australia, and South Africa.

Many of the dry climate regions throughout the West have relatively mild winter temperatures. These conditions have enabled us to import a rich and diverse palette of plants for ornamental landscape use without a great deal of concern for frost. Studies also indicate that temperatures ranging between 77 - 86° F sustain optimum plant growth for many species from

All plants have naturally adapted to climate cycles that result in seasons of growth and seasons of rest.

Many trees and shrubs adapted to Mediterranean climates are evergreen and grow most actively in winter and spring. They often have deep roots and hard, leathery leaves.

Mediterranean and temperate type climates. These plants exhibit minium activity at temperatures below 40°F. In contrast, plants from subtropical and tropical climates often perform best within temperatures ranges between 86-95°F. Such plants show minimum levels of activity below 45-50°F. These conditions are very common in the Mediterranean climate areas of California and provide the basis for long growing seasons, if water is provided.

In regions that have an arid or desert type climate, the influence of temperatures provides more challenging considerations. Some areas, such as the high deserts, experience regular frosts and cold temperatures during the winter. This condition keeps us from using plants that are not tolerant of cold. In another regard, most arid regions experience periods of extremely high temperatures that cause plants to transpire rapidly in an effort to cool their foliage. Some plants cannot transpire moisture quickly enough and become highly stressed and damaged. This situation is further complicated when moisture is not available for the plant to use.

Desert regions are also hard on plants as a result of high levels of aridity that can quickly drain a plant of its internal moisture. When air is dry, it develops a pressure similar to a vacuum that draws up moisture from the surfaces of soil, plant leaves, and exposed water bodies, day or night. Many plants are not adapted to resist arid conditions when moisture is not abundantly available. The impact of aridity is increased with the occurrence of winds. Plants that are not adapted to arid climate conditions are easily stressed, stunted, or otherwise harmed by a combination of cold, heat, and aridity. Often, exotic plant species perform best when located in microclimate areas that help to reduce one or more of these extreme climate conditions.

Topography, Geology, Soils:
The discussion of plants and environment needs to extend beyond climate factors to include other habitat conditions. One of the most

significant examples pertains to the development and management of soils. Soils are initially formed through many centuries of weathering of rock by water, wind, and temperature. Soils result from the breakdown of rock into smaller particle sizes in combination with organic matter from plants. This material sustains a wide range of soil life including fungi and bacteria.

A healthy and viable soil ecology is the foundation for successful plant growth. It is desirable to nurture and manage the soil with the view that it is highly interactive and an extension of the flora and fauna above the surface, and vice versa. It is a medium which also contains a great deal of life that is very important in making nutrients and moisture available to plants. Soil is not simply an inert substance to fill with water and fertilizer to be absorbed by plants.

In natural landscapes the process of soil development and plant growth have occurred together. As a result, there are specific relationships that occur between certain species of plants and various types of fungi and bacteria. In one example, a diverse group of fungi, identified as *Mycorrhiza*, help to convert organic nitrogen and phosphorous into a usable form for plants to absorb and sustain their growth. Individual types of mycorrhizal fungi have evolved with specific plant species and are highly important to them in their nutrient uptake. Many western natives will not grow well in ornamental landscapes until these fungi are established throughout the soil. Another example of soil life and plant growth is illustrated by the symbiotic association between certain plants and nitrogen fixing bacteria. These bacteria, mainly from a group known as *Rhizobium*, associate with certain plant species and take nitrogen from the air in the soil and fix it for use by the host plant. The host plant provides certain nutrients to these bacteria, but in turn receives nitrogen that has been fixed for use by the bacteria. This concept is described further on page 51.

The seasonal availability of moisture is the principal limiting factor in the distribution and growing season of native species and communities.

Plants will absorb as much of the nutrient base from the soil as they can, within the limits of temperature and moisture. When moisture, temperature, and soil nutrients reach good levels of balance, plant growth will often occur at the maximum rate. Plants will sustain this faster growth and reach larger sizes until the conditions change. In dry climate regions, the relationships become quite clear: plants receive moisture from winter rains, foliage and flowers are produced, summer heat and drought lead to plant dormancy and loss of some foliage that lies on the ground until winter rains and various bacteria and fungi help contribute to its decomposition and release of nutrients back to the plants.

In many ornamental landscapes, it would not be as necessary to add fertilizers to shrub and tree plantings as long as surface leaf litter could collect and decompose back into the soil. This litter contains most of the essential nutrients to sustain continued growth and development of the plants. An alternative would be to compost the leaf litter and to use the humus material as a topdressing. Rainfall and irrigation will help the nutrients to leach into the soil.

Adaptations to Moisture Stress:
Water is one of the principal elements that sustains all growth and survival. Within plants, it is the basic building block in the process of photosynthesis and transpiration. It is the medium through which nutrients are carried in solution throughout all parts and activities of plants. When water is absent, growth processes cease to function. The concern for water is visibly important in regions that are warm and dry for several months of the year. When water is scarce, there is less plant growth.

Our western regions and the natural landscapes are very indicative of this situation. The occurrence of coastal sage scrub, chaparral, and desert plant communities reflect the scarcity of water. These are scrub type communities that are dominated by shrubs, perennials, and annuals. Trees are largely confined to washes and seasonal streams where they can benefit from the accumulation of additional moisture. In earlier ages, western regions had greater levels of rainfall and forests comprised of larger tree species existed until the climate began to dry out. Forest landscapes can be seen at higher elevations and in regions that receive greater levels of rainfall, such as the Pacific Northwest.

The environmental conditions in dry climate regions have led to a number of plant adaptations. We have already observed that seasons of growth and dormancy in plants follow the cycle of moisture and drought. Within this broad framework, we can observe other adaptations among annuals, perennials, succulents, shrubs, and trees that help to assure their survival of moisture stress.

Annuals most often grow when conditions of temperature, light, and moisture are best, often from fall through spring. In this manner they escape moisture stress and drought. Their seeds germinate in late fall through winter, and they produce most of their foliage growth during the cooler months when moisture is in greatest supply. They complete their flowering and seed production cycle as moisture becomes scarce. Seeds are produced in abundance and often have the capacity to remain viable for many years until moisture conditions are right again.

Perennial plants are typically vigorous growers with intensive root systems that help the plant to grow very quickly when moisture is available. Their foliage growth can begin in early winter and often results in colorful flowering seasons in mid to late spring. Their growth and flowering is often improved if they receive moisture on a weekly basis throughout the spring. After a long season of productivity, they survive drought by becoming dormant in summer and fall. This dormancy is accompanied by loss of foliage and the dieback of herbaceous stems. In garden settings, perennials are typically cut back after the flowering cycle. This practice concentrates the development of new foliage and leads to more vigorous flowering for the next season.

Succulents such as aloes, agaves, and ice plants are widely known to have the capacity to absorb moisture in their fleshy stems and leaves and to resist drought with the use of this internal supply. Some of these plants develop far reaching root systems to harvest the scant seasonal moisture; others have thick, fibrous roots that are also capable of absorbing and storing adequate supplies of moisture. This group of plants also uses water the most efficiently. They will close the stomata on their leaves during the hot and sunny period of the day and perform photosynthesis activities during the cooler night time temperatures when they will lose less moisture. This capacity enables most succulents and cacti to use as little as 20 percent of the water that is required by most other shrubs, trees, and ground covers.

Woody shrubs have developed many adaptations to endure periods of drought. Often, their foliage is tough and leathery. It is also common to find waxy or hairy coverings on leaves that help to retain moisture and provide shade on the leaf surface. Leaves can be light in color to reflect more light, or be held at certain angles away from the sun to reduce exposure to light. Deep and far reaching rooting habits are also a characteristic of many drought enduring shrubs. However, it should be noted that the development of these roots is highly dependent upon the soil structure that permits such growth. Where soils and fissures in the subgrade permit, the deep roots of young plants are often capable of tapping into far reaching moisture sources.

Trees that are adapted to dry climate regions often have extensive root systems that enable them to have access to moisture in large volumes of soils. Many types will develop deep tap roots in their early stages of growth, but as they mature, they rely more heavily upon the lateral roots that have developed closer to the surface where nutrients and moisture is more readily available. The initial tap roots can eventually lose their significance and decompose. Trees typically are vigorous growers in spring through mid-summer after they have absorbed winter moisture and reached levels of full photosynthesis activity. By late summer and fall, trees become less active and their foliage begins to harden. Some desert tree species have tiny leaves that are shed under drought stress, yet also have green bark that helps continue the process of photosynthesis. In Mediterranean and arid climate regions, the occurrence of deciduous trees and shrubs is found largely in riparian areas that provide good seasonal water conditions. Some of the hardy species such as the western sycamore or palo verde trees are good examples of plants that grow in areas of seasonal or perennial streams and washes. These plants are best adapted to riparian zones, but have proven to be highly tolerant of heat and seasonal drought stress.

Section 4 Estimated Water Needs of Landscape Plants

Introduction:

Determining the precise water needs of landscape plants is very difficult. In natural environments, plants receive water directly or indirectly from rainfall. Part of this is absorbed by the soil, part runs off into seasonal or permanent stream channels and water bodies, and part evaporates into the atmosphere. There is great uncertainty as to the exact amount and complete whereabouts of water at any one time—it is always moving from place to place. To make things even more difficult, we do not have a complete understanding of how much water it takes to sustain levels of healthy growth and viability in plants. In Mediterranean and arid climate regions, the availability of water often is erratic and seasonal; plants adjust to what they get and use it until it runs out and then cease activity. Some of the mechanisms used to survive water stress were discussed in the previous section. Issues regarding water use in landscapes may always be problematic and be a cause for research and study.

One of the principal goals in dry climate regions is to use water in landscaping wisely. Part of our effort involves estimating the water needs of our landscapes in order to help us plan and manage the use of water more accurately. However, we should take care to look at the water needs of plants and water use in landscapes in a wider context of costs and benefits and plant needs. It is very easy to become over specialized and to focus on only one issue at a time. This can lead to an imbalance in decision making. On one hand, conservation of water in landscapes should evolve along with changing attitudes and economics. On the other hand, water is only one part of understanding the full nature of plants. Our efforts to conserve water in ornamental landscapes should emerge with these broader considerations in mind.

This section provides some insight into the issues of water use by plants. A chart has been prepared that lists the estimated supplemental water needs of landscape plants when we use them in ornamental landscapes. We are learning about water needs from many areas including research and scientific studies, weather studies, and the study of plants within their natural habitats. All of these approaches are needed to help us understand landscape water use.

Research and Scientific Studies:

Research and scientific studies have been made for a number of years into the adaptation and evolution of plants. A combination of field and laboratory studies have been used to describe plant growth and adaptation. In some areas, a great deal of specific data and information has been obtained. For instance, research into photosynthesis indicates that virtually all types of plants, including cool season grasses, use between 55-110 gallons of water to grow one pound of biomass such as leaves, stems, or roots. This amount of water use is the same for pines, oaks, or azaleas. There are several significant exceptions to this amount of water use. Warm season grasses such as bermuda will use approximately 30-40 gallons of water; cacti and succulents have a process of photosynthesis that requires only 6-7 gallons to produce each pound of biomass.

The amount of water required for tissue growth, therefore, is relatively straightforward. However, we are very uncertain of how much additional water is needed to sustain a plant for its transpiration needs after other growth processes have been accounted for. This additional water use is highly dependent upon the type of the plant, its foliage, roots, age, and size, and upon seasonal temperature, day light length, and availability of moisture. Fast growing plants such as mature cottonwood trees (*Populus fremontii*) growing in desert regions can transpire hundreds of gallons of water on a warm summer day when they have ample soil moisture. Drought adapted plants such as toyon (*Heteromeles arbutifolia*) growing on a dry chaparral hillside will be in a state of inactivity by late summer and will transpire very little relative to the amount that occurs in mid-spring when moisture is available.

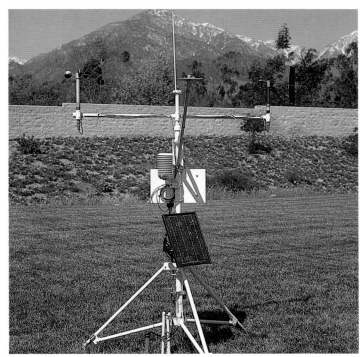

This weather station has been set up to measure various climate data and to help calculate evapotranspiration loss from the tall fescue turfgrass below.

This information helps provide specific types of insight regarding water use by plants. It is quite another thing to be able to combine it into an overview that describes all plants and all types of conditions. At this point, it is desirable to look for other types of assistance.

Using Weather Data to Calculate Evapotranspiration Stress:

In recent years there have been many methods developed to help estimate the supplemental water needs of landscape plants. One approach has been to measure and calculate the potential evapotranspiration of moisture from a landscape with the use of weather stations. Evapotranspiration, also referred to as ET, is a measurement of moisture loss in inches from the landscape. This measurement includes evaporation from soils as well as moisture loss from transpiration from plant foliage.

Measurements of evapotranspiration are done with the use of weather stations that monitor rainfall, air and soil temperature, solar radiation, wind, aridity, humidity, and vapor pressure conditions. With this process, data does not directly account for a number of factors such as soil characteristics, microclimate exposure, or variations among plant types.

It should be noted that potential evapotranspiration loss can only occur from landscapes as long as adequate moisture is available. Many native plant communities within dry climate regions will not lose this amount of moisture because it is not available during the warm summer months. Ornamental landscapes can more readily lose this much moisture if they are provided with regular irrigation.

Currently, several western states operate stations to collect readings regarding evapotranspiration in both urban and agricultural areas. These stations provide a clear picture of the potential evapotranspiration loss that can occur in many coastal, valley, and desert regions. This approach has proven to be effective in estimating the amount of water to provide to agricultural field crops and orchards for high levels of productivity. It

Annual evapotranspiration stress in northern coastal regions ranges 33-35 inches. In low desert areas around Palm Springs, annual evapotranspiration exceeds 70 inches. Turfgrasses can require twice as much water when grown in Palm Springs as San Francisco.

is now being applied to urban areas and is proving to be a valuable basis of estimating and managing the use of water in ornamental landscapes.

In an effort to more closely correlate this data with ornamental landscapes, studies have been conducted with a number of landscape plant species. To date, most of this work evaluates evapotranspiration measurements in comparison to the actual amount of water that is applied to tall fescue turfgrass that is maintained to 4 inches high. This turfgrass is supplied with just enough water to keep it from experiencing moisture stress as it grows in response to the local climate conditions. The measured water use is considered the maximum amount of water needed by the turfgrass to sustain its growth. The evapotranspiration measurements associated with tall fescue are referred to as reference evapotranspiration, or ETo. The map on the opposite page illustrates how many inches of supplemental water that is needed by tall fescue turfgrass each year when it is grown in different western regions. The variations in moisture needs correlate with key climate conditions of rainfall, temperature, aridity, and wind.

Evapotranspiration data is very helpful in managing our use of water, particularly for turfgrass species. Evapotranspiration measurements are recorded in many regions on a daily, weekly, monthly, and annual basis. With this data, it is possible to schedule irrigation to replace the moisture that is lost due to climate conditions. These schedules can be adjusted to fit immediate conditions throughout the year.

Estimating the water needs of trees and shrubs is more complex than turfgrasses. As a result, the need for supplemental water by trees and shrubs is still largely based upon observation and field experience. Until comprehensive field tests are completed on trees and shrubs in relation to evapotranspiration measurements, there will always be a need for a combination of approaches to be used to estimate the water needs of ornamental landscapes.

Estimating Water Needs with Habitat Information:
Knowledge of habitat information regarding landscape plants can be useful in many ways. Perhaps its greatest value is in providing a foundation to help us make better judgements and estimates regarding the basic needs and uses of plants within ornamental landscapes. For example, when we know the natural origin of plants in terms of climate and habitat, it becomes easier to match them with specific regions and sites in new locations. This approach also clarifies the natural seasons of moisture and drought as well as growing and resting cycles that can guide our management efforts.

Many specific facts can be learned about plants regarding their adaptability to sun, moisture, temperature, and soils by studying their habitat. This study naturally includes associated plants—an effort that can broaden our basis of seeing plants as members of groups that grow best within certain types of climate and habitat situations. A successful design will usually draw from this more complete picture of plants.

The study of habitat information also endeavors to keep the issue of water use within a broader perspective of plant needs and adaptations. Water is part of a larger complex of factors and conditions which leads to successful plant growth and survival. It is necessary to always

consider the needs and water use of plants within this broader framework. This will help put into perspective the more detailed and specific information that is provided from scientific studies and weather station measurements.

Several basic observations can be emphasized from a study of plants and habitats regarding their use of water. A number of insights have already been described in Section 3. Other key points to keep in mind when estimating the water needs of plants that come from different types of climates include:

▪ Many plants that have evolved and adapted to Mediterranean and arid climate regions will transition into a state of reduced activity and dormancy during periods of high drought stress. These plants experience various problems of disease and overgrowth when they are stimulated into longer periods of growth with summer watering. Moderate amounts of supplemental water is often most effective when provided to fill the gaps between winter rains, this being especially true during drought years. High amounts of supplemental water in the winter months can encourage overgrowth that cannot be sustained when the conditions become dry during the summer. Deep watering at 3-4 week intervals is often recommended for these plants when they are grown in ornamental landscapes in order to maintain good character.

▪ Plants that have adapted to cool and moist climate conditions, such as the Pacific Northwest or Eastern United States, are widely grown in dry climate regions. In their natural habitats, these plants typically receive an abundance of moisture during winter and spring, as well as experiencing greater frequency of moisture from summer rains. In western

---

Evapotranspiration Map (Right):

In recent years there have been many methods developed to help estimate the supplemental water needs for landscape plants. One approach has been to measure and calculate the evapotranspiration of moisture from a landscape. Evapotranspiration is the measurement of potential moisture loss to the atmosphere as a result of surface evaporation from soils, and moisture that is transpired from plant foliage.

This map illustrates the average annual evapotranspiration loss that can occur from properly irrigated tall fescue turfgrass, referred to as ETo, in different regions of the West. However, it does not fully account for many factors including seasonal variations in rainfall, soil types, slopes, or irrigation efficiency. References cited on page 32 and within the bibliography help to explain how to estimate the water needs of landscapes including trees and shrubs on the basis of evapotranspiration data. This approach to estimating water needs can be done on a daily, weekly, and seasonal basis and can be very helpful in scheduling irrigation applications to replace moisture that is lost from ornamental landscapes.

Evapotranspiration Map for Landscape Regions

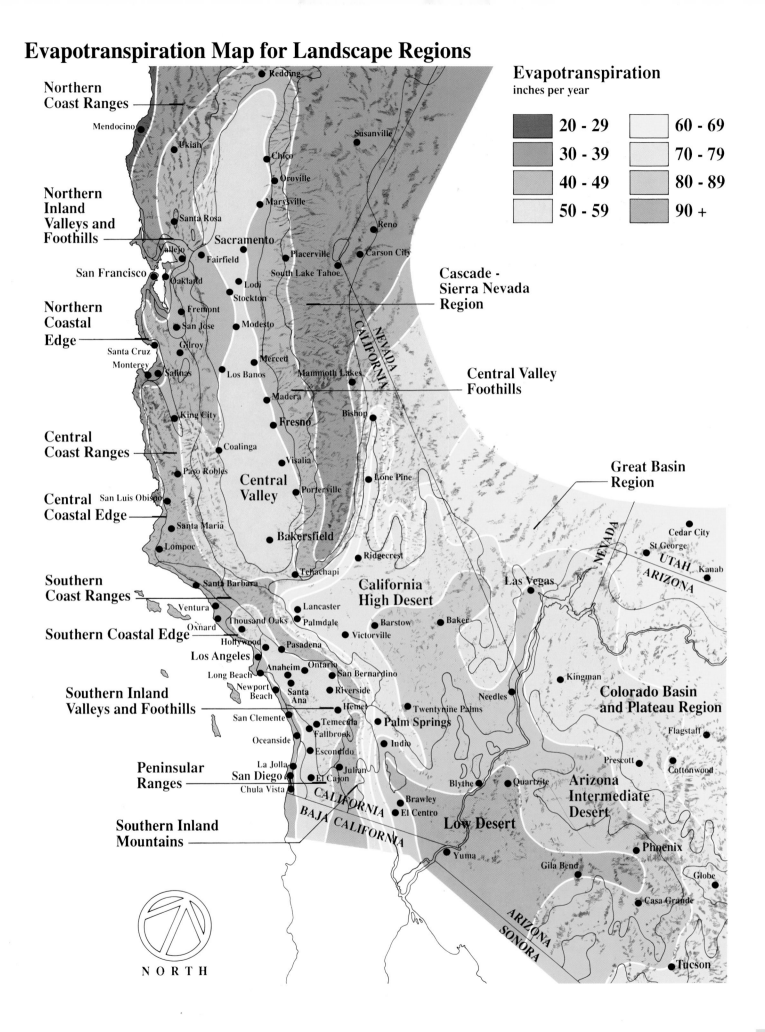

Evapotranspiration
inches per year

■ 20 - 29	□ 60 - 69
■ 30 - 39	□ 70 - 79
■ 40 - 49	■ 80 - 89
□ 50 - 59	■ 90 +

Northern Coast Ranges

Northern Inland Valleys and Foothills

Northern Coastal Edge

Central Coast Ranges

Central Coastal Edge

Southern Coast Ranges

Southern Coastal Edge

Southern Inland Valleys and Foothills

Peninsular Ranges

Southern Inland Mountains

Cascade - Sierra Nevada Region

Central Valley Foothills

Great Basin Region

Colorado Basin and Plateau Region

Arizona Intermediate Desert

Central Valley

California High Desert

Low Desert

NORTH

regions, these plants often grow best with moderate to high amounts of supplemental water particularly from mid-spring through summer. Watering should also occur on a more regular basis to sustain good health and character. Fortunately, many of these plant species can become well established with age and require little supplemental water. Many of these plants also do well when grown in turfgrass and become very appropriate for ornamental use in parks and when grouped together where they can be efficiently irrigated.

▪ Plants that have adapted to subtropical regions such as South America are naturally adapted to cycles of heat combined with periodic moisture stress. In many instances, these species respond to moisture stress by producing a greater abundance of flowers. Subtropical plants tend to be inactive during the winter months and need only low amounts of supplemental water. They respond to more moisture in the spring and to lower amounts during their active growing and flowering season from summer through late fall.

When all of the habitat characteristics and plant adaptations are taken into consideration, it is possible to refine our estimates of the relative moisture needs of landscape plant species that we use in different dry climate regions. The listing on the following pages reflects values that are based upon regional evapotranspiration loss and an understanding of the basic regional adaptability and suitability of the individual plant species. This approach provides helpful insight into projecting the water needs of these plants. It can also help guide our decisions to use plants within similar groupings or hydrozones based upon compatible water needs.

These estimates are not intended to be an absolute and quantitative measurement, rather, an approximation that can help us group plants into similar water use areas within different regions. The plant descriptions provided within the plant compendium section endeavors to provide additional insight into each species and their regional suitabilities and relative water needs.

Helpful References:

Collinson, A. S. Introduction to World Vegetation. London: Unwin Hyman, 1988.

Costello, L. R. and K. S. Jones. WUCOLS Project - Water Use Classification of Landscape Species. Cooperative Extension. University of California. Sacramento: Department of Water Resources, 1992.

Costello, L. R., N. Matheny, and J. Clark. Estimating Water Requirements of Landscape Plantings. Leaflet 21493. Cooperative Extension. University of California.

Gibeault, V. Turfgrass Water Conservation. Leaflet 21405. Cooperative Extension. University of California, 1985.

Gibeault, V. A., J. L. Meyer, R. Strohman, R. Autio, M. Murphy, and D. Monson. Irrigation of Turfgrass for Water Conservation. University of California, Riverside and the Metropolitan Water District of Southern California, 1984.

Snyder, Richard L., Brenda J. Lanini, David A. Shaw, and William O. Pruitt. Using Reference Evapotranspiration (ETo) and Crop Coefficients to Estimate Crop Evapotranspiration (ETc) for Agronomic Crops, Grasses, and Vegetable Crops. Leaflet 21427. Cooperative Extension. University of California. Division of Agriculture and Natural Resources.

_____. Using Reference Evapotranspiration (ETo) and Crop Coefficients to Estimate Crop Evapotranspiration (ETc) for Tree and Vines. Leaflet 21428. Cooperative Extension. University of California. Division of Agriculture and Natural Resources.

Walter, Heinrich. Vegetation of the Earth and Ecological Systems of the Geo-biosphere. Berlin: Springer-Verlag, 1985.

Explanation of Legend for Estimated Water Needs

AL = Adapted to region/Low supplemental water needed.

Plant species that are highly adapted to the indicated region. Once established, these species need little or no supplemental water to sustain good character. Many of these plants can be observed to be growing in areas where they survive only on natural rainfall. In ornamental landscapes, low amounts of supplemental water can be provided, up to 25 percent of the monthly evapotranspiration measurements is recommended. Summer watering can be helpful on a monthly basis, especially during drought cycles.

L = Low supplemental water needed.

Plant species that can sustain good growth and character with approximately 25 percent of the measured evapotranspiration stress. The emphasis on replacing moisture loss should be during fall through spring. A large number of western natives, along with many species from subtropical climates, are included in this group. These plants need only periodic watering in the summer, often on a monthly basis at most.

LM = Low to moderate supplemental water needed.

Plant species that are in need of greater amounts of supplemental water. Many plants that are adapted to dry climate areas come from coastal habitats and are frequently used in warmer inland valley and foothill regions. Their need for supplemental moisture often increases to approximately 25-50 percent of the monthly evapotranspiration measurement. Summer irrigation should be infrequent and adjusted to reflect the occurrences of summer temperatures and drought conditions.

M = Moderate supplemental water needed.

Plant species that will grow in a region with regular amounts of supplemental moisture that equals approximately 50 percent of the measured evapotranspiration loss. These plants are often from climates that have greater levels of moisture and will suffer in the dry climate regions if they are not sustained with moisture on a more regular schedule. Additionally, many exotic species that are used in desert regions are cited on this list. These plants need additional moisture to offset the increased level of evapotranspiration stress.

MH = Moderate to high supplemental water needed.

Plants that are more fully adapted to regular moisture than to drought stress conditions. These plants often come from cool and moist climate areas and will perform best with weekly or bimonthly watering throughout the year. Supplemental water can range from 50 to 75 percent of the measured evapotranspiration. These plants often grow well in turfgrass and in microclimate areas that are cooler and retain their moisture for longer periods of time.

— = Not well suited to this region

This symbol indicates that a specific plant species is not well suited to grow in this region. This is often a result of temperature and moisture extremes that adversely affect plant growth. Exceptions can occur when these plants are grown in microclimate locations that offset the regional climate conditions.

Estimated Water Needs for Landscape Plants

Legend:
AL = Adapted to region—Little or low water needs
L = Low supplemental water needs
LM = Low to moderate supplemental water needs
M = Moderate supplemental water needs
MH = Moderate to high supplemental water needs
— = Not well suited to this region
NCN = No common name

Trees:

		Northern Coastal	Northern Inland Valleys & Foothills	Southern Coastal	Southern Inland Valleys & Foothills	Central Valley	Low Deserts	Intermediate Deserts	High Deserts
Acacia baileyana	*Bailey Acacia*	AL	L	AL	L	L	—	—	—
Acacia dealbata	*Silver Wattle*	AL	AL	AL	AL	L	—	—	—
Acacia decurrens	*Green Wattle*	AL	AL	AL	L	L	—	—	—
Acacia farnesiana	*Sweet Acacia*	—	—	L	L	L	L	—	—
Acacia longifolia	*Sydney Golden Wattle*	AL	L	AL	L	L	—	—	—
Acacia melanoxylon	*Blackwood Acacia*	AL	AL	AL	AL	L	—	—	—
Acacia pendula	*Weeping Myall*	L	L	L	M	M	M	M	—
Acacia retinodes	*Water Wattle*	L	L	L	M	M	—	—	—
Acacia saligna	*Willow Acacia*	L	L	L	M	M	M	—	—
Acacia smallii	*NCN*	—	—	L	L	L	L	L	—
Acacia stenophylla	*Shoestring Acacia*	—	L	L	L	LM	LM	LM	—
Aesculus californica	*California Buckeye*	AL	AL	AL	AL	L	—	—	—
Agonis flexuosa	*Peppermint Tree*	M	M	M	M	—	—	—	—
Albizia julibrissin	*Silk Tree*	L	L	L	M	M	M	M	M
Angophora costata	*Gum Myrtle*	L	L	L	LM	—	—	—	—
Arbutus menziesii	*Madrone*	AL	AL	L	—	—	—	—	—
Arbutus unedo	*Strawberry Tree*	L	L	L	M	M	M	M	M
Brachychiton populneus	*Kurrajong Bottle Tree*	L	L	L	M	M	M	M	—
Broussonetia papyrifera	*Paper Mulberry*	L	L	L	M	M	M	M	M
Callistemon citrinus	*Lemon Bottlebrush*	L	L	L	M	M	M	M	—
Callistemon viminalis & cvs	*Weeping Bottlebrush*	L	L	L	M	M	M	M	—
Calocedrus decurrens	*Incense Cedar*	LM	M	M	M	M	—	—	—
Carnegiea gigantea	*Saguaro*	—	—	—	—	—	L	L	L
Casuarina cunninghamiana	*River She-oak*	L	L	L	M	M	M	M	—
Casuarina equisetifolia	*Horsetail Tree*	AL	L	AL	M	M	—	—	—
Casuarina stricta	*Drooping She-oak*	AL	L	AL	L	M	M	—	—
Ceanothus arboreus	*Feltleaf Ceanothus*	AL	L	L	L	L	—	—	—
Ceanothus 'Ray Hartman'	*NCN*	AL	AL	AL	L	L	—	—	—
Ceanothus thyrsiflorus	*Blue Blossom*	AL	AL	AL	L	L	—	—	—
Cedrus atlantica & cvs	*Atlas Cedar*	L	M	M	M	M	M	M	M
Cedrus deodara & cvs	*Deodar Cedar*	L	L	M	M	M	M	M	M
Ceratonia siliqua	*Carob Tree*	AL	AL	AL	AL	L	M	M	M
Cercidium floridum	*Blue Palo Verde*	—	—	—	L	L	LM	LM	LM
Cercidium microphyllum	*Little Leaf Palo Verde*	—	—	—	L	—	LM	LM	LM
Cercidium praecox	*Sonoran Palo Verde*	—	—	—	L	L	LM	LM	LM
Cercis canadensis & cvs	*Eastern Redbud*	M	M	M	MH	MH	MH	MH	MH
Cercis occidentalis	*Western Redbud*	AL	AL	L	M	M	—	—	—
Chilopsis linearis	*Desert Willow*	L	L	L	L	M	M	M	M
Chitalpa tashkentensis	*Chitalpa*	L	L	L	M	M	M	M	—
Cordyline australis	*Giant Dracaena*	L	L	L	LM	M	M	M	M
Cupressus arizonica	*Arizona Cypress*	L	L	L	L	L	LM	LM	LM
Cupressus forbesii	*Tecate Cypress*	L	L	L	L	L	—	—	—
Cupressus glabra	*Smooth Arizona Cypress*	L	L	L	L	L	LM	LM	LM
Cupressus macrocarpa	*Monterey Cypress*	AL	AL	L	—	—	—	—	—
Cupressus sempervirens	*Italian Cypress*	AL	AL	L	L	L	LM	LM	LM
Dalea spinosa	*Smoke Tree*	—	—	—	—	—	L	L	—
Dodonaea viscosa	*Hopseed Bush*	L	L	LM	LM	LM	LM	LM	LM
Dracaena draco	*Dragon Tree*	L	—	L	L	—	—	—	—
Eucalyptus caesia	*Gungurru*	L	L	L	L	—	—	—	—
Eucalyptus camaldulensis	*River Red Gum*	AL	AL	AL	LM	LM	M	M	—
Eucalyptus cinerea	*Argyle Apple*	AL	AL	AL	LM	LM	—	—	—
Eucalyptus citriodora	*Lemon-scented Gum*	L	L	L	M	—	—	—	—
Eucalyptus cladocalyx	*Sugar Gum*	AL	AL	AL	L	—	—	—	—
Eucalyptus erythrocorys	*Red-cap Gum*	L	L	L	M	M	—	—	—
Eucalyptus ficifolia	*Red Flowering Gum*	AL	AL	AL	LM	—	—	—	—

Estimated Water Needs for Landscape Plants

Legend:
AL = Adapted to region—Little or low water needs
L = Low supplemental water needs
LM = Low to moderate supplemental water needs
M = Moderate supplemental water needs
MH = Moderate to high supplemental water needs
— = Not well suited to this region
NCN = No common name

Trees (Cont.):

		Northern Coastal	Northern Inland Valleys & Foothills	Southern Coastal	Southern Inland Valleys & Foothills	Central Valley	Low Deserts	Intermediate Deserts	High Deserts
Eucalyptus globulus & cv	*Blue Gum*	AL	AL	AL	LM	LM	—	—	—
Eucalyptus lehmannii	*Lehmann's Mallee*	AL	AL	AL	LM	—	—	—	—
Eucalyptus leucoxylon & cv	*White Ironbark*	AL	AL	AL	LM	LM	M	—	—
Eucalyptus maculata	*Spotted Gum*	AL	AL	AL	LM	—	—	—	—
Eucalyptus microtheca	*Coolibah*	AL	AL	AL	L	LM	M	M	—
Eucalyptus nicholii	*Willow Peppermint*	AL	AL	AL	LM	LM	M	M	—
Eucalyptus papuana	*Ghost Gum*	L	L	L	LM	LM	M	M	—
Eucalyptus polyanthemos	*Silver Dollar Gum*	AL	AL	AL	LM	LM	M	M	M
Eucalyptus rudis	*Flooded Gum*	AL	AL	AL	LM	LM	M	M	M
Eucalyptus sideroxylon & cv	*Red Ironbark*	AL	AL	AL	LM	LM	M	M	M
Eucalyptus spathulata	*Narrow-leaved Gimlet*	AL	AL	L	LM	L	LM	LM	LM
Eucalyptus torquata	*Coral Gum*	L	L	L	LM	LM	M	—	—
Eucalyptus viminalis	*Manna Gum*	AL	AL	L	LM	M	M	—	—
Feijoa sellowiana	*Pineapple Guava*	L	L	L	LM	M	M	M	—
Ficus carica & cvs	*Common Fig*	LM	LM	LM	M	M	MH	MH	MH
Geijera parviflora	*Australian Willow*	L	L	L	LM	LM	M	M	—
Grevillea robusta	*Silky Oak*	L	L	L	LM	LM	M	MH	—
Juglans californica	*S. Calif. Black Walnut*	AL	AL	AL	AL	—	—	—	—
Juniperus chinensis 'Torulosa'	*Hollywood Juniper*	L	L	L	LM	LM	M	M	M
Juniperus virginiana	*Eastern Redcedar*	LM	LM	LM	M	M	—	—	—
Lagerstroemia indica & cvs	*Crape Myrtle*	L	L	L	LM	LM	M	M	M
Laurus nobilis	*Sweet Bay*	L	L	L	LM	M	M	M	M
Leptospermum laevigatum	*Australian Tea Tree*	AL	AL	AL	L	M	—	—	—
Leptospermum scoparium	*New Zealand Tea Tree*	LM	LM	LM	M	M	—	—	—
Lyonothamnus floribundus & var.	*Catalina Ironwood*	AL	AL	AL	LM	—	—	—	—
Lysiloma m. var. Thornberi	*Feather Bush*	—	—	—	L	—	M	M	M
Melaleuca armillaris	*Drooping Melaleuca*	L	L	L	LM	LM	—	—	—
Melaleuca linariifolia	*Flaxleaf Paperbark*	L	L	L	M	M	—	—	—
Melaleuca quinquenervia	*Cajeput Tree*	L	L	L	LM	M	M	M	—
Melia azedarach & cv	*Chinaberry*	AL	AL	AL	AL	AL	M	M	M
Metrosideros excelsus	*New Zealand Christmas Tree*	L	LM	LM	M	—	—	—	—
Morus alba	*White Mulberry*	AL	AL	AL	AL	AL	—	—	—
Myoporum laetum	*Myoporum*	AL	L	L	LM	M	—	—	—
Myrica californica	*Pacific Wax Myrtle*	L	L	LM	M	—	—	—	—
Nerium oleander & cvs	*Oleander*	AL	AL	AL	L	LM	M	M	M
Olea europaea & cvs	*Olive*	AL	AL	AL	L	LM	M	M	M
Olneya tesota	*Desert Ironwood*	—	—	—	—	LM	LM	LM	LM
Parkinsonia aculeata	*Mexican Palo Verde*	L	L	L	LM	LM	LM	LM	LM
Pinus brutia	*Calabrian Pine*	L	L	L	LM	LM	M	M	M
Pinus canariensis	*Canary Island Pine*	L	L	L	LM	LM	MH	MH	MH
Pinus coulteri	*Coulter Pine*	L	L	L	L	LM	—	—	—
Pinus eldarica	*Afghan Pine*	L	L	L	LM	LM	LM	LM	LM
Pinus halepensis	*Aleppo Pine*	AL	AL	AL	AL	L	LM	LM	LM
Pinus monophylla	*Single-leaf Pinon Pine*	—	—	—	L	L	L	LM	LM
Pinus pinea	*Italian Stone Pine*	L	L	L	L	LM	M	M	M
Pinus radiata	*Monterey Pine*	AL	AL	AL	LM	—	—	—	—
Pinus sabiniana	*Digger Pine*	AL	AL	L	L	AL	—	—	—
Pinus torreyana	*Torrey Pine*	AL	AL	AL	LM	—	—	—	—
Pithecellobium flexicaule	*Texas Ebony*	—	—	—	—	—	LM	LM	LM
Pittosporum phillyraeoides	*Willow Pittosporum*	L	L	L	LM	LM	LM	LM	—
Platanus racemosa	*Western Sycamore*	M	M	M	MH	MH	MH	—	—
Prosopis alba	*Argentine Mesquite*	—	—	—	L	L	LM	LM	LM
Prosopis chilensis	*Chilean Mesquite*	—	—	—	L	L	LM	LM	LM
Prosopis glandulosa	*Texas Mesquite*	—	—	—	L	L	LM	LM	LM
Prosopis juliflora	*Mesquite*	—	—	—	L	L	LM	LM	LM

Trees (Cont.):

		Northern Coastal	Northern Inland Valleys & Foothills	Southern Coastal	Southern Inland Valleys & Foothills	Central Valley	Low Deserts	Intermediate Deserts	High Deserts
Prosopis pubescens	*Screw Bean Mesquite*	—	—	—	—	—	LM	LM	LM
Prunus caroliniana	*Carolina Laurel Cherry*	L	L	L	LM	M	M	M	M
Prunus lyonii	*Catalina Cherry*	AL	AL	AL	LM	LM	—	—	—
Punica granatum & cvs	*Pomegranate*	L	L	L	LM	M	M	M	M
Quercus agrifolia	*Coast Live Oak*	AL	AL	AL	AL	LM	—	—	—
Quercus douglasii	*Blue Oak*	AL	AL	AL	AL	AL	—	—	—
Quercus engelmannii	*Mesa Oak*	—	—	AL	AL		—	—	—
Quercus ilex	*Holly Oak*	L	L	L	LM	LM	M	M	M
Quercus lobata	*Valley Oak*	L	L	L	L	AL	—	—	—
Quercus suber	*Cork Oak*	L	L	L	L	L	M	M	M
Rhus lancea	*African Sumac*	L	L	L	LM	LM	M	M	M
Robinia ambigua & cvs	*Locust*	L	L	L	LM	LM	M	M	M
Robinia pseudoacacia	*Black Locust*	L	L	L	LM	LM	LM	LM	M
Sambucus caerulea	*Blue Elderberry*	AL	AL	AL	AL	LM	—	—	—
Schinus molle	*Pepper Tree*	AL	AL	AL	AL	AL	LM	LM	LM
Schinus polygamus	*Peruvian Pepper*	L	L	L	L	LM	LM	LM	—
Schinus terebinthifolius	*Brazilian Pepper*	LM	LM	LM	M	M	MH	—	—
Sophora secundiflora	*Mescal Bean*	—	—	—	L	—	LM	LM	LM
Tamarix aphylla	*Athel Tree*	AL	AL	AL	AL	L	LM	LM	LM
Tristania conferta & cv	*Brisbane Box*	M	M	M	MH	—	—	—	—
Vitex angus-castus	*Chaste Tree*	L	L	L	LM	LM	M	M	M
Xylosma congestum	*Shiny Xylosma*	L	L	LM	LM	LM	M	M	M
Yucca brevifolia	*Joshua Tree*	—	—	—	—	—	L	L	AL
Yucca gloriosa	*Spanish Dagger*	L	L	L	L	L	L	L	L

Palms:

		Northern Coastal	Northern Inland Valleys & Foothills	Southern Coastal	Southern Inland Valleys & Foothills	Central Valley	Low Deserts	Intermediate Deserts	High Deserts
Brahea armata	*Blue Hesper Palm*	L	L	L	L	LM	LM	LM	LM
Brahea edulis	*Guadalupe Palm*	L	L	L	LM	LM	LM	LM	LM
Butia capitata	*Pindo Palm*	L	L	L	L	LM	LM	LM	LM
Chamaerops humilis	*Mediterranean Fan Palm*	L	L	L	L	LM	LM	LM	LM
Phoenix canariensis	*Canary Island Date Palm*	L	L	L	LM	LM	M	M	M
Phoenix dactylifera	*Date Palm*	—	—	L	L	LM	M	M	M
Trachycarpus fortunei	*Windmill Palm*	L	L	L	LM	M	—	M	—
Washingtonia filifera	*California Fan Palm*	L	L	L	LM	M	M	M	M
Washingtonia robusta	*Mexican Fan Palm*	L	L	L	LM	M	M	M	M

Shrubs & Vines:

		Northern Coastal	Northern Inland Valleys & Foothills	Southern Coastal	Southern Inland Valleys & Foothills	Central Valley	Low Deserts	Intermediate Deserts	High Deserts
Acacia berlandieri	*Berlandier Acacia*	—	—	—	—	—	LM	LM	—
Acacia cultriformis	*Knife Acacia*	AL	AL	AL	L	L	—	—	—
Acacia cyclops	*Western Coastal Wattle*	AL	AL	AL	L	—	—	—	—
Acacia farnesiana	*Sweet Acacia*	—	—	L	L	L	L	—	—
Acacia greggii	*Catclaw Acacia*	—	—	—	—	—	AL	AL	AL
Acacia longifolia	*Sydney Golden Wattle*	AL	L	AL	L	L	—	—	—
Acacia retinodes	*Water Wattle*	L	L	L	M	M	—	—	—
Aesculus californica	*California Buckeye*	AL	AL	AL	AL	L	—	—	—
Alyogyne huegelii	*Blue Hibiscus*	L	L	L	LM	LM	LM	—	—
Anisacanthus thurberi	*Desert Honeysuckle*	—	—	—	L	—	LM	LM	—
Anisodontea hypomandarum	*Dwarf Pink Hibiscus*	L	L	LM	LM	—	M	—	—
Arbutus unedo 'Compacta'	*Dwarf Strawberry Tree*	L	L	L	LM	LM	M	M	M
Arctostaphylos densiflora & cvs	*Sonoma Manzanita*	L	L	L	L	LM	—	—	—
Arctostaphylos edmundsii	*Little Sur Manzanita*	AL	L	L	LM	—	—	—	—
Arctostaphylos hookeri	*Monterey Manzanita*	AL	AL	L	L	LM	—	—	—
Artemisia arborescens	*Shrubby Wormwood*	AL	AL	AL	L	—			

Estimated Water Needs for Landscape Plants

Legend:
- **AL** = Adapted to region—Little or low water needs
- **L** = Low supplemental water needs
- **LM** = Low to moderate supplemental water needs
- **M** = Moderate supplemental water needs
- **MH** = Moderate to high supplemental water needs
- **—** = Not well suited to this region
- *NCN* = No common name

Shrubs & Vines (Cont.):

		Northern Coastal	Northern Inland Valleys & Foothills	Southern Coastal	Southern Inland Valleys & Foothills	Central Valley	Low Deserts	Intermediate Deserts	High Deserts
Artemisia californica & cvs	*California Sagebrush*	AL	AL	AL	AL	—	—	—	—
Artemisia 'Powis Castle'	*NCN*	AL	AL	AL	L	—	—	—	—
Atriplex canescens	*Four-wing Saltbush*	—	—	—	—	L	L	L	L
Atriplex hymenelytra	*Desert Holly*	—	—	—	—	—	L	L	L
Atriplex lentiformis	*Quail Bush*	—	—	—	—	—	L	L	L
Atriplex l. var. breweri	*Brewer Saltbush*	AL	L	L	AL	L			
Baccharis p. consahguinea	*Chaparral Broom*	AL	AL	AL	AL	L	—	—	—
Baccharis sarothroides	*Desert Broom*	—	—	L	L	L	L	AL	AL
Bougainvillea species & cvs	*Bougainvillea*	LM	LM	LM	LM	LM	LM	LM	—
Buddleia marrubiifolia	*Woolly Butterfly Bush*	—	—	—	—	—	L	L	L
Caesalpinia species	*Bird-of-paradise Bush*	—	—	L	L	—	L	L	—
Calliandra californica	*Baja Fairy Duster*	—	—	—	L	—	L	L	L
Calliandra eriophylla	*Fairy Duster*	—	—	—	L	—	L	L	—
Calliandra peninsularis	*NCN*	—	—	—	L	—	L	L	—
Callistemon citrinus	*Lemon Bottlebrush*	L	L	L	M	M	M	M	—
Callistemon rigidus	*Stiff Bottlebrush*	L	L	L	L	L	LM	—	—
Calocephalus brownii	*Cushion Bush*	L	L	LM	M	—	—	—	—
Carpenteria californica	*Bush Anemone*	L	L	L	LM	LM	—	—	—
Cassia artemisioides	*Feathery Cassia*	L	L	L	L	L	L	L	L
Cassia nemophila	*Desert Cassia*	—	—	L	L	L	L	L	L
Cassia odorata	*Spreading Cassia*	—	—	L	L	—	L	—	—
Cassia phyllodinea	*Silvery Cassia*	—	—	L	L	L	L	L	—
Ceanothus arboreus	*Feltleaf Ceanothus*	AL	L	L	L	L	—	—	—
Ceanothus 'Concha'	*NCN*	AL	AL	L	L	L	—	—	—
Ceanothus 'Dark Star'	*NCN*	AL	AL	AL	L	L	—	—	—
Ceanothus 'Frosty Blue'	*NCN*	AL	AL	AL	L	L	—	—	—
Ceanothus gloriosus & cvs	*Point Reyes Ceanothus*	AL	AL	AL	L	L	—	—	—
Ceanothus griseus & cvs	*Carmel Ceanothus*	AL	AL	AL	L	L	—	—	—
Ceanothus impressus	*Santa Barbara Ceanothus*	AL	L	L	L	L	—	—	—
Ceanothus 'Joyce Coulter'	*NCN*	AL	AL	AL	L	L	—	—	—
Ceanothus 'Julia Phelps'	*NCN*	AL	AL	AL	L	L	—	—	—
Ceanothus maritimus & cvs	*Maritime Ceanothus*	AL	AL	AL	L	L	—	—	—
Ceanothus 'Ray Hartman'	*NCN*	AL	AL	AL	L	L	—	—	—
Ceanothus rigidus & cvs	*Monterey Ceanothus*	AL	AL	AL	L	L	—	—	—
Ceanothus thyrsiflorus & cvs	*Blue Blossom Ceanothus*	AL	AL	AL	L	L	—	—	—
Ceanothus 'Wheeler Canyon'	*NCN*	AL	L	L	L	LM	—	—	—
Cercis occidentalis	*Western Redbud*	AL	AL	L	M	M	—	—	—
Chamelaucium uncinatum	*Geraldton Wax Flower*	L	L	L	LM	—	M	—	—
Chilopsis linearis	*Desert Willow*	L	L	L	L	M	M	M	M
Cistus species & cvs	*Rockrose*	L	L	L	LM	LM	LM	LM	LM
Cleome isomeris	*Bladderpod*	AL	AL	AL	L	LM	AL	AL	AL
Comarostaphylis diversifolia	*Summer Holly*	AL	AL	AL	L	—	—	—	—
Cordia species	*Cordia*	—	—	—	—	L	L	L	L
Correa species & cvs	*Correa*	L	L	L	LM	LM	—	—	—
Cotoneaster apiculatus	*Cranberry Cotoneaster*	L	L	LM	LM	LM	—	—	—
Cotoneaster buxifolius	*NCN*	L	L	L	LM	LM	M	M	M
Cotoneaster congestus	*NCN*	L	L	L	M	M	M	M	M
Cotoneaster horizontalis	*Rock Cotoneaster*	L	L	L	M	M	M	M	M
Cotoneaster lacteus	*Red Clusterberry*	L	L	L	LM	LM	M	M	M
Cotoneaster salicifolius	*Willowleaf Cotoneaster*	L	L	L	LM	M	M	M	M
Cowania mexicana	*Cliff Rose*	—	—	—	—	—	L	L	L
Dalea frutescens	*Black Dalea*	—	—	LM	LM	—	M	M	M
Dalea pulchra	*Indigo Bush*	—	—	LM	LM	—	M	M	M
Dendromecon species	*Bush Poppy*	L	L	AL	L	L	—	—	—
Dodonaea viscosa	*Hopseed Bush*	L	L	LM	LM	LM	LM	LM	LM

	Northern Coastal	Northern Inland Valleys & Foothills	Southern Coastal	Southern Inland Valleys & Foothills	Central Valley	Low Deserts	Intermediate Deserts	High Deserts
Echium fastuosum — *Pride of Madeira*	L	L	L	LM	LM	—	—	—
Elaeagnus pungens — *Silverberry*	L	L	L	L	L	LM	LM	LM
Encelia californica — *California Encelia*	L	L	AL	L	—	—	—	—
Encelia farinosa — *Desert Encelia*	—	—	—	L	L	L	L	L
Eriogonum arborescens — *Santa Cruz Island Buckwheat*	L	L	AL	L	L	—	—	—
Eriogonum cinereum — *Asyleaf Buckwheat*	L	L	AL	L	L	—	—	—
Eriogonum fasciculatum — *Common Buckwheat*	AL	AL	AL	AL	L	L	—	—
Eriogonum giganteum — *St. Catherine's Lace*	AL	AL	AL	AL	L	—	—	—
Eriogonum parvifolium — *Coastal Buckwheat*	AL	AL	AL	L	L	—	—	—
Eucalyptus lehmannii — *Bushy Yate*	AL	AL	AL	LM	—	—	—	—
Fallugia paradoxa — *Apache Plume*	—	—	—	L	—	L	L	L
Feijoa sellowiana — *Pineapple Guava*	L	L	L	LM	M	M	M	—
Fremontodendron species & cvs — *California Flannel Bush*	AL	AL	AL	AL	L	—	—	—
Galvezia speciosa — *Island Bush-snapdragon*	L	L	L	LM	M	—	—	—
Garrya elliptica — *Coast Silktassel*	AL	AL	AL	L	LM	—	—	—
Grevillea species & cvs — *Grevillea*	L	L	L	LM	LM	M	M	—
Hakea suaveolens — *Sweet-scented Hakea*	L	L	L	LM	LM	—	—	—
Hardenbergia violacea — *False Sarsaparilla*	L	L	L	LM	—	—	—	—
Heteromeles arbutifolia — *Toyon*	AL	AL	AL	AL	L	—	—	—
Hibiscus syriacus — *Rose of Sharon*	L	LM	L	LM	M	M	M	M
Iva hayesiana — *Hayes Iva*	L	L	AL	L	—	—	—	—
Jasminum species — *Jasmine*	L	LM	LM	LM	M	M	M	—
Juniperus californica — *California Juniper*	—	—	—	—	L	L	L	L
Juniperus chinensis & cvs — *NCN*	L	L	L	LM	LM	M	M	M
Juniperus sabina & cvs — *Savin Juniper*	L	L	L	L	LM	M	M	M
Juniperus scopulorum & cvs — *Rocky Mountain Juniper*	L	L	L	L	L	—	L	L
Justicia californica — *Chuparosa*	—	—	L	L	—	L	L	—
Justicia spicigera — *Mexican Honeysuckle*	—	—	—	L	—	LM	LM	—
Keckiella species — *Native Penstemon*	AL	AL	AL	AL	—	—	—	—
Lagerstroemia indica & cvs — *Compact Crape Myrtle*	L	L	L	LM	LM	M	M	M
Lantana camara — *Yellow Sage*	L	LM	LM	LM	M	M	M	—
Larrea tridentata — *Creosote Bush*	—	—	—	—	—	AL	AL	AL
Lavandula species & cvs — *Lavender*	L	L	L	LM	LM	M	M	M
Lavatera species — *Mallow*	AL	L	AL	LM	M	—	—	—
Leonotis leonurus — *Lion's Tail*	L	L	L	LM	LM	M	M	M
Leptospermum laevigatum — *Australian Tea Tree*	AL	AL	AL	L	M	—	—	—
Leptospermum scoparium — *New Zealand Tea Tree*	LM	LM	LM	M	M	—	—	—
Leucophyllum species & cvs — *Cenizo*	L	L	L	LM	L	LM	LM	LM
Lupinus albifrons — *Silver Lupine*	L	L	L	L	L	—	—	—
Lupinus arboreus — *Coastal Bush Lupine*	AL	AL	AL	L	—	—	—	—
Macfadyena unguis-cati — *Cat's Claw*	L	L	L	L	L	L	L	L
Mahonia aquifolium — *Oregon Grape*	LM	LM	M	M	M	—	—	—
Mahonia 'Golden Abundance' — *NCN*	L	L	L	LM	LM	—	—	—
Mahonia nevinii — *Nevin Mahonia*	L	L	L	AL	L	—	—	—
Mahonia pinnata & cvs — *California Grape*	AL	AL	L	LM	LM	—	—	—
Malosma laurina — *Laurel Sumac*	L	L	AL	AL	—	—	—	—
Melaleuca armillaris — *Drooping Melaleuca*	L	L	L	LM	LM	—	—	—
Melaleuca nesophila — *Pink Melaleuca*	AL	AL	AL	LM	LM	M	—	—
Metrosideros excelsus — *New Zealand Christmas Tree*	L	LM	LM	M	—	—	—	—
Myoporum laetum & cvs — *NCN*	AL	L	L	LM	M	—	—	—
Myrica californica — *Pacific Wax Myrtle*	L	L	LM	M	—	—	—	—
Myrtus communis & cvs — *True Myrtle*	L	L	L	LM	LM	M	M	M
Nerium oleander & cvs — *Oleander*	AL	AL	AL	L	LM	M	M	M
Plecostachys serpyllifolia — *NCN*	L	L	L	LM	—	—	—	—
Plumbago auriculata — *Cape Plumbago*	L	L	L	LM	LM	M	M	—

Estimated Water Needs for Landscape Plants

Legend:
- **AL** = Adapted to region—Little or low water needs
- **L** = Low supplemental water needs
- **LM** = Low to moderate supplemental water needs
- **M** = Moderate supplemental water needs
- **MH** = Moderate to high supplemental water needs
- **—** = Not well suited to this region
- *NCN* = No common name

Shrubs & Vines (Cont.):

		Northern Coastal	Northern Inland Valleys & Foothills	Southern Coastal	Southern Inland Valleys & Foothills	Central Valley	Low Deserts	Intermediate Deserts	High Deserts
Polygonum aubertii	*Silver Lace Vine*	L	L	L	L	LM	—	—	—
Prosopis pubescens	*Screw Bean Mesquite*	—	—	—	—	—	LM	LM	LM
Prunus caroliniana cvs	*Carolina Laurel Cherry*	L	L	L	LM	M	M	M	M
Prunus ilicifolia	*Hollyleaf Cherry*	AL	AL	AL	AL	L	—	—	—
Prunus lyonii	*Catalina Cherry*	AL	AL	AL	LM	LM	—	—	—
Punica granatum & cvs	*Pomegranate*	L	L	L	LM	M	M	M	M
Pyracantha species & cvs	*Firethorn*	L	L	L	LM	M	M	M	M
Rhamnus alaternus	*Italian Buckthorn*	L	L	L	LM	M	—	—	—
Rhamnus californica	*California Coffeeberry*	AL	AL	L	LM	—	—	—	—
Rhamnus crocea & var.	*Redberry*	AL	AL	AL	AL	—	—	—	—
Rhaphiolepis indica & cvs	*India Hawthorn*	L	L	L	LM	LM	M	M	M
Rhaphiolepis 'Majestic Beauty'	*NCN*	L	L	L	LM	LM	M	M	M
Rhaphiolepis umbellata & cv	*Yedda Hawthorn*	L	L	L	LM	LM	—	—	—
Rhus integrifolia	*Lemonade Berry*	AL	AL	AL	L	LM	—	—	—
Rhus ovata	*Sugar Bush*	AL	AL	AL	L	M	—	M	M
Ribes aureum	*Golden Currant*	AL	AL	AL	AL	L	—	—	—
Ribes indecorum	*White-flowered Currant*	AL	AL	AL	AL	—	—	—	—
Ribes malvaceum	*Chaparral Currant*	AL	AL	AL	AL	—	—	—	—
Ribes speciosum	*Fuchsia-flowering Gooseberry*	LM	LM	LM	LM	M	—	—	—
Rosa banksiae	*Lady Banks' Rose*	LM	LM	LM	LM	LM	M	M	M
Rosmarinus officinalis & cvs	*Rosemary*	L	L	L	L	LM	M	M	M
Ruellia species	*Ruellia*	—	—	—	—	—	M	M	M
Salvia apiana	*White Sage*	L	L	AL	AL	L	—	—	—
Salvia chamaedryoides	*Blue Sage*	L	L	L	L	LM	M	—	—
Salvia clevelandii & cvs	*Cleveland Sage*	AL	AL	AL	AL	L	—	—	—
Salvia greggii	*Autumn Sage*	L	L	L	LM	LM	LM	LM	LM
Salvia leucantha	*Mexican Bush Sage*	L	L	L	LM	LM	LM	LM	—
Salvia leucophylla	*Purple Sage*	AL	AL	AL	AL	L	—	—	—
Salvia mellifera & cvs	*Black Sage*	AL	AL	AL	AL	—	—	—	—
Sambucus caerulea	*Blue Elderberry*	AL	AL	AL	AL	LM	—	—	—
Santolina species	*Lavender Cotton*	L	L	L	L	LM	LM	LM	LM
Schinus molle	*Pepper Tree*	AL	AL	AL	AL	AL	LM	LM	LM
Schinus terebinthefolius	*Brazilian Pepper*	LM	LM	LM	M	M	MH	—	—
Simmondsia chinensis	*Jojoba*	L	L	L	L	LM	LM	LM	LM
Sollya heterophylla	*Australian Blue-bell Creeper*	L	L	L	LM	LM	—	—	—
Sophora secundiflora	*Mescal Bean*	—	—	—	L	—	LM	LM	LM
Tecoma stans var. angustata	*Hardy Yellow Trumpet Flower*	—	—	—	L	—	LM	LM	LM
Tecomaria capensis	*Cape Honeysuckle*	LM	LM	LM	M	M	MH	MH	—
Teucrium chamaedrys	*NCN*	L	LM	LM	LM	M	—	—	—
Teucrium fruticans	*Bush Germander*	L	L	L	L	L	—	—	—
Trichostema lanatum	*Woolly Blue Curls*	AL	AL	AL	AL	L	—	—	—
Vitex agnus-castus	*Chaste Tree*	L	L	L	LM	LM	M	M	M
Westringia species	*NCN*	L	L	L	LM	M	M	—	—
Xylosma congestum	*Shiny Xylosma*	L	L	LM	LM	LM	M	M	M

Ground Covers:

		Northern Coastal	Northern Inland Valleys & Foothills	Southern Coastal	Southern Inland Valleys & Foothills	Central Valley	Low Deserts	Intermediate Deserts	High Deserts
Acacia redolens & cvs	*NCN*	L	L	L	LM	LM	LM	LM	—
Achillea millefolium	*Common Yarrow*	L	L	L	LM	LM	—	—	—
Adenostoma fasciculatum 'Prostrata'	*Chamise*	L	L	L	L	—	—	—	—
Aptenia 'Red Apple'	*NCN*	L	L	L	LM	M	M	M	—
Arctostaphylos edmundsii & cvs	*Little Sur Manzanita*	L	L	L	LM	L	—	—	—
Arctostaphylos 'Emerald Carpet'	*NCN*	L	L	L	LM	L	—	—	—
Arctostaphylos hookeri & cvs	*Monterey Manzanita*	L	L	L	LM	L	—	—	—

Ground Covers (Cont.):

		Northern Coastal	Northern Inland Valleys & Foothills	Southern Coastal	Southern Inland Valleys & Foothills	Central Valley	Low Deserts	Intermediate Deserts	High Deserts
Arctostaphylos 'Pacific Mist'	*NCN*	L	L	L	LM	L	—	—	—
Arctostaphylos uva-ursi & cvs	*Bearberry*	L	LM	LM	LM	LM	—	—	—
Arctotheca calendula	*Cape Weed*	LM	LM	LM	M	M	M	—	—
Artemisia californica & cvs	*Prostrate California Sagebrush*	AL	AL	AL	L	—	—	—	—
Atriplex glauca	*NCN*	AL	AL	AL	AL	L	—	—	—
Atriplex semibaccata	*Creeping Saltbush*	AL	AL	AL	AL	L	—	—	—
Baccharis 'Centennial'	*NCN*	L	L	L	LM	LM	LM	LM	LM
Baccharis pilularis & cvs	*Prostrate Coyote Brush*	L	L	L	LM	M	—	—	—
Bougainvillea cultivars	*Bougainvillea*	L	L	L	LM	—	LM	LM	—
Carpobrotus species	*Sea Fig*	AL	AL	AL	LM	M	LM	—	—
Ceanothus gloriosus & cvs	*Point Reyes Ceanothus*	AL	AL	L	LM	LM	—	—	—
Ceanothus g. var. horizontalis	*Carmel Creeper*	AL	AL	L	LM	LM	—	—	—
Ceanothus g. var. h. 'Yankee Point'	*NCN*	AL	AL	L	LM	LM	—	—	—
Ceanothus 'Joyce Coulter'	*NCN*	AL	AL	L	LM	LM	—	—	—
Ceanothus maritimus & cvs	*Maritime Ceanothus*	AL	AL	L	LM	LM	—	—	—
Cephalophyllum 'Red Spike'	*Red Spike Ice Plant*	L	L	L	L	LM	—	—	—
Cistus salviifolius	*Sageleaf Rockrose*	L	L	L	L	LM	—	—	—
Cistus 'Sunset'	*NCN*	L	L	L	L	LM	—	—	—
Coprosma kirkii	*NCN*	L	LM	L	LM	LM	—	—	—
Coprosma 'Verde Vista'	*NCN*	L	L	L	LM	M	—	—	—
Cotoneaster adpressus	*Creeping Cotoneaster*	L	L	L	M	M	—	—	—
Cotoneaster dammeri & cvs	*NCN*	L	L	L	M	M	—	—	—
Cotoneaster horizontalis	*Rock Cotoneaster*	L	L	L	M	M	—	—	—
Cotoneaster salicifolius 'Repens'	*NCN*	L	L	L	LM	M	—	—	—
Crassula multicava	*NCN*	L	L	L	L	—	—	L	—
Dalea greggii	*Trailing Indigo Bush*	—	—	—	—	—	L	L	L
Delosperma 'Alba'	*White Trailing Ice Plant*	L	L	L	LM	M	LM	—	—
Drosanthemum floribundum	*Rosea Ice Plant*	L	L	L	L	LM	L	—	—
Dymondia margaretae	*NCN*	L	L	L	L	LM	—	—	—
Eriogonum fasciculatum & cvs	*Common Buckwheat*	AL	AL	AL	AL	L	L	—	—
Festuca ovina glauca	*Blue Fescue*	L	L	L	LM	M	M	M	M
Gazania species & cvs	*Gazania*	LM	LM	LM	LM	M	M	M	—
Hardenbergia violacea & cvs	*False Sarsaparilla*	L	L	L	LM	M	—	—	—
Iva hayesiana	*Hayes Iva*	L	L	AL	L	—	—	—	—
Juniperus chinensis & cvs	*NCN*	L	L	L	LM	LM	M	M	M
Juniperus conferta	*Shore Juniper*	L	LM	L	LM	M	M	M	—
Juniperus horizontalis & cvs	*Creeping Juniper*	L	L	L	LM	LM	M	M	M
Juniperus sabina & cvs	*Tamarix Juniper*	L	L	L	L	LM	M	M	M
Lampranthus species	*Ice Plant*	L	L	L	LM	LM	LM	LM	—
Lantana montevidensis & cvs	*Trailing Lantana*	L	L	L	L	LM	LM	LM	—
Lonicera japonica 'Halliana'	*Hall's Japanese Honeysuckle*	LM	LM	LM	LM	M	M	M	M
Mahonia aquifolium 'Compacta'	*Compact Oregon Grape*	LM	LM	LM	M	M	—	—	—
Mahonia repens	*Creeping Mahonia*	L	L	L	LM	M	—	—	—
Maleophora species	*Ice Plant*	L	L	L	L	L	LM	—	—
Myoporum hybrids	*NCN*	L	L	L	LM	LM	—	—	—
Myoporum parvifolium & cvs	*Prostrate Myoporum*	L	L	L	L	L	LM	LM	—
Pyracantha species & cvs	*Firethorn*	L	L	L	LM	M	M	M	M
Ribes viburnifolium	*Evergreen Currant*	L	L	L	LM	LM	—	—	—
Rosmarinus officinalis & cvs	*Prostrate Rosemary*	L	L	L	L	LM	M	M	M
Salvia mellifera & cvs	*Prostrate Black Sage*	AL	AL	AL	AL	—	—	—	—
Scaevola 'Mauve Clusters'	*NCN*	L	L	L	LM	LM	—	—	—
Sedum species	*Stonecrop*	L	L	L	L	L	L	—	—
Senecio mandraliscae	*NCN*	L	L	L	L	L	L	—	—
Teucrium cossonii	*NCN*	LM	LM	LM	LM	—	—	—	—
Verbena species & cvs	*Verbena*	L	L	L	LM	LM	LM	LM	LM

Estimated Water Needs for Landscape Plants

Legend:
- **AL** = Adapted to region—Little or low water needs
- **L** = Low supplemental water needs
- **LM** = Low to moderate supplemental water needs
- **M** = Moderate supplemental water needs
- **MH** = Moderate to high supplemental water needs
- **—** = Not well suited to this region
- *NCN* = No common name

Perennials:

		Northern Coastal	Northern Inland Valleys & Foothills	Southern Coastal	Southern Inland Valleys & Foothills	Central Valley	Intermediate Deserts	Low Deserts	High Deserts
Achillea species & cvs	*Yarrow*	L	L	L	LM	LM	—	—	—
Anigozanthos species & cvs	*Kangaroo Paw*	LM	LM	LM	M	M	M	M	—
Armeria maritima	*Sea Pink*	M	M	M	M	M	—	—	—
Artemisia pycnocephala & cvs	*Sandhill Sage*	L	L	LM	LM	M	—	—	—
Asteriscus species	*NCN*	L	L	L	LM	M	—	—	—
Baileya multiradiata	*Desert Marigold*	—	—	—	L	—	L	L	L
Brachycome multifida	*Cut-leaf Daisy*	LM	LM	LM	M	M	—	—	—
Centaurea species	*Dusty Miller*	L	L	L	LM	M	M	M	—
Centranthus ruber	*Red Valerian*	AL	AL	AL	AL	LM	M	M	—
Cheiranthus 'Bowles Mauve'	*Shrubby Wallflower*	LM	LM	LM	M	M	—	—	—
Convolvulus cneorum	*Bush Morning Glory*	L	L	L	LM	M	M	M	—
Convolvulus mauritanicus	*Ground Morning Glory*	L	L	L	LM	M	—	—	—
Coreopsis species & cvs	*Coreopsis*	L	L	L	LM	M	M	M	M
Cortaderia selloana	*Pampas Grass*	L	L	L	L	LM	LM	LM	LM
Dietes species & cvs	*Fortnight Lily*	L	L	L	LM	LM	—	—	—
Diplacus species & hybrids	*Monkey Flower*	AL	AL	AL	L	LM	—	—	—
Elymus species & cvs	*Giant Wild Rye*	L	L	L	L	LM	—	—	—
Epilobium species & cvs	*California Fuchsia*	L	L	L	L	L	—	—	—
Erigeron glaucus & cvs	*Beach Aster*	L	L	L	M	—	—	—	—
Erigeron karvinskianus	*Mexican Daisy*	L	L	LM	LM	M	M	M	M
Eriogonum crocatum	*Conejo Buckwheat*	L	L	L	LM	M	—	—	—
Eriogonum grande ssp. rubescens	*Red Buckwheat*	L	L	L	L	M	—	—	—
Eriogonum umbellatum & cv	*Sulfur Flower*	L	L	LM	LM	M	—	—	—
Eschscholzia californica	*California Poppy*	AL	AL	AL	L	L	—	—	—
Euphorbia milii	*Crown of Thorns*	L	L	L	L	L	M	M	—
Euphorbia rigida	*NCN*	L	L	L	L	LM	M	M	M
Euryops pectinatus & cv	*Euryops*	L	L	L	LM	M	M	M	M
Gaillardia grandiflora	*Blanket Flower*	L	L	L	LM	LM	M	M	M
Gaura lindheimeri	*Gaura*	LM	LM	LM	LM	LM	M	M	M
Helianthemum nummularium & cvs	*Sunrose*	LM	LM	LM	LM	M	—	—	—
Helictotrichon sempervirens	*Blue Oat Grass*	L	L	L	LM	M	M	M	—
Heuchera species & cvs	*Coral Bells*	M	M	M	M	M	—	—	—
Iris douglasiana & cvs	*Pacific Coast Iris*	LM	LM	LM	M	M	—	—	—
Kniphofia uvaria & cvs	*Red-hot Poker*	L	L	L	LM	M	M	M	—
Limonium perezii	*Sea Lavender*	AL	L	AL	LM	LM	M	M	—
Lobelia laxiflora	*Mexican Bush Lobelia*	—	—	L	L	—	LM	—	—
Melampodium leucanthum	*Blackfoot Daisy*	—	—	—	L	—	L	L	L
Muhlenbergia species	*NCN*	L	L	L	LM	LM	—	—	—
Oenothera species	*Mexican Evening Primrose*	L	L	L	LM	LM	M	M	M
Pennisetum setaceum & cv	*Fountain Grass*	L	L	L	LM	LM	LM	LM	LM
Penstemon species & cvs	*Western Natives*	L	L	L	L	L	L	L	L
Perovskia atriplicifolia	*Russian Sage*	L	L	L	LM	M	M	—	—
Phlomis species	*NCN*	L	L	L	LM	M	M	M	M
Phormium tenax & cvs	*New Zealand Flax*	L	L	L	LM	M	M	M	—
Romneya coulteri & cvs	*Matilija Poppy*	AL	AL	AL	AL	L	LM	LM	LM
Salvia species & cvs	*Sage*	AL	AL	AL	AL	LM	LM	LM	LM
Senecio cineraria	*Dusty Miller*	L	L	L	LM	LM	M	M	—
Sisyrinchium bellum	*Blue-eyed Grass*	AL	AL	AL	AL	L	—	—	—
Sphaeralcea ambigua	*Desert Mallow*	—	—	—	L	—	L	L	L
Stachys byzantina	*Lamb's Ear*	L	L	LM	LM	M	M	M	M
Tagetes lemmonii	*Mountain Marigold*	L	L	L	LM	LM	LM	LM	LM
Thymus species & cvs	*Thyme*	LM	LM	LM	LM	M	M	M	M
Tulbaghia violacea & cv	*Society Garlic*	LM	M	M	M	M	MH	—	—
Verbena species & cvs	*Verbena*	L	L	L	LM	LM	LM	M	—
Xanthorrhoea species	*Grass Tree*	L	L	L	LM	—	—	—	—

Agave, Cacti, Succulents and Yucca:

		Northern Coastal	Northern Inland Valleys & Foothills	Southern Coastal	Southern Inland Valleys & Foothills	Central Valley	Low Deserts	Intermediate Deserts	High Deserts
Aeonium species & cvs	*NCN*	L	L	L	L	—	LM	—	—
Agave americana	*Century Plant*	L	L	L	L	L	L	L	L
Agave attenuata	*Foxtail Agave*	L	L	L	L	—	—	—	L
Agave deserti	*Desert Agave*	—	—	L	L	—	L	AL	L
Agave shawii	*Shaw's Century Plant*	—	—	L	L	—	L	AL	L
Agave victoriae-reginae	*NCN*	L	L	L	L	L	L	L	—
Agave vilmoriniana	*Octopus Agave*	L	L	L	L	L	L	L	L
Aloe arborescens	*Tree Aloe*	AL	AL	AL	L	—	LM	LM	—
Aloe bainesii	*NCN*	AL	AL	AL	AL	—	—	—	—
Aloe candelabrum	*Candelabra Aloe*	L	L	L	L	L	L	L	—
Aloe ciliaris	*NCN*	L	—	L	LM	—	—	—	—
Aloe ferox	*NCN*	L	L	L	L	L	—	—	—
Aloe marlothii	*NCN*	L	L	L	L	L	—	—	—
Aloe nobilis	*NCN*	L	L	L	L	L	L	—	—
Aloe plicatilis	*NCN*	L	L	L	L	—	—	—	—
Aloe striata	*Coral Aloe*	L	L	L	L	LM	L	—	—
Aloe vera	*Medicinal Aloe*	L	L	L	LM	LM	LM	LM	—
Beaucarnea recurvata	*Ponytail Tree*	—	—	L	L	LM	LM	—	—
Carnegiea gigantea	*Saguaro*	—	—	—	—	—	L	L	L
Cereus peruvianus	*Peruvian Apple*	L	—	L	L	—	—	—	—
Cordyline australis	*Dracaena Palm*	L	L	L	LM	M	M	M	M
Cotyledon species	*NCN*	L	L	L	L	L	—	—	—
Crassula species	*Jade Plant*	L	L	L	L	L	L	—	—
Dasylirion species	*Desert Spoon*	—	—	L	L	—	L	L	L
Dracaena draco	*Dragon Tree*	L	L	L	LM	—	LM	—	—
Dudleya species	*Live-forever*	AL	L	AL	L	—	—	—	—
Echeveria species	*Echeveria*	L	L	L	L	L	LM	—	—
Euphorbia ingens	*Candelabra Tree*	—	—	L	L	—	—	—	—
Euphorbia tirucalli	*Milkbush*	L	L	L	L	—	L	—	—
Fouquieria splendens	*Ocotillo*	—	—	—	—	—	L	L	L
Hesperaloe parviflora	*Red Yucca*	—	—	L	L	L	LM	LM	LM
Kalanchoe species	*NCN*	L	L	L	L	L	L	—	—
Nolina species	*Bear Grass*	—	—	L	L	L	L	L	L
Opuntia species	*Prickly Pear, Cholla*	—	—	L	L	L	L	L	L
Portulacaria afra	*Elephant's Food*	L	L	L	L	L	L	—	—
Yucca aloifolia	*Spanish Bayonet*	L	L	L	L	L	L	L	L
Yucca baccata	*Datil Yucca*	—	—	—	—	L	L	L	L
Yucca brevifolia	*Joshua Tree*	—	—	—	—	—	L	L	L
Yucca elata	*Soaptree Yucca*	—	—	—	—	—	L	L	L
Yucca gloriosa	*Spanish Dagger*	L	L	L	L	L	L	L	L
Yucca recurvifolia	*NCN*	—	—	—	—	—	L	L	L
Yucca rigida	*NCN*	—	—	—	—	—	L	L	L
Yucca rostrata	*Beaked Yucca*	—	—	—	—	—	L	L	L
Yucca schidigera	*Mohave Yucca*	—	—	—	—	—	L	L	L
Yucca whipplei	*Our Lord's Candle*	—	—	AL	AL	L	AL	—	—

Section 5 Design Checklists

Introduction:

One of the most basic goals of landscape planting is to select plants that can be combined and used to achieve visual and aesthetic character along with cultural compatibility. Meeting these goals is not always easy. In many situations, satisfying aesthetic character often reflects criteria that are different than the cultural compatibility of various plants. The planning and design process must develop a clear set of guidelines for the selection of plants that address these goals.

The approach recommended in this book begins with an ecological foundation. Plants must be selected with a strong understanding of their adaptation to sun, water, temperature, and soil conditions. This effort should begin with a study of the regional environment and then extend to the soil and microclimate conditions at the site level. After this process is complete, an attempt should be made to develop groupings of plants that can fit these conditions. These groupings of plants should be developed with a solid understanding of their natural origins and adaptations. This approach emphasizes the compatible preferences and needs of plants.

The goal of this approach is to select groupings that can be organized as associations of plants that have a likeness to natural plant communities. It is very important to stress the idea of visualizing groups of plants — plants should not be viewed just as individual species. With this view, it is possible to imagine landscapes that work with the region, site, and each other with greater levels of ecological and cultural compatibility. This results in a greater chance of establishing landscapes that grow and function with less need for excessive levels of energy, water, fertilizer, and maintenance.

This section provides a number of plant lists and specialty topics that can address a number of landscape situations. These lists are intended to assist in the selection of plants that are suited to both regional and local conditions.

Cultural and Aesthetic Compatibility:

The emphasis that is placed upon cultural compatibility and plant groupings can bring many ideas into greater practice. At one level, we can moderate our use of plants that are not highly suited to our regions and that will always require high levels of support and care. Further, landscapes can be designed with plants that are better adapted to each other and that require similar maintenance and watering practices. At a minimum, we can separate plants that have high water needs from plants that have low water needs. And, in some projects, we can design for increased levels of species diversity and then manage the landscape with greater appreciation for natural cycles of growth and rest. The practice of composting and the use of efficient irrigation systems, edible plants, and plants for wildlife can be highly appropriate.

Achieving strong ecological and cultural compatibility within our landscapes will have a major influence upon the visual and aesthetic goals. Ideally, the visual and aesthetic character that emerges from groupings of plant species that are adapted to regional and site conditions are part of the project goals. There are many good examples of Mediterranean landscapes that are comprised of groupings of plants such as oaks, olives, pines, and bay trees that are highly attractive and regionally appropriate. Similarly, there are very good examples of desert landscapes that are founded upon groupings of palo verde, saguaro, ocotillo, and jojoba plants. This visual and aesthetic character should be encouraged and perhaps become a greater part of the landscape identity on a larger scale.

It is also very apparent that there is a great demand for green and lush landscapes in dry climate regions. This type of visual and aesthetic character is difficult to achieve with many of the species that are from Mediterranean and desert regions. Wherever possible, this green and lush planting should be located in areas where it provides optimum value, and be kept to an appropriate scale. As we are discovering, the

Ornamental landscapes should be visualized and designed as associations of plants, not as individual species.

widespread development of landscapes that do not reflect the regional ecology and resources are not sustainable.

Plant Associations and Specialty Plant Groupings:

Presented on the following pages are several plant association groupings that are intended to serve as examples of the ideas discussed above. These groupings are conceived to fit certain landscape regions in the West and include a variety of plants that have a good cultural and visual compatibility.

In the process of reviewing these lists, it can be seen that many groupings are organized on the basis of their natural origin such as: western natives, Mediterranean plants, Australian plants, Asian plants, and South African plants. Often, plants of the same origin have high levels of cultural and visual compatibility, and provide a strong starting point for the preparation of a plant palette. Additionally, in this approach, tree species have first been selected to fit a particular region such as coastal, inland, valley, or desert. The tree species and region provide the strongest basis for each plant association grouping comprised of compatible shrubs, vines, ground covers, and perennials.

These groupings are not rigidly restricted to native species or plants from precisely the same origin. All of the example lists include some plants from other regions or natural communities on the basis of their compatible cultural and visual character. These plants add diversity and greater design choice while retaining overall group character and integrity. These lists are not intended to provide a rigid palette, but to offer a range of plant choices that have a basis for working together.

In this effort to develop groupings of plants, a great deal of consideration, experience, and judgement is always required. This is one of the most demanding and creative aspects of working with landscape plants. Hopefully, these plant association lists, in combination with the illustrated plant compendium, can be used to design landscapes that are both pleasing and have improved levels of sustainability.

Specialty Plant Groupings — Western Natives

Quercus agrifolia association — Coast Live Oak

This association is designed to complement the coast live oak as it naturally occurs in coastal and adjacent inland regions from northern to southern California. Large stands as well as individual specimens are often encountered in urban areas and have become part of ornamental landscapes. Established trees can survive on rainfall, however some trees in warmer inland areas can benefit from periodic deep watering in the summer. Understory shrubs and ground covers must tolerate a mixture of sun and shade and survive without frequent surface irrigation in order to avoid disease problems. The visual character of this association is dominated by plants having mounding forms and deep forest green foliage. This consistency helps provide visual continuity. The flower cycle occurs in late winter through spring; colors are principally blue, yellow, and white. This grouping has strong evergreen character and includes some of the most widely grown California native species and cultivars.

Companion Trees in Northern California:
Arbutus menziesii
Arbutus unedo
Lyonothamnus f. asplenifolius
Myrica californica
Pinus radiata

Companion Trees in Southern California:
Arbutus unedo
Lyonothamnus f. asplenifolius
Quercus engelmannii

Perimeter & Background Shrubs:
Arbutus unedo 'Compacta'
Arctostaphylos hookeri
Arctostaphylos 'Howard McMinn'
Carpenteria californica
Ceanothus griseus varieties
Ceanothus 'Concha'
Ceanothus 'Dark Star'
Ceanothus 'Ray Hartman'
Ceanothus 'Wheeler Canyon'
Dendromecon harfordii
Eriogonum species
Fremontodendron cvs
Garrya elliptica
Heteromeles arbutifolia
Mahonia aquifolium
Mahonia 'Golden Abundance'
Myrica californica
Prunus ilicifolia
Prunus lyonii
Rhamnus californica
Rhamnus crocea
Rhus integrifolia
Rhus ovata
Ribes indecorum
Ribes malvaceum
Salvia clevelandii

Understory Shrubs & Ground Covers:
Arctostaphylos edmundsii & cvs
Arctostaphylos hookeri & cvs
Baccharis pilularis cvs
Ceanothus griseus horizontalis
Ceanothus 'Joyce Coulter'
Ceanothus maritimus & cvs
Cotoneaster dammeri 'Lowfast'
Cotoneaster salicifolius 'Repens'
Galvezia speciosa
Keckiella cordifolia
Mahonia aquifolium 'Compacta'
Mahonia repens
Ribes speciosum
Ribes viburnifolium

Perennials & Accent Plants:
Centranthus ruber
Diplacus species
Epilobium species & cvs
*Heuchera maxima & hybrids
*Iris douglasiana
Penstemon species
Romneya coulteri & cultivars
Salvia sonomensis
Salvia spathacea
Sisyrinchium bellum

*Prefer locations that receive periodic summer water

cvs = cultivars
cv = cultivar

Pinus radiata association — Monterey Pine

This plant grouping is designed for coastal climate areas from the San Francisco Bay areas to central California including San Luis Obispo and south to Santa Barbara. Winters experience little frost; summers are cool and foggy with daily onshore breezes. Ornamental landscapes in these regions can become established and survive with only low amounts of supplemental water during the summer.

Some of the most popular California native species and cultivars of manzanita, wild lilac, and pacific coast iris are ideally suited to these areas. Additionally, a wide variety of plants from coastal habitats of Australia, New Zealand, Europe, and South Africa that are tender to hard frosts can be grown.

The visual character of this plant palette is dominated by evergreen and coniferous tree species. Flower character provided by many types of native shrubs and ground covers is dominated by blue with accent values of pink, red, and yellow. A number of accent plants provide an extended flowering season.

Companion Trees:
Cupressus macrocarpa
Eucalyptus cladocalyx
Quercus agrifolia

Shrubs & Vines:
Acacia cyclops
Acacia longifolia
Arctostaphylos edmundsii
Arctostaphylos hookeri
Arctostaphylos 'Howard McMinn'
Ceanothus 'Concha'
Ceanothus g. 'Louis Edmunds'
Ceanothus 'Ray Hartman'
Hardenbergia violacea & cvs
Lavatera assurgentiflora
Mahonia aquifolium
Mahonia pinnata
Metrosideros excelsus
Myoporum laetum

Ground Covers:
Arctostaphylos edmundsii & cvs
Arctostaphylos hookeri & cvs
Baccharis pilularis cultivars
Carpobrotus species
Ceanothus gloriosus & cvs
Ceanothus griseus horizontalis
Ceanothus maritimus
Mahonia aquifolium 'Compacta'
Mahonia repens
Ribes viburnifolium

Perennials:
Armeria maritima
Centranthus ruber
Diplacus species
Heuchera species & cvs
Limonium perezii
Lupinus albifrons
Penstemon species

Accent Plants:
Acacia baileyana
Bougainvillea species & cvs
Eucalyptus ficifolia
Fremontodendron cultivars
Leptospermum scoparium & cvs

Specialty Plant Groupings — Western Natives

Pinus torreyana association — Torrey Pine

This association is developed with an emphasis on species that are highly suited to southern coastal environments in California. This region is warmer and drier than northern coastal areas: annual rainfall is as little as 10 inches, soils are often fine textured and calcareous, leading to chlorosis in many species. Many of the plants, including the Torrey pine, are naturally adapted to these conditions, but also show good tolerance and adaptability to ornamental landscapes. Many plants from Australia and Mediterranean regions of Europe are highly suited to this habitat. Emphasis in this case is placed upon species that are native to California. The visual character includes grey-green to sage foliage color and many flower colors, with a flowering season heaviest in late winter to spring.

Associated Trees:
Agonis flexuosa
Arbutus unedo
Feijoa sellowiana
Melaleuca quinquenervia
Metrosideros excelsus
Quercus ilex

Shrubs & Vines:
Artemisia arborescens
Cistus hybridus
Cistus purpureus
Dendromecon rigida
Encelia californica
Eriogonum arborescens
Eriogonum giganteum
Eriogonum fasciculatum
Heteromeles arbutifolia
Lavatera bicolor
Leptospermum laevigatum
Metrosideros excelsus
Rhus integrifolia
Rosmarinus officinalis & cvs
Salvia clevelandii & cvs
Salvia leucantha
Salvia munzii
Simmondsia chinensis
Westringia fruticosa

cvs = cultivars
cv = cultivar

Ground Covers:
Arctostaphylos 'Pacific Mist'
Artemisia 'Powis Castle'
Cistus salviifolius
Cistus 'Sunset'
Delosperma 'Alba'
Eriogonum fasciculatum cvs
Iva hayesiana
Salvia mellifera 'Terra Seca'
Salvia sonomensis 'Dara's Choice'
Senecio mandraliscae
Rosmarinus officinalis cvs

Perennials:
Achillea species & cvs
Centaurea cineraria
Convolvulus maritimus
Coreopsis gigantea
Coreopsis maritima
Diplacus longiflorus
Epilobium species & cvs
Erigeron glaucus
Eriogonum crocatum
Eriogonum grande spp. rubescens
Helianthemum nummularium
Limonium perezii

Accent Plants:
Brahea armata
Dracaena draco
Fremontodendron hybrids
Opuntia species
Romneya coulteri
Yucca schidigera
Yucca whipplei

Platanus racemosa association — Western Sycamore

The western sycamore is one of the most picturesque and characteristic trees of riparian areas throughout low elevation foothills and washes in California. It survives in dry climate regions with the additional moisture that occurs as runoff from seasonal rains. The plant grouping listed below is highly suited to northern coastal and inland regions where winter rains and cooler summer temperatures provide better growing conditions for many of the shrub and ground cover species. This palette is also well suited to southern coastal and inland regions in microclimate areas that provide additional moisture and shade during the heat and dryness of summer. Often, a mature tree or grouping of western sycamores provides ample overstory protection for the associated perimeter and ground cover plants. Periodic deep irrigation is desirable during summer months. This listing includes some of the most colorful and attractive California natives for foliage and flowering character.

Associated Trees:
Cercis canadensis
Cercis occidentalis
Lyonothamnus f. asplenifolius
Prunus caroliniana
Prunus lyonii
Quercus agrifolia

Perimeter & Background Shrubs:
Arctostaphylos edmundsii
Arctostaphylos hookeri
Arctostaphylos 'Howard McMinn'
Carpenteria californica & cvs
Ceanothus 'Concha'
Ceanothus 'Frosty Blue'
Ceanothus 'Wheeler Canyon'
Galvezia speciosa & cv
Heteromeles arbutifolia
Keckiella cordifolia
Mahonia aquifolium
Myrica californica
Prunus ilicifolia
Rhamnus californica 'Eve Case'
Rhus ovata

Understory Shrubs & Ground Covers:
Ceanothus griseus horizontalis
Mahonia aquifolium 'Compacta'
Mahonia 'Repens'
Ribes viburnifolium

Perennials:
Heuchera species & cvs
Iris douglasiana & cvs

Accent Plants:
Eschscholzia californica
Fremontodendron cultivars
Mahonia 'Golden Abundance'
Romneya coulteri
Sisyrinchium bellum

Cercidium floridum association — Blue Palo Verde

A number of exciting plant species are native to southwestern deserts. This listing brings emphasis to species suited to intermediate and low desert regions. Many of these plants, particularly trees and large shrubs, have developed in sandy washes where they can obtain moisture with deep reaching root systems. In ornamental landscapes, these plants often are grouped together into "mini-oases" to provide periodic deep watering. This grouping approach also enables trees to provide microclimate benefit to understory shrubs and perennials. Smaller species often benefit greatly when placed where larger plants, boulders, and slopes provide protection from extreme heat and sun conditions. Drip irrigation is highly recommended. Many trees, shrubs, and perennials produce bright flowering character in the spring; agaves and cacti provide year around accent and sculptural character.

Associated Trees:
Cercidium microphyllum
Cercidium praecox
Chilopsis linearis
Dalea spinosa
Lysiloma microphylla var. Thornberi
Olneya tesota
Pithecellobium flexicaule
Prosopis glandulosa
Prosopis juliflora
Prosopis pubescens

Palms:
Brahea armata
Brahea edulis
Phoenix dactylifera
Washingtonia filifera
Washingtonia robusta

Shrubs:
Anisacanthus thurberi
Atriplex canescens
Atriplex lentiformis
Buddleia marrubiifolia
Caesalpinia species
Calliandra species
Cleome isomeris
Cordia boissieri
Cordia parvifolia
Dalea pulchra
Dalea spinosa
Encelia farinosa
Fallugia paradoxa
Justicia californica
Justicia spicigera
Larrea tridentata
Leucophyllum species & cvs
Prosopis pubescens
Salvia greggii
Simmondsia chinensis
Sophora secundiflora
Tecoma stans var. angustata

Ground Covers:
Baccharis 'Centennial'
Dalea greggii
Myoporum parvifolium
Verbena species & cvs

Perennials:
Baileya multiradiata
Gaura lindheimeri
Lobelia laxiflora
Melampodium leucanthum
Oenothera species
Penstemon species & cvs
Sphaeralcea ambigua & cvs
Tagetes lemmonii
Verbena species & cvs

cvs = cultivars
cv = cultivar

Agave, Succulents, Yucca:
Agave americana & cultivars
Agave deserti
Agave shawii
Agave victoriae-reginae
Agave vilmoriniana
Aloe vera
Beaucarnea recurvata
Carnegiea gigantea
Dasylirion species
Fouquieria splendens
Hesperaloe parviflora
Nolina species
Opuntia species
Yucca aloifolia
Yucca baccata
Yucca brevifolia
Yucca elata
Yucca recurvifolia
Yucca rostrata
Yucca schidigera

Yucca brevifolia association — Joshua Tree

Ornamental landscaping in the high desert regions of the Southwest poses a highly difficult challenge. The combination of cold winters, aridity, wind, heat, and poor soils is very hard on many exotic as well as native species. The careful planning of building orientation and microclimate development underlies much of the success of these landscapes by providing protection from the elements and manageable spaces for improving soil and moisture conditions. Some of the most widely used exotic species include hardy coniferous species of pine and juniper as well as tough deciduous species including mulberry and ash trees. This listing brings emphasis to native species from high desert habitats as well as hardy varieties from intermediate regions.

Associated Trees:
Acacia smallii
Cercidium floridum
Chilopsis linearis
Olneya tesota
Pinus monophylla
Pithecellobium flexicaule
Prosopis species

Palms:
Brahea armata
Brahea edulis
Washingtonia filifera
Washingtonia robusta

Shrubs:
Acacia greggii
Anisacanthus thurberi
Atriplex canescens
Atriplex lentiformis
Buddleia marrubiifolia
Calliandra species
Cleome isomeris
Cordia boissieri
Cordia parvifolia
Cowania mexicana
Dalea pulchra
Encelia farinosa
Fallugia paradoxa
Juniperus californica
Justicia californica
Larrea tridentata
Salvia greggii
Simmondsia chinensis
Sophora secundiflora

Ground Covers:
Baccharis 'Centennial'
Dalea greggii
Myoporum parvifolium
Verbena species & cvs

Perennials:
Baileya multiradiata
Euphorbia rigida
Gaura lindheimeri
Lobelia laxiflora
Melampodium leucanthum
Oenothera berlandieri
Penstemon species & cvs
Sphaeralcea ambigua & cvs
Tagetes lemmonii
Verbena species & cvs

Agave, Succulents, Yucca:
Agave americana & cvs
Agave deserti
Dasylirion species
Fouquieria splendens
Hesperaloe parviflora
Nolina species
Yucca aloifolia
Yucca baccata
Yucca elata
Yucca schidigera
Yucca whipplei

Specialty Plant Groupings — Mediterranean Species

Olea europaea association — Olive Tree

The olive tree is one of the most widely associated plant species within Mediterranean regions around the world. It is a highly adaptable plant that can be grown in coastal, inland, valley, and desert regions. This listing is designed to work best in warm and sunny coastal and inland habitats, particularly in southern California and in areas of little frost. Once established, most of these plants can survive with low amounts of supplemental water. Many of the plants included on this list reflect the classical plant species that have been used for many years in Mediterranean gardens. The oils of many plants such as the cypress, myrtle, lavender, and rosemary become highly fragrant on warm summer days or when crushed. Trees are largely evergreen; shrubs and perennials provide many bright colors from spring through summer.

Associated Trees:
Arbutus unedo
Cupressus sempervirens
Pinus halepensis
Pinus pinea
Quercus agrifolia
Quercus ilex
Quercus suber

Shrubs & Vines:
Alyogyne huegelii & cvs
Bougainvillea cultivars
Cistus hybridus
Cistus purpureus
Eriogonum giganteum
Hardenbergia violacea & cv
Lavandula species & cvs
Myrtus communis
Nerium oleander & cvs
Rosa banksiae cvs
Rosmarinus officinalis & cvs
Salvia clevelandii & cvs
Santolina chamaecyparissus
Teucrium chamaedrys
Teucrium fruticans
Vitex angus-castus
Westringia fruticosa

Ground Covers & Vines:
Bougainvillea cultivars
Cistus salviifolius
Cistus 'Sunset'
Gazania rigens leucolaena
Rosmarinus officinalis cvs
Teucrium cossonii

Perennials:
Achillea taygetea & cvs
Dietes species & cvs
Euryops pectinatus
Festuca ovina glauca
Helictotrichon sempervirens
Limonium perezii
Perovskia atriplicifolia
Phlomis species

Accent Elements:
Agave americana
Agave attenuata
Aloe species
Brahea armata
Butia capitata
Chamaerops humilis
Dracaena draco
Kniphofia uvaria
Phoenix canariensis
Romneya coulteri & cvs

cvs = cultivars
cv = cultivar

Quercus ilex association — Holly Oak

The holly oak is native to coastal and inland areas throughout the Mediterranean region. It is tolerant of heat, cold, and seasonal drought and is widely used throughout Europe as a tree or large clipped hedge in highly urban areas. This listing of plants features a number of Mediterranean species in combination with a diverse range of hardy plants that are well adapted to inland and valley regions of California. These species tolerate areas with regular winter frost and high summer temperatures. Most of the tree species can become monumental in size when grown in deeper valley soils and provided with periodic deep watering throughout the year.

This palette is well suited to commercial landscapes and large spaces such as parks. A strong coniferous character can be achieved by emphasizing pines and juniper species, or the evergreen oaks can be featured along with other broadleaf shrubs and ground covers.

Associated Trees:
Acacia baileyana & cv
Arbutus unedo
Cedrus atlantica & cvs
Cedrus deodara & cvs
Laurus nobilis
Olea europaea
Pinus halepensis
Pinus pinea
Quercus agrifolia
Quercus suber
Schinus molle

Shrubs & Vines:
Acacia species
Carpenteria californica
Ceanothus 'Concha'
Ceanothus 'Ray Hartman'
Cercis occidentalis
Cotoneaster species & cvs
Dodonaea viscosa & cv
Grevillea species & cvs
Heteromeles arbutifolia
Jasminum mesnyi
Juniperus species
Myrtus communis & cvs
Nerium oleander & cvs
Prunus ilicifolia
Pyracantha species & cvs
Rhaphiolepis indica & cvs
Rhamnus alaternus
Rosa banksiae & cvs
Teucrium fruticans

Ground Covers & Vines:
Baccharis pilularis & cvs
Cotoneaster salicifolius 'Repens'
Juniperus species & cvs
Lonicera japonica 'Halliana'
Rosmarinus officinalis cvs

Perennials:
Centranthus ruber
Dietes species
Gaura lindheimeri
Perovskia atriplicifolia
Phormium tenax & cultivars
Tagetes lemmonii

Accent Plants:
Agave americana
Fremontodendron species & cvs
Phoenix canariensis
Romneya coulteri
Yucca recurvifolia

Laurus nobilis association — Sweet Bay

The sweet bay tree has been cultivated for many years as an ornamental tree and clipped hedge plant as well as for its leaves that are widely used as a seasoning in cooking. This listing of plants is designed to include many species that offer edible and culinary value that are suited to small and medium size spaces. Many successful designs can be achieved by combining edible plants with those that are grown strictly for ornamental purposes. In this list, a strong emphasis has been placed upon a variety of perennials that can be used to add diverse foliage and flowering character to the garden. Many of these plants are also selected for their attraction to hummingbirds, butterflies, and for foliage and flower fragrance.

Associated Trees:
Arbutus unedo
Feijoa sellowiana
Ficus carica
Olea europaea & cvs
Punica granatum & cvs

Shrubs:
Anisodontea hypomandarum
Arbutus unedo 'Compacta'
Eriogonum arborescens
Eriogonum giganteum
Lavandula species & cvs
Lavatera species
Leonotis leonurus
Rosmarinus officinalis & cvs
Salvia apiana
Salvia 'Allen Chickering'
Salvia clevelandii & cvs
Salvia greggii
Salvia leucophylla
Trichostema lanatum
Vitex angus-castus

Ground Covers:
Mahonia repens
Rosmarinus officinalis cvs
Teucrium cossonii
Thymus species
Verbena species & cvs

Perennials:
Achillea species
Diplacus species & cvs
Erigeron karvinskianus
Eschscholzia californica
Lupinus species
Penstemon species & cvs
Romneya coulteri
Salvia officinalis

Chamaerops humilis association — Mediterranean Fan Palm

Palms are very often used as accent elements in ornamental landscapes. They are typically placed in raised planters or in restricted planting locations. One of the most attractive palms for use in courtyard and large scale spaces is the Mediterranean fan palm. Large, multiple trunk specimens can become the most significant landscape element and require only a few colorful background shrubs and perennials.

This listing brings attention to many trees and shrubs that can work exceptionally well as specimen and color accent elements in courtyard and entry settings. The trees in particular can be pruned to reveal interesting bark and branching character. These plants always seem to get better with age. Due to their sculptural and dramatic character, many of these plants can be featured at night with lights and be placed in areas where their silhouette value can be appreciated. Plants on this list do best in warm and sunny coastal and frost free inland areas of California.

Specimen Type Tree Species:
Arbutus unedo
Cupressus sempervirens & cvs
Dracaena draco
Ficus carica
Olea europaea
Quercus suber

Shrubs & Vines:
Alyogyne huegelii & cvs
Bougainvillea species & cvs
Fremontodendron cvs
Lavandula species & cvs
Myrtus communis
Nerium oleander & cvs
Rhaphiolepis indica & cvs
Rosa banksiae cvs
Salvia clevelandii & cvs
Salvia leucantha
Trichostema lanatum
Westringia species & cvs

Ground Covers:
Delosperma 'Alba'
Drosanthemum hispidum
Sedum rubrotinctum
Senecio mandraliscae

Perennials:
Anigozanthos cvs
Convolvulus mauritanicus
Dietes species & cvs
Helictotrichon sempervirens
Kniphofia uvaria
Leonotis leonurus
Phlomis fruticosa
Phormium tenax
Romneya coulteri
Tagetes lemmonii

Accent Plants:
Agave americana & cvs
Agave attenuata
Aloe arborescens
Butia capitata
Cereus peruvianus
Dasylirion wheeleri
Euphorbia ingens
Kalanchoe beharensis
Opuntia robusta

Specialty Plant Groupings — Australian Species

Eucalyptus cladocalyx association — Sugar Gum

A great variety of plants that are adapted to dry climate regions come from Australia. Perhaps the most highly visible and widely recognized species are the eucalypts. However, upon closer inspection, there are many other trees, shrubs, ground covers, and perennials that have been introduced into cultivation. In our efforts to work with these plants, a distinction should be made regarding their adaptation to different regions of the West. The list of plants presented below emphasizes Australian natives and associated plants that are best suited to warm and dry coastal environments of California where winter frosts are infrequent nor too severe. Many of these plants provide colorful flowering character and require only low amounts of supplemental water for good performance.

Associated Trees:
Acacia baileyana & cv
Acacia longifolia
Acacia melanoxylon
Agonis flexuosa
Angophora costata
Callistemon citrinus
Callistemon viminalis
Casuarina equisetifolia
Eucalyptus citriodora
Eucalyptus ficifolia
Eucalyptus globulus & cv
Eucalyptus lehmannii
Eucalyptus leucoxylon & cv
Eucalyptus maculata
Eucalyptus nicholii
Eucalyptus polyanthemos
Eucalyptus spathulata
Eucalyptus torquata
Grevillea robusta
Melaleuca quinquenervia
Tristania conferta & cvs

Shrubs & Vines:
Acacia cultriformis
Acacia cyclops
Acacia longifolia
Alyogyne cuneiformis
Alyogyne hakeifolia
Alyogyne huegelii & cvs
Artemisia 'Powis Castle'
Callistemon citrinus
Chamelaucium uncinatum
Correa species & cvs
Echium fastuosum
Eucalyptus lehmannii
Galvezia speciosa
Grevillea species & cvs
Hakea suaveolens
Hardenbergia violacea & cv
Lantana camara & cvs
Leptospermum laevigatum & cvs
Melaleuca armillaris
Melaleuca nesophila
Myoporum laetum
Plumbago auriculata
Sollya heterophylla & cvs
Tecomaria capensis
Westringia species & cvs

Ground Covers:
Acacia redolens & cv
Bougainvillea cultivars
Delosperma 'Alba'
Gazania rigens leucolaena
Lantana montevidensis
Myoporum cultivars
Plumbago auriculata
Sollya heterophylla

Perennials:
Anigozanthos species & cvs
Asteriscus maritimus
Brachycome multifida
Calocephalus brownii
Coreopsis species & cvs
Dietes species & cvs
Euryops pectinatus & cv
Leonotis leonurus
Limonium perezii
Xanthorrhoea species

Accent Plants:
Agave americana
Agave attenuata
Aloe arborescens
Aloe bainesii
Cordyline australis
Dracaena draco
Echium fastuosum
Phormium tenax
Romneya coulteri

cvs = cultivars
cv = cultivar

Eucalyptus camadulensis association — River Red Gum

Many Australian plant species come from inland habitats where they are adapted to heat and moisture stress as well as cool winters that have a number of frosts each winter. This listing of plants brings attention to many Australian and associated species that do well in inland valley and foothill regions throughout northern and southern California and the Central Valley. This list includes many of the frost hardy species from Australia as well as a number of shrubs and perennials that come from Mediterranean regions that grow well in association.

Associated Trees:
Acacia pendula
Acacia stenophylla
Brachychiton populneus
Casuarina cunninghamiana
Eucalyptus cinerea
Eucalyptus erythrocorys
Eucalyptus globulus & cv
Eucalyptus leucoxylon & cv
Eucalyptus papuana
Eucalyptus polyanthemos
Eucalyptus rudis
Eucalyptus sideroxylon & cv
Eucalyptus spathulata
Eucalyptus viminalis
Geijera parviflora
Grevillea robusta
Pinus halepensis

Shrubs:
Dodonaea viscosa & cv
Grevillea species & cvs
Nerium oleander
Rhamnus alaternus
Rhaphiolepis 'Majestic Beauty'

Ground Covers:
Acacia redolens & cv
Carpobrotus hybrids
Myoporum parvifolium cvs

Perennials:
Cheiranthus 'Bowles Mauve'
Dietes species & cvs
Helictotrichon sempervirens
Muhlenbergia species
Perovskia atriplicifolia
Phormium tenax
Tagetes lemmonii

Agonis flexuosa association — Peppermint Tree

This association of plants emphasizes Australian species that are suited to courtyard and feature plantings in both residential and commercial landscapes. Most of the tree species that are identified develop canopy shapes and can easily be pruned to reveal interesting bark and branching habits. These trees, as well as a number of the shrubs, are sensitive to frost and are best suited to coastal and mild inland locations. A number of other plants from subtropical regions have been added to this list due to their suitability to these same climate conditions. Many of the subtropical species have extended flowering seasons that help to make this a colorful plant palette.

Associated Trees:
Arbutus unedo
Callistemon citrinus
Eucalyptus ficifolia
Eucalyptus torquata
Feijoa sellowiana
Leptospermum laevigatum

Shrubs & Vines:
Alyogyne huegelii & cvs
Callistemon citrinus
Chamelaucium uncinatum
Cistus 'Doris Hibberson'
Cistus purpureus
Correa species & cvs
Hardenbergia violacea & cv
Lavandula species
Lavatera bicolor
Leptospermum laevigatum & cvs
Leptospermum scoparium & cvs
Melaleuca armillaris
Melaleuca nesophila
Santolina species
Sollya heterophylla & cvs
Westringia species & cvs

Ground Covers:
Cistus 'Sunset'
Cistus salviifolius
Delosperma 'Alba'
Gazania species & cvs
Sedum species
Senecio mandraliscae

Perennials:
Anigozanthos species & cvs
Asteriscus species
Brachycome multifida
Convolvulus mauritanicus
Coreopsis species & cvs
Dietes species & cvs
Euryops pectinatus 'Viridis'
Leonotis leonurus
Limonium perezii
Phlomis fruticosa
Tulbaghia violacea & cv

Accent Plants:
Agave attenuata
Cereus peruvianus
Dracaena draco
Kalanchoe beharensis

cvs = cultivars
cv = cultivar

Acacia stenophylla association — Shoestring Acacia

There are a number of hardy Australian plants that show good tolerance of desert climate and habitat conditions. These plants are proving to be very helpful in developing low water requiring landscapes in low and intermediate desert regions of the Southwest. Shoestring acacia is a relatively recent introduction and is featured in this list below. All species on this list are adapted to high levels of heat and aridity as well as iron poor soils. Drip irrigation has helped with the success of these plants by providing moisture close to the root zone. Careful irrigation management is necessary to avoid stimulating too much growth that can be damaged by high summer temperatures or early frosts in the fall.

These Australian plants combine very effectively with southwestern natives. A number of these natives are included on this list, others can be found on page 45.

Associated Trees:
Acacia pendula
Acacia smallii
Acacia stenophylla
Brachychiton populneus
Callistemon viminalis & cvs
Eucalyptus cinerea
Eucalyptus microtheca
Eucalyptus papuana
Eucalyptus rudis
Geijera parviflora
Lysiloma microphylla var. Thornberi
Pittosporum phillyraeoides
Rhus lancea

Shrubs & Vines:
Anisacanthus thurberi
Buddleia marrubiifolia
Caesalpinia mexicana
Caesalpinia pulcherrima
Callistemon citrinus & cvs
Cassia artemisioides
Cassia nemophila
Cassia phyllodinea
Cordia boissieri
Leucophyllum candidum & cvs
Leucophyllum frutescens & cvs
Leucophyllum laevigatum
Macfadyena unguis-cati
Nerium oleander & cvs
Ruellia peninsularis
Salvia greggii

Ground Covers:
Acacia redolens & cvs
Baccharis 'Centennial'
Dalea greggii
Myoporum parvifolium & cvs
Verbena species & cvs

Perennials:
Baileya multiradiata
Melampodium leucanthum
Muhlenbergia rigens
Penstemon species & cvs
Sphaeralcea ambigua & cvs
Tagetes lemmonii

Accent Plants:
Agave vilmoriniana
Carnegiea gigantea
Dasylirion species
Fouquieria splendens
Opuntia species

Specialty Plant Groupings

Asian Species — Lagerstroemia indica association — Crape Myrtle

A great variety of plants that are native to cool and moist temperate climates are grown throughout western regions. Once established, many of these have proven to be highly tolerant of heat, aridity, and low amounts of supplemental water. This list identifies a number of plants that are native to Asia that are tolerant of a wide range of conditions. This list is supplemented with other species from temperate regions of the Midwest through northeastern United States. This listing has a greater mixture of deciduous and coniferous plants than previous lists.

Deciduous plants in particular are most strongly adapted to cool winters that establishes winter dormancy. Such environments also receive ample rainfall. This palette works very well in the Central Valley of California and cooler climates associated with northern California and higher elevations in foothill locations.

Trees:
Broussonetia papyrifera
Cercis canadensis
Chitalpa tashkentensis cvs
Juniperus chinensis 'Torulosa'
Juniperus virginiana & cvs
Lagerstroemia indica & cvs
Melia azedarach & cv
Morus alba
Robinia a. 'Idahoensis'
Robinia pseudoacacia

Shrubs & Vines:
Cotoneaster species & cvs
Elaeagnus pungens & cvs
Hibiscus syriacus
Jasminum humile
Jasminum mesnyi
Jasminum officinale
Juniperus chinensis & cvs
Juniperus sabina & cvs
Juniperus scopulorum and cvs
Lagerstroemia indica cvs
Polygonum aubertii
Pyracantha species & cvs
Rhaphiolepis indica & cvs
Rosa banksiae & cvs
Xylosma congestum

Ground Covers:
Cotoneaster adpressus
Cotoneaster dammeri & cvs
Cotoneaster horizontalis
Cotoneaster salicifolius 'Repens'
Juniperus chinensis cvs
Juniperus conferta
Juniperus horizontalis
Juniperus sabina 'Tamariscifolia'
Lonicera japonica 'Halliana'

cvs = cultivars
cv = cultivar

Perennials:
Centranthus ruber
Festuca ovina glauca
Perovskia atriplicifolia
Stachys byzantina
Teucrium chamaedrys & cv

Accent Plants:
Cedrus atlantica 'Glauca'
Trachycarpus fortunei
Vitex angus-castus

South Africa Species — Dietes vegeta association — Fortnight Lily

Most of the landscape plants from South Africa that are grown in western gardens are ground covers, perennials, and succulents. A few trees and shrubs come from this region of the world, but not enough to develop a well rounded plant palette of just South African species. As a result, this list also contains a number of plants that come from coastal habitats of the Mediterranean region in an effort to provide additional choices for trees and shrubs. This listing of plants includes plants that are most naturally suited to southern coastal and frost free inland

regions of California. Some of the South African species are also grown in low desert regions in microclimate spaces that provide protection from intense sunlight and periodic frost, but their main preference is for coastal habitats. This palette is highly adaptable: many can be used together on coastal slopes and bluffs, others can be grown in small patio spaces or in containers. A number of the succulent species provide striking winter flowering character.

Trees:
Aloe bainesii
Feijoa sellowiana
Olea europaea
Rhus lancea

Shrubs & Vines:
Anisodontea hypomandarum
Cistus species & cvs
Echium fastuosum
Lantana camara & cvs
Lavatera bicolor
Plecostachys serpyllifolia
Plumbago auriculata & cv
Tecomaria capensis & cvs

Ground Covers:
Arctotheca calendula
Carpobrotus edulis
Cephalophyllum 'Red Spike'
Crassula multicava
Delosperma 'Alba'
Drosanthemum species
Dymondia margaretae
Gazania species & cvs
Lampranthus spectabilis
Lantana montevidensis
Maleophora species
Senecio mandraliscae

Perennials:
Dietes bicolor
Dietes vegeta & cvs
Euphorbia milii
Euryops pectinatus & cv
Gazania species & cvs
Kniphofia uvaria
Leonotis leonurus
Tulbaghia species & cvs

Succulents & Accent Plants:
Aloe species and hybrids
Cereus peruvianus
Crassula species & cvs
Dracaena draco
Euphorbia ingens
Euphorbia tirucalli
Kalanchoe species
Portulacaria afra

Nitrogen Fixing Plant Species

Introduction:

Nitrogen is a principal element used in the development of proteins essential to sustaining metabolism in living cells within both plants and animals. Fortunately, it is highly abundant in air as a free molecule where it comprises almost 80 percent of the earth's atmosphere. However, in this free form it is not useful to plants or other organisms. In order to become useful, it must be combined or 'fixed' with hydrogen or oxygen.

In terrestrial environments, the biological process of fixing nitrogen involves special bacteria. One group of bacteria is known as *Rhizobium*. These bacteria grow in symbiotic association within the roots of many species of plants. Most plants that function in association with this bacteria are known as legumes, and are part of the *Fabaceae* family (Synonym: *Leguminosae*). These plants provide key nutrients to sustain the bacteria and in turn can absorb part of the 'fixed' nitrogen that is produced.

An adequate supply of nitrogen is necessary for healthy plant growth and photosynthesis activities. Nitrogen fixing plants are able to obtain most of their nitrogen from their bacteria while providing benefit to other plants as they shed their leaves. This leaf litter breaks down during decomposition and releases nitrogen into the soil for use by plants and other organisms.

In Mediterranean and desert climate regions, the availability of fixed nitrogen for plants is usually limited. Therefore, it is desirable to include nitrogen fixing species in ornamental plant groupings and to retain their leaf litter for mulching in an effort to sustain a balanced soil ecology for all plant and soil organisms.

Listed below are key landscape plant genera and species that are noted for their association with nitrogen fixing bacteria.

Cercis occidentalis, Western Redbud, is one of the many western native plants that help fix nitrogen.

Principal nitrogen fixing plant genera & species count

Acacia	1100 species
Albizia	150 species
Alnus	30 species
Atriplex	100+ species
Bauhinia	300 species
Caesalpinia	70 species
Calliandra	150 species
Caragana	60 species
Cassia	500 species
Castanospermum	1 species
Casuarina	40 species
Ceanothus	55 species
Ceratonia	1 species
Cercidium	10 species
Cercis	7 species
Cercocarpus	8-10 species
Cytisus	50 species
Dalea	200 species
Elaeagnus	40 species
Erythrina	10 species
Genista	70+ species
Gleditsia	12 species
Hardenbergia	3 species
Lotus	100 species
Lupinus	200 species
Myrica	50 species
Parkinsonia	2 species
Pithecellobium	100+ species
Prosopis	25 species
Purshia	2 species
Robinia	20 species
Sophora	50 species
Spartium	1 species
Tipuana	1 species
Trifolium	300 species
Ulex	25 species
Vigna	200 species
Wisteria	9 species

Nitrogen fixing plant species described in plant compendium

Trees:

Acacia baileyana & cv
Acacia dealbata
Acacia decurrens
Acacia farnesiana
Acacia longifolia
Acacia melanoxylon
Acacia pendula
Acacia retinodes
Acacia saligna
Acacia smallii
Acacia stenophylla
Albizia julibrissin & cv
Ceanothus 'Ray Hartman'
Ceanothus arboreus
Ceratonia siliqua
Cercidium floridum
Cercidium microphyllum
Cercidium praecox
Cercis canadensis & cvs
Cercis occidentalis
Dalea spinosa
Lysiloma microphylla var. Thornberi
Myrica californica
Olneya tesota
Parkinsonia aculeata
Pithecellobium flexicaule
Prosopis alba
Prosopis chilensis
Prosopis glandulosa
Prosopis juliflora
Prosopis pubescens
Robinia ambigua & cultivars
Robinia pseudoacacia & cultivars
Sophora secundiflora

Shrubs & Vines:

Acacia berlandieri
Acacia cultriformis
Acacia cyclops
Acacia dealbata
Acacia decurrens
Acacia farnesiana
Acacia greggii
Acacia longifolia
Caesalpinia gilliesii
Caesalpinia mexicana
Caesalpinia pulcherrima
Calliandra californica
Calliandra eriophylla
Calliandra peninsularis
Cassia artemisioides
Cassia nemophila
Cassia odorata
Cassia phyllodinea
Ceanothus 'Concha'
Ceanothus 'Dark Star'
Ceanothus 'Frosty Blue'
Ceanothus 'Joyce Coulter'
Ceanothus 'Julia Phelps'
Ceanothus 'Ray Hartman'
Ceanothus 'Wheeler Canyon'
Ceanothus arboreus
Ceanothus gloriosus & cvs
Ceanothus g. 'Louis Edmunds'
Ceanothus g. 'Santa Ana'
Ceanothus impressus
Ceanothus maritimus & cvs
Ceanothus rigidus 'Snowball'
Ceanothus thyrsiflorus & cvs
Cercis occidentalis

Shrubs & Vines:

Dalea pulchra
Dalea spinosa
Hardenbergia violacea & cv
Lupinus albifrons
Lupinus arboreus
Lysiloma microphylla var. Thornberi
Prosopis pubescens
Sophora secundiflora

Ground Covers:

Acacia redolens & cultivar
Ceanothus gloriosus & cvs
Ceanothus griseus v. horizontalis
Ceanothus g. h. 'Yankee Point'
Ceanothus maritimus & cvs
Dalea greggii

Perennials:

Lupinus species

Helpful References:

Brill, Winston J. "Biological Nitrogen Fixation." Scientific American 236 (March 1977): 68-81.

Delwiche, C. C. "The Nitrogen Cycle." Scientific American 223 (September 1970): 136-146.

Landscaping with Western Natives

Introduction:
A large number of plants described in this book are California native species that come from Mediterranean type climate regions. In recent years there has been renewed interest in growing these plants in ornamental landscapes. In this effort, it has been necessary to understand a number of planting guidelines and concepts. Many of these ideas have been reviewed in other sections. A concise summary of key recommendations and guidelines that should be considered when using native plants is provided below.

Plant Selection and Grouping Recommendations:
▪ Identify the basic region and plant community that native species grow within; respect the differences among plants adapted to coastal, inland, and valley areas. Identify other species that grow within the same community and adjacent communities.

▪ Develop a list of species that can be possible choices in new landscape situations. Separate this list into composite groupings of trees, shrubs, vines, ground covers, and perennials. Think of developing lists into communities of plants.

▪ Identify more detailed information on each plant species including sun exposure, adaptation to moisture or drought, growing season, growth rate, size, and visual character. Be very conscious of the microclimate needs of native plants. Plants that are native to coastal regions often grow better in partial shade when they are planted in warmer locations.

▪ Landscapes that begin without any mature plants will take several years to develop. The landscape should be planned in stages. Allow for landscapes to change and mature. Tree species are often most critical in developing visual character and microclimate conditions for understory shrubs and ground covers. Faster growing plants can be used to achieve more immediate visual character.

Planting Recommendations:
▪ Container grown plants transplant best when they are small in size and do not have coiled roots.

▪ Many native plants can now be purchased from nurseries that have inoculated them with desirable *Mycorrhiza* and *Rhizobium* bacteria that will help the plants absorb nutrients from the soil.

▪ The best planting season for most western natives is the late fall into early winter. Plants need a minimum of 2-3 months of establishment time prior to the full growing season.

▪ Soils for most native plants do not require amendment. At most, small amounts of slow release or organic fertilizer can be used.

▪ Planting holes should be dug 2-3 times wider than the diameter of the container, but equal in depth. The rootball should be set slightly higher than the surrounding finish soil level; a water basin can be formed from excess soil. Do not allow soil or dense mulch to build up around the stem of young plants to reduce susceptibility to bacteria and soil diseases. Drip irrigation is highly recommended where possible.

▪ Like container plants, root balls of native plants should never be allowed to dry out on the site before or during the planting operations. Plants should be watered immediately after installation and the process should assure that the soil is firmly compacted around the root ball and that the plant has not settled below the surrounding natural grade.

▪ A 3-4 inch layer of mulch material can be used to cover the planting area and around newly installed plants. Many materials do well and include chipped branches and foliage of plants, rocks, or leaf litter. Mulch helps to reduce loss of moisture from soils, suppress weedy plant growth, and cool plant roots.

▪ Native plants can be installed in the cooler months of spring, however expect little new growth and weaker flowering character. These plants will appear relatively dormant until the following spring. Avoid planting during high temperatures in mid-summer.

Management Recommendations:
▪ Plants that are established in the fall benefit from regular supplemental water during the first winter, particularly if seasonal rains are erratic. Most native trees and shrubs planted in the fall can become established

Western natives provide great diversity and character for ornamental landscape use. Santa Barbara Botanic Garden, California.

well enough to need only one or two waterings during the summer depending upon temperature and heat conditions. In the summer months, always avoid watering that leads to root rot and active fungus growing conditions.

▪ Plants that are successfully established for 1-2 years can often survive with little supplemental water and need no fertilizer applications. In practice, many plants will grow faster and to larger sizes if supplemental water is applied after they are established. This takes good judgement and experience with each of the species involved. Supplemental water is often most helpful to established plants from late fall through early spring as a complement to winter rains and their natural growing cycle.

▪ Plants that become too large or are stimulated to grow excessively can be pruned. This pruning often works best after a plant has completed its flowering cycle and new foliage shoots are in the beginning stages of growth.

▪ The ongoing practice of mulching with organic materials can lead to significant changes in the soil conditions. This material will steadily improve the water holding capacity of the soils as well as increase the amount of organic matter that is subject to decomposition. However, these changes to the soil can lead to long term disease problems, particularly during the summer months when organic materials in soils can become warm and moist and subject to active bacteria and fungi.

Helpful References:

Fremontia. Journal of the California Native Plant Society. (published quarterly) Sacramento: California Native Plant Society.

Lenz, Lee W., and John Dourley. California Native Trees and Shrubs. Claremont, California: Rancho Santa Ana Botanic Garden, 1981.

Perry, Bob. Trees and Shrubs for Dry California Landscapes. Claremont, California: Land Design Publishing, 1989.

Schmidt, Marjorie G. Growing California Native Plants. Berkeley: University of California Press, 1980.

Tree of Life Nursery. Plants of el Camino Real: Catalog and Planting Guide, 1990-91. San Juan Capistrano, California, 1990.

Landscaping for Wildlife

Introduction:
The transformation of natural landscapes to accommodate population growth and urban development is causing a significant impact on all forms of natural wildlife. The loss of habitat leads to both displacement and population loss of many species.

Research is being conducted to help understand the relationships between urban areas and wildlife. This effort is greatly needed since many people choose to live where they have some contact with native plants and animals.

Even among people who wish to sustain wildlife, there are certain types of wildlife that are preferred more than others. Species of birds and butterflies are often viewed as being safe, colorful, and even friendly. Other species such as opossums and raccoons are tolerable, but tend to be seen as pests and are more problematic. Coyotes and snakes are often viewed as hazardous and are not wanted near populated areas. A number of ideas involving landscapes have been discovered that can increase the habitat and populations of various types of wildlife in urban and suburban areas. A summary of key points regarding planning and design are listed below. Species that are noted for specific wildlife value can be found within the design checklist on pages 55-63.

Planning:
- Wildlife species are part of the total fabric of natural ecosystems. Wherever possible, landscapes that are being considered for development should identify the wildlife species and populations and their habitat requirements. Sustaining viable wildlife populations is most successful when the entire habitat or ecosystem can be preserved and protected.

- Landscapes that are set aside to help maintain wildlife within urban areas should be planned as networks of corridors and habitat sites. Isolated patches and discontinuous landscapes are not as effective in supporting movement and interaction necessary among species.

- Water in dry climate regions is particularly necessary. The preservation of natural sources of water is usually preferred. However, introduced water elements are often highly successful in increasing local populations of wildlife.

Design:
- Landscapes that support wildlife are comprised of elements that provide food, water, cover for nourishment, protection, and nesting. Often, the most successful landscapes provide these elements in many diverse ways.

- Landscapes should be designed with a variety of different plant types, particularly those species known to have high wildlife value. Select native species to help replace those being lost.

- Select plants with different flowering and fruiting times for year around benefit. In natural environments, the combination of annuals, perennials, shrubs, and trees provides distinct seasonal patterns.

- Planting patterns should emphasize differing heights, low, medium, and high. This vertical diversity gives wildlife many opportunities to select optimum habitat locations.

- Landscape plants should be located in random patterns with gaps between masses. This form of diversity provides better opportunity for wildlife to use spaces and edges for forage and cover.

- Provide places where wildlife can get water.

- If people are to visit or use areas designed for wildlife, locate pathways in a manner to create separation and distance from various areas in order to reduce disturbance and create more of a sanctuary.

Management:
- Avoid the indiscriminate use of insecticides and other toxic chemicals. These can cause many disruptions to the natural balance of many food chains, for example, from insects to caterpillars and birds. Chemicals can be as harmful to beneficial wildlife as to those we consider to be pests.

- Reduce the impact of domestic predators, such as cats and dogs by separating them from wildlife areas. Or, as a lesser measure, put bells on their collars to warn wildlife of their presence.

- Try to lessen the impacts associated with human activity. Manage the

An area of high wildlife value at Rancho Santa Ana Botanic Garden, Claremont, California. Plant diversity and a nearby pond combine to provide a variety of elements for food, shelter, and water.

use of wildlife spaces by regulating the frequency of visits by people and the sizes of groups. Screen and buffer areas that are subject to traffic and noise.

- Once a well balanced landscape is developed, try to maintain it without too many major changes. This will help prevent disruptions to the life-cycle of wildlife and allow for succession and maturation in the landscape.

Helpful References:
Bontrager, David. "Ecological Landscaping: Creating Bird Habitat in Suburban California Gardens and Public Landscapes." Endangered Wildlife and Habitats in Southern California: Memoirs of the Natural History Foundation of Orange County, vol. 3. Natural History Foundation of Orange County, 1990, 26-35.

Brinkmann-Busi, Angelika, comp. Guidelines to Select Native Plants for Various Aesthetic and Ecological Considerations as Well as Garden Situations. California Native Plant Society, Santa Monica Mountains Chapter, 1989.

Gardening With Wildlife: A Complete Guide to Attracting and Enjoying the Fascinating Creatures in Your Backyard. Washington, D.C.: National Wildlife Federation, 1974.

Hirschman, Joan. "Bird Habitat Design For People: A Landscape Ecological Approach." M.L.A. Thesis, University of Colorado at Denver, 1988.

Lyle, John T. "A General Approach to Landscape Design for Wildlife Habitat." In Integrating Man and Nature in the Metropolitan Environment: Proceedings of the National Symposium on Urban Wildlife Held in Chevy Chase, Md. 4-7 November 1986, L. W. Adams and D. L. Leedy, ed. Columbia, Maryland: National Institute for Urban Wildlife, 1987, 87-91.

Merilees, Bill. Attracting Backyard Wildlife: A Guide for Nature Lovers. Stillwater, Minneapolis: Voyageur Press, 1989.

Rodiek, Jon E., and Eric G. Bolen, ed. Wildlife and Habitats in Managed Landscapes. Washington, D.C.: Island Press, 1991.

Soule, Michael E. "Land Use Planning and Wildlife Maintenance: Guidelines for Conserving Wildlife in an Urban Landscape." Journal of the American Planning Association 57 (Summer 1991): 313.

Restoration and Escaped Exotics

Introduction:

The protection and restoration of natural landscapes involves many needs and concerns that should be addressed at all levels of planning, design, and management. Ecological restoration is becoming increasingly important in light of the many impacts development and other land uses have on our environment. Restoration involves many complex ideas and processes that lead to the renewal of areas that have been damaged. On one hand, this involves strong application of ecological principles and processes, particularly in the effort to help mitigate development impacts. On the other, concepts being explored within this discipline are far reaching and highly philosophical regarding our attitudes and beliefs about the environment.

Environmental protection and restoration goals are now being fostered by a growing number of organizations and agencies, both public and private. Many of the issues and concepts far exceed the scope of this book as well as the range of practice by many people in landscaping. However, it is necessary to become aware of such relevant issues. Many exotic species pose serious threats to our natural environments. At the same time, we must realize that the practice of environmental restoration is a field in need of expert understanding.

One very important example of environmental protection pertains to exotic plant species that have escaped from cultivation. Over the years, a great diversity of exotic plants have been introduced into western regions for landscaping, grazing, and crop production purposes. Unfortunately, some of these have escaped to become pests of great significance in urban, agricultural, and natural landscapes. The likelihood of plants escaping cultivation can increase when we use exotic species that are highly adapted to western regions. A number of plants that are described within this publication are identified in this regard. Care must be exercised in selecting these plants and understanding their potential for escaping.

A partial listing of commonly used exotic species that have become pests in natural landscapes is provided below.

Spartium junceum, Spanish Broom, escaped and naturalized in the San Gabriel Mountains of southern California.

Acacia cyclops, Southern coastal regions
Acacia dealbata, Northern coastal to southern inland regions
Acacia decurrens, Northern coastal
Acacia melanoxylon, Northern coastal & inland to southern coastal
Acacia retinodes, Southern coastal foothills & canyons
Achillea millefolium, Coastal & inland areas in moist places
Ailanthus altissima, Urban & natural areas around the world
Aptenia cordifolia, Coastal zones
Arctotheca calendula, Northern & southern coastal bluffs, foothills
Arundo donax, All regions in moist areas, seasonal water courses
Atriplex glauca, Southern coastal foothills
Atriplex semibaccata, Coastal to inland areas of California
Carpobrotus edulis, Coastal & inland regions throughout California
Centranthus ruber, Inland & foothill regions throughout California
Cortaderia atacamensis, Coastal & inland regions of California
Cortaderia sellowana, Southern coastal regions
Cynodon dactylon, All warm regions
Cytisus canariensis, Foothill regions, northern California & Central Valley
Cytisus racemosus, Foothill regions, northern California & Central Valley
Eucalyptus camaldulensis, Southern coastal canyons & foothills
Eucalyptus globulus, Coastal canyons & foothills of California
Hedera canariensis, Coastal & inland regions in moist & shady places
Hedera helix, Coastal & inland regions in moist & shady places
Limonium perezii, Southern coastal beaches & bluffs
Lobularia maritima, All regions in moist places
Lonicera japonica 'Halliana', Coastal & inland regions; moist, shady places
Myoporum laetum, Northern & southern coastal foothills of California
Olea europaea, Southern coastal & inland foothills
Oxalis pes-caprae, Urban areas all regions
Pennisetum setaceum, All dry climate regions
Ricinus communis, Disturbed areas, coastal & inland areas of California
Robinia pseudoacacia, Northern California valleys & foothills to southern
      California mountains & foothills

Schinus molle, Coastal canyons & foothills statewide
Schinus terebinthifolius, Coastal lowlands, wet places
Senecio mikanioides, Coastal canyons & moist areas statewide
Spartium junceum, Southern coastal & inland foothills
Tamarix aphylla, Coastal through desert regions in wet places
Tamarix chinensis, Coastal through desert regions in wet places
Tropaeolum majus, Moist coastal areas
Ulex europaeus, Northern coastal & inland foothills
Vinca major, Foothills, canyons, riparian areas all regions

Helpful References:

Berger, John J., ed. Environmental Restoration: Science and Strategies for Restoring the Earth. Washington, D.C.: Island Press, 1990.

Hughes, H. Glenn, and Thomas M. Bonnicksen, ed. The Society for Ecological Restoration; Restoration '89: the New Management Challenge: Proceedings of the 1st Annual Conference Held in Oakland, California 16-20 January 1989. Madison: Society for Ecological Restoration, 1990.

Jordan, William R. III, ed. Restoration & Management Notes. (published bi-annually) Madison: University of Wisconsin Press.

Niering, William, ed. Restoration Ecology. (published quarterly) Cambridge, Mass.: Blackwell Scientific Publications, Inc.

Design Checklist: Character, Size, Flowering, Wildlife Value

Introduction:

The design of ornamental landscapes involves a wide range of conditions and expectations. Checklists are always helpful in stimulating ideas and thoughts as well as assisting in selecting plants that satisfy specific criteria. This design checklist provides descriptive data on plants that are described in greater detail within the plant compendium section.

The seasonal character and eventual size of landscape plants is a consideration in virtually every landscape. Plant sizes can be highly variable and often can be managed by pruning practices. The sizes provided in this chart reflect the average mature size for each plant. In the situation regarding ground covers, the recommended spacing for planting is provided in place of the actual width of the plant. The spread of ground covers is provided within the individual plant descriptions in the compendium section.

A series of columns are provided to display the principle flowering periods for plants including fall, winter, spring, and summer. A number of plants have insignificant flowers which is also indicated. Perhaps one of the most informative lists in this chart is related to the wildlife value of each plant species. This column is a composite data summary that has been combined from a wide variety of sources. Information on wildlife planning and plant species value is in need of further study. Some helpful guidelines for improving the wildlife value of landscapes are provided on page 53.

Legend for Design Checklist:

Character: E = Evergreen D = Deciduous

Height and Width: Average mature size of each species

Flower Season: F = Fall, W = Winter, Sp = Spring, Su = Summer

Flower Color:

B = Blue		Pu = Purple
G = Green		R = Red
L = Lavender		Ro = Rose
M = Magenta		W = White
O = Orange		Y = Yellow
Pi = Pink		

Wildlife Value:
- H = Habitat value for native revegetation projects
- F = Edible fruit and nuts for birds, squirrels, etc.
- L = Leaves for caterpillars, browse value
- N = Nectar for hummingbirds and butterflies
- P = Pollen for honey production
- S = Seed for birds, etc.

NCN = No common name

Trees:

Species	Common Name	Character	Height	Width	F	W	Sp	Su	Insig.	Flower Color	Wildlife Value
Acacia baileyana	Bailey Acacia	E	20-30 ft.	20-30 ft.	■	■				Y	P,S
Acacia dealbata	Silver Wattle	E	25-40 ft.	25-45 ft.	■	■				Y	P,S
Acacia decurrens	Green Wattle	E	25-40 ft.	25-45 ft.			■			Y	P,S
Acacia farnesiana	Sweet Acacia	D	15-20 ft.	15-20 ft.			■			Y	H,P,S
Acacia longifolia	Sydney Golden Wattle	E	15-20 ft.	15-20 ft.	■	■				Y	P,S
Acacia melanoxylon	Blackwood Acacia	E	25-50 ft.	20-25 ft.					■		P,S
Acacia pendula	Weeping Myall	E	15-25 ft.	10-15 ft.			■			Y	
Acacia retinodes	Water Wattle	E	15-20 ft.	12-15 ft.	■	■				Y	P,S
Acacia saligna	Willow Acacia	E	15-35 ft.	12-20 ft.			■			Y	P,S
Acacia smallii	NCN	D	15-20 ft.	15-20 ft.			■			Y	H,P,S
Acacia stenophylla	Shoestring Acacia	E	20-45 ft.	10-20 ft.	■	■				Y	
Aesculus californica	California Buckeye	D	20-40 ft.	20-40 ft.			■			W,Pi	H
Agonis flexuosa	Peppermint Tree	E	25-35 ft.	25-35 ft.					■		S
Albizia julibrissin	Silk Tree	D	25-40 ft.	25-40 ft.			■	■		Pi	N
Angophora costata	Gum Myrtle	E	40-55 ft.	35-40 ft.					■		N
Arbutus menziesii	Madrone	E	30-50 ft.	30-40 ft.			■			W	H,F,L,N,P,S
Arbutus unedo	Strawberry Tree	E	15-30 ft.	15-30 ft.	■	■				W,Pi	H,F,S
Brachychiton populneus	Kurrajong Bottle Tree	E	30-45 ft.	25-30 ft.			■			W	
Broussonetia papyrifera	Paper Mulberry	D	30-40 ft.	25-40 ft.					■		F
Callistemon citrinus	Lemon Bottlebrush	E	10-20 ft.	10-15 ft.			■			R	N,P,S
Callistemon viminalis & cvs	Weeping Bottlebrush	E	20-30 ft.	10-15 ft.			■			R	N
Calocedrus decurrens	Incense Cedar	E	40-80 ft.	10-20 ft.					■		H,S
Carnegiea gigantea	Saguaro	E	25-50 ft.	6-12 ft.				■		W	H,F
Casuarina cunninghamiana	River She-oak	E	50-70 ft.	20-30 ft.					■		
Casuarina equisetifolia	Horsetail Tree	E	40-60 ft.	20-25 ft.					■		
Casuarina stricta	Drooping She-oak	E	25-35 ft.	20-25 ft.					■		
Ceanothus arboreus	Feltleaf Ceanothus	E	15-25 ft.	12-15 ft.			■			B	H,L,N,S
Ceanothus 'Ray Hartman'	NCN	E	10-15 ft.	10-15 ft.			■			B	L,N,S
Ceanothus thyrsiflorus	Blue Blossom	E	15-20 ft.	10-15 ft.			■			B,W	H,L,N,S
Cedrus atlantica & cvs	Atlas Cedar	E	50-70 ft.	40-50 ft.					■		
Cedrus deodara & cvs	Deodar Cedar	E	60-80 ft.	40-50 ft.					■		
Ceratonia siliqua	Carob Tree	E	25-50 ft.	25-50 ft.			■			W	
Cercidium floridum	Blue Palo Verde	D	25-30 ft.	25-30 ft.			■			Y	H,P,S
Cercidium microphyllum	Little Leaf Palo Verde	D	15-25 ft.	15-25 ft.			■			W,Y	H,S
Cercidium praecox	Sonoran Palo Verde	D	20-25 ft.	20-25 ft.			■			Y	H,S
Cercis canadensis & cvs	Eastern Redbud	D	25-35 ft.	20-25 ft.			■			M,Pi	N

Design Checklist: Character, Size, Flowering, Wildlife Value

Legend for Design Checklist:

Character: E = Evergreen
D = Deciduous

Height and Width: Average mature size

NCN = No common name

Flower Season: F = Fall
Sp = Spring
Su = Summer
W = Winter

Flower Color: B = Blue
G = Green
L = Lavender
M = Magenta
O = Orange
Pi = Pink
Pu = Purple
R = Red
Ro = Rose
W = White
Y = Yellow

Wildlife Value:
H = Habitat value for native revegetation projects
F = Edible fruit and nuts for birds, squirrels, etc.
L = Leaves for caterpillars, browse value
N = Nectar for hummingbirds and butterflies
P = Pollen for honey production
S = Seed for birds, etc.

Trees (Cont.):

		Character	Height	Width	F	W	Sp	Su	Insig.	Flower Color	Wildlife Value
Cercis occidentalis	*Western Redbud*	D	15-20 ft.	15-20 ft.			■			M,Pi,W	H,N,S
Chilopsis linearis	*Desert Willow*	D	15-40 ft.	15-30 ft.			■	■		Pi,Pu,W	H,N
Chitalpa tashkentensis	*Chitalpa*	D	20-30 ft.	20-30 ft.				■		Pi,W	
Cordyline australis	*Giant Dracaena*	E	20-30 ft.	10-12 ft.			■			W	
Cupressus arizonica	*Arizona Cypress*	E	35-50 ft.	20-30 ft.					■		H
Cupressus forbesii	*Tecate Cypress*	E	20-30 ft.	15-20 ft.					■		H
Cupressus glabra	*Smooth Arizona Cypress*	E	30-40 ft.	20-25 ft.					■		H
Cupressus macrocarpa	*Monterey Cypress*	E	30-40 ft.	30-40 ft.					■		H
Cupressus sempervirens	*Italian Cypress*	E	40-60 ft.	10-15 ft.					■		
Dalea spinosa	*Smoke Tree*	D	20-25 ft.	15-20 ft.			■	■		Pu	H,P
Dodonaea viscosa	*Hopseed Bush*	E	12-18 ft.	10-12 ft.					■		S
Dracaena draco	*Dragon Tree*	E	12-25 ft.	6-15 ft.			■			W	
Eucalyptus caesia	*Gungurru*	E	15-20 ft.	10-15 ft.		■	■			R	N,S
Eucalyptus camaldulensis	*River Red Gum*	E	60-100 ft.	40-60 ft.					■		N
Eucalyptus cinerea	*Argyle Apple*	E	20-40 ft.	20-30 ft.					■		N
Eucalyptus citriodora	*Lemon-scented Gum*	E	70-100 ft.	25-40 ft.					■		N,S
Eucalyptus cladocalyx	*Sugar Gum*	E	45-75 ft.	35-50 ft.					■		N,S
Eucalyptus erythrocorys	*Red-cap Gum*	E	15-25 ft.	10-15 ft.	■					R	N,S
Eucalyptus ficifolia	*Red Flowering Gum*	E	25-40 ft.	25-40 ft.				■		Pi,R	N,S
Eucalyptus globulus & cv	*Blue Gum*	E	60-120 ft.	35-50 ft.					■		N,P,S
Eucalyptus lehmannii	*Lehmann's Mallee*	E	20-30 ft.	20-30 ft.					■		N,P,S
Eucalyptus leucoxylon & cv	*White Ironbark*	E	30-50 ft.	15-40 ft.	■					R,W	N,P,S
Eucalyptus maculata	*Spotted Gum*	E	60-80 ft.	30-40 ft.					■		N,P,S
Eucalyptus microtheca	*Coolibah*	E	30-40 ft.	20-30 ft.					■		N,P,S
Eucalyptus nicholii	*Willow Peppermint*	E	30-40 ft.	20-30 ft.					■		N,P,S
Eucalyptus papuana	*Ghost Gum*	E	30-50 ft.	25-40 ft.					■		N,P,S
Eucalyptus polyanthemos	*Silver Dollar Gum*	E	45-60 ft.	30-45 ft.			■			W	N,P,S
Eucalyptus rudis	*Flooded Gum*	E	30-50 ft.	25-40 ft.					■		N,P,S
Eucalyptus sideroxylon & cv	*Red Ironbark*	E	35-70 ft.	25-40 ft.		■				Ro,W	N,P,S
Eucalyptus spathulata	*Narrow-leaved Gimlet*	E	15-25 ft.	15-20 ft.					■		P
Eucalyptus torquata	*Coral Gum*	E	15-25 ft.	15-25 ft.				■		Pi,Ro	N,P,S
Eucalyptus viminalis	*Manna Gum*	E	40-120 ft.	40-50 ft.					■		N,P,S
Feijoa sellowiana	*Pineapple Guava*	E	15-25 ft.	15-25 ft.				■		R,W	F,P
Ficus carica & cvs	*Common Fig*	D	15-30 ft.	15-30 ft.					■		F
Geijera parviflora	*Australian Willow*	E	20-35 ft.	20-30 ft.					■		
Grevillea robusta	*Silky Oak*	E	40-75 ft.	30-40 ft.			■			O	N
Juglans californica	*S. Calif. Black Walnut*	D	20-35 ft.	20-40 ft.					■		H,F
Juniperus chinensis 'Torulosa'	*Hollywood Juniper*	E	15-25 ft.	15-20 ft.					■		
Juniperus virginiana	*Eastern Redcedar*	E	40-70 ft.	10-20 ft.					■		
Lagerstroemia indica & cvs	*Crape Myrtle*	D	15-25 ft.	15-25 ft.				■		many	
Laurus nobilis	*Sweet Bay*	E	15-40 ft.	15-25 ft.					■		
Leptospermum laevigatum	*Australian Tea Tree*	E	15-25 ft.	15-25 ft.			■			W	S
Leptospermum scoparium	*New Zealand Tea Tree*	E	10-12 ft.	8-10 ft.		■	■			many	
Lyonothamnus floribundus & var.	*Catalina Ironwood*	E	30-60 ft.	25-35 ft.			■	■		W	H,S
Lysiloma thornberi	*Feather Bush*	E/D	12-15 ft.	12-15 ft.			■			W	
Melaleuca armillaris	*Drooping Melaleuca*	E	12-15 ft.	15-30 ft.			■			Pi,W	N
Melaleuca linariifolia	*Flaxleaf Paperbark*	E	20-30 ft.	20-25 ft.			■	■		W	N
Melaleuca quinquenervia	*Cajeput Tree*	E	25-40 ft.	15-20 ft.	■					W	N
Melia azedarach & cv	*Chinaberry*	D	30-50 ft.	40-50 ft.			■			Pu	
Metrosideros excelsus	*N. Z. Christmas Tree*	E	15-30 ft.	15-30 ft.			■	■		R	N
Morus alba	*White Mulberry*	D	30-60 ft.	30-50 ft.					■		F
Myoporum laetum	*Myoporum*	E	20-30 ft.	15-25 ft.					■		
Myrica californica	*Pacific Wax Myrtle*	E	15-25 ft.	15-20 ft.					■		F,S
Nerium oleander & cvs	*Oleander*	E	15-20 ft.	10-15 ft.			■	■		many	N
Olea europaea & cvs	*Olive*	E	20-35 ft.	20-30 ft.			■			Y	F

Trees (Cont.):

Name	Common Name	Character	Height	Width	F	W	Sp	Su	Insig.	Flower Color	Wildlife Value
Olneya tesota	*Desert Ironwood*	E	25-30 ft.	20-25 ft.			■	■		L,W	H,L
Parkinsonia aculeata	*Mexican Palo Verde*	D	20-30 ft.	20-30 ft.	■		■	■		Y	
Pinus brutia	*Calabrian Pine*	E	30-60 ft.	30-50 ft.					■		S
Pinus canariensis	*Canary Island Pine*	E	40-60 ft.	20-35 ft.					■		S
Pinus coulteri	*Coulter Pine*	E	30-60 ft.	25-40 ft.					■		H,S
Pinus eldarica	*Afghan Pine*	E	30-60 ft.	25-40 ft.					■		S
Pinus halepensis	*Aleppo Pine*	E	30-60 ft.	20-40 ft.					■		S
Pinus monophylla	*Single-leaf Pinon Pine*	E	10-25 ft.	15-20 ft.					■		H,S
Pinus pinea	*Italian Stone Pine*	E	40-80 ft.	30-50 ft.					■		S
Pinus radiata	*Monterey Pine*	E	60-80 ft.	20-35 ft.					■		H,S
Pinus sabiniana	*Digger Pine*	E	30-50 ft.	25-40 ft.					■		H,S
Pinus torreyana	*Torrey Pine*	E	40-60 ft.	25-40 ft.					■		H,S
Pithecellobium flexicaule	*Texas Ebony*	E	20-25 ft.	20-25 ft.			■	■		Y	H,N,S
Pittosporum phillyraeoides	*Willow Pittosporum*	E	15-25 ft.	15-20 ft.			■			Y	N,S
Platanus racemosa	*Western Sycamore*	D	50-90 ft.	30-50 ft.					■		H,L,S
Prosopis alba	*Argentine Mesquite*	E/D	25-30 ft.	25-30 ft.			■			Y	N,P,S
Prosopis chilensis	*Chilean Mesquite*	E/D	20-25 ft.	20-25 ft.			■			Y	N,P,S
Prosopis glandulosa	*Texas Mesquite*	D	25-30 ft.	25-30 ft.			■			Y	H,N,P,S
Prosopis juliflora	*Mesquite*	D	40-50 ft.	30-40 ft.			■			Y	H,N,P,S
Prosopis pubescens	*Screw Bean Mesquite*	D	15-25 ft.	15-25 ft.			■			Y	H,N,P,S
Prunus caroliniana	*Carolina Laurel Cherry*	E	20-35 ft.	20-30 ft.		■	■			W	F,N
Prunus lyonii	*Catalina Cherry*	E	30-45 ft.	20-30 ft.			■			W	H,F,N
Punica granatum & cvs	*Pomegranate*	D	12-18 ft.	15-20 ft.			■	■		O,R,W	F,S
Quercus agrifolia	*Coast Live Oak*	E	30-60 ft.	40-70 ft.					■		H,F,L
Quercus douglasii	*Blue Oak*	D	25-50 ft.	30-50 ft.					■		H,F,L
Quercus engelmannii	*Mesa Oak*	E	20-50 ft.	30-50 ft.					■		H,F
Quercus ilex	*Holly Oak*	E	40-50 ft.	30-50 ft.					■		F
Quercus lobata	*Valley Oak*	D	50-70 ft.	50-70 ft.					■		H,F,L
Quercus suber	*Cork Oak*	E	60-80 ft.	40-50 ft.					■		F
Rhus lancea	*African Sumac*	E	20-30 ft.	20-35 ft.					■		S
Robinia ambigua & cvs	*Locust*	D	30-40 ft.	20-25 ft.			■			Pi,Pu	N
Robinia pseudoacacia	*Black Locust*	D	40-70 ft.	30-40 ft.			■			W	N
Sambucus caerulea	*Blue Elderberry*	D	15-30 ft.	20-30 ft.			■	■		Y	H,F,N
Schinus molle	*Pepper Tree*	E	25-40 ft.	30-40 ft.					■		S
Schinus polygamus	*Peruvian Pepper*	E	20-30 ft.	20-30 ft.					■		S
Schinus terebinthifolius	*Brazilian Pepper*	E	20-30 ft.	20-30 ft.				■		Y	F,N
Sophora secundiflora	*Mescal Bean*	E	25-35 ft.	20-25 ft.			■			L	H,N
Tamarix aphylla	*Athel Tree*	E	20-35 ft.	20-30 ft.				■		Pi,W	
Tristania conferta & cv	*Brisbane Box*	E	40-70 ft.	25-35 ft.					■		
Vitex angus-castus	*Chaste Tree*	D	15-25 ft.	15-20 ft.				■		Pi,Pu	N
Xylosma congestum	*Shiny Xylosma*	E	15-25 ft.	15-20 ft.					■		N
Yucca brevifolia	*Joshua Tree*	E	20-30 ft.	15-25 ft.			■			W	H,L,N
Yucca gloriosa	*Spanish Dagger*	E	15-20 ft.	10-15 ft.			■			W	L,N

Palms:

Name	Common Name	Character	Height	Width	F	W	Sp	Su	Insig.	Flower Color	Wildlife Value
Brahea armata	*Blue Hesper Palm*		25-45 ft.	10-12 ft.				■		Y	
Brahea edulis	*Guadalupe Palm*		20-30 ft.	10-12 ft.			■	■		Y	F
Butia capitata	*Pindo Palm*		10-20 ft.	15-20 ft.			■			R	
Chamaerops humilis	*Mediterranean Fan Palm*		10-20 ft.	10-25 ft.		■				Y	
Phoenix canariensis	*Canary Island Date Palm*		50-60 ft.	40-50 ft.					■		F
Phoenix dactylifera	*Date Palm*		50-60 ft.	30- 40 ft.					■		F
Trachycarpus fortunei	*Windmill Palm*		20-30 ft.	6-8 ft.					■		
Washingtonia filifera	*California Fan Palm*		60-75 ft.	10-15 ft.			■			W	F
Washingtonia robusta	*Mexican Fan Palm*		60-100 ft.	10-12 ft.			■			W	F

Design Checklist: Character, Size, Flowering, Wildlife Value

Shrubs & Vines:

Species	Common Name	Character	Height	Width	F	W	Sp	Su	Insig.	Flower Color	Wildlife Value
Acacia berlandieri	Berlandier Acacia	D	10-12 ft.	6-12 ft.			■			W	P,S
Acacia cultriformis	Knife Acacia	E	6-12 ft.	6-15 ft.			■			Y	P,S
Acacia cyclops	Western Coastal Wattle	E	6-15 ft.	10-20 ft.					■		S
Acacia farnesiana	Sweet Acacia	D	15-20 ft.	15-20 ft.			■			Y	H,P,S
Acacia greggii	Catclaw Acacia	D	15-25 ft.	15-25 ft.	■		■	■		Y	H,N,P,S
Acacia longifolia	Sydney Golden Wattle	E	15-20 ft.	15-20 ft.		■	■			Y	P,S
Acacia retinodes	Water Wattle	E	15-20 ft.	12-15 ft.		■	■			Y	P,S
Aesculus californica	California Buckeye	D	20-40 ft.	20-40 ft.			■			Pi,W	H
Alyogyne huegelii	Blue Hibiscus	E	6-10 ft.	6-10 ft.			■	■		B,M,Pu	
Anisacanthus thurberi	Desert Honeysuckle	E/D	3-6 ft.	3-6 ft.			■			O,R	
Anisodontea hypomandarum	Dwarf Pink Hibiscus	E	5-7 ft.	5-7 ft.	■	■	■	■		Pi	N
Arbutus unedo 'Compacta'	Dwarf Strawberry Tree	E	6-12 ft.	6-12 ft.	■	■				Pi,W	F,S
Arctostaphylos densiflora & cvs	Sonoma Manzanita	E	6-8 ft.	6-12 ft.		■	■			Pi,W	F,N,P
Arctostaphylos edmundsii	Little Sur Manzanita	E	2-3 ft.	4-6 ft.			■			Pi,W	F,N,P
Arctostaphylos hookeri	Monterey Manzanita	E	2-4 ft.	4-6 ft.		■	■			Pi,W	F,N,P
Artemisia arborescens	Shrubby Wormwood	E	5-6 ft.	6-8 ft.			■			Y	P,S
Artemisia californica & cvs	California Sagebrush	E	3-5 ft.	3-5 ft.					■		H,P,S
Artemisia 'Powis Castle'	NCN	E	2-3 ft.	3-4 ft.					■		
Atriplex canescens	Four-wing Saltbush	E	4-8 ft.	4-8 ft.			■			Y	H,L,S
Atriplex hymenelytra	Desert Holly	E	1-3 ft.	1-3 ft.					■		H,L
Atriplex lentiformis	Quail Bush	E	8-10 ft.	12-15 ft.					■		H,L,S
Atriplex l. var. breweri	Brewer Saltbush	E	6-10 ft.	8-12 ft.					■		H,L,S
Baccharis p. consanguinea	Chaparral Broom	E	4-12 ft.	6-8 ft.					■		H,N,S
Bougainvillea species & cvs	Bougainvillea	E	10-25 ft.	10-25 ft.	■			■	■	many	N
Buddleia marrubiifolia	Woolly Butterfly Bush	E	3-4 ft.	3-4 ft.				■		O,Y	N
Caesalpinia species	Bird-of-paradise Bush	E/D	6-15 ft.	10-20 ft.			■	■		O,R,Y	N
Calliandra californica	Baja Fairy Duster	E/D	3-4 ft.	4-5 ft.	■		■			R	S
Calliandra eriophylla	Fairy Duster	E/D	1-3 ft.	4-6 ft.	■			■		Pi	S
Calliandra peninsularis	NCN	E/D	5-6 ft.	5-6 ft.			■			R	S
Callistemon citrinus	Lemon Bottlebrush	E	10-15 ft.	10-15 ft.			■			R	N,P,S
Calocephalus brownii	Cushion Bush	E	1-2 ft.	3-4 ft.			■			Y	
Carpenteria californica	Bush Anemone	E	4-6 ft.	6-8 ft.			■			W	
Cassia artemisioides	Feathery Cassia	E	3-5 ft.	3-5 ft.		■	■			Y	P
Cassia nemophila	Desert Cassia	E	5-8 ft.	4-6 ft.		■	■			Y	P
Cassia phyllodinea	Silvery Cassia	E	3-5 ft.	4-6 ft.			■			Y	
Ceanothus arboreus	Feltleaf Ceanothus	E	15-25 ft.	12-15 ft.			■			B	H,L,N,P,S
Ceanothus 'Concha'	NCN	E	5-7 ft.	6-10 ft.			■			B	L,N,P,S
Ceanothus 'Dark Star'	NCN	E	4-6 ft.	5-6 ft.			■			B	L,N,P,S
Ceanothus 'Frosty Blue'	NCN	E	8-10 ft.	10-12 ft.			■			B	L,N,P,S
Ceanothus gloriosus & cvs	Point Reyes Ceanothus	E	1-2 ft.	4-6 ft.			■			B,Pu	H,L,N,P,S
Ceanothus griseus & cvs	Carmel Ceanothus	E	4-6 ft.	6-12 ft.		■	■			B	H,L,N,P,S
Ceanothus impressus	Santa Barbara Ceanothus	E	6-10 ft.	6-10 ft.			■			B	H,L,N,P,S
Ceanothus 'Joyce Coulter'	NCN	E	3-5 ft.	8-10 ft.			■			B	L,N,P,S
Ceanothus 'Julia Phelps'	NCN	E	5-6 ft.	6-8 ft.			■			Pu	L,N,P,S
Ceanothus 'Ray Hartman'	NCN	E	10-15 ft.	10-15 ft.			■			B	L,N,P,S
Ceanothus rigidus & cvs	Monterey Ceanothus	E	3-4 ft.	3-4 ft.			■			B	H,L,N,P,S
Ceanothus thyrsiflorus & cvs	Blue Blossom Ceanothus	E	15-20 ft.	10-15 ft.			■			B,W	H,L,N,P,S
Ceanothus 'Wheeler Canyon'	NCN	E	5-6 ft.	5-6 ft.			■			B	L,N,P,S
Cercis occidentalis	Western Redbud	D	15-20 ft.	15-20 ft.			■			M,Pi,W	N,S
Chamelaucium uncinatum	Geraldton Wax Flower	E	8-10 ft.	6-12 ft.		■	■			Ro,W	
Chilopsis linearis	Desert Willow	D	15-20 ft.	15-20 ft.			■	■		Pi,Pu,W	N
Cistus species & cvs	Rockrose	E	3-7 ft.	3-7 ft.			■			Pi,Pu,W	
Cleome isomeris	Bladderpod	E	3-6 ft.	3-6 ft.			■	■		Y	N
Comarostaphylis diversifolia	Summer Holly	E	6-10 ft.	6-8 ft.			■			W	H,F,N
Cordia species	Cordia	E/D	10-25 ft.	10-25 ft.			■			W	N

Shrubs & Vines (Cont.):

Botanical Name	Common Name	Character	Height	Width	F	W	Sp	Su	Insig.	Flower Color	Wildlife Value
Correa species & cvs	*Correa*	E	3-4 ft.	3-5 ft.	■	■	■			many	N
Cotoneaster apiculatus	*Cranberry Cotoneaster*	E/D	3-4 ft.	5-6 ft.					■		F,N
Cotoneaster buxifolius	*NCN*	E	3-4 ft.	5-6 ft.					■		F,N
Cotoneaster congestus	*NCN*	E	2-3 ft.	3-4 ft.					■		F,N
Cotoneaster lacteus	*Red Clusterberry*	E	8-10 ft.	10-12 ft.	■	■	■			W	F,N
Cotoneaster salicifolius	*Willowleaf Cotoneaster*	E	12-15 ft.	12-18 ft.					■		F,N
Cowania mexicana	*Cliff Rose*	E	2-6 ft.	3-6 ft.			■			W	H,L
Dalea frutescens	*Black Dalea*	E	1-3 ft.	2-3 ft.	■			■		Pu	
Dalea pulchra	*Indigo Bush*	E	3-5 ft.	5-7 ft.			■			Pu	
Dendromecon species	*Bush Poppy*	E	8-10 ft.	10-15 ft.			■	■		Y	H
Dodonaea viscosa	*Hopseed Bush*	E	6-12 ft.	6-10 ft.					■		S
Echium fastuosum	*Pride of Madeira*	E	4-6 ft.	4-6 ft.			■			B,Pu	P
Elaeagnus pungens	*Silverberry*	E	6-15 ft.	6-15 ft.					■		F
Encelia californica	*California Encelia*	E	3-5 ft.	3-5 ft.		■	■			Y	L,S
Encelia farinosa	*Desert Encelia*	E	2-4 ft.	2-4 ft.			■			Y	S
Eriogonum arborescens	*Santa Cruz Is. Buckwheat*	E	3-5 ft.	4-6 ft.			■	■		Pi	H,N,S
Eriogonum cinereum	*Asyleaf Buckwheat*	E	4-6 ft.	4-6 ft.				■		Pi	N,S
Eriogonum fasciculatum	*Common Buckwheat*	E	2-3 ft.	2-3 ft.				■		Pi,W	H,N,P,S
Eriogonum giganteum	*St. Catherine's Lace*	E	5-8 ft.	6-10 ft.			■	■		W	H,L,S
Eriogonum parvifolium	*Coastal Buckwheat*	E	1-2 ft.	5-6 ft.			■	■		Pi,W	H,N
Eucalyptus lehmannii	*Bushy Yate*	E	15-20 ft.	15-20 ft.					■		N,S
Fallugia paradoxa	*Apache Plume*	D	3-8 ft.	6-10 ft.			■			W	H,N
Feijoa sellowiana	*Pineapple Guava*	E	15-20 ft.	15-20 ft.			■			R,W	F,N
Fremontodendron species & cvs	*California Flannel Bush*	E	10-20 ft.	10-20 ft.			■			Y	H,S
Galvezia speciosa	*Island Bush-snapdragon*	E	6-8 ft.	8-12 ft.			■	■		R	H,F,N
Garrya elliptica	*Coast Silktassel*	E	8-12 ft.	8-12 ft.		■				W	H,F
Grevillea species & cvs	*Grevillea*	E	3-8 ft.	5-10 ft.			■	■		many	N,S
Hakea suaveolens	*Sweet-scented Hakea*	E	10-18 ft.	8-12 ft.					■		N
Hardenbergia violacea	*False Sarsaparilla*	E	10-12 ft.	10-12 ft.			■			Pu	
Heteromeles arbutifolia	*Toyon*	E	12-18 ft.	15-20 ft.			■	■		W	H,F
Hibiscus syriacus	*Rose of Sharon*	D	8-12 ft.	6-12 ft.	■			■		Pu,W	L
Iva hayesiana	*Hayes Iva*	E	2-3 ft.	4-5 ft.					■		H
Jasminum species	*Jasmine*	E/D	6-8 ft.	10-15 ft.	■		■	■		W,Y	N
Juniperus californica	*California Juniper*	E	5-15 ft.	10-15 ft.					■		H,F
Juniperus chinensis & cvs	*NCN*	E	2-12 ft.	5-20 ft.					■		
Juniperus sabina & cvs	*Savin Juniper*	E	1-3 ft.	5-15 ft.					■		
Juniperus scopulorum & cvs	*Rocky Mountain Juniper*	E	5-20 ft.	5-10 ft.					■		
Justicia californica	*Chuparosa*	D	3-5 ft.	6-8 ft.			■			R	H,N,S
Justicia spicigera	*Mexican Honeysuckle*	E/D	2-3 ft.	2-3 ft.			■	■		O	H,N,S
Keckiella species	*Native Penstemon*	E	5-6 ft.	6-8 ft.			■	■		R,Y	H,N,S
Lagerstroemia indica & cvs	*Compact Crape Myrtle*	D	15-20 ft.	15-20 ft.				■		many	
Lantana camara	*Yellow Sage*	E	4-6 ft.	5-7 ft.	■			■	■	many	F,L,N
Larrea tridentata	*Creosote Bush*	E	5-10 ft.	5-10 ft.			■			Y	H,S
Lavandula species & cvs	*Lavender*	E	1-3 ft.	1-3 ft.	■		■	■		B,LPu	N
Lavatera species	*Mallow*	E	8-12 ft.	8-12 ft.	■		■	■		Pu,Ro,W	L,N,S
Leonotis leonurus	*Lion's Tail*	E	5-6 ft.	5-6 ft.			■	■		O	
Leptospermum laevigatum	*Australian Tea Tree*	E	10-15 ft.	15-25 ft.			■			W	S
Leptospermum scoparium	*New Zealand Tea Tree*	E	5-10 ft.	4-6 ft.		■	■			Pi,R,W	
Leucophyllum species & cvs	*Cenizo*	E	4-8 ft.	4-5 ft.	■		■			B,L,W	H
Lupinus albifrons	*Silver Lupine*	E	3-5 ft.	3-5 ft.			■	■		B,Pu	H,L,N,S
Lupinus arboreus	*Coastal Bush Lupine*	E	3-6 ft.	3-6 ft.			■			Y	H,L,S
Macfadyena unguis-cati	*Cat's Claw*	E/D	30-40 ft.	N.A.			■			Y	
Mahonia aquifolium	*Oregon Grape*	E	5-6 ft.	4-5 ft.			■			Y	H,F,N
Mahonia 'Golden Abundance'	*NCN*	E	5-6 ft.	5-6 ft.			■			Y	F,N
Mahonia nevinii	*Nevin Mahonia*	E	8-12 ft.	8-12 ft.			■			Y	H,F,N

Design Checklist: Character, Size, Flowering, Wildlife Value

Shrubs & Vines (Cont.):

Name	Common Name	Character	Height	Width	F	W	Sp	Su	Insig.	Flower Color	Wildlife Value
Mahonia pinnata & cvs	*California Grape*	E	4-5 ft.	4-5 ft.			■			Y	H,F,N
Malosma laurina	*Laurel Sumac*	E	12-20 ft.	12-20 ft.			■	■		W	H,S
Melaleuca armillaris	*Drooping Melaleuca*	E	12-15 ft.	15-30 ft.			■			Pi,W	N
Melaleuca nesophila	*Pink Melaleuca*	E	10-18 ft.	15-20 ft.				■		Pi,W	N
Metrosideros excelsus	*N. Z. Christmas Tree*	E	15-20 ft.	15-20 ft.			■	■		R	N
Myoporum laetum & cvs	*NCN*	E	15-20 ft.	15-20 ft.					■		
Myrica californica	*Pacific Wax Myrtle*	E	10-15 ft.	10-15 ft.					■		F,S
Myrtus communis & cvs	*True Myrtle*	E	8-10 ft.	8-10 ft.				■		W	
Nerium oleander & cvs	*Oleander*	E	5-10 ft.	5-10 ft.			■	■		many	
Plecostachys serpyllifolia	*NCN*	E	1-3 ft.	3-4 ft.					■		
Plumbago auriculata	*Cape Plumbago*	E	6-8 ft.	8-12 ft.	■		■	■		B,W	N
Polygonum aubertii	*Silver Lace Vine*	E	30-40 ft.	N.A.				■		W	
Prosopis pubescens	*Screw Bean Mesquite*	D	10-25 ft.	10-25 ft.			■			Y	H,P,S
Prunus caroliniana & cvs	*Carolina Laurel Cherry*	E	15-20 ft.	12-15 ft.		■	■			W	F,N,P
Prunus ilicifolia	*Hollyleaf Cherry*	E	15-20 ft.	15-20 ft.			■			W	H,F,L,N
Prunus lyonii	*Catalina Cherry*	E	15-30 ft.	15-20 ft.			■			W	H,F,N
Punica granatum & cvs	*Pomegranate*	D	12-18 ft.	12-18 ft.			■	▪		O,R,W	F,S
Pyracantha species & cvs	*Firethorn*	E	4-8 ft.	4-8 ft.			■			W	F,P
Rhamnus alaternus	*Italian Buckthorn*	E	12-15 ft.	12-15 ft.					▪		F
Rhamnus californica	*California Coffeeberry*	E	8-10 ft.	8-10 ft.					▪		H,F,L,P
Rhamnus crocea & var.	*Redberry*	E	6-8 ft.	6-8 ft.					▪		H,F,L,P
Rhaphiolepis indica & cvs.	*India Hawthorn*	E	3-8 ft.	3-8 ft.			■			Pi,W	
Rhaphiolepis 'Majestic Beauty'	*NCN*	E	6-10 ft.	6-10 ft.			■			Pi	
Rhaphiolepis umbellata & cv	*Yedda Hawthorn*	E	3-8 ft.	3-8 ft.			■			W	
Rhus integrifolia	*Lemonade Berry*	E	6-15 ft.	6-15 ft.					▪		H,F
Rhus ovata	*Sugar Bush*	E	15-20 ft.	15-20 ft.			■			Pi,W	H,F
Ribes aureum	*Golden Currant*	D	4-6 ft.	4-6 ft.			■			Y	H,F,L,N
Ribes indecorum	*White-flowered Currant*	D	5-6 ft.	4-6 ft.	■	■				W	H,F,L,N
Ribes malvaceum	*Chaparral Currant*	D	6-8 ft.	4-6 ft.		■	■			Pi,W	H,F,L,N
Ribes speciosum	*Fuchsia-flr. Gooseberry*	D	4-8 ft.	5-8 ft.			■			R	H,F,L,N
Rosa banksiae	*Lady Banks' Rose*	E	10-20 ft.	20-25 ft.			■	■		W,Y	
Rosmarinus officinalis & cvs	*Rosemary*	E	4-7 ft.	5-8 ft.		■	■			B,L	N,P,S
Ruellia species	*Ruellia*	E	2-4 ft.	3-4 ft.			■	■		Pu	
Salvia apiana	*White Sage*	E	3-5 ft.	3-5 ft.				■		W	H,N,S
Salvia chamaedryoides	*Blue Sage*	E	2-3 ft.	3-4 ft.	■		■	■		B	N,S
Salvia clevelandii & cvs	*Cleveland Sage*	E	3-4 ft.	4-5 ft.			■	▪		B	H,N,P,S
Salvia greggii	*Autumn Sage*	E	2-3 ft.	2-3 ft.	■		■			R	H,N,S
Salvia leucantha	*Mexican Bush Sage*	E	3-5 ft.	3-5 ft.	■		▪	■		Pu,W	N,S
Salvia leucophylla	*Purple Sage*	E	5-6 ft.	5-6 ft.			■			L	H,N,P,S
Salvia mellifera & cvs	*Black Sage*	E	4-5 ft.	4-5 ft.				■		B,W	H,N,P,S
Sambucus caerulea	*Blue Elderberry*	D	15-20 ft.	15-20 ft.			■	■		Y	H,F,N,P
Santolina species	*Lavender Cotton*	E	1-2 ft.	3-4 ft.			■	■		G,Y	
Schinus molle	*Pepper Tree*	E	20-30 ft.	30-35 ft.					▪		F
Schinus terebinthifolius	*Brazilian Pepper*	E	15-20 ft.	15-20 ft.				■		Y	F,N
Simmondsia chinensis	*Jojoba*	E	8-10 ft.	10-12 ft.					▪		S
Sollya heterophylla	*Australian Blue-bell Cr.*	E	2-3 ft.	6-8 ft.			■	■		B	
Sophora secundiflora	*Mescal Bean*	E	10-20 ft.	10-15 ft.			■			L	H,N
Tecoma stans var. angustata	*Hardy Yellow Trumpet Flr.*	E/D	12-18 ft.	10-15 ft.				■		Y	H
Tecomaria capensis	*Cape Honeysuckle*	E	6-8 ft.	12-15 ft.	■	■		■		O,R	
Teucrium chamaedrys	*NCN*	E	12-15 in.	1-2 ft.				■		L,Pu	P
Teucrium fruticans	*Bush Germander*	E	4-8 ft.	8-10 ft.		■	■			B,L	
Trichostema lanatum	*Woolly Blue Curls*	E	2-3 ft.	3-4 ft.	■			■	▪	B,Pu,W	N
Vitex agnus-castus	*Chaste Tree*	D	10-15 ft.	10-12 ft.				■		L,Pu,W	
Westringia species	*NCN*	E	5-7 ft.	6-12 ft.	▪	▪	▪	▪		L,W	
Xylosma congestum	*Shiny Xylosma*	E	15-25 ft.	15-20 ft.					▪		N

Ground Covers:

		Character	Height	Spacing for planting	F	W	Sp	Su	Insig.	Flower Color	Wildlife Value
Acacia redolens & cvs	NCN	E	3-12 ft.	15-30 ft.			■			Y	
Achillea millefolium	Common Yarrow	E	18-30 in.	18-30 in.			■	■		Pi,R,W	N,S
Aptenia 'Red Apple'	NCN	E	6-12 in.	2 ft.	■		■	■		Pu,R	P
Arctostaphylos edmundsii & cvs	Little Sur Manzanita	E	2-3 ft.	4-6 ft.			■			Pi,W	F,N,P
Arctostaphylos 'Emerald Carpet'	NCN	E	6-12 in.	4-6 ft.					■		F,N,P
Arctostaphylos hookeri & cvs	Monterey Manzanita	E	1-2 ft.	4-6 ft.		■	■			Pi,W	F,N,P
Arctostaphylos 'Pacific Mist'	NCN	E	1-2 ft.	5-6 ft.					■		F,N,P
Arctostaphylos uva-ursi & cvs	Bearberry	E	6-12 in.	5-6 ft.		■	■			Pi,W	F,N,P
Arctotheca calendula	Cape Weed	E	3-6 in.	12-15 in.	■	■	■	■		Y	P
Artemisia californica & cvs	Prostrate Calif. Sagebrush	E	15-18 in.	4-8 ft.					■		H
Baccharis 'Centennial'	NCN	E	2-3 ft.	5-6 ft.					■		H,N
Baccharis pilularis & cvs	Prostrate Coyote Brush	E	2-3 ft.	4-6 ft.					■		H,N
Bougainvillea cultivars	Bougainvillea	E	3-5 ft.	8-20 ft.	■		■	■		many	N
Carpobrotus species	Sea Fig	E	6-12 in.	24-30 in.			■	■		Ro,Y	
Ceanothus gloriosus & cvs	Point Reyes Ceanothus	E	1-2 ft.	4-5 ft.			■			B,Pu	F,L,N,P,S
Ceanothus griseus varieties	Prostrate Carmel Creeper	E	2-3 ft.	8-10 ft.		■	■			B	F,L,N,P,S
Ceanothus 'Joyce Coulter'	NCN	E	3-5 ft.	6-8 ft.			■			B	F,L,N,P,S
Ceanothus maritimus & cvs	Maritime Ceanothus	E	1-3 ft.	4-5 ft.		■	■			B,W	F,L,N,P,S
Cephalophyllum 'Red Spike'	Red Spike Ice Plant	E	4-6 in.	8-12 in.		■	■			M	P
Cistus species	Rockrose	E	1-2 ft.	4-5 ft.			■			many	
Coprosma kirkii	NCN	E	2-3 ft.	4-5 ft.					■		
Coprosma 'Verde Vista'	NCN	E	2-3 ft.	3-4 ft.					■		
Cotoneaster adpressus	Creeping Cotoneaster	D	12-18 in.	4-5 ft.					■		F,N
Cotoneaster dammeri & cvs	NCN	E	6-9 in.	4-6 ft.					■		F,N
Cotoneaster horizontalis	Rock Cotoneaster	E/D	2-3 ft.	6-8 ft.					■		F,N
Cotoneaster salicifolius 'Repens'	NCN	E	1-2 ft.	5-6 ft.					■		F,N
Crassula multicava	NCN	E	6-8 in.	1-2 in.		■				Pi	
Dalea greggii	Trailing Indigo Bush	E	12-18 in.	6-8 ft.				■		Pu	
Delosperma 'Alba'	White Trailing Ice Plant	E	6-12 in.	12-18 in.				■		W	P
Drosanthemum floribundum	Rosea Ice Plant	E	4-6 in.	12-15 in.			■			Pi,Pu	P
Dymondia margaretae	NCN	E	1-3 in.	6-12 in.				■		Y	
Eriogonum fasciculatum & cvs	Common Buckwheat	E	1-2 ft.	2-3 ft.			■			Pi,W	H,N,P,S
Festuca ovina glauca	Blue Fescus	E	10-12 in.	12-18 in.			■	■		W	
Gazania species & cvs	Gazania	E	6-12 in.	18-24 in.	■	■	■	■		many	N
Iva hayesiana	Hayes Iva	E	2-3 ft.	4-5 ft.					■		H
Juniperus chinensis cvs	NCN	E	1-3 ft.	varies					■		F,S
Juniperus conferta	Shore Juniper	E	8-12 in.	4-5 ft.					■		F,S
Juniperus horizontalis & cvs	Creeping Juniper	E	8-12 in.	5-10 ft.					■		F,S
Juniperus sabina & cvs	Tamarix Juniper	E	1-3 ft.	10-15 ft.					■		F,S
Lampranthus species	Ice Plant	E	12-18 in.	18-24 in.			■			many	P
Lantana montevidensis & cvs	Trailing Lantana	E	12-18 in.	4-6 ft.	■		■	■		Pu,W	F,L,N
Lonicera japonica 'Halliana'	Japanese Honeysuckle	E	18-24 in.	2-4 ft.			■	■		W,Y	F,L,N
Mahonia aquifolium 'Compacta'	Compact Oregon Grape	E	18-24 in.	3-4 ft.			■			Y	F
Mahonia repens	Creeping Mahonia	E	8-12 in.	3-4 ft.		■	■			Y	F
Maleophora species	Ice Plant	E	6-12 in.	18-24 in.			■			Ro,Y	
Myoporum hybrids	NCN	E	1-2 ft.	6-8 ft.			■			W	
Myoporum parvifolium & cvs	Prostrate Myoporum	E	6-8 in.	8-10 ft.			■	■		W	
Pyracantha species & cvs	Firethorn	E	2-3 ft.	6-8 ft.			■			W	F,P
Ribes viburnifolium	Evergreen Currant	E	2-3 ft.	3-4 ft.		■	■			R	F,N
Rosmarinus officinalis cvs	Prostrate Rosemary	E	1-3 ft.	3-4 ft.		■				B,L	N,S
Salvia mellifera & cvs	Prostrate Black Sage	E	2-3 ft.	6-8 ft.				■		B,W	H,N,P
Scaevola 'Mauve Clusters'	NCN	E	4-6 in.	12-18 in.			■	■		Pu	
Sedum species	Stonecrop	E	varies	varies		■	■			Y	L
Senecio mandraliscae	NCN	E	12-15 in.	15-24 in.				■		W	
Teucrium cossonii	NCN	E	4-6 in.	18-24 in.			■	■		Pu	
Verbena species & cvs	Verbena	E	18-24 in.	2-3 ft.	■		■	■		L,Pi,R,W	L,N

Design Checklist: Character, Size, Flowering, Wildlife Value

Perennials:

		Height	Width	F	W	Sp	Su	Insig.	Flower Color	Wildlife Value
Achillea species & cvs	*Yarrow*	1-3 ft.	2-3 ft.			■	■		Pi,R,W,Y	N,S
Anigozanthos species & cvs	*Kangaroo Paw*	1-3 ft.	1-2 ft.			■	■		Pi,R,Y	N
Armeria maritima	*Sea Pink*	8-12 in.	8-12 in.			■			Pi	N
Artemisia pycnocephala & cvs	*Sandhill Sage*	12-18 in.	18-24 in.			■			Y	P
Asteriscus species	*NCN*	1-3 ft.	3-4 ft.				■		Y	N
Baileya multiradiata	*Desert Marigold*	12-18 in.	12-18 in.			■	■		Y	H,S
Brachycome multifida	*Cut-leaf Daisy*	6-12 in.	12-18 in.			■	■		B,Pi	
Centaurea species	*Dusty Miller*	1-3 ft.	1-3 ft.			■	■		Pu,Y	N,P
Centranthus ruber	*Red Valerian*	2-3 ft.	2-3 ft.	■		■	■		Pi,R,W	N
Cheiranthus 'Bowles Mauve'	*Shrubby Wallflower*	2-3 ft.	2-3 ft.			■			L	
Convolvulus cneorum	*Bush Morning Glory*	2-3 ft.	2-4 ft.	■		■	■		W	
Convolvulus mauritanicus	*Ground Morning Glory*	1-2 ft.	2-3 ft.	■			■		B	
Coreopsis species & cvs	*Coreopsis*	1-3 ft.	2-3 ft.	■			■		O,Y	N,S
Cortaderia selloana	*Pampas Grass*	10-12 ft.	10-12 ft.	■	■				Pi,W	
Dietes species & cvs	*Fortnight Lily*	3-4 ft.	3-4 ft.			■	■		W,Y	
Diplacus species & hybrids	*Monkey Flower*	1-3 ft.	1-3 ft.			■	■		many	H,N
Elymus species & cvs	*Giant Wild Rye*	2-3 ft.	1-2 ft.				■		W	
Epilobium species & cvs	*California Fuchsia*	1-2 ft.	1-3 ft.	■			■		Pi,R	N
Erigeron glaucus & cvs	*Beach Aster*	10-18 in.	10-18 in.			■			Pu	N
Erigeron karvinskianus	*Mexican Daisy*	10-18 in.	10-18 in.			■	■		Pi,W	N
Eriogonum crocatum	*Conejo Buckwheat*	12-18 in.	15-24 in.			■			Y	N,S
Eriogonum grande ssp. rubescens	*Red Buckwheat*	6-10 in.	2-3 ft.	■		■	■		R,Ro	N,S
Eriogonum umbellatum & cv	*Sulfur Flower*	6-12 in.	1-3 ft.				■		Y	N,S
Eschscholzia californica	*California Poppy*	6-15 in.	6-15 in.			■	■		O,Y	S
Euphorbia milii	*Crown of Thorns*	1-4 ft.	3-4 ft.				■		R	
Euphorbia rigida	*NCN*	3-4 ft.	4-5 ft.			■			G	
Euryops pectinatus & cv	*Euryops*	3-6 ft.	3-6 ft.	■		■	■		Y	
Gaillardia grandiflora	*Blanket Flower*	2-3 ft.	2-3 ft.	■		■	■		R,Y	
Gaura lindheimeri	*Gaura*	3-4 ft.	3-4 ft.	■		■	■		W	
Helianthemum nummularium	*Sunrose*	6-8 in.	2-3 ft.			■			many	
Helictotrichon sempervirens	*Blue Oat Grass*	2-3 ft.	2-3 ft.					■		
Heuchera species & cvs	*Coral Bells*	12-18 in.	12-18 in.			■	■		Pi,R,W	N
Iris douglasiana & cvs	*Pacific Coast Iris*	12-18 in.	12-24 in.			■			B,Pu,W,Y	
Kniphofia uvaria & cvs	*Red-hot Poker*	1-3 ft.	1-3 ft.				■		O,R,W,Y	
Limonium perezii	*Sea Lavender*	12-18 in.	12-18 in.	■		■	■		Pu	
Lobelia laxiflora	*Mexican Bush Lobelia*	2-3 ft.	4-6 ft.			■	■		O,R	N
Melampodium leucanthum	*Blackfoot Daisy*	12-15 in.	2-3 ft.	■		■	■		W	
Muhlenbergia species	*NCN*	24-30 in.	24-30 in.					■		
Oenothera species	*Mex. Evening Primrose*	12-18 in.	1-2 ft.	■		■	■		Pi,W,Y	
Pennisetum setaceum & cvs	*Fountain Grass*	2-3 ft.	1-2 ft.	■			■		Pi,Pu,W	
Penstemon species & cvs	*Western Natives*	2-3 ft.	2-3 ft.			■			many	N,S
Perovskia atriplicifolia	*Russian Sage*	3-4 ft.	3-4 ft.				■		B	
Phlomis species	*NCN*	3-4 ft.	3-4 ft.			■	■		Y	
Phormium species & cvs	*New Zealand Flax*	4-10 ft.	4-6 ft.				■		R,Y	
Romneya coulteri & cvs	*Matilija Poppy*	5-8 ft.	5-10 ft.			■	■		W	
Salvia species & cvs	*Sage*	1-4 ft.	3-4 ft.	■			■		many	H,N,P,S
Senecio cineraria	*Dusty Miller*	4-6 in.	3-4 ft.			■			Y	N
Sisyrinchium bellum	*Blue-eyed Grass*	12-18 in.	12-18 in.			■			B,Pu	S
Sphaeralcea ambigua	*Desert Mallow*	3-4 ft.	3-4 ft.				■		O,Pi,R	L,N,S
Stachys byzantina	*Lamb's Ear*	6-12 in.	2-3 ft.				■		Pu	
Tagetes lemmonii	*Mountain Marigold*	3-5 ft.	8-12 in.	■	■	■			O	L,S
Thymus species & cvs	*Thyme*	3-12 in.	12-18 in.				■		Ro,W	
Tulbaghia violacea & cv	*Society Garlic*	15-18 in.	18-24 in.	■		■	■		L	

Agave, Cacti, Succulents, & Yucca:

		Height	Width	F	W	Sp	Su	Insig.	Flower Color	Wildlife Value
Aeonium species & cvs	NCN	12-24 in.	12-24 in.			■			Y	
Agave americana	Century Plant	5-6 ft.	5-6 ft.				■		Y	F,N,P
Agave attenuata	Foxtail Agave	3-5 ft.	3-5 ft.	■	■				Y	F,N,P
Agave deserti	Desert Agave	3-4 ft.	3-4 ft.				■		Y	H,F,L,N,P
Agave shawii	Shaw's Century Plant	2-3 ft.	3-4 ft.			■	■		Y	H,F,N,P
Agave victoriae-reginae	NCN	1-2 ft.	1-2 ft.			■	■		Y	F,N,P
Agave vilmoriniana	Octopus Agave	3-4 ft.	3-4 ft.			■			Y	F,N,P
Aloe arborescens	Tree Aloe	6-12 ft.	10-12 ft.			■	▌		O,R	
Aloe bainesii	NCN	8-12 ft.	6-12 ft.	■	■				O,Ro	
Aloe candelabrum	Candelabra Aloe	8-12 ft.	5-7 ft.		■				O,R	
Aloe ferox	NCN	6-10 ft.	4-6 ft.		■				R	N
Aloe marlothii	NCN	8-12 ft.	4-6 ft.		■				O	N
Aloe plicatilis	NCN	8-12 ft.	6-8 ft.			■			O,R	
Aloe striata	Coral Aloe	10-15 in.	10-15 in.			■			O	N
Aloe vera	Medicinal Aloe	18-24 in.	18-24 in.			■			Y	N
Beaucarnea recurvata	Ponytail Tree	12-25 ft.	8-12 ft.				■		W	
Carnegiea gigantea	Saguaro	25-50 ft.	6-12 ft.			■			W	H,F
Cereus peruvianus	Peruvian Apple	12-18 ft.	12-15 ft.			■	■		W	
Cordyline australis	Dracaena Palm	20-30 ft.	10-12 ft.			■			W	
Cotyledon species	NCN	1-4 ft.	1-4 ft.			■	■		O	
Crassula species	Jade Plant	2-4 ft.	2-4 ft.	▌	■				Pi,R,W	
Dasylirion species	Desert Spoon	4-8 ft.	4-8 ft.	■					W	
Dracaena draco	Dragon Tree	12-25 ft.	6-15 ft.			■			W	
Dudleya species	Live-forever	6-12 in.	6-12 in.	■		■	■		Pi,R,Y	
Echeveria species	Hen-and-chickens	6-18 in.	6-18 in.			■	■		O,Pi,R,Y	
Euphorbia species	Euphorbia	varies	varies					▌		
Fouquieria splendens	Ocotillo	15-20 ft.	10-15 ft.			■			R	N
Hesperaloe parviflora	Red Yucca	3-4 ft.	3-4 ft.			■	▌		Pi,R	N
Kalanchoe species	NCN	1-5 ft.	1-5 ft.			■			O,R,Y	
Nolina species	Bear Grass	5-10 ft.	5-8 ft.			■			W	S
Opuntia species	Prickly Pear, Cholla	varies	varies			■			M,Pi,W,Y	F,S
Portulacaria afra	Elephant's Food	6-8 ft.	3-5 ft.				■		Pu	
Yucca aloifolia	Spanish Bayonet	8-10 ft.	4-5 ft.				■		W	N,P
Yucca baccata	Datil Yucca	3-4 ft.	8-10 ft.			■			W	H,F,N,P
Yucca brevifolia	Joshua Tree	20-30 ft.	20-30 ft.			■			W	H,F,N,P,S
Yucca elata	Soaptree Yucca	10-20 ft.	4-6 ft.			■			W	H,N,P,S
Yucca gloriosa	Spanish Dagger	10-15 ft.	8-12 ft.			■			W	N,P
Yucca recurvifolia	NCN	4-6 ft.	3-5 ft.			■			W	N,P
Yucca rigida	NCN	10-12 ft.	3-5 ft.			■			W	H,N,P,S
Yucca rostrata	Beaked Yucca	8-12 ft.	3-5 ft.			■			W	H,N,P,S
Yucca schidigera	Mohave Yucca	6-12 ft.	3-5 ft.			■			W	H,F,N,P
Yucca whipplei	Our Lord's Candle	6-12 ft.	4-5 ft.			■	■		W	H,N,P,S

Section 6 Plant Compendium

Introduction:

The following pages present more than 650 species of plants that are suited for use in ornamental landscapes within dry climate regions of the West. Each plant is described in terms of its physical characteristics and cultural adaptations. Most species are illustrated by two color photographs to help with the identification and recognition of their character. In addition to this photographic effort, consistent attention has been placed upon describing the origin and natural habitat conditions of each species. This habitat information provides valuable insight regarding the suitability of the plants to grow within different regions of the West.

The compendium is organized alphabetically by scientific name to assist in finding information. Individual plant species as well as plant groups can be found by both their scientific and common names within the index at the end of this section. An extensive bibliography of important references is also provided at the end of the compendium.

In the description of plants on the following pages, a number of terms are used on a regular basis. These terms are used with consistency and are intended to carry the same meaning from one plant to the next. A brief definition of these terms is provided below.

Commonly Used Terms:

▪ **'Calcareous', 'Limestone', 'Chlorosis'** — These are soils terms that describe the relative abundance of calcium within the soil. These soils are often of marine origin and contain the skeletal remains of millions of tiny organisms that are largely comprised of calcium. This type of soil often lacks the necessary amounts of micronutrients that are important for many types of landscape plants, particularly iron. These deficiencies often impact plant growth. Plants that suffer from iron deficiency will show signs of yellowing, or chlorosis.

▪ **'Coastal', 'Inland', 'Valley'**, and **'Desert'**— These terms describe the basic habitat types that are found in western regions. It is possible to describe the general suitability or preference of many species according to these simple categories. More detailed descriptions of these habitats and regions are provided in Section 2.

▪ **'Evapotranspiration stress'** — The potential amount of moisture that can be lost from a landscape. This moisture loss occurs from the surface of the soils and from the transpiration processes of plants. Evapotranspiration stress is measured in terms of inches of moisture lost for a given period of time. In most cases, the figures used in this book indicate the amount of moisture that is needed by tall fescue turfgrass to replace moisture lost to the combined influence of temperature, sun, wind, and aridity.

Evapotranspiration can be measured on a daily, monthly, and seasonal basis. A more complete description of this term and an evapotranspiration map of western regions is provided in Section 2.

▪ **'Low amounts of supplemental water'** — This statement describes the approximate amount of additional water that is needed to sustain an established plant in healthy condition. This estimate is based upon a percentage of the measured evapotranspiration stress of the region the plant is growing in.

Plants that require low amounts of water need up to 25% of the measured evapotranspiration stress

Plants that require moderate amounts of water need between 25-50% of the measured evapotranspiration stress

Plants that require high amounts of water need between 50-75% of the measured evapotranspiration stress

These water use estimates need to reflect the natural growing and resting cycle of each species in an effort to avoid unnecessary growth and excessive watering. This concept and ideas pertaining to evapotranspiration stress are discussed in greater detail in Section 4.

▪ **'Microclimate'** — A term that indicates a small scale climate or site condition that is different from the general regional climate. Microclimate conditions are highly significant in providing opportunities for many types of plant species to be grown in regions that they are not naturally suited. Many designs are highly successful as a result of developing microclimate conditions that shelter plants from the full intensity of sun, wind, and high temperatures.

▪ **'Once established'**— All plants need a period of time after they have been planted to become well rooted and capable of growth without the same frequency of supplemental watering. Most perennials, sub-shrubs, succulents, and cacti can become established after one complete growing season. Larger shrubs and trees can take between 1-2 years.

▪ **'Periodic Deep Watering'**— A statement that describes a watering schedule that allows for the slow application of water to encourage infiltration to deep soil levels. Water can be applied at two, three or four week intervals depending upon climate and site conditions. This approach is often recommended for the summer months for the watering of adapted and established plants in order to reduce drought stress and to maintain good visual character in ornamental landscapes.

▪ **'Well drained'** — A term that describes the manner in which water moves through soil. Water typically moves quickly through well drained soils. These soils do not stay saturated long after water is applied. Most sandy and loam type soils have a well drained nature; clay soils lose their moisture more slowly. Too much water in the soil can lead to disease problems, particularly for plants that are adapted to Mediterranean climate regions. These problems are made worse during the summer months when soils are warm and fungi and bacteria growth can be very active.

Acacia
Wattle
Fabaceae

Introduction:
Acacias are evergreen or deciduous trees and shrubs that are most often valued for their fast growth and prolific flowering quality. Over 20 species are used in western gardens as ground covers, visual screens, and accent elements. This represents a very small percentage of the more than 1,100 species believed to exist in warm regions of the world. Their many forms and wide tolerance of soils, exposure, and moisture conditions enable them to be used for many purposes. When considered for landscaping, there is a distinction to be made between acacias that are best suited to low desert regions, as compared to those that succeed best in coastal and inland areas. Many of the species naturally adapted to arid regions are native to the Southwest United States, Mexico, and Africa. Most of the species that are highly suited to coastal and inland environments come from Australia. New species of acacia are continuing to be introduced into the trade and can be found at specialty growers.

Character:
Foliage and flower character vary widely among acacias. Species that have evolved within desert regions are typically deciduous, have finely divided leaves, and sharp thorns on their branches. Australian species are evergreen, lack thorns, and can have leaves that are soft and bipinnately divided, or have phyllodes that look and function like leaves. These phyllodes harden as they mature, enabling the plant to resist greater levels of heat, aridity, and drought. Flowers range in color from white to golden yellow and occur from late winter to early spring. The early flower season is widely appreciated in landscapes, and in some instances, the intense yellow flower color on some plants provides a strikingly beautiful contrast to the dark rainstorm clouds of late winter and early spring.

Most species from Australia grow into large plants with a woody branching structure. With age, the interiors of shrub species become filled with dead branches and are exposed when heavily pruned or sheared. This woody buildup provides fuel that make many acacias poor choices for high fire hazard areas.

Habitat and Culture:
Acacias prefer full sun and fast drainage conditions. They are best adapted to sandy soil types, neutral pH, and an average range of nutrients. Chlorosis is often observed under boggy conditions and in iron poor soils. Some species in landscape use are damaged by frost; young plants can be killed by cold below 20°F.

Acacias will tolerate regular watering and respond with faster growth. This can lead to a weaker branching structure and earlier deaths from excessive growth. Most species can survive with little or no supplemental water after they are established, and have proven to be among the best adapted trees and shrubs to the basic Mediterranean and arid climate conditions of the West.

Uses and Considerations:
Acacias quickly come to mind for use in many difficult and challenging landscape situations. Most species are highly tolerant of poor soils, wind, drought, aridity, and have the ability to survive with low amounts of supplemental water. The flower value of these plants makes them good for background and mass accent plantings in both commercial and residential landscapes. Many species can be sheared to form hedges and screens; others are planted along highways as ground covers and in large, shrubby masses.

Acacias are relatively pest free with only occasional problems with borers. Root systems are often shallow; this being very characteristic in areas that receive surface irrigation. Larger growing tree species can uplift pavement, while fast growing shrub species can become top heavy and contribute to surface slope failure on newly constructed slopes during heavy winter rains. Many types produce a high quantity of pollen that bees harvest for honey production. However, this pollen can be highly allergenic to some people. The seeds have food value for many bird species.

Supplemental watering for established plants is seldom needed in coastal areas; plants in warmer inland and desert locations perform best with periodic deep watering. Most species are fast growing and often short-lived, from 15-25 years. Life spans can be increased by restricting the amount of summer water and pruning after the flowering cycle.

A number of Australian species such as *A. baileyana*, *A. cyclops*, *A. dealbata*, *A. decurrens*, *A. longifolia*, and *A. melanoxylon* can reseed and have escaped cultivation along coastal and inland areas of California. These species should only be considered with great care.

Associated Plantings:
Species highly suited to both coastal and inland regions include *A. baileyana*, *A. dealbata*, *A. decurrens*, *A. cultriformis*, *A. cyclops*, *A. longifolia*, *A. melanoxylon*, *A. pendula*, *A. redolens*, and *A. saligna*. These species perform well as companion trees or understory shrubs to species of eucalyptus. Other adapted plant types include *Nerium oleander*, *Grevillea robusta*, *Myoporum laetum*, and *Melaleuca* species. In these plantings, shredded organic mulch and leaf litter is often used as a ground cover on slopes and in large spaces. This mulch helps control weeds and reduces the need for ground covers that often require overhead spray irrigation.

Species adapted to low desert regions include *A. berlandieri*, *A. constricta*, *A. farnesiana*,

1. **Acacia baileyana**

A. greggii, *A. pendula*, *A. redolens*, *A. smallii*, and *A. stenophylla*. These species combine well with *Cassia nemophila*, *Encelia farinosa*, and *Myoporum parvifolium*.

Most acacias do not adapt well to high desert regions of the Southwest due to cold temperatures. *A. constricta* and *A. greggii* are two species native to high desert habitats and are sometimes found in ornamental landscape use.

Helpful References:
Elliot, W. Rodger and David L. Jones, Encyclopaedia of Australian Plants, Volume 2. Melbourne: Lothian Publishing Company, 1982.

Vines, Robert A. Trees, Shrubs, and Woody Vines of the Southwest. Austin: University of Texas Press, 1986.

Benson, Lyman and Robert A. Darrow. Trees and Shrubs of the Southwestern Deserts. Tucson: The University of Arizona Press, 1981.

Acacia baileyana
Bailey Acacia, Cootamundra Wattle

A small to medium size evergreen tree, 20-30 ft. tall with an equal spread. Soft textured foliage is comprised of grey-green leaves that are bipinnately divided; large quantities of sulphur yellow flowers occur in early spring.

This species is native to a limited area in southeastern Australia, where it grows in inland foothill locations within woodland and savanna landscapes. It has proven to be well adapted to many conditions, and is widely grown in warm regions around the world. In western gardens, this species is planted in coastal, inland, valley, and low desert regions. It often performs best in areas having a coastal influence that moderates summer temperatures and reduces the occurrence of heavy frost.

Bailey acacia is commonly planted as a fast growing canopy and flowering accent tree on slopes, in parking lots, and background settings. It performs best for 10-15 years, after which some plants show signs of dieback and aging. Pruning after the flower cycle ends can increase both its character and life span. Once established, this species needs little or no supplemental water in coastal or inland locations, and low to moderate amounts in valley and desert landscapes. Experience has shown that this species naturalizes, particularly in coastal regions, and should be managed carefully. A cultivar, *A. baileyana* 'Purpurea', has a pleasant purple color cast to the new growth. Plates 1 - 3.

2. **Acacia baileyana, Santa Maria, California**

3. **Acacia baileyana 'Purpurea'**   4. **Acacia berlandieri**

Acacia berlandieri
Berlandier Acacia

A medium size deciduous shrub or small tree, mounding 10-12 ft. tall, spreading 10-20 ft. Foliage is comprised of bipinnately divided leaves that are light green in color and produce a feathery, soft textured appearance. Clusters of showy, round, white flowers are fragrant and occur in loose clusters in early spring.

This species is native to southern Texas and adjacent parts of Mexico in low elevation drainage plains along the Gulf of Mexico. It grows in sandy and limestone soils and in areas that receive 20-40 in. of annual rainfall. Within its natural range, this species is widely noted as a source for high quality honey and as a species for cultivation in ornamental gardens. It has a distinctively delicate, fern-like appearance and seldom has thorns that are so typical of other desert species. It can be used in courtyards, planters, and in background locations where both its foliage, character, and flower value can be appreciated. Established plants are easily sustained with periodic deep watering. Plates 4 - 5.

5. **Acacia berlandieri, Tucson, Arizona**

6. Acacia cultriformis

Acacia cultriformis
Knife Acacia, Knife-leaf Wattle

A mounding evergreen shrub, 6-12 ft. high, 6-15 ft. spread. Phyllodes are triangular in shape and an attractive grey-green in color. Bright yellow flowers produce a showy display on the ends of branches in early to mid-spring.

This species comes from arid climate regions of eastern Australia where it is found on dry, rocky ridges. Within its natural habitat, it prefers full sun exposure and requires well drained soils. In western gardens, it has proven to be both frost and drought resistant. Established plants can survive in coastal and inland landscapes with little or no supplemental water; low amounts are needed in valley and low desert regions.

Knife acacia performs very well on slopes and banks for erosion control, barrier, and screening purposes. It is often used along highways and on large slopes in housing developments where its foliage character contrasts nicely with other plants. It is also useful as a foliage and flowering accent element in mixed plantings in both commercial and residential landscapes. Plates 6 - 7.

7. Acacia cultriformis

8. Acacia cyclops

Acacia cyclops
Western Coastal Wattle

A dense, mounding, evergreen shrub, 6-15 ft. high, 6-15 ft. wide. Phyllodes are 3-5 in. long, linear, and pale to dark emerald green. Inconspicuous flowers are pale yellow and hidden within the foliage; seed pods persist and split as they dry to reveal an interesting red seed stalk around the seed.

This species comes from dry coastal plains of South and Western Australia. In this habitat, it occurs on both calcareous and lightly saline soils and is exposed to wind and salt spray. It also tolerates poor drainage and short periods of flooding but is damaged by periodic frosts.

This species has been used in both coastal and inland areas of California with good results. It is most often used as an alternative to *A. longifolia*, for screening and erosion control along highways, on large slopes, and for windbreaks. Once established, it survives with little or no supplemental water and provides 10-15 years of good foliage character before becoming quite open and sprawling in form. It is tender to temperatures below 25°F. This species has reseeded itself in coastal and intermediate foothills and should be used with care. Plates 8 - 9.

9. Acacia cyclops

Acacia dealbata
Silver Wattle

A large shrub to small evergreen tree, 25-40 ft. high, 25-45 ft. wide. Foliage is comprised of finely divided, grey-green leaves that produce a soft, feathery texture. Flowers are round, pale to bright yellow, and produce an intensive and colorful display in early spring.

This is a species from southeastern Australia and Tasmania where its natural habitat is along stream banks and within open forest associations. In this region, annual rainfall ranges from 23-40 in., and numerous frosts occur each year. This species develops on many soils including clays, gravelly clays, and sandstone and is found in association with *Eucalyptus viminalis*.

This is a highly adaptable species of *Acacia* that has been planted for many years in western gardens. During this period, it has proven to be quite adaptable to coastal and inland regions, where established plants survive with little or no supplemental water other than from rainfall. Unfortunately, it has naturalized in both coastal regions and inland areas of California, particularly from San Luis Obispo to Monterey, in disturbed and semi-natural landscapes. It is noted for quick growth and soft, billowy texture and is often used as a screen and park tree. Plates 10 - 12.

10. Acacia dealbata

11. Acacia dealbata

12. Acacia dealbata

13. Acacia decurrens

Acacia decurrens
Green Wattle

A small to medium size evergreen tree, 25-40 ft. tall, spreading 25-40 ft. Foliage is comprised of finely divided, dark green leaves. Flowers are intense yellow and occur in large, showy clusters in mid-spring.

This species comes from both moist and dry coastal and inland habitats of eastern Australia. In western gardens, it tolerates a wide range of conditions but shows a preference for moist locations and slightly acid soils. As with *A. dealbata*, it is highly adapted to coastal areas, particularly northern California, where it is prone to naturalizing and should be used with caution. In warmer and drier locations, it grows best with low to moderate amounts of supplemental water.

Green wattle is a fast growing species that develops into a shapely tree. It is useful as a shade tree and for spring flower character in parks and large garden spaces. Plates 13 - 14.

14. Acacia decurrens

Acacia farnesiana
Sweet Acacia

A large shrub to small size deciduous tree, 15-20 ft. high and as wide. Branches have numerous short spines; small, bipinnately divided leaves produce a soft and open character. Fragrant and showy round flowers are bright yellow and occur in early to mid-spring.

This species is native to the Southwest, Mexico, and Chile in desert and foothill regions. Due to its wide range of distribution, different tolerances and adaptations have been noted. Plants in the trade known as *A. farnesiana* are from milder and more subtropical habitats and are tender to frosts. A hardier selection known as *A. smallii* is similar in character but tolerates more cold.

Sweet acacia has long been recognized for its value as a native forage plant and honey plant, and for the production of perfume from its flowers. In residential and commercial landscapes, it is used as an accent shrub or small canopy tree in courtyards and in medians. Sweet acacia prefers well drained soils and is best suited to low desert regions where it can survive with low to moderate amounts of supplemental water. Plates 15 - 16.

15. Acacia farnesiana, Palm Desert, California

16. Acacia farnesiana

17. Acacia greggii

18. Acacia greggii

Acacia greggii
Catclaw Acacia

A many branched shrub to small deciduous tree, 15-25 ft. high and as wide. Branches have numerous curved spines; small, bipinnate leaves are divided into tiny leaflets. Noticeable flowers are fragrant, creamy yellow, occurring mostly in spring and continuously throughout summer and fall.

Catclaw acacia is a very widespread species throughout the southwestern deserts of United States, Mexico, and Baja California. It establishes dense thickets on dry rocky mesas, canyon slopes, and in deep, sandy soils along arroyos. Wildlife uses this species for shelter and for its seed, foliage and honey production value.

This species is well adapted to high and low desert regions where it is very tolerant of heat, aridity, and drought. Plants growing along washes develop into handsome tree specimens; plants on drier slopes and mesas are typically shrubby in habit. Catclaw acacia often provides its best value among other native desert species as part of the natural desert landscape flora. It will tolerate garden conditions and, with age, can mature into a screen or patio tree. Plates 17 - 18.

Acacia longifolia
Sydney Golden Wattle

A large shrub to small evergreen tree, 15-20 ft. high, 15-20 ft. wide. Foliage is comprised of 3-6 in. long, bright green phyllodes. Intense yellow flowers occur in brush-like spikes along branchlets and produce a showy display in early to mid-spring.

This species is widespread throughout eastern and southern Australia in both coastal and inland habitats. In western gardens, it has proven adaptable to coastal, inland, and low desert regions where it tolerates heat, aridity, wind, salt spray, and drought. It needs well drained soils and frequently becomes chlorotic with either too much moisture or when grown in iron poor soils.

Sydney golden wattle has been widely used as a screen plant along highways and in commercial and housing developments. Often, it grows too fast and becomes too heavy with frequent watering and contributes to slope failure. This species performs quite well for 10-15 years as a large shrub; older plants become large enough to be pruned into small trees. Plates 19 - 20.

19. Acacia longifolia

20. Acacia longifolia

21. Acacia melanoxylon

Acacia melanoxylon
Blackwood Acacia

A large, upright tree, 25-50 ft. high, 20-25 ft. wide. Its dense foliage is comprised of dull, forest green phyllodes, 3-4 in. long. Creamy white flowers are inconspicuous.

Blackwood acacia is widely distributed throughout eastern Australia and Tasmania in cool and moist habitats. Rainfall is frequent and ranges from 30-60 in. annually.

Blackwood acacia has shown widespread adaptation to coastal, inland, valley, and low desert habitats throughout California. It grows best in moist, well drained soils with cool climate conditions. However, it has proven to be highly tolerant of heat and extended periods of drought in warm valley and foothill locations. This species will sucker from its many surface roots and will naturalize in coastal and inland areas when moisture is present. These tendencies cause it to be undesirable in many locations and for uses around pavement. Over the years, it has been successfully used as a tree in parks and along highways where many handsome specimens have matured. It is the largest species of *Acacia* in landscape use and lives 40-50 years in good character. Plates 21 - 22.

22. Acacia melanoxylon

23. **Acacia pendula, Phoenix, Arizona**

24. **Acacia pendula**

25. **Acacia redolens**

26. **Acacia redolens, Laguna Hills, California**

Acacia pendula
Weeping Myall

A small to medium tree, 15-25 ft. tall, spreading 10-15 ft. Distinctive foliage is comprised of long, silvery grey-green phyllodes that hang from drooping branches. Dull yellow flowers are noticeable in early spring.

This species comes from warm and dry interior plains and low hillsides in Australia. These are areas of limited rainfall, from 15-20 in. annually, but also where seasonal ground water is sometimes available. Soil conditions vary from rich and heavy on the plains, to gravelly and stony clays with good drainage on hillsides. Within its range, it associates with *A. stenophylla*, *Eucalyptus microtheca*, and with *E. camaldulensis* along seasonal water courses.

This is one of the most attractive and ornamental species for use in both residential and commercial landscapes. With age it becomes a handsome planter and entry specimen that is appreciated for its form and foliage character. It is relatively slow growing for an acacia but provides ample grace and interest as it matures. Established plants can thrive on low to moderate levels of supplemental irrigation in coastal and inland areas and moderate amounts in low desert regions. Plates 23 - 24.

Acacia redolens
(Acacia ongerup)

A large spreading shrub that grows 3-12 ft. high, spreading 15-30 ft. wide. Foliage is comprised of grey-green phyllodes. Round, yellow flowers become more profuse and noticeable as plants age.

This species comes from warm and dry inland areas of Western Australia. In western landscapes, it has proven adaptable to many habitats ranging from the coast to inland valleys and low deserts. It tolerates slightly saline to alkaline soils, full sun, cold temperatures to 15° F, and extended periods of drought.

Acacia redolens is used as an erosion control and ground cover plant along highways and on large slopes. This is a fast growing and large plant that needs ample room to spread. Plants become taller with age or when they are sheared to contain their growth along walkways and curbs. In coastal and inland areas, it requires little or no supplemental water after it is established. Low to moderate amounts of water are desirable in low desert regions. A number of lower growing selections that stay below 3 ft. high for many years, including *A. r.* 'Desert Carpet', have been introduced into the trade. Plates 25 - 26.

Acacia retinodes
Water Wattle, Swamp Wattle

A large shrub or small tree, 15-20 ft. high, 12-15 ft. wide. Narrow, blue-green phyllodes are 5-7 in. long. Numerous clusters of showy, deep yellow flowers occur in late winter to early spring.

This species comes from coastal and inland habitats of southern Australia and Tasmania. It is one of the few species that tolerates clayey soils and poorly drained conditions. It also tolerates calcareous soils and salt spray along the coast. It is fast growing and often not long lived.

In western gardens, water wattle is often established through hydroseeding for slope and open space plantings in coastal habitats. It germinates readily from seed and has become established in natural landscape areas. This species is often used for quick planting effects and can be removed as slower growing species become established. Plates 27 - 28.

27. Acacia retinodes

28. Acacia retinodes

29. Acacia saligna

Acacia saligna
(Acacia cyanophylla)
Willow Acacia, Orange Wattle

A large shrub to small tree, 15-35 ft. high, 12-20 ft. wide. Phyllodes are very long and narrow, 5-10 in., and hang in a weeping habit from branches. Color of the phyllodes ranges from deep green to blue-green. Very showy clusters of golden yellow flowers occur in early spring.

This is a species native to southwestern Australia where it grows in dry climate regions in calcareous soils. It is widely adapted to coastal and inland locations and to light or heavy soils if the drainage is good. It grows very fast in moist conditions, or it can successfully adapt to drier conditions, where it receives little or low amounts of supplemental water.

Willow acacia is often used in hydroseed applications for slope planting, erosion control, and in open spaces and greenbelts. Older plants can be pruned into trees that provide striking flowering accent value. Plates 29 - 30.

30. Acacia saligna

Acacia smallii
(Acacia minuta)

A large shrub to small tree, 15-20 ft. high and as wide. Branches have numerous short spines; bipinnately divided leaves produce a fine texture and open foliage character. Fragrant and showy round flowers are bright yellow and occur in early to mid-spring.

This species is likely a selected form of *A. farnesiana* that has greater cold tolerance. It is recognized in the trade as a separate species and is more widely used in low desert areas that experience periodic frost. It is often grown as a small canopy tree within desert landscapes and is tolerant of heat, aridity, and drought. It can easily survive on low amounts of supplemental water, however, it can accept more water and grow faster to larger sizes. Plates 31 - 32.

31. Acacia smallii, Carefree, Arizona

32. Acacia smallii

33. Acacia stenophylla

Acacia stenophylla
Shoestring Acacia

A small to medium tree, 20-45 ft. tall, 10-20 ft. wide. Phyllodes are dull green, very long and narrow, and hang from weeping branches. Noticeable clusters of pale yellow flowers occur in winter and early spring.

Shoestring acacia is widely distributed throughout all of Australia, particularly within warm interior regions. It is adapted to light or heavy soils and even to those with some alkalinity and salinity. Annual rainfall is limited, 15-20 in.; some areas experience short periods of seasonal flooding and frost. In its range, it grows with *Eucalyptus camaldulensis* and *Acacia pendula*.

This species is becoming valued in low desert regions throughout Arizona and California, where it thrives on low to moderate amounts of supplemental water. Its open habit and hanging foliage produce a quite graceful appearance. It develops an upright form that makes it useful for tight spaces, for filtering views, and in small groupings. It is now being introduced to coastal and inland areas where it is expected to provide equal value. Plates 33 - 35.

34. Acacia stenophylla, Carefree, Arizona

35. Acacia stenophylla, Carefree, Arizona

Achillea

Yarrow
Asteraceae

A large group of herbaceous perennials that are noted for their feathery foliage and brightly colored flower heads. Approximately 100 species are believed to exist, principally in the Northern Hemisphere, and in habitats ranging from dry foothills to alpine slopes. Currently, only 8-10 species are found in landscape use. However, many cultivars have been produced from these species and provide a wide range of garden choices. Local nurseries should be consulted regarding the many yarrow choices that are becoming available.

Yarrows range in size and character, from spreading, mat-like forms to clumping, upright plants. Foliage is comprised of featherlike divided leaves that are often aromatic when crushed. Tiny flowers are clustered into broad heads and range in color from white to pink, red, and yellow. Flowers occur mainly in late spring through early fall, with intermittent blooming all year.

Yarrows are among the most adaptable and easy to grow perennials for western gardens. They can be started from seed or transplanted from containers. They prefer full sun and moderate amounts of supplemental moisture. However, within one to two years of planting, they can develop strong tap roots to enable them to withstand periods of dryness. They are well adapted to sandy, clayey, and calcareous soils. Most species will provide several years of good character and value in coastal and inland habitats before needing to be replaced; plants grown in desert regions are often used as annuals.

Mat-like forms of yarrow are best suited to small scale rock garden spaces. Taller forms can be used in border and mixed planting beds. The foliage texture and flower colors of yarrows often contrast well with succulents such as *Sedum* species, *Aloe striata, Aloe arborescens*, and *Echeveria imbricata*. Other successful combinations include *Helianthemum nummularium, Artemisia* 'Powis Castle', *Romneya coulteri*, and *Santolina chamaecyparissus*. Flowers are good for fresh or dry cut arrangements. Old flower heads on plants become unsightly and should be removed after they are spent.

Achillea clavennae

Silvery Yarrow

A small plant that develops as a spreading mat, 6-8 in. high, 12-24 in. across. Bright white flower clusters occur in mid-spring and contrast nicely with its silvery grey foliage. Plate 36.

Achillea filipendulina

Fernleaf Yarrow

This is the largest species, growing in upright clumps to 3-4 ft. high. Coarsely divided leaves are medium green and 8-10 in. long. Flowers are deep golden yellow clustering into large heads, 3-5 in. across. This is a very popular species for perennial gardens; there are also several cultivated varieties available. Plates 38 - 39.

36. **Achillea clavennae**

37. **Achillea tomentosa**

38. **Achillea filipendulina**

39. **Achillea filipendulina**

40. **Achillea taygetea 'Moonshine'**

41. **Achillea taygetea 'Moonshine'**

42. Achillea millefolium

44. Achillea millefolium 'Rosea'

43. Achillea millefolium 'Paprika'

45. Achillea millefolium 'Rosea'

Achillea millefolium
Common Yarrow

This is a clumping species of intermediate size, 18-30 in. high. Foliage is comprised of finely divided, medium green leaves, 6-8 in. long. Numerous cultivars of this species have been introduced offering a wide range of flower colors from white, to pink or red.

This species comes from many climate types and regions of the world. In western gardens, it has proven to be highly adaptable to several landscape uses. It is often planted by seed on slopes where it is quick to germinate and function as an erosion control plant during the initial stages of slope stabilization. In such cases, it can be combined with *Eschscholzia californica, Lupinus* species, *Alyssum saxatilis*, and *Gazania* species. It can also be used as a low ground cover on dry slopes that transition into natural landscapes in an effort to improve fire safety. One of its unique uses is as a substitute for turfgrass. It can be seeded on flat or sloping sites and be attractively maintained with as few as 6-8 mowings each year. Moderate amounts of supplemental water on a regular basis is recommended in lawn situations. Plants on slopes need seasonal trimming of taller flower heads and foliage with a weed whip to maintain good character. Plates 42 - 46.

Achillea taygetea

A species from Greece that develops into a clumping plant, 12-18 in. high. Pinnately divided, grey-green leaves are 4-6 in. long and contrast nicely with bright yellow flower heads that reach 2-3 in. across. Several varieties of this intermediate size species are popular for use in perennial gardens. Plates 40 - 41.

Achillea tomentosa
Woolly Yarrow

A small spreading plant, 6-12 in. high, 18-24 in. across. Foliage is comprised of finely divided, grey-green leaves, 1-2 in. long. Colorful yellow flower heads cover the plant in mid-spring. Plate 37.

46. Achillea millefolium 'Rosea' - the "lawn" at the Lummis Home, Pasadena, California

Left: *Achillea millefolium* 'Rosea' is used as a lawn substitute at the Charles F. Lummis historical home in Los Angeles. This planting was established in 1987 from seed on fast draining sandy soil. It receives low to moderate amounts of water and is mowed about 4-6 times each year. It easily tolerates the foot traffic of garden visitors and periodic open house events; many people use the space for book sales and demonstrations. Common yarrow is a practical water and energy conserving alternative to turfgrass in such settings, yet it is not found to be as durable and refined as turfgrass for a playing surface or in areas of shade.

Adenostoma fasciculatum
Chamise
Rosaceae

A medium to large evergreen shrub growing 5-12 ft. high, 5-8 ft. wide. Foliage is comprised of small, needle-like leaves to 1/4 in. long; noticeable clusters of creamy white flowers develop at the ends of branches from early spring into summer.

Chamise is one of the dominant species of the chaparral plant community throughout California, from coastal foothills to slopes of the Sierra Nevada, south into Mexico. It grows in sunny and dry locations in well drained soils and is highly tolerant of heat and drought. However, its foliage contains oils that are highly flammable, increasing the fire risk in dry foothill areas. As a result, it is frequently removed from natural areas around housing developments to reduce the fuel load on slopes.

Chamise is not valued for cultivation in ornamental landscapes. It is a primary habitat species in natural environments on dry south and west facing slopes. In these areas, it develops deep roots that are useful for erosion control and slope stabilization. Its foliage, flowers, and seed provide habitat and food value to wildlife. A prostrate form, *A. f.* 'Prostrata', grows 2-3 ft. high, has been introduced into the trade, and can be used as a slope plant in natural areas. Plates 47-48.

47. Adenostoma fasciculatum 'Prostrata'

48. Adenostoma fasciculatum

Aeonium
Crassulaceae

A small group of succulents with distinctive foliage character and colorful flowers. Leaves are fleshy and grow in rosettes on succulent stems. About 38 species are known to exist, most coming from the Canary Islands and around the Mediterranean Sea.

Several species and cultivars are used in western gardens. They perform best in coastal regions where they prefer full sun, mild temperatures, humidity, and well draining soils. They do not tolerate frost and can burn in full sun in inland landscapes on hot days. Aeoniums are used as foliage and flowering accent plants in small garden spaces and containers. They are easy to grow and survive on low amounts of supplemental water.

49. Aeonium arboreum 'Atropurpureum'

Aeonium arboreum
An upright plant, 2-3 ft. high, that has medium green leaves on succulent stems and colorful yellow flowers. This species is available in two varieties: *A. a.* 'Atropurpureum' offers dark purple foliage, *A. a.* 'Zwartkop' has nearly black foliage. Plate 49.

Aeonium floribundum
This species develops into a low, dense form, 12-15 in. high, spreading 24-20 in. across. This species produces numerous yellow flower heads that cover the plant in spring. Plate 50.

Aeonium 'Pseudotabulaeforme'
A hybrid that develops into clumping groups that have large, light green foliage rosettes. Flowers on this variety are light yellow and extend 12-15 in. above the foliage. Plate 51.

50. Aeonium floribundum

51. Aeonium 'Pseudotabulaeforme'

52. Aesculus californica　　　　**53. Aesculus californica**

54. Aesculus californica in leaf and bloom.

55. Aesculus californica in winter deciduous stage.

Aesculus
Horse Chestnut, Buckeye
Hippocastanaceae

A small group of deciduous shrubs and trees that includes some 13 species. Most species and cultivars come from cool and moist climates and do best with regular water when planted in the Southwest. *Aesculus hippocastanum*, common horse chestnut, is a large tree to 45 ft. high with deep green, palmately divided leaves that produces an edible nut. *A. carnea*, Red Horse Chestnut, grows to 30-40 ft. and is valued for its rich foliage and striking pink to red flowers. Several cultivated varieties of this hybrid also exist. Both of these trees prefer rich, deep, and moist soils. One species is native to California and is considered to be drought tolerant and very colorful within its natural range.

Aesculus californica
California Buckeye

A large deciduous shrub to medium tree, 20-40 ft. high and as wide. Medium green leaves are palmately divided and reach 8-10 in. across. Showy spikes of creamy white to pale pink flowers range 6-10 in. long, cover these plants in mid-spring, and are noticeably fragrant. Large, pear-shaped seed pods develop by late summer. In natural areas where drought stress increases through summer, leaves will turn papery brown and persist until wind or rain removes them.

This plant is native to dry slopes and foothills around the San Joaquin Valley and the coast ranges from northern to southern California. It is a member of the foothill woodland plant association and can be found growing with such plants as *Pinus sabiniana*, *Cercis occidentalis*, *Quercus agrifolia*, *Sambucus caerulea* var. *mexicana*, *Fremontodendron californica*, and others. In cooler and more northern regions, it grows principally on south facing foothill slopes and canyon bottoms. In warmer and drier locations of the south, it often develops dense thickets on north facing slopes and in areas that receive more moisture from runoff. Throughout its range, this species grows in sun to partial shade, in well drained soils, and endures heat with long periods of drought.

California buckeye is a highly attractive woodland plant. Its spring flower character is among the most colorful and striking of western native plants. In addition, during the winter its branches often are silvery white, standing out in contrast to darker background areas. Unfortunately, all parts of this plant are poisonous: leaves, flowers, and the large pear-shaped fruit. This limits its use in ornamental gardens to a great extent. Its best landscape value is usually within its natural range where it can be used as a background and slope plant, or as a focal element in large spaces. Young plants tend to develop as multi-stemmed shrubs unless pruned into tree forms. One cultivated variety, *A. c.* 'Canyon Pink', has deeper pink coloration in the flowers. Plates 52-55.

Agave

Century Plant

Agavaceae

A large group of succulents with more than 300 known species. These plants are native to many habitats from the southwestern United States to upper South America, with the greatest diversity and number occurring in Mexico. They are easily recognized by their highly distinctive blade-like foliage and tall flower stalks.

Most species of *Agave* are naturally adapted to arid regions and Mediterranean climates of the Southwest. They most frequently develop upon rocky slopes of hills and mountains above the valley floor and sandy plains, at elevations ranging from sea level to above 7,000 ft. Annual rainfall is highly varied; some areas receive as little as 4-5 in., other regions receive over 30 in. They need fast draining conditions, thrive in limestone soils, and are well adapted to sun, heat, aridity, and seasonal frost. Leaves are long and linear, often grow from basal rosettes, and can be armed with teeth on the margins and have spines on the tips. Both leaves and roots can absorb large amounts of moisture which can sustain them through long periods of drought. Stomates on leaves close during the heat of the day and when soil moisture is low.

Colorful flowers are prominently displayed on tall stalks that can last from weeks to months. Several species of hummingbirds are attracted to these flowers. However, before flowering, individual plants need to grow and mature for many years, and the combination of seasonal temperatures and moisture must be correct. Plants die after they flower, but will produce a ring of new pups by underground stems. Other plants are started by seed, principally during decades when rainfall is higher than average for several years in a row.

Agaves have been widely cultivated as accent plants throughout coastal, inland, valley, and desert regions. In coastal and inland gardens, they easily survive on natural rainfall; plants in desert landscapes need only periodic deep watering. Over the years, a number of species have been introduced into the trade providing a range of sizes and leaf characteristics. Their striking forms offer bold line and textural contrast to foliage plants. They provide distinctive silhouette and sculptural character against smooth walls. Smaller varieties work in rockery and bank plantings and can be used to create gardens with intricate patterns of color and texture. All species do well in containers. Care should be taken to avoid injury from sharp spines on the tips and margins of leaves.

Agave americana

Century Plant

A large species, 5-6 ft. high and as wide. Large leaves are dull sea-green, have hooked spines on the margins, and a sharp spine on the tip. Clusters of showy yellow-green flowers are displayed on branched stalks, 20-40 ft. high. Flowers occur on mature plants in early to late summer and take 1-2 months to develop.

This species comes from arid regions of central Mexico. It is the most widely recognized agave and has been widely planted in warm regions around the world. Numerous hybrids and cultivars can be found in the trade, including *A. a.* 'Variegata' and *A. a.* 'Medio-picta'. These provide a range of sizes and variations in foliage markings. They are easy to grow in containers, raised planters, against walls, and once estab-

56. Agave americana 'Variegata', Santa Barbara, California

57. Agave attenuata

58. Agave attenuata

59. Agave deserti

60. Agave deserti

61. Agave shawii

62. Agave shawii

63. Agave victoriae-reginae

64. Agave victoriae-reginae

65. Agave vilmoriniana

66. Agave vilmoriniana

lished, have been able to develop into large groupings and naturalize on dry hillsides. Plate 56.

Agave attenuata
Foxtail Agave

A medium size species, 3-5 ft. high and as wide. Grey-green leaves are soft, fleshy, and do not have spines on the margins or tips. Striking clusters of light yellow-cream flowers are distinctively displayed on 10-12 ft. long arching spikes during the fall.

This species is unlike most others in the trade. The soft foliage color and habit, in combination with the distinctive flower stalks and spineless foliage, make it well suited to many garden uses. It is a popular container plant and accent element in both subtropical and water conserving gardens. It is tender to cold and grows best in coastal and frost free inland areas, where it needs only low amounts of supplemental water. Plates 57 - 58.

Agave deserti
Desert Agave

A small species that grows 3-4 ft. high and as wide. Leaves are light grey-green and have spines on the margins and tips. Flowers are bright yellow and occur in early summer on branched stalks, 10-15 ft. high.

This species comes from the Colorado Desert of California and Arizona, where it grows on dry rocky hills and gravelly slopes. It is well suited to planting schemes that include other desert trees and shrubs which reflect the natural desert landscape character. Plates 59 - 60.

Agave shawii
Shaw's Century Plant

A small species, growing 2-3 ft. high, spreading 3-4 ft. wide. Leaves are stiff, deep green, and have spines on the margins and tips. Colorful flowers are yellow with red and are displayed on 10-12 ft. tall branched stalks.

This is an endangered species that comes from dry and warm coastal bluffs and hillsides from Tijuana to El Rosario in northern Baja California. With its smaller size and rich foliage character, it is well suited to bank, container, and accent planting uses. Plates 61 - 62.

Agave victoriae-reginae

A small species, growing 1-2 ft. high and into a tight, rounded form. Distinctive foliage is comprised of deep green leaves that have striking white accent lines on the margins. Showy yellow flowers develop on single 8-12 ft. tall stalks.

This species is a popular choice for use in containers and as small accent elements in rock gardens where its distinctive foliage markings can be enjoyed. It is slow growing and develops for many years before flowering and dying. Plates 63 - 64.

Agave vilmoriniana
Octopus Agave

A medium species, 3-4 ft. high and as wide. Foliage is comprised of long, twisting leaves that are blue-green and pointed on the tips. Creamy yellow flowers are prominently displayed on single stalks, 10-12 ft. high.

This species, from northwest Mexico, grows on cliffs where it has evolved without the protective spines necessary to ward off browsing from wildlife. It provides unique arching and twisting foliage character for specimen and sculptural uses in landscapes. It grows relatively fast and adapts well to container conditions. Plates 65 - 66.

Agonis
Myrtaceae

A small group of evergreen trees and shrubs coming from Western Australia. Eleven species are known to exist; one is widely used in western gardens. This genus is related to *Melaleuca* and *Leptospermum* and shows similar affinity and adaptation to coastal environments. Most species come from mild and moist habitats but show good adaptability to periods of drought as they mature.

Agonis flexuosa
Peppermint Tree, Australian Willow Myrtle

A small to medium evergreen tree, eventually reaching 25-35 ft. high, and developing an equal spread. Long, narrow leaves are pale green, fragrant when crushed, and hang gracefully from drooping branches. Inconspicuous white flowers develop in spring. Trunks and branches are covered with distinctive, coarse, red-brown bark.

This species grows within shrublands on coastal sand dunes and as an understory tree within forest associations of Western Australia. In its natural range, it grows at elevations from sea level to 750 ft. and in areas that receive 32-40 in. of annual precipitation. The climate is very moderate; mean maximum temperatures range, 79-86°F; mean minimums range, 44-48°F with little or no occurrence of frost. Soils range from calcareous deposits to beach sands and sandy loams.

Peppermint tree develops into a handsome canopy tree for both residential and commercial landscapes. It is best adapted to frost free coastal regions from northern to southern California, where it needs low amounts of supplemental water after it becomes established. It also performs well in warmer and drier inland areas, in locations that are protected from intense heat, and with regular moisture. This is a slow to moderate growing species that can take 8-10 years before developing good size and spread. However, it provides very handsome foliage and bark characteristics and is highly useful as a street, lawn, and patio tree. Plates 67 - 70.

67. Agonis flexuosa

68. Agonis flexuosa bark

70. Agonis flexuosa, Newport Beach, California

69. Agonis flexuosa

71. Albizia julibrissin

72. Albizia julibrissin 'Rosea'

Albizia
Fabaceae

A large group of deciduous trees and shrubs including between 100-150 species. They are native to many regions of the world including India, Australia, Guatemala, West Indies, and Africa. Most types come from tropical climate regions and are characterized by large bipinnately divided leaves. These leaves have many small leaflets that produce a soft, feathery quality. Showy flowers are comprised of many stamens and range in color from white or yellow, to pink and rose.

Only two species of *Albizia* are commonly found in western gardens, *A. julibrissin* and *A. lophantha*. The first plant is considered very ornamental and useful as a canopy tree; the latter plant is a problematic shrub that has become naturalized in coastal areas of California.

Albizia julibrissin
Silk Tree, Mimosa

A deciduous tree developing low and broad branching habits, growing 25-40 ft. high, with an equal width. Soft, feathery leaves are bipinnately divided and create a light and airy canopy. Large numbers of showy flowers cover the tops of these trees in late spring to mid-summer, varying in intensity from pale pink to deep rose. Numerous brown seed pods, 2-3 in. long, develop in late fall, persist into winter, and are considered unsightly by many.

This species is native to many parts of Iran, India, China, and Japan. Throughout its natural range in China, it grows in foothills and valleys at elevations ranging from 1,000-5,000 ft. within broad leaved deciduous forests. Annual rainfall ranges 40-60 in.; winter frost is very common. It is a highly adaptable plant that can grow in temperate or subtropical climate regions around the world, becoming easily naturalized in some areas.

Silk tree is widely grown as an ornamental shade tree in coastal, inland, valley, and desert regions throughout the western states. It tolerates many types of soils, including clayey and calcareous, and grows with lots or little amounts of supplemental water. This is a fast growing plant that thrives in warm valley and foothill areas and tolerates heat, sun, and aridity. It is the only species of *Albizia* that tolerates heavy winter frost and, as a result, is also grown in southeastern states where it has naturalized due to moist climate conditions. A variety, *A. j.* 'Rosea', is a cultivar with very pink flower color.

Silk tree is one of the most colorful canopy trees for urban landscapes. It can be grown as a single or multiple trunk specimen in lawns, patios, parking lots, and in raised planters. Young plants often have a low branching structure that need pruning to attain greater height; mature plants produce ample leaf and seed pod litter. Plates 71 - 73.

73. Albizia julibrissin, San Dimas, California

Aloe

Aloe

Liliaceae

A large and varied group of succulent plants, including an estimated 250 species. These plants range in size from clumping and ground hugging forms to shrubs and trees. Most species have thick, fleshy foliage and stems. Leaves are arranged in rosettes and often have toothed margins. They produce colorful and striking tubular flowers that are clustered on long spikes and range from pale yellow to bright red-orange. Flowering on many species occurs in mid-winter to early spring and provides some of the best winter color value in western gardens.

Most species of *Aloe* come from arid and subtropical climates of the Cape and Natal regions of south and east Africa. They are best adapted to coastal habitats and frost free zones, in full sun, and on well drained bluffs and rocky soils. They are extensively damaged by temperatures below 25°F and can suffer from root rot in heavy or poorly drained soils. Plants used in low desert regions perform best in microclimate areas that provide protection from extreme heat, sun, and frost.

Aloes are striking foliage and flowering plants. Larger species are useful as accent and specimen elements; others can be used for ground covers in dry rock gardens. These larger species are slow to develop, but age to provide unique shape and character. Smaller species easily hybridize and often develop into dense clumps that can be divided every 2-3 years. Aloes are very effective in containers or when combined with other succulents such as *Sedum*, *Agave*, and *Crassula*. Unlike agaves, these plants do not die after flowering. Established plants need very little care or attention and only periodic deep watering. Many interesting and obscure hybrids and species are available through specialized nurseries. Some of the more popular choices are discussed below.

Aloe arborescens

Tree Aloe

A large mounding shrub, 6-12 ft. high, spreading 10-12 ft. and wider. Fleshy leaves are medium green and have spines on the margins. Colorful flowers are deep red-orange and occur on stems in early winter. Tree aloe is one of the largest and most popular shrub forms in landscape use. It takes many years to become large, and can be pruned to any desirable size. It is highly suited to coastal bluffs and gardens, where it tolerates salt spray and summer drought. It is also popular in inland and low desert gardens where it needs protection from frost and extreme sun. Plates 75 - 76.

Aloe bainesii

A small to medium tree, slowly growing, 8-12 ft. high. Thick, fleshy leaves grow 2-3 ft. long and are curved and dull dark green. Flowers are rose-pink to orange and occur on branched stems. This is a slow growing species that can eventually become a medium size tree with a heavy, thickened trunk, and several main branches. It is often grown in containers or located in garden spaces to function as a sculptural accent element. Plate 77.

Aloe candelabrum

Candelabra Aloe

A large single trunked shrub, slowly growing 8-12 ft. high and developing a massive rosette of thick, downward arching foliage. Leaves are dull green and have reddish edges with small teeth;

74. Aloe species, Los Angeles County Arboretum, California

75. Aloe arborescens, Monterey Coast, California

76. Aloe arborescens

77. Aloe bainesii

78. Aloe candelabrum

79. Aloe ciliaris

80. Aloe nobilis

81. Aloe plicatilis

82. Aloe striata hybrid

83. Aloe vera

flower colors range from scarlet, rose-pink, to orange and occur on upright spikes in late winter. An excellent container plant and sculptural element in courtyard settings. Plate 78.

Aloe ciliaris
A vining and climbing plant that can grow to 10 ft. long. Medium green leaves grow 8-10 in. long; orange flowers with yellow tips occur on short stems. This species is popular in coastal landscapes on walls, in planters, and around the base of palm trees. It can be maintained to grow as a mounding shrub or meandering vine. Plate 79.

Aloe ferox
A large shrub with a single trunk, developing a large rosette of upward arching foliage. Mature plants can reach 6-10 ft. high. Leaves are dull green and have stout brown-red teeth on the surface; striking scarlet flowers occur on upright spikes in late winter. This species needs space to develop and is very tolerant of heat and drought once established. Good in containers, raised planters, and courtyards.

Aloe marlothii
An upright species, developing a single stalk trunk, eventually reaching 8-12 ft. high. Leaves are large and thick, dull green, and have reddish brown teeth and spines over their margins and surfaces. Colorful orange flowers develop on horizontally branched spikes above the foliage in winter. A large species that is well suited for use in containers, raised planters, and for sculptural effects.

Aloe nobilis
A small clumping species, 8-12 in. high. Short, stout leaves are rich green and covered with hooked spines on the margins. Orange-red flowers occur on 6-12 in. tall stalks in late spring. A species well suited to rock gardens and mixed succulent plantings. In 2-3 years time, it will develop into a clump 2-3 ft. high and 3-4 ft. across. Plate 80.

Aloe plicatilis
A slow growing species that can eventually reach tree-like sizes, 8-12 ft. high. Pale grey-green leaves range 10-12 in. long and curve upward in opposite groupings. Colorful orange to scarlet flowers occur in early spring. A striking plant due to its intriguing foliage arrangement, flower color, and branching habit. It is useful in containers and in planters as a sculptural accent plant. Plate 81.

Aloe striata
Coral Aloe

A clumping species, 10-15 in. high. Long leaves are grey-green and have smooth margins. Dense clusters of colorful coral to orange flowers occur in early spring. Coral aloe is a very popular species that is used either as accent clumps or in mass ground cover plantings. It hybridizes easily and often has small teeth on the margins. Plate 82.

Aloe vera
(Aloe barbadensis)
Medicinal Aloe

A clumping species, growing to 18 in. high. Long, spineless leaves grow upright, and are pale green. Colorful yellow flowers develop high above the foliage. This species is widely known for its treatment of burns and bites. It is often a container plant and is more tolerant of low desert heat, sun, and aridity than other types. Plate 83.

Alyogyne
Malvaceae

A small group of evergreen shrubs that includes only 4 species. All are native to Australia, where they are principally found in dry coastal and frost free inland habitats. Three species have been introduced into western gardens and provide widely varying foliage and flower character for ornamental use. They have proven to perform best in warm coastal and inland gardens with good drainage and with mild winter temperatures.

Alyogyne cuneiformis

A mounding shrub to 5 ft. high, spreading 5-10 ft. wide. Foliage is comprised of 3-6 in. long, medium green leaves. Showy white flowers occur throughout spring and summer and are comprised of tightly rolled petals that are accented with a red spot at their base. This species is native to the coastline of Western Australia and adjacent offshore islands. In western regions, it is useful for slope, screen, and background areas. Plate 84.

Alyogyne hakeifolia
Red Centered Hibiscus

An upright shrub reaching 5-9 ft. high. Foliage is comprised of stiff, narrow, dark green needle-like leaves that produce a broom-like texture. Colorful flowers can be blue or yellow and have a bright red spot at the base of the petals. This species grows throughout many parts of South Australia into Western Australia in well drained soils and in areas having little winter frost. In western regions, it can be used as a fast growing tall screen and background plant. Plate 85.

Alyogyne huegelii
(Hibiscus huegelii)
Blue Hibiscus

A medium shrub to small tree, 6-10 ft. tall, equal in width. Pale green leaves are deeply lobed and create an open and coarse textured appearance. Showy flowers range in color from light blue and magenta to deep purple and occur for many months from mid-spring through summer.

Blue hibiscus is native to many parts of South Australia and Western Australia, where it grows in dry habitats in sandy and gravelly soils. The climate throughout this range is typically mild in the winter and has extended periods of drought; rainfall ranges 10-25 in. annually.

This species is the most popular choice of *Alyogyne* for western gardens. It grows very fast and produces an abundance of rich purple flowers for many months making it useful for color accent value in many landscape situations. It tolerates many types of soil, but drainage must be fast in order to avoid water related diseases and early deaths. It prefers a sunny exposure and easily survives with low to moderate amounts of supplemental water in coastal and inland regions. Mature plants are heavily damaged by temperatures below 25° F; young plants are often killed. Several cultivars have been introduced including *A. h.* 'Santa Cruz' and *A. h.* 'Monterey Bay', which have striking deep purple-blue flower color. *A. h.* 'Purple Haze' has lighter purple flowers. Blue hibiscus is often used as a flowering accent shrub on slopes, for screening, and as a small patio tree. Plates 86 - 89.

84. Alyogyne cuneiformis

85. Alyogyne hakeifolia

86. Alyogyne huegelii

87. Alyogyne huegelii 'Santa Cruz'

88. Alyogyne huegelii

89. Alyogyne huegelii

90. Angophora costata

91. Angophora costata, Qld., Australia

Angophora costata
(Angophora lanceolata)
Gum Myrtle, Smooth-barked Apple
Myrtaceae

A medium evergreen tree with an open crown growing moderately fast, 40-55 ft. tall, 35-40 ft. wide. Bark on trunks is similar to *Eucalyptus citriodora*, very smooth, grey to pink in color, and deciduous. Foliage is comprised of pointed leaves, 4-6 in. long, that occur in opposite pairs on the branches. Large clusters of creamy white flowers occur on mature trees and are relatively inconspicuous.

Gum myrtle comes from mild coastal and inland habitats in southeast Australia. It is native to foothills and plains at elevations ranging from sea level to over 1,000 ft. Throughout its natural range, annual rainfall varies from 25-50 in. Plants occurring in inland locations experience higher temperatures, seasonal drought, and frequent winter frosts. It grows in open forests with various species of *Eucalyptus* and is commonly found in sandy, well drained soils.

In western gardens, it grows well in both coastal and inland valleys and foothills. It shows good tolerance of many soil conditions, including calcareous, and grows well with low to moderate amounts of supplemental water. This species is not as widely known as the more popular *Eucalyptus* group but is of equal character and value. It is useful for parkways, open space areas, and parks, where its distinctive bark and open canopy provides handsome landscape character. Plates 90 - 92.

92. Angophora costata, Cal Poly University, Pomona, California

Anigozanthos

Kangaroo Paw

Haemodoraceae

Herbaceous perennials with strap-like leaves, a clumping growth habit, and varying in size from 6-24 in. tall. Unique flowers are tubular in shape, fuzzy, and can occur on branched or unbranched stems that grow several feet above the foliage. Flower color ranges from red, pink, green, yellow, and orange, make striking displays from mid-spring to early summer, and produce nectar for birds.

The genus *Anigozanthos* is comprised of 11 species, all of which are endemic to the southwestern edge of Western Australia. They grow in warm, dry areas, in full sun, and in well drained soils. In western landscapes, they do best in mild coastal and inland locations in sandy loams with regular watering while flowering. Some of the more vigorous species and cultivars can tolerate low desert conditions if protected from extreme heat and sun, and when provided with regular summer irrigation. Most types are short lived and will become dormant under dry conditions of late summer and fall. Drip irrigation is highly recommended; poor drainage often causes early death.

Kangaroo paws are highly successful as container plants, cut flowers, and as flowering accents along borders. Many new cultivated hybrids, particularly the Bush Gems series, are being introduced into the trade that provide many flower colors, sizes, and greater resistance to frost and water related diseases. Larger varieties can be divided in the late fall; all are easily damaged by snails and slugs.

Anigozanthos flavidus

Tall Kangaroo Paw

Deep green leaves reach 15-18 in. high; Flowers can be yellow, pink, or red and occur on stalks that reach 5-6 ft. high and last for 1-2 months. The most commonly cultivated species; large, robust, and more tolerant of frost, heavier soils, and moisture. It prefers loam soils and endures seasonal drought when established. Good for containers and in perennial gardens; a species to divide in early spring every 2-3 years to maintain vigor. Plate 94.

Anigozanthos humilis

Cat's Paw

One of the smallest species, growing 3-6 in. high, with grey-green sickle-shaped leaves. Flowers are chartreuse green with yellow and occur in clusters of 10-15. A short lived species that can die back under drought stress, regrowing again each winter. Plate 95.

Anigozanthos manglesii

Red and Green Kangaroo Paw

A small species, reaching 8-12 in. high, having light grey-green leaves. Striking flowers are deep green with bright red bases and stems. This species is the floral emblem of Western Australia and is very demanding of good drainage conditions, but provides spectacular flower character in small spaces. Plate 96.

Anigozanthos rufus

Red Kangaroo Paw

An intermediate species, growing 1-2 ft. high. Dark green foliage grows upright; showy deep red flowers occur on branched stalks from spring into summer. Tolerant of light frost and many soils, but frequently short lived. Plate 97.

93. Anigozanthos cultivars

94. Anigozanthos flavidus

95. Anigozanthos humilis

96. Anigozanthos manglesii

97. Anigozanthos rufus

98. Anisacanthus thurberi

99. Anisacanthus thurberi

100. Anisodontea hypomandarum

101. Anisodontea hypomandarum

102. Aptenia 'Red Apple'

103. Aptenia 'Red Apple'

Anisacanthus thurberi
Desert Honeysuckle, Chuparosa
Acanthaceae

A small mounding shrub growing 3-6 ft. high and as wide. Light green leaves are clustered on arching branches; showy clusters of red to orange flowers occur in spring.

This plant comes from desert regions throughout the Southwest, from Arizona to New Mexico, south into central Mexico. It grows in sandy washes and canyon bottoms, as well as in the desert grassland plant community at elevations ranging from 2,000-5,000 ft. It is adapted to heat, sun, and aridity and survives drought by shedding some of its leaves and becoming dormant.

Desert honeysuckle is an attractive flowering shrub in desert gardens around such plants as *Chilopsis linearis, Ruellia peninsularis, Beloperone californica,* and *Encelia farinosa.* It grows best in well drained soils and with periodic deep watering that helps to enhance the foliage and flower character. Plates 98 - 99.

Anisodontea hypomandarum
Dwarf Pink Hibiscus
Malvaceae

An upright perennial, 5-7 ft. high and as wide. Small green leaves are deeply lobed and occur on long, upright branches. Colorful pink to rose flowers occur for many months, beginning in winter and continuing through late fall.

This plant is a hybrid of unknown origin. The genus *Anisodontea* contains 19 species, all from subtropical climates of South Africa. In western gardens, it is well adapted to coastal and inland regions, in full sun, and in well drained soils. It performs best with low to moderate amounts of supplemental water. It is also very adaptable to frost free areas in low deserts but needs regular water to maintain good character.

This plant is recognized for its prolific flowering character that is ongoing throughout the warm season of the year. It is fast growing and is used in mixed garden plantings, containers, and in background areas. It is easy to grow and performs well for 2-3 years before needing pruning to remove some of the overgrown stems. Plates 100 - 101.

Aptenia 'Red Apple'
Aizoaceae

A low growing succulent perennial, 6-12 in. high, spreading more than 2 ft. wide. Fleshy, heart-shaped leaves are light green; showy purple-red flowers begin in spring and continue through fall.

This succulent is a hybrid resulting from crossing *Aptenia cordifolia* with *Platythyra haeckeliana,* both from South Africa. Similar to other succulents, it is capable of absorbing moisture and resisting drought for long periods at a time. It is highly adapted to coastal areas and frost free inland zones, where it grows best in well drained soils, in full sun, and with low amounts of supplemental water. It also tolerates salt spray but becomes chlorotic in iron-poor soils.

Aptenia 'Red Apple' is widely planted on slopes, banks, and in planters as a carefree ground cover. It grows quickly from unrooted cuttings and provides a long season of flower character. Flowers are very attractive to bees. Plates 102 - 103.

Arbutus
Ericaceae

A small group of evergreen trees and shrubs that includes about 14 species. Two species are commonly cultivated in western regions, one native to the Mediterranean region of Europe, the other from California and the Pacific Northwest. These plants are known for their handsome foliage, distinctive bark, attractive urn-shaped flowers, and colorful red fruit. Mature specimens take many years to develop, but are among the most highly valued plants in ornamental landscapes.

Arbutus menziesii
Madrone, Madrono

A large evergreen shrub or medium to large tree with many growth habits. In warmer and drier landscapes, it grows 20-30 ft. high and as wide; in cooler and moister climate areas, it grows 60-100 ft. high. Leaves vary from 3-6 in. long, are dark glossy green above, pale green below. Showy clusters of white urn-shaped flowers occur in early spring and are followed by bright red to orange berries. Trunks and branches are covered by very attractive smooth, mahogany-red bark that peels off each year.

Madrone is native to the western United States, where it is most commonly established within mixed evergreen and Douglas fir forests and the oak woodland plant communities. Its habitat extends throughout the coastal foothill regions from western British Columbia to northern California and the Sierra Nevada foothills, where annual precipitation ranges from 40-100 in. Several small stands exist in the coastal mountains of southern California, where rainfall ranges from 25-40 in. Within its range, it grows in both sun and shade and at many elevations but always within slightly acid and well drained soils. In drier regions, it establishes best along streams, on north facing slopes, and in partial shade.

Madrone is considered by many to be the most handsome native broadleaf evergreen tree in California. Even within natural woodland and forest settings, this species provides distinctive form, flowers, and bark character

104. **Arbutus menziesii**

105. **Arbutus menziesii**

106. **Arbutus menziesii**

107. **Arbutus menziesii, Marin County, California**

Photo by Jeffrey K. Olson

108. Arbutus unedo, Sardinia, Italy

Photo by Robert Black

109. Arbutus unedo

110. Arbutus unedo

111. Arbutus unedo, Pomona, California

among other native plants. However, it has proven to be a difficult plant to grow in cultivation. Young plants need protection from extreme heat and aridity and are highly susceptible to root rot when given regular summer water, particularly in areas of poor drainage. The best success for this species can be expected in northern California and foothill regions that are within the principal range of its native habitat. They dislike calcareous or saline soils and will take many years to develop into larger sizes. Madrone can be used in park and garden landscapes in areas where space and time permit long term growth and size. As plants become established, periodic deep summer watering is recommended. Plates 104 - 107.

Arbutus unedo
Strawberry Tree

A large shrub to medium tree, 15-30 ft. high and as wide. Leathery, dark green leaves have toothed margins and range from 2-3 in. long. Clusters of white to pink, urn-shaped flowers are modestly showy in late fall and early winter. Showy red to yellow fruit occur in winter and create a noticeable litter problem. Fruit is edible and is used in preserves. Trunks and branches are twisting and covered with rough brown bark.

The strawberry tree comes from Europe and North Africa, where it is principally native to dry foothills, canyons, and slopes around the Mediterranean Sea. Annual rainfall ranges from 15-30 in. and occurs largely in the winter months. Some stands extend northward into cooler climate regions, including Ireland. Within this broad range of distribution, it has become widely adapted to many climate conditions, ranging from cool and moist to warm and dry. It grows in both slightly acid to slightly alkaline soils but always prefers well drained conditions.

This plant is perhaps one of the best large shrubs or small trees for western gardens. This species grows slowly but provides ongoing value for many years. Younger plants need time and pruning to develop good shape and character. Large specimens can be seen in older gardens where they are highly valued for their interesting form, trunk, and bark characteristics. It is often used as a specimen plant in courtyards and raised planters, and around lawns. It grows well in coastal, inland, and valley habitats, as well as in high and low desert areas where it needs microclimate protection from extreme heat, wind, and aridity.

Two cultivated varieties are available in the trade. *A. u.* 'Compacta' grows 8-12 ft. high, *A. u.* 'Elfin King' is a dwarf selection, growing 4-6 ft. high. These varieties provide excellent flower, fruit, and foliage character. They perform well in smaller spaces for background and screening uses and in large containers where they can be pruned into interesting specimens. Plates 108 - 111.

Arctostaphylos
Manzanita
Ericaceae

Introduction:
A diverse group of evergreen shrubs that vary from spreading ground cover forms to small, multi-branched trees. Over 50 species are native to Central and North America; more than 45 of these are found in California where they achieve their greatest occurrence. Manzanitas are recognized and appreciated for their smooth and colorful mahogany-red bark and for their profuse clusters of urn-shaped flowers. Several species, and their cultivars, are among the most prized California native plants for use in ornamental gardens. Careful consideration needs to be given to soil and watering conditions in order to achieve the best performance from these plants.

Character:
Manzanitas provide handsome foliage, bark, and flower character. Leaves are often pointed and grow upright. New growth is soft and light green, becoming hard and tough as it matures, making it capable of resisting drought stress through summer and fall. Mature plants often have twisting branches that are covered by smooth, mahogany-red to brown bark. Bark will shed by late spring through summer to reveal lighter color and smoother new bark. Most species also develop large numbers of urn-shaped flowers that characterize the *Ericaceae* family. Flowers are small, to 1/4 in. in size, range in color from white to deep rose, and occur from winter to early spring. The development of berry-like fruit is highly variable among species and is seldom ornamental. Both flowers and fruit are of value to bees, birds, and other wildlife.

Botanists have divided manzanitas into two basic groups. One group of species develops deep roots and a basal burl that helps them withstand drought and fires. A second group lacks this basal burl and tends to develop shallow root systems. Most species and cultivars in cultivation do not have the basal burl or deep roots. Manzanita species hybridize easily in nature, which has led to a number of natural varieties and selections for ornamental landscape use.

Habitat and Culture:
A variety of manzanitas are adapted to habitats in California, from coastal bluffs to inland mountains and desert edges. They typically grow on slightly acid, well drained soils and can endure warm temperatures and dry summer conditions within their natural range.

Most species and cultivars selected for their ornamental value and landscape use are native to the coastal counties of northern and central California. Summer heat and drought conditions in these regions are mitigated by cool sea breezes and fog. Species native to these coastal habitats receive winter rainfall between 20-25 in. and easily survive the dry season from May to November without supplemental moisture. When these plants, or their cultivars, are used in inland locations or in southern California, they prefer microclimate areas that provide some relief from the intense sun and heat. Soils should be light and

well drained. Some varieties will grow in heavier soils, including clayey conditions, as long as they are on slopes that help moisture to drain.

Manzanitas found in cultivation do best with drip irrigation. Most varieties planted in coastal habitats need only low amounts of supplemental water, principally in the summer. Varieties used in inland areas perform well with monthly deep watering that should be provided at intervals that let the soil dry out between applications. Drip irrigation is strongly advised to limit the wetting of foliage, branches, and surface leaf litter. Too much moisture, particularly in the summer months, often leads to disease and root rot problems.

Uses and Considerations:
Manzanitas are valued for many landscape uses. Their popularity and success in landscapes is far greater in northern California than in southern areas. This is due in part to poor soils and to the greater heat and relative dryness of southern California, which often leads to too much watering. Many species are relatively slow to mature but are then among the best long term shrubs in garden settings.

Low growing and spreading forms often are planted as ground covers on small to medium size banks and slopes. These should not be planted in heavy organic mulch in order to limit the possibility of moisture and bacteria related diseases. These spreading forms often do not grow to the same size and will take several years to achieve a solid cover. However, once an area becomes established, manzanita ground covers are highly ornamental in character. Several successful choices for ground cover uses include *A. edmundsii* and cultivars, *A.* 'Emerald Carpet', *A. hookeri* 'Monterey Carpet', *A.* 'Pacific Mist', *A.* 'Point Reyes', and *A. uva-ursi* cultivars.

Upright and mounding forms of manzanita are useful as screen, slope, and background plants. As these plants mature, their branching habit and bark character provides greater interest for specimen value in the garden. Popular shrub type manzanitas include *A. densiflora* cultivars and *A. hookeri*. These shrub forms often appear best when used individually or in small groupings.

Many species of manzanita in landscape use are susceptible to a disease called branch dieback or stem canker. This disease is caused by the fungus *Botryosphaeria ribis* and can severely disfigure and slowly kill both young and mature plants. Overhead watering is known to increase the spread of this disease and should be discontinued in favor of drip systems. Infected parts of the plant should immediately be removed several inches below the occurrence of the disease. Diligent

112. **Arctostaphylos Manzanita, Common Manzanita**

attention to this condition has been successful in maintaining the health and vigor of the plants.

Associated Plantings:
Manzanitas are most successful when used in conjunction with other California native plant species. Their dependence upon well drained soils and restricted summer water is often overlooked when combined with other ornamentals and in areas adjacent to lawns. They grow well within the partial shade of native pines and oaks and in association with *Heteromeles arbutifolia*, *Prunus ilicifolia*, and various *Ceanothus* species and cultivars. A number of native annuals and perennials also combine well within these plantings. Suggestions include *Eschscholzia californica*, *Sisyrinchium bellum*, *Lupinus* species, and *Penstemon* species.

Helpful References:
Munz, Philip A. A Flora of Southern California. Berkeley: University of California Press, 1974.

Lenz, Lee W. and John Dourley. California Native Trees and Shrubs. Claremont: Rancho Santa Ana Botanic Garden, 1981.

Schmidt, Marjorie G. Growing California Native Plants. Berkeley: University of California Press, 1980.

Everett, Percy C. A Summary of the Culture of California Plants at the Rancho Santa Ana Botanic Garden. Claremont: Rancho Santa Ana Botanic Garden, 1957.

McMinn, Howard E. An Illustrated Manual of California Shrubs. Berkeley: University of California Press, 1974.

Arctostaphylos densiflora
Sonoma Manzanita

A low spreading shrub that is native to a very limited area in the coastal foothills of Sonoma County. This species is not commonly used in landscapes. Instead, several attractive hybrids have been discovered during the process of germinating seed from this parent that produce colorful flowers and have proven to be among the best shrub choices for ornamental uses. *A. d.* 'Howard McMinn' is a large mounding shrub, 5-6 ft. high, with an equal spread. Leaves are medium green, elliptical and grow to 1 in. long. It develops striking mahogany-red bark color and showy clusters of light pink or white flowers in early spring. This selection is the most popular shrub form of manzanita for coastal and inland regions throughout California. In coastal zones, it grows well in full sun; in warmer inland locations, it performs best in areas that are shaded from hot afternoon sun. It shows greater tolerance to traditional garden care and watering than most varieties of manzanita, but soils must still be well drained, and periodic deep watering is strongly advised. *A. d.* 'Sentinel' is a taller and wider selection than *A. d.* 'Howard McMinn', with an upright branching habit, 6-8 ft. high, and to 8 ft. across. Branches have mahogany-purple bark; leaves reach 1 1/2 in. long and are pale green. Clear white to light pink flowers are showy during early spring. This cultivar has a strong branching habit and more irregular shape in its early stages of development. Mature plants become more mounding in habit, and can be pruned to reveal colorful bark and twisting branches. It is quite sensitive to poor drainage and excessive water, and is suited for slope, screen, background and accent plantings. Plates 113 - 114.

113. Arctostaphylos densiflora 'Howard McMinn'

114. Arctostaphylos d. 'Howard McMinn'

115. Arctostaphylos edmundsii

116. Arctostaphylos edmundsii

Arctostaphylos edmundsii
Little Sur Manzanita

A spreading shrub, 2-3 ft. high, reaching 4-6 ft. across. Leaves are rounded with red tinged edges; flowers are light pink to white and occur in spring to provide pleasing accent value.

This species comes from Monterey County, where it grows on ocean facing bluffs near the Little Sur River. It has proven to be a very durable and attractive species in coastal areas for use on banks, along borders, and in mixed plantings. It shows tolerance to heavy loam soils and prefers periodic deep irrigation. Place in partial shade when used in warm inland locations. This species has produced several seedling hybrids that have been selected for landscape use. *A. e.* 'Little Sur', *A. e.* 'Carmel Sur', and *A. e.* 'Danville' are slower and lower growing forms with smaller leaves. These perform well in small spaces as ground covers. Plates 115 - 116.

Arctostaphylos 'Emerald Carpet'

A very low, compact, and spreading shrub, to 1 ft. high, reaching 4-6 ft. across. Small, deep green leaves provide rich foliage character; inconspicuous clusters of light pink flowers occur in spring.

This selection is a hybrid between *A. uva-ursi* and *A. nummularia,* which are species of coastal origin. It shows a cultural preference for loam soils that are rich, slightly acid, and well drained. This cultivar is quite popular in northern California, where it is used as a ground cover in small planters and on slopes and banks. In these zones, it does well in full sun and requires low amounts of supplemental water. When planted in southern California and in warmer inland locations, it needs some protection from intense heat and sun and periodic deep watering. Avoid using overhead spray systems and do not plant in heavy mulch in order to avoid disease problems. Plates 117 - 118.

117. Arctostaphylos 'Emerald Carpet'

118. Arctostaphylos 'Emerald Carpet'   119. Arctostaphylos hookeri

Arctostaphylos hookeri
Monterey Manzanita

A low mounding shrub, growing 1-4 ft. high, spreading 4-6 ft. across. Small, medium green leaves are held erect and have minute barbs on their margins. Clusters of pink to white flowers are showy in late winter to early spring.

This species is native to Monterey Bay, where it grows on sandy flats and in forest locations in openings under *Pinus radiata*. It is a handsome plant that has been used for many years in coastal and inland regions on banks and in mixed shrub plantings. In inland areas, it needs protection from heat and sun and grows better with low to moderate amounts of supplemental water. Light, well drained soils are needed. Several excellent hybrid selections also have been selected from seedlings of this species for landscape use. *A. h.* 'Monterey Carpet' grows to 1 ft. tall and spreads 5-8 ft. *A. h.* 'Wayside' is an intermediate mounding shrub, 2-3 ft. high and spreads up to 8 ft. Both of these cultivars are highly suited as ground covers on slopes and in understory areas in sun to partial shade. Plates 119 - 120.

120. Arctostaphylos hookeri

Arctostaphylos 'Pacific Mist'

A spreading shrub with twisting branches, reaching 2 ft. high, 5-6 ft. across. Foliage is distinctively grey-green; 1-2 in. long leaves are attached to reddish stems. Flowers are white and mostly inconspicuous.

This plant is a hybrid seedling of unknown parentage that has become recognized for its rapid growth, light foliage color, and prostrate growth. As a result, it often is used for ground cover applications on banks and in raised planters. It has shown good adaptation to both coastal and inland regions in sun or partial shade and grows with low amounts of supplemental water. It is taller and more robust than other types of manzanita ground covers. Drip irrigation is recommended. Plates 121 - 122.

121. Arctostaphylos 'Pacific Mist'

122. Arctostaphylos 'Pacific Mist'

123. Arctostaphylos uva-ursi 'Point Reyes'

124. Arctostaphylos uva-ursi 'Point Reyes'

Arctostaphylos uva-ursi
Bearberry, Kinnikinnick

A prostrate shrub, 6-12 in. high and spreading as much as 10-12 ft. Glossy green leaves attach to dark red-brown branches; flowers are white to light pink in late winter to early spring. Berries are bright red and valuable to wildlife.

Bearberry is a species that comes from cool, moist, and coastal habitats in many parts of the world. It is found throughout the Pacific Northwest and extends into northern California from Del Norte to Point Reyes in Marin County. This species is not considered to be drought tolerant, but selections from seedling hybrids have shown moderate tolerance to coastal and inland areas that experience heat and dry conditions. These selections often have denser foliage and include A. u. 'Point Reyes', A. u. 'Radiant', A. u. 'Wood's Compact', and A. u. 'Wood's Red'. Plates 123 - 124.

Arctotheca calendula
Cape Weed
Asteraceae

A low growing herbaceous perennial, 3-6 in. high, 12-15 in. across. Leaves are deeply lobed, dull green above, silvery white below. Colorful yellow daisy-like flowers occur with greatest intensity in spring and intermittently during warm periods throughout the year.

Cape weed comes from coastal desert regions of South Africa. It is a very fast growing plant that spreads over large areas by underground runners. It performs best in sunny locations on sandy, well drained soils. It thrives in warm coastal and frost free inland regions and with low amounts of supplemental water. Poor drainage and too much water leads to root rot diseases that can damage large areas of a planting. This plant often escapes into lawn and adjacent planting areas and can be difficult to contain. Problems with naturalizing into native landscapes have occurred in northern coastal regions. Mass plantings last best for 2-3 years before some areas die out, making it difficult to achieve long term uniform character. Plates 125 - 126.

125. Arctotheca calendula, L. A. County Arboretum, California

126. Arctotheca calendula

127. Armeria maritima

Armeria maritima
(Statice armeria, Armeria vulgaris)
Sea Pink, Thrift
Plumbaginaceae

A small clumping perennial, 8-12 in. high. Deep green leaves are narrow and linear; showy deep pink, ball-shaped flowers develop on stems above the foliage in mid to late spring.

This plant is native to coastal bluffs, rocks, and sand dunes in both North America and Europe. Throughout this range, many local forms and variations exist. Plants native to the West Coast can be found in San Luis Obispo County north to British Columbia, Canada. It is a popular choice for border and container uses and can be planted 15-18 in. apart and serve as a ground cover in small spaces. It develops a deep tap root that enables it to perform well with moderate amounts of supplemental water through the summer months. It is highly suited to coastal gardens in full sun and performs best when protected from intense heat and drought conditions when used in inland locations. Plates 127 - 128.

128. Armeria maritima

129. Artemisia arborescens

130. Artemisia arborescens

131. Artemisia californica 'Montara'

132. Artemisia californica 'Canyon Grey'

Artemisia
Sagebrush, Mugwort, Wormwood
Asteraceae

A large group of herbaceous annuals, perennials, or shrubs, including about 200 species, that are mostly native to dry areas throughout the Northern Hemisphere. These plants are widely known for their grey-green aromatic foliage. They range in character from garden herbs with culinary and medicinal value, to large shrubs occurring in arid regions of the Southwest that are well suited to natural landscapes and restoration plantings.

Species discussed below are evergreen shrubs and perennials that grow best in coastal and inland regions and prefer sunny locations, well drained soils, and require low amounts of supplemental water. These plants grow rapidly and provide good character for 3-5 years; seasonal pruning is recommended to remove spent flower heads and to keep foliage habit dense. They are most often used a foliage accent plants in contrast to other plants, on slopes, and in combination with other western natives.

Artemisia arborescens
Shrubby Wormwood

A medium shrub, 5-6 ft. high, spreading 6-8 ft. across. Deeply divided leaves are silvery green and produce a fine textured appearance. Noticeable clusters of dull yellow flowers occur in late spring.

This species comes from rocky slopes and bluffs in calcareous soils around the Mediterranean Sea. It is highly adapted to salt air, wind, heat, and periods of summer drought. In western gardens, it is useful as a background, slope and foliage contrast plant. It grows very fast, and maintains good character for several years before pruning is needed to maintain shape and density. Plants grow well in inland areas that are sunny and hot, but are damaged by frosts below 25° F. Plates 129 - 130.

Artemisia californica
California Sagebrush

A small to medium shrub, 3-5 ft. high and as wide. Grey-green leaves are finely divided into narrow segments and are highly aromatic when crushed. Flowers are inconspicuous.

California sagebrush is a dominant member of the coastal sage plant community throughout California and Baja California. This species is most useful for restoration projects and is seldom used in ornamental landscapes. However, in recent years, prostrate selections have been introduced into cultivation for use as ground covers and slope plants in dry landscape situations. A. c. 'Canyon Grey' is a selection from San Miguel Island. It is very prostrate, growing 15-18 in. high, and spreading 6-12 ft. across. It provides striking silver-grey foliage character, but will become partially dormant in early summer and will shed much of its leaves. Rapid growth in late summer and fall provides renewed character. A. c. 'Montara' is a selection from the coastal foothills of San Mateo County, and has a mounding form, 12-24 in. high and 3-5 ft. across. Plates 131 - 132.

Artemisia 'Powis Castle'
(Artemisia arborescens 'Powis Castle')

A small mounding shrub, 2-3 ft. high, 3-4 ft. across. Silvery grey-green foliage is finely divided; flowers are inconspicuous.

This selection is a seedling hybrid of *A. arborescens* that was discovered in Powis Castle, Wales. It has been recently introduced to western gardens and is proving to be very popular as a foliage accent plant on slopes, in perennial gardens, and in small spaces in both residential and commercial landscapes. It is one of the few shrub-type species of *Artemisia* that retains good foliage character and size for several years. It tolerates calcareous soils and grows best in frost free coastal and inland habitats in full sun or partial shade. Plates 133 - 134.

Artemisia pycnocephala
Sandhill Sage

A herbaceous perennial, 12-18 in. high, spreading 18-24 in. across. Soft foliage is finely divided and silvery grey-green. Flowers develop on upright spikes and produce a modestly attractive display in late spring.

This species is native to coastal regions of California, where it grows on bluffs and in sandy soils. It is used along borders and as a foliage accent plant in both coastal and inland regions. Its best performance occurs in well drained soils, full sun, and with low amounts of supplemental water. New cultivars are being introduced, including, *A. p.* 'David's Choice', which provide more consistent growth and stronger flowering character. This is a short-lived species that performs best for 2-3 years before needing to be replaced. Plates 135 - 137.

133. Artemisia 'Powis Castle'

134. Artemisia 'Powis Castle'

135. Artemisia pycnocephala 'David's Choice'

136. Artemisia pycnocephala 'David's Choice'

137. Artemisia pycnocephala

138. Asteriscus maritimus

139. Asteriscus maritimus

140. Asteriscus sericeus

141. Atriplex canescens

Asteriscus
(Odontospermum)
Asteraceae

A small group of herbaceous perennials that come from the Canary Islands and Mediterranean region. Two species have been recently introduced to western gardens and are useful as bank and border plants, in containers, and for small garden spaces. Both species are easy to grow and are best suited to coastal habitats in full sun and on well draining soils. They tolerate salt spray and need low amounts of supplemental water in the summer. They need protection from frost, extreme heat, and drought in inland areas.

Asteriscus maritimus
Gold Chip

A low spreading perennial, reaching 12 in. high, to 3-4 ft. across. Bright yellow-gold flowers, growing 1 1/2 in. in dia., cover the plant in mid-summer. This species is native to coastal bluffs of North Africa to the eastern Mediterranean region. Very good flowering character and tolerance of short periods of drought. Plates 138 - 139.

Asteriscus sericeus

A mounding species, growing 2-3 ft. high and as wide. Flowers become 2-3 in. across and occur heaviest in summer. This species comes from the Canary Islands where it is adapted to mild coastal climates and seasonal drought. Plate 140.

Atriplex
Saltbush
Chenopodiaceae

A diverse group of herbaceous perennials and woody shrubs, including an estimated 100 species. These plants are native to many climates and continents from Europe, Asia, and Australia to the southwestern regions of the United States. Many types are characterized by grey-green foliage color and inconspicuous flowering habits.

Saltbushes are principally noted for their tolerance of difficult soils and harsh growing conditions. Many species tolerate levels of alkalinity and salinity far beyond those of other ornamental plants. Species from coastal regions are adapted to wind and salt spray and require little or no supplemental water once established. Species from desert regions are widely adapted to heat, drought, and aridity.

This group of plants often is valued for utilitarian roles in difficult situations. They are useful for slope and soil stabilization, for screening, and restoration plantings. In desert regions, range animals and wildlife are attracted to the protein rich foliage and seed. Species introduced from Australia are popular in coastal areas for slope and erosion control plantings but frequently escape cultivation and naturalize.

Atriplex canescens
Four-wing Saltbush

A large mounding shrub, 4-8 ft. high and as wide. A very densely branched species with long, narrow, grey-green leaves that drop off under extended drought stress. Creamy yellow flowers occur in late spring and become golden-brown as they mature into seeds.

This is the most widely distributed species of *Atriplex* in North America. It is adapted to a variety of very difficult climatic and alkaline conditions within many states of the west and Mexico. It grows in alkaline soils within a variety of plant communities including creosote bush, sagebrush scrub, and desert grassland.

This species is widely adapted to many conditions but is not considered to be useful for ornamental landscapes. It is mainly used for roadside stabilization, range, and revegetation projects where it is a valuable habitat species for erosion control and wildlife value. Plate 141.

Atriplex glauca

A low spreading perennial, 12-18 in. tall, growing 8-10 ft. across and more. Herbaceous stems are densely covered with small, 1/2 in. long, grey leaves. Flowers are inconspicuous.

This species comes from dry climate regions of South Australia. It is highly adapted to dry coastal regions of California where it tolerates both calcareous and saline soils. It is a fast growing species that often is established by seed for quick erosion control and slope stabilization. It is not highly ornamental in character and develops a loose, sprawling habit in 2-3 years.

Atriplex hymenelytra
Desert Holly

A small mounding shrub, 1-3 ft. high and as wide. Striking foliage is comprised of silvery, triangularly shaped leaves; flowers are insignificant.

This species is native to high and low desert regions of the Southwest, where it is found in alkaline soils and adjacent to washes. This species is occasionally cultivated in desert gardens as a foliage accent plant. Well drained soils and periodic deep watering is desirable. Plate 142.

Atriplex lentiformis
Quail Bush

A large spreading shrub, 8-10 ft. high, 12-15 ft. across. The branching habit is very dense and is covered by grey-green, heart-shaped leaves.

This species comes from the high and low deserts of the Southwest, often from alkali sink habitats. It is useful for habitat improvement and erosion control within its natural range. A subspecies, *A. l.* ssp. *breweri*, is from coastal and inland areas of California, where it has similar uses. It is often found on saline soils and easily tolerates salt spray and wind. In its range, it is commonly found on coastal slopes, bluffs, and disturbed areas, where it survives without supplemental water. Plates 143 - 144.

Atriplex semibaccata
Creeping Saltbush

A low spreading perennial, 6-12 in. high, 3-4 ft. across. Herbaceous stems are densely covered with small, grey leaves; flowers are insignificant.

This species comes from many dry climate areas throughout Australia. It is highly adapted to coastal and inland foothill regions in California, where it has reseeded and become widely naturalized. Like other herbaceous species of *Atriplex*, it establishes easily from seed and can be used on slopes for erosion control. It will grow vigorously for 2-3 years before plants age and decline. Plates 145.

142. **Atriplex hymenelytra**

143. **Atriplex lentiformis ssp. breweri**

144. **Atriplex lentiformis ssp. breweri**

145. **Atriplex semibaccata**

146. Baccharis 'Centennial'

147. Baccharis 'Centennial'

148. Baccharis pilularis 'Twin Peaks'

149. Baccharis pilularis 'Twin Peaks'

150. Baccharis pilularis 'Pigeon Point'

Baccharis
Asteraceae

A large group of evergreen and deciduous shrubs, including an estimated 350 species that are found throughout North and South America. Several species are native to western states, ranging from the northern California coast and into the desert regions of Arizona and Nevada. These plants provide significant wildlife and habitat value within their respective areas of natural distribution. A few species and varieties are very successful as ground covers and slope plants in residential and commercial landscapes. These are appreciated for their tolerance of many soil and moisture conditions.

Baccharis 'Centennial'

A low mounding evergreen shrub, 2-3 ft. high, 5-6 ft. wide. Small, narrow green leaves have several teeth on the margins and grow on green stems. Flowers are insignificant; seed heads on female plants are white to tan and are noticeable in late fall.

This plant is a hybrid between *B. pilularis* and *B. sarathroides*. It combines the prostrate habit of the former with the tolerance of desert conditions of the latter. As a result, this cultivar is highly suited to low and high desert regions, where it is one of the few heat, sun, and frost tolerant ground covers that provides a rich green and fresh appearance. It prefers light, well drained soils, and needs low to moderate amounts of supplemental water. Periodic removal of branches that grow upright will help keep this plant from mounding over 3 ft. high. Plates 146 - 147.

Baccharis pilularis
Coyote Brush

A prostrate evergreen shrub, 2-3 ft. high, spreading 4-6 ft. across. Small green leaves, to 1/2 in. long, are round and have irregular teeth on the margins. Insignificant flowers occur in summer and are lightly scented. Cotton-like seed capsules on female plants are quite numerous and can become unsightly in late fall.

This species comes from coastal bluffs and sand dunes along central California, from Monterey to Marin counties. It is well suited for use in coastal, inland, and valley regions, where it tolerates moderate levels of heat, drought, aridity, and calcareous soils. Being of coastal origin, this species can suffer from drought when grown in hotter and drier areas, particularly on south and west facing slopes. It has also been used within protected microclimate areas of high and low desert regions but is not as well adapted to full sun, heat, and aridity as *B.* 'Centennial' and needs regular supplemental water.

Coyote brush and its several cultivars have proven to be among the best western native plants for use as ground covers on large banks and slopes. *B. p.* 'Pigeon Point' is a selection from San Mateo County that has round foliage and a billowy, mounding growth habit. *B. p.* 'Twin Peaks' is a selection taken from coastal areas in San Francisco County. It has small, 1/4 in. size leaves, with distinctly toothed margins, and develops a low, prostrate branching habit. Rooted cuttings of these selections should be spaced at least 3-4 ft. apart to accommodate their mature size.

After 4-5 years of growth, these varieties develop a woody interior and will start to mound higher. They can be revitalized by pruning the stems back to the ground in mid-winter. Plates 148 - 150.

B. p. ssp. *consanguinea,* Chaparral Broom, is a subspecies that is widely distributed throughout the coastal strand and coastal grassland communities from San Diego to Oregon. It is a taller, upright plant, 4-12 ft. high. It is often planted by seed in restoration and revegetation projects where it is recognized for its soil stabilization and habitat value. Plates 151 - 152.

Baccharis sarothroides
Desert Broom

An upright shrub, 6-12 ft. high, 4-8 ft. wide. Tiny green leaves occur on numerous slender, 4-sided stems, producing a broom-like appearance. Large numbers of tan flower heads occur in fall and mature into noticeable cottony seed clusters.

Desert broom is native to many parts of the arid Southwest. It grows within the coastal sage plant community in San Diego and Riverside counties and within the creosote bush scrub, desert grassland, and other desert plant communities in Arizona, Nevada, and northern Mexico. This species offers limited use in ornamental plantings but is valued in revegetation and erosion control in intermediate and high desert regions.

151. Baccharis pilularis ssp. consanguinea

152. Baccharis pilularis ssp. consanguinea

153. Baileya multiradiata

Baileya multiradiata
Desert Marigold
Asteraceae

A small clumping biennial or perennial, growing 12-18 in. high. Foliage develops from the base; leaves are grey-green, divided at the base, and mostly entire at the tops. Colorful yellow flowers occur for 1-2 months during spring and early summer.

This species is native to most arid regions of the Southwest, including Utah, California, Nevada, Arizona, Texas, and northern Mexico. It commonly grows along washes, roadsides, and rocky slopes throughout all desert zones. It is a popular flowering accent plant for both ornamental and natural gardens along walkways, on banks, and in wildflower plantings. It is easily established from seed and grows in sandy soils, as well as caliche. It is often combined with other desert perennials, including *Penstemon superbus, Penstemon barbatus, Melampodium leucanthum,* and *Sphaeralcea ambigua.* It also makes an excellent cut flower. Plates 153 - 155.

154. Baileya multiradiata

155. Baileya multiradiata

Beaucarnea recurvata
(Nolina tuberculata)
Ponytail, Bottle Palm
Agavaceae

A unique tree-like plant with a swollen base, stout trunks and branches, and long, strap-like leaves. This is a slow growing species that can eventually reach sizes of 12-25 ft. Leaves grow to 6 ft. long; large plumes of showy creamy white flowers occur in early summer above the clumps of foliage.

Ponytail comes from warm and dry regions of Mexico and is well adapted to heat and drought. *B. r.* var. *intermedia* has leaves that grow to 3 ft. long and is a more commonly cultivated variety in western gardens. It performs best in coastal and inland regions, in well drained soils, and with little supplemental water. Due to its slow growth rate, it is often used as a container specimen and accent element in dry garden schemes. It takes 15-20 years and more before tree sizes are attained; the enlarged base and number of stems become more pronounced and interesting with age. It also can be grown in low desert regions in protected microclimates, as well as in interior spaces that receive ample light. Plates 156 - 158.

156. Beaucarnea recurvata

157. Beaucarnea recurvata

158. Beaucarnea recurvata, Cal Poly University, Pomona, California

Bougainvillea
Nyctaginaceae

A small group of evergreen shrubs and vines that are among the most widely known flowering plants in subtropical regions around the world. Bougainvilleas come from many parts of South America and are ideally suited to warm coastal habitats but perform with equal success in most frost free regions, including the low and intermediate deserts. They provide many landscape uses from vines on trellises, in containers, as ground covers on slopes, and for cascading over walls.

All types thrive in full sun and heat, require well drained soils, and low amounts of supplemental water. Too much water, particularly during late spring and summer, encourages more foliage growth and less flowering. Young plants should be installed with care. Root balls are easily broken and careful handling is often recommended to reduce root damage and shock. Once established, bougainvilleas can be quite carefree. Fertilizing and pruning in early spring can help improve growth and shapes of these plants. All varieties are damaged by frost; young plants are often killed. Watering in late summer also can stimulate additional growth that is highly sensitive to frost.

Most cultivars available in nurseries are hybrids among three closely related species: *B. glabra*, *B. peruviana*, and *B. spectabilis* (*B. brasiliensis*). These species vary in size, produce bright rose to purple-red flower bracts, and usually have sharp spines on their stems. Widespread interest in these species has led to the development of new hybrids that now provide many flower, foliage, and growth characteristics for garden use. Flowers are actually small and white; the color value of these plants is caused by brightly colored leaf bracts. These bracts can be single or double and range from pink, purple, white, rose, and orange. Plants vary in habit, from dense, mounding shrubs to vigorous woody vines. The wide array of choices has led to some confusion among certain names and plants. Several popular varieties are noted below. Plates 159 - 171.

Mounding shrub types:
B. 'Crimson Jewel' - Brilliant glowing red bracts.
B. 'La Jolla' - Fluorescent red bracts, compact, bush form, 12-20 ft.
B. 'Raspberry Ice' (*B.* 'Hawaii') - Variegated leaves, bright magenta bracts, 10-20 ft.
B. 'Rosenka' - Fluorescent pink-orange bracts, mounding and spreading from, 12-20 ft.
B. 'Temple Fire' - Bronzy red bracts, bush form.

Large, vining types:
B. 'Barbara Karst' - Brilliant crimson red, strong bloomer.
B. 'California Gold' (Sunset) - Deep golden bracts.
B. 'Don Mario' - Large, deep purple-red bracts, vigorous, 15-25 ft.
B. glabra - Maroon-purple flowers, cold hardy and vigorous, 15-25 ft.
B. 'Jamaica White' - White bracts with pink tinge.
B. 'James Walker' - Small, reddish purple bracts, vigorous, 15-20 ft.
B. 'Orange King' - Bronzy orange bracts, open growth, 15-20 ft.
B. 'San Diego Red' - Large, bright red bracts, vigorous, 15-25 ft.
B. 'Texas Dawn' - Purplish pink bracts, vigorous.

159. Bougainvillea spectabilis, Newport Beach, California

160. Bougainvillea 'Don Mario'

161. Bougainvillea 'Don Mario'

162. Bougainvillea glabra

163. Bougainvillea glabra

164. Bougainvillea 'Jamaica White'

165. Bougainvillea 'Orange King'

166. Bougainvillea 'Rosenka'

167. Bougainvillea 'Raspberry Ice'

168. Bougainvillea 'Raspberry Ice'

169. Bougainvillea 'Texas Dawn'

170. Bougainvillea 'San Diego Red', San Juan Capistrano Mission, California

171. Bougainvillea species

Brachychiton

Bottle Tree

Sterculiaceae

A varied group of evergreen and deciduous trees that includes some 31 species. Most species come from Australia, where they exist in widely varying habitats, from rainforests to dry inland regions along seasonal water courses. Three species are commonly found in landscape use in western gardens, one being best adapted to arid and warm landscapes.

Brachychiton populneus

(Sterculia diversifolia)

Kurrajong Bottle Tree

A small to medium evergreen tree, 30-45 ft. tall. Young trees develop an upright habit; mature plants have a round dome shape. Foliage is comprised of glossy, medium green leaves, 2-3 in. long; inconspicuous bell-shaped flowers are creamy white with rose inside and are produced in large numbers in early spring. Large clusters of woody seed pods are produced in summer.

Kurrajong bottle tree is native to foothills and plains throughout inland parts of eastern Australia, where it is adapted to humid and semi-arid climates, warm temperatures, and seasonal drought. The mean annual rainfall within its natural habitat averages 17-30 in. and occurs evenly all year. Plants will grow in drier areas along seasonal water courses, where they can obtain additional moisture for larger growth. Soils are often rocky, poor in value, and well drained.

This species is appreciated for its fresh green foliage, shimmering leaf character, and tolerance for heat, sun, and aridity. It is widely used in coastal and inland areas as a street tree, in parks, and as a shade tree in residential gardens. Young plants do best with low to moderate amounts of supplemental water; established plants are quite drought tolerant. It is also a very popular shade tree in lawn areas in low and intermediate desert regions, where warm temperatures and regular water stimulate very fast growth. Good drainage is preferred; excessive watering can lead to root rot problems in poorly drained areas. Litter from leaves, flowers, and pods can be objectionable. Plates 172 - 175.

172. **Brachychiton populneus**

173. **Brachychiton populneus**

174. **Brachychiton populneus, Australia**

175. **Brachychiton populneus**

Brachycome multifida
(Brachyscome multifida)
Cut-leaf Daisy
Asteraceae

A small herbaceous perennial, 6-12 in. high, 12-18 in. wide. Bright green leaves are divided into narrow leaflets and create a soft textured appearance. Numerous daisy-like flowers vary in color, from deep blue to pale pink, and occur in showy masses from late spring through summer.

Cut-leaf daisy belongs to a group of annual and perennial plants that includes over 60 species, mostly from Australia. This species has become popular in landscape use in recent years as a compact flowering accent element in mixed perennial plantings, on banks, rock gardens, and other small landscape spaces. It occurs naturally in open forest and rocky areas where it performs best in warm, sunny locations. It has shown good tolerance of clayey soils as long as drainage conditions are good. In coastal and inland gardens, it needs low to moderate amounts of supplemental water and performs best for 2-3 years before needing to be replaced. Plates 176 - 177.

176. Brachycome multifida

177. Brachycome multifida

Brahea
(Erythea)
Palmae

A group of 12 species of palms occurring mainly in Mexico, with two species extending into Guatemala. Several species occur in coastal and inland areas that have a low annual rainfall and infrequent frosts. They often inhabit oases or hillsides and steep gullies on rocky, calcareous soils. Two species are common in western gardens.

Brahea armata
(Erythea armata)
Blue Hesper Palm

A single trunk fan palm that grows very slowly to 45 ft. high. Distinctive foliage is chalky blue-green in color and has spines on the petiole. Very showy flower inflorescences are creamy yellow, extend 10-12 ft. long, and occur in mid-summer.

This species is quite rare in nature and is restricted to several small canyons and desert slope areas of northwestern Baja California. It has always been a popular accent element in landscape plantings due to its distinctive flower and foliage character. It is often used as a focal plant and entry accent in containers and raised planters. It prefers full sun, well drained soils, and periodic deep watering. It grows well in coastal, inland, valley, and all desert regions. Plates 178 - 179.

178. Brahea armata

179. Brahea armata

Brahea edulis
(Erythea edulis)
Guadalupe Palm

A medium size fan palm, developing single trunks, and slowly growing to 30 ft. Leaves are medium green in color and have no spines on the petiole. Light yellow flower inflorescences are partially hidden among leaf bases and occur in late spring to early summer; large amounts of orange fruit are occasionally produced.

This species is native to rocky ledges at the north end of Guadalupe Island, off of western Mexico. It often is used as a small accent plant and as an understory to taller *Washingtonia* palms in commercial landscapes. It is not as hazardous as other species since there are no spines on the fronds, and its size makes it much more suited to fit residential scale gardens. Plates 180 - 181.

180. Brahea edulis

181. Brahea edulis

Broussonetia papyrifera
Paper Mulberry
Moraceae

A deciduous tree of medium size, 30-40 ft. high, 25-40 ft. wide. Hard, papery foliage is comprised of variable heart-shaped, deeply lobed leaves. Leaves are dull green above, silvery grey and tomentose below. Noticeable flowering catkins occur in early spring.

This tree comes from temperate deciduous forests on foothills and plains from east Asia to central China. It is highly adapted to long, cold winters and many types of soils, including clayey and calcareous. In western landscapes, it has proven to be among the most adaptable and tolerant trees for difficult conditions in high desert, interior valley, and warm inland regions. It has been widely used as a fast growing shade tree around homesteads and in rural communities where landscapes are seldom cared for. It accepts any amount of water and can survive in most areas with natural rainfall and periodic watering. Young plants develop quickly and often out compete and crowd out other plants. Plate 182.

182. Broussonetia papyrifera

Buddleia marrubiifolia
Woolly Butterfly Bush
Loganiaceae

A small evergreen shrub, 3-4 ft. high and as wide. Foliage is comprised of distinctive grey leaves that have serrated margins; colorful yellow to orange flower heads occur in spring.

Woolly butterfly bush is a member of a diverse group of evergreen and deciduous shrubs that includes about 100 species. The most popular species come from temperate climates of Asia, prefer regular moisture, and produce colorful flower spikes during spring. In contrast, this species is native to low desert regions of Texas and northern Mexico. It inhabits sunny sites on well drained soils and survives long periods of drought stress. It is used principally in low desert regions as a bank and median plant in combination with other desert species. It is sensitive to frost and requires low amounts of supplemental water for best performance. Plates 183 - 184.

183. Buddleia marrubiifolia

184. Buddleia marrubiifolia

Butia capitata
Pindo Palm, Jelly Palm
Palmae

A stout feather palm with a single trunk, slowly reaching 10-20 ft. high. Distinctive foliage is grey-green and recurves downward toward the trunk. Bases of old leaves persist; noticeable inflorescences of reddish flowers occur in spring. Edible fruit grow to 1 1/2 in. dia. and are occasionally produced in large quantities.

Pindo palm is one of 12 species within the genus *Butia* that are native from Brazil to Argentina. This species is the best known, and is widely cultivated for landscape use in western gardens. It comes from central Brazil and northern Argentina, from woodlands and grasslands that have periods of seasonal drought. It grows in all zones, from the coast to interior valleys and in sheltered microclimates within low and intermediate deserts. It shows good tolerance to frost, heat, and aridity, and does best in well drained soils with periodic deep irrigation. Plates 185 - 186.

185. Butia capitata

186. Butia capitata

187. Caesalpinia gilliesii

188. Caesalpinia gilliesii

189. Caesalpinia mexicana

190. Caesalpinia mexicana

191. Caesalpinia pulcherrima

192. Caesalpinia pulcherrima

Caesalpinia
(Poinciana)
Fabaceae

Evergreen and deciduous shrubs and trees that include about 70 species coming from tropical and subtropical regions. Most species in cultivation are used widely as foliage and flowering accent plants in tropical zones, from southern Florida to South America and islands in the Caribbean and Pacific Ocean. Three shrub species are popular flowering accent plants in low desert and warm inland gardens of the Southwest. They are fast growing, prefer well drained soils, and need periodic deep watering. They respond well to summer heat and do not thrive in cool, humid environments along the coastal edge of northern and central California.

Caesalpinia gilliesii
Bird of Paradise Bush

A deciduous shrub mounding 6-8 ft. high, or small tree that can reach 10-12 ft. high. Large, feathery leaves are bipinnately divided; large terminal clusters of showy yellow flowers are accented by long, red stamens. Flowers occur for several months through spring and summer and attract hummingbirds.

This species originally comes from central and western Argentina and Uruguay but has been widely planted and naturalized throughout much of South America and southern Texas. In dry inland and low desert regions of the Southwest, it has proven to be a remarkably durable plant and can survive with low to moderate amounts of supplemental water. It grows best in sandy soils and tolerates alkaline conditions. It often is used in background areas and, when trained as a tree, is nicely suited to small entry and patio spaces. Leaves will drop after periods of frost. Plates 187 - 188.

Caesalpinia mexicana
Mexican Poinciana

A large evergreen shrub or small tree, mounding 15-25 ft. high and as wide. Bipinnately divided leaves have round leaflets; strongly fragrant flowers are deep yellow and showy during mid-spring.

Mexican poinciana is native to northern Mexico, where it grows along washes and slopes in arid regions. It is a handsome flowering shrub that frequently is used as a screen and background plant to enclose garden spaces. Mature plants can be pruned to become a small canopy tree for use in courtyards and patios. Plates 189 - 190.

Caesalpinia pulcherrima
Dwarf Poinciana, Barbados Pride

A deciduous shrub, 6-10 ft. high and as wide. Deep green foliage is bipinnately divided into numerous small leaflets; striking orange and yellow flowers occur in terminal clusters during spring and summer.

This species comes from the West Indies and shows remarkable adaptation to low desert landscapes, even naturalizing in parts of the Sonoran desert of Arizona. It is one of the most colorful flowering accent shrubs for median, courtyard, and background landscapes in both commercial and residential settings. It is easily damaged by frost but regrows quickly to bloom in summer. Plates 191 - 192.

Calliandra
Powder Puff
Fabaceae

A varied group of evergreen and deciduous shrubs or trees including over 150 species. Most types come from tropical regions of South America, however, several come from desert regions of California, Arizona, Texas, and Mexico and are adapted to heat, drought, aridity, and calcareous soils.

Species of *Calliandra* that are indigenous to desert regions have small, bipinnately divided leaves and colorful red to pink flowers. Foliage is largely evergreen but plants become sparse and shed many leaves under drought stress. Flowers occur after winter rains as well as after summer thunderstorms in low and intermediate deserts. The species discussed below are used in residential and commercial landscapes in desert regions, where they prefer well drained soils and low amounts of supplemental water during the summer months.

Calliandra californica
Baja Fairy Duster

A small shrub with a dense branching habit, 3-4 ft. high, 4-5 ft. across. Dull green leaves are divided into many tiny leaflets; numerous, showy purple-red to rose colored flowers cover the plant after rains occur in late spring and fall.

This species is native to sandy washes, flats, and hillsides in the Cape region of Baja California. It is a densely branched shrub that looks best when provided with periodic deep watering. It is useful as an accent and background plant in small scale spaces and among other desert wash and cacti species. Plates 193 - 194.

Calliandra eriophylla
Fairy Duster

A small spreading shrub, 1-3 ft. high, 4-6 ft. wide. Leaves are dull green and pinnately divided into tiny leaflets; colorful pink to rose and white colored flowers occur in summer and fall.

This species is native to many parts of the southwestern deserts, where it is considered to be one of the most important habitat plants for erosion control and for browse and seed value to wildlife. It is common in limestone soils on slopes, hillsides, and drainage washes in high and low desert regions at elevations ranging from 2,000-5,000 ft. In ornamental gardens it prefers well drained soils, full sun, and periodic deep watering. It is often used as a border and rockery plant along dry stream features. Plates 195 - 196.

Calliandra peninsularis

A medium shrub with an open habit, 5-6 ft. high and as wide. Showy red stamens can become 1 in. long and produce the showiest flower character among the various species from southwestern deserts.

This species is native to the Cape region of Baja California where it grows on rocky hillsides and in canyons. It is similar in distribution and character to *C. californica* but becomes a larger plant and produces brighter flower character. It is used as a background, screen, and accent plant in residential and commercial gardens. Plates 197 - 198.

193. **Calliandra californica**

194. **Calliandra californica**

195. **Calliandra eriophylla**

196. **Calliandra eriophylla**

197. **Calliandra peninsularis**

198. **Calliandra peninsularis**

199. Callistemon citrinus

200. Callistemon citrinus

201. Callistemon rigidus

202. Callistemon viminalis

203. Callistemon viminalis

Callistemon
Bottlebrush
Myrtaceae

A diverse group of evergreen shrubs and trees that are known for their bright red flower character and tolerance of many landscape conditions. This genus comes from Australia and includes 25 known species. Most are native to areas of ample rainfall, or to edges of streams and swamps. Several species and numerous cultivars are commonly used in western gardens and have proven to be tolerant of many types of soil, moisture, and exposure conditions. Their best performance occurs in warm, sunny locations, with low to moderate amounts of regular moisture. Chlorosis can occur in iron poor soils; and frost damage can be extensive when temperatures drop below 25° F.

Bottlebrush plants are often used for patio and small scale street trees, as well as shrubs on slopes, screens, and highway plantings. They respond well to pruning; flowers occur on new growth and are valuable to birds for nectar.

Callistemon citrinus
(Callistemon lanceolatus)
Lemon Bottlebrush

A large shrub to small tree, 10-20 ft. tall, 10-15 ft. wide. Pointed leaves grow 3-4 in. long; new growth is reddish, turns medium green when mature. Striking red flowers occur in large brush-like spikes, 4-5 in. long, during early spring and intermittently all year.

Lemon bottlebrush comes from wet, swampy areas in coastal habitats in eastern Australia. It is a highly adaptable plant and is widely used in coastal, inland, and low desert regions, where it is appreciated for its tolerance of sun, heat, wind, and highway conditions. It can be trained as a small, single trunk tree or clipped into a dense hedge and does best with moderate amounts of supplemental water. Several cultivars are available, including compact forms and red-purple flowers. Plates 199 - 200.

Callistemon rigidus
Stiff Bottlebrush

A medium shrub to small tree, 10-15 ft. high, 8-10 ft. wide. Foliage is comprised of stiff, narrow, medium green leaves. Showy deep red flowers occur in spring.

This is a slow growing species that is adapted to both moist and dry conditions. In western gardens, it is used in coastal, inland, valley, and low desert landscapes. It is quite tolerant of heat, aridity, and cold to 20° F. This species is good for bank, background, and screening in difficult areas, where it needs only low amounts of supplemental water and little care. Plate 201.

Callistemon viminalis
Weeping Bottlebrush

A small to medium size tree of narrow and upright habit, 20-30 ft. tall, 10-15 ft. wide. Soft, narrow leaves hang from drooping branches to create a weeping appearance. Red flowers are showy in early to mid-spring.

Weeping bottlebrush comes from stream bank habitats in mild coastal climate regions of eastern Australia where moisture is constantly available. It is a widely adaptable plant in cultivation and is planted in coastal, inland, valley, and low desert regions as a lawn and street tree. It tolerates heat and aridity but prefers regular water. Plates 202 - 203.

Calocedrus decurrens
(Libocedrus decurrens)
Incense Cedar
Cupressaceae

A large coniferous tree, growing upright and columnar, 40-80 ft. high. Foliage is comprised of dark green, scale-like leaves that develop on flat branchlets and is aromatic when crushed. Flowers are insignificant; seeds develop in pairs and are of value to wildlife in late fall.

Incense cedar is native to western states from central Oregon to Baja California. It inhabits mountain slopes in both coastal and inland ranges, with its best development occurring in the central Sierra Nevada on moist, slightly acid, sandy loam soils. In this range, annual precipitation is usually 20 in. and more, but summers are dry, often with less than 1 in. of rainfall per month. Plants that grow in inland ranges and at higher elevations experience winter snow and extended periods of cold temperatures.

Incense cedar is a very handsome western tree. It shows remarkable adaptation to a wide range of conditions and can be grown in ornamental landscapes from coastal to high desert regions. It performs best in areas where it can receive ample winter moisture to help it endure drier summer months. Deep, sandy loam soils produce the best growth. However, this species adapts to clayey and calcareous conditions as well. Over the years, this species has been used for many landscape purposes including street and lawn trees, in parks, and in residential and commercial landscapes. It is slow growing and well suited to civic and institutional landscapes where it can be appreciated for many years after it matures. Young plants grow best with moderate amounts of supplemental water; mature plants do well with low or moderate amounts. This species grows well with other natives including *Cercis occidentalis, Mahonia aquifolium, Ribes speciosum, Heuchera* hybrids, and *Iris douglasiana*. Plates 204 - 207.

204. Calocedrus decurrens

205. Calocedrus decurrens

206. Calocedrus decurrens

207. Calocedrus decurrens

Calocephalus brownii
Cushion Bush
Asteraceae

A small evergreen shrub, growing 1-2 ft. high, spreading 3-4 ft. across, with a dense, mounding habit. Distinctive silvery grey, scale-like leaves cover finely divided branchlets. Conspicuous round-headed flowers are pale yellow and develop above the foliage during late spring.

Cushion bush is native to coastal cliffs and bluffs from South to Western Australia and Tasmania. It grows under full coastal conditions including salt spray, wind, frost, drought, and in calcareous soils.

In western landscapes, this species is used as a striking foliage accent plant and is well suited to rock gardens, banks, and mixed plantings. It requires well drained soils, prefers full sun, and can be lightly pruned to retain shape. It thrives in coastal regions where established plants can withstand considerable drought. Low amounts of supplemental water is recommended when planted in drier, inland locations. Plates 208 - 209.

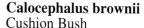

208. Calocephalus brownii

209. Calocephalus brownii, South Australia

210. Carnegiea gigantea

Carnegiea gigantea
Saguaro
Cactaceae

A large tree-like cactus, developing a solitary trunk and several side branches. This is a slow growing species, taking many years to reach 25-50 ft. high. Trunk and branches are deeply ribbed and covered with many sharp spines. Showy white flowers grow 4-5 in. long, occur late spring, are strongly scented, and are followed by large, oval shaped, red fruit.

The saguaro is the only species of this genus and is one of the most distinctive plants of the Sonoran desert in Arizona, Mexico, and parts of California. Within its range, it is a member of several desert plant communities where it associates with species such as *Acacia greggii*, *Cercidium floridum*, *C. microphyllum*, *Fouquieria splendens*, *Larrea tridentata,* and *Olneya tesota*. It is commonly found on slopes and bajadas in coarse, well draining soils, and at intermediate desert zones above the valley floors. It is very slow growing, often taking over 100 years to develop into a branched specimen. It survives extended periods of heat and drought by storing large amounts of water from seasonal rains in its fleshy tissue.

This species is widely appreciated for its habitat and wildlife value throughout its range and is carefully protected from damage or removal without permit to assure its ongoing survival. It is a monumental plant of the intermediate desert zone throughout Arizona, where it has become a highly symbolic image of the Old West. In cultivation, it is a popular specimen and accent plant for low and intermediate desert regions in Arizona, Nevada, and California. Transplanting and follow-up care for this species should be done with the help of experienced people. Plates 210 - 212.

211. Carnegiea gigantea

212. Carnegiea gigantea

Carpenteria californica
Bush Anemone
Saxifragaceae

A medium evergreen shrub, growing to 8 ft. high, 6-8 ft. wide. Leaves are dark green on top, white below, reach 2-4 in. long. Showy clusters of white flowers with yellow centers occur in early spring.

This plant is the only species of this genus. It is native to a restricted area in the foothills of the Sierra Nevada, where it grows on ridges and sunny slopes at the lower limits of snowline. Rainfall ranges 18-20 in. per year and occurs principally in the winter. Extended periods of summer drought and warm summer temperatures are common.

Bush anemone is a very popular and successfully cultivated California native plant. It is grown in ornamental gardens in coastal, inland and valley regions throughout the state. It prefers well drained, slightly acidic soils, and periodic deep watering. Flowering is best when plants are located in mostly sunny areas that have some afternoon shade. *C. c.* 'Elizabeth' is a vigorous selection with deep green leaves, growing to 8 ft. high, 5-6 ft. wide and produces a greater abundance of flowers. Plates 213 - 214.

213. Carpenteria californica

214. Carpenteria californica

Carpobrotus

(Mesembryanthemum)

Ice Plant

Aizoaceae

A small group of succulents including some 29 species that come from many regions of the world including Africa, Australia, and the west coast of North and South America. These plants are characterized by fleshy, angular stems and bright colorful flowers. Two species and various hybrids are common in western gardens where they are best suited to coastal conditions. However, they have proven to be strong growers in frost free inland and low desert areas. Over the years, they have been used extensively for large areas including bank and slope plantings along highways and in housing developments. In recent years, these plants have become widely infested with several species of scale, causing death to large areas within existing plantings. Both chemical and biological methods of control have been investigated and provide a partial control to this problem. But, it is still common to find large slope and highway plantings with scale problems.

Carpobrotus species and hybrids are quick to root from cuttings and grow very quickly to cover the soil. Care should be taken to avoid planting on steep slopes as this is a shallow rooted and heavy ground cover. It can contribute to surface slope failure on steep slopes, particularly when excessive irrigation or rainfall create saturated conditions. Plates 215 - 216.

Carpobrotus chilensis

A species native to the west coast of Oregon, California, and Baja California. It grows on bluffs and sand dunes and has straight 3-sided foliage to 2 in. long. Showy red-purple flowers occur in the summer.

Carpobrotus edulis

Native to South Africa, it has curved foliage to 4-5 in. long and produces showy yellow to rose colored flowers in summer. This species has become widely naturalized throughout coastal edges of California where it is considered to be an invasive exotic plant. Plate 217.

Cassia

Senna

Fabaceae

Cassia is a very large genus of evergreen and deciduous plants that contains over 500 species, mostly of tropical and subtropical origin. A number of tree and shrub species are grown in western gardens where they are appreciated for their showy yellow flower character. Species that are valued for drought tolerance are evergreen shrub types that mostly come from warm and dry areas of Australia. They grow on slopes, ridges, and ravines in foothills and are well adapted to calcareous soils.

Australian cassias are widely used as foliage and flowering accent shrubs in low and intermediate desert regions of the Southwest. They can also survive in some parts of the high desert if they are protected from frosts below 28° F. They are often combined with such species as *Agave deserti, Opuntia* species, *Cercidium floridum, Fouquieria splendens, Acacia stenophylla,* and *Myoporum parvifolium.* Some species are also successful in coastal and inland gardens, where they prefer warm, sunny loca-

215. Carpobrotus hybrid

216. Carpobrotus hybrid

217. Carpobrotus edulis, Morro Bay, California

218. Cassia artemisioides

219. Cassia artemisioides

220. Cassia nemophila

221. Cassia nemophila

222. Cassia odorata

223. Cassia phyllodinea

224. Cassia phyllodinea

tions. They produce an abundance of yellow flowers in early spring and intermittently all year. They need good drainage conditions and grow well with low amounts of supplemental water. They develop into handsome mounding shapes and can be kept to many sizes by pruning after they flower.

Cassia artemisioides
Feathery Cassia

A rounded to mounding shrub, 3-5 ft. high and as wide. Soft grey-green foliage is finely divided into linear segments. Heavy clusters of clear yellow flowers provide striking color value for many weeks in mid-winter to early spring. Numerous 2-3 in. long seed pods develop and persist for several months.

This species is native to semi-arid interior regions of Australia that are hot and dry and where rainfall rarely exceeds 20 in. Feathery cassia is a popular foliage and flowering accent shrub in coastal, inland, and desert landscapes. It has been the most widely known and cultivated shrub species of *Cassia* for many years. It is tender to frost and needs good drainage when planted in clayey and calcareous soils. Plates 218 - 219.

Cassia nemophila
(Cassia eremophila)
Desert Cassia

A rounded to upright shrub, 5-8 ft. high, 4-6 ft. wide. Medium green leaves are finely divided into linear segments; numerous clusters of showy yellow flowers occur in late winter and early spring.

This species comes from desert regions and plains in central Australia. It has proven to be an excellent choice for desert landscapes, where it tolerates hot, dry conditions, while always looking fresh and green. It has a higher tolerance to cold than *C. artemisioides* and can be used in high desert gardens in areas protected from temperatures below 22° F. Plates 220 - 221.

Cassia odorata

A small spreading shrub, 2-3 ft. high, 4-5 ft. across. Deep green foliage is divided into many leaflets; bright yellow flowers are heaviest in spring and continue intermittently through fall.

This species is a relatively unknown species that is native to the south coast of Australia. In western gardens, it is well suited to coastal areas and other frost free locations. It prefers part to full sun and needs well draining soils. It performs well on banks and slopes and needs low to moderate amounts of supplemental water. Plate 222.

Cassia phyllodinea
Silvery Cassia

A mounding shrub, 3-5 ft. high, 4-6 ft. across. Foliage is comprised of long flattened phyllodes that are silver-grey in color. Showy yellow flowers occur in clusters at the ends of the branches in spring.

This species comes from inland plains of Australia, where it tolerates heat, drought, and seasonal frosts. It grows in sunny locations and has a low tolerance for poor drainage, humidity, or wet areas. Silvery cassia is similar to *C. artemisioide*s, but has a heavier texture due to its bolder leaf structure. It is well suited to low and intermediate desert conditions and can survive in protected areas in high deserts. It often is used in medians, on slopes, and mixed plantings with other desert species. Plates 223 - 224.

Casuarina

She-oak

Casuarinaceae

A unique group of evergreen trees and shrubs that are characterized by a wispy, pine-like appearance. Leaves do not exist; photosynthesis occurs on long, thin, green branchlets. Flowers and seed cones are inconspicuous. Some 40 species are currently known, most coming from Australia. Three tree species are currently used in western landscapes.

Most species are fast growing, prefer well draining soils, and tolerate ample amounts of water. However, they easily adapt to many types of dry and arid areas with little care and support. Certain species are best suited to coastal habitats, others tolerate inland valleys and low desert conditions. These plants are often seen in rural and agricultural landscapes where they tolerate neglect, frost, and soils contaminated by livestock waste.

She-oaks can be planted in groves and as individual specimens for accent character in landscapes. They are used as street trees, for tall screens, as windbreaks, and in parks. Young plants often develop upright branching habits; mature trees become more rounded.

Casuarina cunninghamiana

River She-oak, River Oak

A large, upright tree, 50-70 ft. high, 20-30 ft. wide. It is native to banks and edges along fresh water river courses throughout eastern Australia. Soils range from fine textured sand and alluvial gravels to calcareous.

River she-oak is the largest tree in this group and is one of the most widely used species in inland and interior valley landscapes. It shows the greatest tolerance to cool, damp winters and high summer temperatures. It has proven to be a strong performer in tough areas, with low to moderate amounts of supplemental water. Plates 227 - 228.

Casuarina equisetifolia

Horsetail Tree, Beach She-oak

An upright tree, reaching 40-60 ft. high. Horsetail tree is a coastal species that comes from eastern Australia, as well as from around the Pacific in subtropical and tropical climates. It is fully adapted to sandy soils, sea spray, and calcareous and moderately saline soils.

This species is used in many coastal landscapes in subtropical and tropical regions around the world for sand stabilization on beaches, windbreaks, and for street tree and park plantings. Plates 225 - 226.

Casuarina stricta

Drooping She-oak

A highly variable species. Some plants grow upright to 45 ft. high or become more rounded in shape to 35 ft. high with a drooping character. This species is native to coastal zones of southeast Australia, where it tolerates salt spray, calcareous and saline soil conditions, and wind. It is one of the climax species on coastal sands and is associated with *Leptospermum laevigatum*. In drier inland sites, it grows as an understory to *Eucalyptus leucoxylon*.

In western gardens, this species shows good adaptation to coastal, interior valley, and low desert conditions. Its tolerance of heat and aridity is impressive, as is its capability to survive with low to moderate amounts of supplemental water. Plate 229.

225. Casuarina equisetifolia

226. Casuarina equisetifolia, Oahu, Hawaii

227. Casuarina cunninghamiana

228. Casuarina cunninghamiana

229. Casuarina stricta, southern Australia

Ceanothus
Wild Lilac, California Lilac
Rhamnaceae

Introduction:

A diverse group of evergreen shrubs and trees from North America. Of the 50 to 60 species known to exist, more than 40 are native to California and adjacent states. Species come from coastal as well as inland regions throughout the West. They hybridize easily in nature and in cultivation which has led to many cultivated varieties and selections for landscape use.

California lilacs are among the most popular western native plants and are widely appreciated for their many forms and profuse flowering character. Most species come from foothill settings and are found within coastal sage, chaparral, oak woodland, and yellow pine forest plant communities. They provide excellent habitat value for wildlife by providing shelter, nectar, and seeds. They are also a key group of plants that help to improve soil fertility in natural areas by fixing nitrogen.

Character:

California lilacs vary greatly in form and size, from low and spreading to tall and upright. Botanists have recognized two distinct sections within this plant group, the *Euceanothus* and the *Cerastes*. The first group, *Euceanothus*, typically has larger leaves that alternate on stems and often grow more upright and to larger sizes. Leaves are typically a rich forest green with a shiny upper surface. Species within the *Cerastes* group have smaller, thicker leaves, opposite on stems, and frequently grow into mounding and spreading forms. Plants within this group are often better adapted to heat and drought stress after they are established.

Wild lilacs are best known for their showy flowering character. Individual flowers are tiny, but they are grouped into round or plume-like clusters and often cover the entire plant. Flower colors range from white, lilac, or purple, to pale and deep blue. They are often fragrant and useful to bees for honey production. Flowering begins in some species in late winter and occurs for others in early to late spring.

Habitat and Culture:

Species and cultivars of *Ceanothus* most commonly found in nurseries come from coastal regions throughout California. These plants often grow on slightly acidic, well drained soils, and can endure coastal sun, heat, and drought. When used in garden plantings, they can easily survive with low amounts of supplemental water. Overwatering, in combination with heavier soils and poor drainage, often leads to early deaths due to root rot conditions. These plants also prefer some protection from the intense heat and dryness that occurs in inland areas of southern California.

Wild lilacs are established best by planting them from small container sizes in the late fall through early winter. Winter rains are often enough to sustain new plants during the first six months of establishment. Supplemental water can be provided in the summer months, but should be applied at intervals that let the soil dry out between applications. Estab-

230. **Ceanothus griseus var. horizontalis (foreground) Point Lobos State Reserve, California**

lished plants can survive with little or no supplemental water.

Uses and Considerations:

Wild lilacs are used as ground covers, bank plantings, and for background and flowering accent elements. Many types are very fast growing and provide flowering color character within the first 1-2 years of growth. Experience also shows that most types are relatively short lived. The best value and character occurs within the first ten years; older plants may then need to be replaced. Quick growth rates and uncertain long term performance, lead some to use *Ceanothus* more for the initial establishment of garden character, while providing slower growing species time to mature.

Low growing forms suited to ground cover uses include *C. gloriosus* & cultivars, *C. griseus* varieties, *C.* 'Joyce Coulter', and *C. maritimus* & cultivars. Mounding forms suited to slopes and mixed shrub plantings include *C.* 'Concha', *C.* 'Dark Star', *C. griseus* 'Louis Edmunds', *C. impressus*, *C.* 'Julia Phelps', and *C. thyrsiflorus* & cultivars. Upright forms suited to screening and pruning into small trees include *C. arboreus* and *C.* 'Ray Hartman'.

Associated Plantings:

California lilacs are most successful when used in combination with other natives. They require well drained soils, limited summer water, and prefer sunny locations. They grow well with many plants including *Lyonothamnus floribundus* var. *asplenifolius*, *Quercus agrifolia*, *Heteromeles arbutifolia*, *Mahonia aquifolium* & cultivars, *Fremontodendron* cultivars, and *Cercis occidentalis*. A number of native annuals and perennials also combine well including *Eschscholzia californica*, *Lupinus* species, *Sisyrinchium bellum*, and *Penstemon* species.

Helpful References:

Munz, Philip A. A Flora of Southern California. Berkeley: University of California Press, 1974.

Lenz, Lee W. and John Dourley. California Native Trees and Shrubs. Claremont: Rancho Santa Ana Botanic Garden, 1981.

Schmidt, Marjorie G. Growing California Native Plants. Berkeley: University of California Press, 1980.

McMinn, Howard E. An Illustrated Manual of California Shrubs. Berkeley: University of California Press, 1974.

Ceanothus arboreus
Island Ceanothus, Catalina Ceanothus

A large evergreen shrub to small tree, 15-25 ft. high, 12-15 ft. wide, usually developing a single trunk. Large leaves, to 3 in. long, have three distinct veins and are glossy dark green above, whitish below. Showy pale blue flowers occur in large 4-6 in. long clusters and produce a noticeable musky fragrance.

Island ceanothus is a member of the *Euceanothus* group that occurs naturally on the coastal islands of California including Santa Rosa, Santa Catalina, and Santa Cruz. It grows in well drained soils on slopes within the island chaparral plant community.

Island ceanothus is the largest growing species of *Ceanothus*, as well as produces the largest leaves and flower clusters that are valued for ornamental character. It grows very fast and works well in background, slope, and screen planting situations. It can also be trained into a small tree. Well drained soils are preferred; regular summer water should be avoided. Plants grow and perform better in partial shade when used in warm inland and foothill regions. This species has been used for hybridization to develop other popular cultivars, including *C.* 'Ray Hartman'. Plates 231 - 232.

231. Ceanothus arboreus

232. Ceanothus arboreus   **233. Ceanothus 'Concha'**

Ceanothus 'Concha'

A medium to large mounding shrub, 5-7 ft. high, 6-10 ft. wide. Narrow leaves grow to 1 in. long, are dark glossy green and heavily wrinkled. Very showy flowers are dark cobalt blue, and occur in numerous tight, round clusters.

Ceanothus 'Concha' is one of the most striking flowering accent cultivars for landscape use. It is a seedling hybrid from two members of the *Euceanothus* group, *C. papillosus* var. *roweanus* and *C. impressus*. It produces a very heavy flower display in mid-spring which can last 2-3 weeks. This plant is well suited to slope plantings and in large scale natural plantings around native oaks and pines. It has also shown greater tolerance to heavy soils than many other species, but good drainage and care with summer watering is still advised. Plates 233 - 234.

234. Ceanothus 'Concha'

Ceanothus 'Dark Star'

A mounding shrub with a stiff branching habit, growing 4-6 ft. high, and 5-6 ft. wide. Plants develop an upright form when young, then become more rounded with age. Leaves are tiny, 1/4 in. to 1/2 in. long, and produce a stiff textural character to the plant. Striking cobalt blue flowers develop in early spring.

Ceanothus 'Dark Star' is often chosen for its fast growth and vibrant flower value. It is among the best California native flowering accent plants for garden use and is well suited to slope and background areas, away from close-up viewing when not in flower. This species often performs best for the 3-5 years, and then can loose its shape or die quickly, particularly if watered too regularly. Plates 235 - 236.

235. Ceanothus 'Dark Star'

236. Ceanothus 'Dark Star'　　　　**237. Ceanothus 'Frosty Blue'**

238. Ceanothus 'Frosty Blue'

Ceanothus 'Frosty Blue'

A medium to large mounding shrub, 8-10 ft. tall, 10-12 ft. across. Leaves are dark glossy green on top, grow to 1/2 in. in size, and have serrated edges. Medium blue flowers with white frosted appearance develop into showy 3-4 in. long clusters in early spring.

Ceanothus 'Frosty Blue' is a seedling hybrid of uncertain origin. It is a large variety that works well as a background and screen plant for garden spaces with room. Its foliage can be sheared, and is appreciated for its rich color and density. It produces prolific numbers of flower clusters for several weeks that are very showy. This variety shows good tolerance of clayey soils, but needs well drained conditions. It is fast growing and performs best for 10-12 years. Plates 237 - 238.

Ceanothus gloriosus
Point Reyes Ceanothus

An evergreen shrub of varying habit, ranging from low and spreading, 12-24 in. high by 6 ft. wide, to a more mounding form, 24-36 in. and taller. Deep green leaves grow to 1 in. in dia., are thick, heavily toothed, and occur on arching branches. Showy flowers are deep blue to purple and grow in large clusters along the branches.

Point Reyes ceanothus is a member of the *Cerastes* group and is native to coastal bluffs and adjacent flats from Point Reyes to Point Arena, California. It occurs naturally within the coastal strand, coastal sage scrub, and closed-cone pine forest plant communities in sandy, well drained soils. This species is quite variable in character throughout its range; plants exposed to coastal winds are more prostrate than plants growing within protective shelter. As a result, numerous forms and seedling hybrids have been discovered and introduced into the trade. These cultivars provide several variations in size, form, and foliage character and include *C. g.* var. *gloriosus*, *C. g.* var. *exaltatus*, *C. g.* var. *exaltatus* 'Emily Brown', and *C. g.* var. *porrectus*. All of these choices are considered excellent bank and slope plants in coastal habitats, particularly within central to northern coastal counties. Well drained soils are essential, as well as partial shade, when planted in warm inland locations of southern California, where these varieties are not considered to be reliably heat or drought tolerant. Plates 239 - 240.

239. Ceanothus gloriosus

240. Ceanothus gloriosus

241. Ceanothus griseus 'Louis Edmunds'

Ceanothus griseus
Carmel Ceanothus

A medium shrub with stiff branching, growing to 8 ft. tall, equal in spread. Handsome rounded leaves are dark glossy green, reach 1-2 in. in size. Showy light to medium blue flowers grow in 1-2 in. long clusters, and occur in late winter to early spring.

Carmel ceanothus is a member of the *Euceanothus* section and comes from the central to northern coast ranges and terraces, from Santa Barbara to Mendocino counties. It grows under many conditions within the northern coastal sage scrub and closed-cone pine forest communities. Interestingly, this upright species is rarely used in landscapes. Instead, there are several naturally occurring varieties and seedling selections that have proven to be very popular due to their many forms and reliability in garden situations. *C. g.* var. *horizontalis* has long been one of the favorite spreading shrubs, reaching 2-3 ft. high and 10-12 across. Flowers form rounded clusters to 1 in., are pale blue, and occur in early to mid-spring. Several selections have been taken from this variety for landscape use

242. Ceanothus griseus 'Louis Edmunds'

243. Ceanothus griseus var. horizontalis

including *C. g. h.* 'Hurricane Point' and *C. g. h.* 'Yankee Point'. All of these prostrate varieties are widely used for slope and bank plantings, as well as for low shrub masses under trees and in large landscape areas. They grow fast, respond well to pruning and prefer well drained conditions, particularly when planted in heavier soils. These plants are excellent performers in full sun in coastal regions. They grow best in partial shade in southern and warm inland locations, and are not considered to be very heat or drought tolerant.

Other varieties of Carmel ceanothus are large shrub forms. These include, *C. g.* 'Louis Edmunds' and *C. g.* 'Santa Ana'. The former is a stiffly branched shrub to 6 ft. tall, and usually spreads 10-15 ft. or larger. The latter selection can also become quite large, over 10 ft. high with a larger spread, and has deep purple-blue flowers. Pruning can be done to maintain these taller selections to desirable heights. Plates 230, 241 - 247.

244. Ceanothus griseus var. horizontalis

245. Ceanothus griseus 'Santa Ana'

246. Ceanothus griseus horizontalis 'Yankee Point'

247. Ceanothus griseus horizontalis 'Yankee Point'

Ceanothus impressus
Santa Barbara Ceanothus

A densely branched shrub, growing 6-10 ft. high with an equal spread. Small round leaves are dark green, very wrinkled, and occur on rigid branches. Flowers are deep blue and develop in ball-like clusters, 1 in. dia., for good ornamental character during the early spring.

Santa Barbara ceanothus comes from the coastal foothills and chaparral plant communities in sporadic populations between Santa Barbara and San Luis Obispo counties. It is a member of the *Euceanothus* section and grows naturally on sandy soils and sandstone hills and is adapted to extended periods of drought. This species is quite sensitive to garden conditions, requiring well drained soils and little or no summer water. It is well suited to slope and background areas that are adjacent to natural landscape open spaces. Plates 248 - 249.

248. Ceanothus impressus

249. Ceanothus impressus

250. Ceanothus 'Joyce Coulter'

Ceanothus 'Joyce Coulter'

A medium to large mounding shrub growing 3-5 ft. high, 8-10 ft. across. Leaves are medium to dark green, 1/2 in. wide by 1 1/2 in. long, and are quite wrinkled. Medium blue flower clusters occur in mid-spring.

Ceanothus 'Joyce Coulter' is a hybrid from *C. papillosus roweanus* and *C. thyrsiflorus*, both members of the *Euceanothus* group. This cultivar is very useful as a spreading ground cover and bank plant, where it provides generous flower value and handsome foliage character. It also shows a high tolerance to garden moisture and heavy soils, although well drained conditions are still recommended. Plants prefer partial shade in warm inland locations. Plates 250 - 251.

251. Ceanothus 'Joyce Coulter'

Ceanothus 'Julia Phelps'

A densely branched shrub that develops into a mounded shape, 5-6 ft. tall, 6-8 ft. across. Leaves are small, to 1/2 in. long, heavily wrinkled, and attach to numerous intertwining branches. Numerous dark purple-blue flowers in 1 in. rounded clusters cover the plant for a very showy display in mid-spring.

Ceanothus 'Julia Phelps' is a hybrid of uncertain origin. Part of its parentage appears to be *C. impressus,* where it reflects the small leaf size and rich flower character. Due to its large size, stiff foliage, and branch habit; this plant is well suited for background, screen, and slope planting purposes. It grows in both coastal and inland locations and in all cases requires good drainage. This variety shows less garden tolerance than other cultivars. Plates 252 - 253.

252. Ceanothus 'Julia Phelps'

253. Ceanothus 'Julia Phelps'

254. Ceanothus maritimus 'Popcorn'

Ceanothus maritimus
Maritime Ceanothus

A low spreading shrub, 1-3 ft. tall, reaching 5-6 ft. across. Small, thick leaves, have 1-3 teeth, are dark shiny green above, and pale white below. Pale lavender-blue flowers occur in showy brush-like clusters along stems from mid-winter to early spring.

Maritime ceanothus comes from coastal areas in San Luis Obispo County. It is a member of the *Cerastes* section and is a species that is highly variable in its flower color. Several selections and cultivars have been introduced into the trade that provide flower colors from white, rose, and deep blue to purple. These include *C. m.* 'Frosty Dawn', *C. m.* 'Point Sierra', *C. m.* 'Popcorn', and others.

Maritime ceanothus and selections can be used as bank and rock garden plants and can be managed as a ground cover in coastal landscapes. Partial shade is recommended when used in warm inland locations, where this group is not considered to have long term tolerance of heat and drought. The small heavy foliage and branching habit is similar to *Cotoneaster dammeri.* Plates 254 - 255.

255. Ceanothus maritimus

Ceanothus 'Ray Hartman'

A large mounding shrub, to 15 ft. tall, 10-15 ft. across. Leaves are large, 1-2 in. long, and dark glossy green. Large plumes of medium blue flowers create a striking display in early spring.

Ceanothus 'Ray Hartman' is a hybrid between *C. griseus* and *C. arboreus*, both members of the *Euceanothus* group. It is widely recognized for its handsome foliage and heavy flower production. It is a vigorous grower that can be trained into a small tree, as well as be used for specimen, screen, and in slope plantings. It shows good tolerance to heat and full sun in warmer, inland locations. Established plants need only periodic deep watering and are considered to be moderately drought tolerant. Plates 256 - 257.

256. Ceanothus 'Ray Hartman'

257. Ceanothus 'Ray Hartman'

258. Ceanothus rigidus 'Snowball'

Ceanothus rigidus
Monterey Ceanothus

A stiffly branched shrub, growing to 4 ft. tall and as wide. Leaves are small, to 1/2 in. long, and dark green. Flowers are bright blue to purple and occur in early spring.

Monterey ceanothus comes from the sandy flats and slopes of Monterey Bay and is a member of the *Cerastes* section. This species is not often used for ornamental landscapes, instead a white flowering variety was discovered and has been successfully introduced into the trade. *C. rigidus* 'Snowball' is a compact mounding shrub, 3-4 ft. tall, that produces a dense layer of white flower clusters in early spring. This selection is best adapted to coastal locations, in well drained soils, and with restricted summer water. It is useful as a bank and background plant, where it provides seasonal flower value. Plates 258-259.

259. Ceanothus rigidus 'Snowball'

Ceanothus thyrsiflorus
Blue Blossom

A large shrub to small tree with upright branching, growing to 20 ft. tall. Leaves are large, to 2 in. long, are dark green, and have three prominent veins. Showy flowers range in color from blue to white and occur in 3 in. large clusters in mid to late spring.

Blue blossom ceanothus comes from the foothills of the outer coast ranges from Santa Barbara County north into Oregon. In drier regions, it is found within protected canyons; in cooler and moister regions it grows within woodland forests. This species is a member of the *Euceanothus* section and is noted for its rich foliage character and large flower clusters.

This species is used for screen and background plantings in large spaces and on slopes. Several selections have been introduced for landscape use including *C. t.* 'Skylark', a compact form, 3-6 ft. tall, with blue flowers and *C. t.* 'Snow Flurry', which grows 8-10 ft. high and produces an abundance of large, white flower clusters. This species and its varieties are not very tolerant of heat and drought conditions when used in warmer inland regions of southern California. Plates 260-262.

260. **Ceanothus thyrsiflorus 'Snow flurry'**

261. **Ceanothus thyrsiflorus 'Skylark'**

262. **Ceanothus thyrsiflorus 'Snow Flurry'**

263. **Ceanothus 'Wheeler Canyon'**

264. **Ceanothus 'Wheeler Canyon'**

Ceanothus 'Wheeler Canyon'

A medium shrub, growing 5-6 ft. tall and as wide. Heavily veined leaves are narrow, to 1 in. long, and dark glossy green. Showy flowers are deep blue and occur in 1-2 in. long clusters at the ends of branches in early spring.

Ceanothus 'Wheeler Canyon' is a selection from *C. papillosus* var. *roweanus* taken from the south coast in Ventura County. It has handsome deep green foliage character and produces intense flower color for ornamental use in both coastal and inland locations. It is useful on slopes and for accent and understory plantings in light shade. It needs well drained soils and periodic deep watering to offset the heat and drought in inland locations. Plates 263 - 264.

Cedrus
Cedar
Pinaceae

A small group of coniferous trees that includes only four species. Cedars are known for their stately character and large pyramidal shapes, and are highly popular for landscape use throughout the world. They perform best in deep, well drained soils, rich in nutrients, and with regular moisture. In these conditions, they grow relatively fast, become monumental in size, and live for hundreds of years. Fortunately, these plants show wide tolerance of many types of climate and soil conditions and are widely grown throughout the western states. They are highly suited to valley conditions, yet can be successfully grown in coastal areas, as well as desert regions. In drier regions, they can do well with low amounts of supplemental water once established and are quite tolerant of heat and aridity.

Cedrus atlantica
Atlas Cedar

An upright tree growing slowly to 50-70 ft. high. Deep green needles are stiff, short, and held in tight clusters on the stems. Branches on this species grow outward and upward, and do not droop at the tips.

This species of cedar is native to foothill slopes of the Atlas mountains in North Africa. It grows at elevations ranging from 4,500-7,200 ft. within a semi-Mediterranean climate that is characterized by cool, moist winters, including some snow, and warm, dry summers.

This species with green needles is frequently used in Pacific Northwest landscapes and in other cool temperate regions. However, it is not as widely planted as the grey foliaged form, *C. a.* 'Glauca', sometimes called the blue atlas cedar, that is perhaps the most popular conifer planted for ornamental use today. These trees are popular choices for parks, commercial spaces, and as accent specimens. Other cultivated varieties exist that provide weeping shapes and foliage color choices. These include *C. a.* 'Aurea' that has a yellow foliage cast; *C. a.* 'Compacta', a denser and slower growing cultivar; *C. a.* 'Fastigiata' that grows into narrow, columnar forms; and *C. a.* 'Pendula', a form with drooping branchlets. All species and cultivars perform best in rich, well drained soils and with regular moisture. Plants that are grown in drier areas and in poorer soils will grow less quickly and to smaller sizes. However, established plants show good resistance to drought and can survive with low amounts of supplemental water. Plates 265 - 267.

265. Cedrus atlantica, Seattle, Washington

266. Cedrus atlantica 'Glauca'

267. Cedrus atlantica 'Glauca', Ontario, California

268. Cedrus deodara

269. Cedrus deodara, left, C. a. 'Glauca', right

Cedrus deodara
Deodar Cedar

A large tree developing a pyramidal form, 60-80 ft. and higher. Needles are dull green; tips of branches and the top of tree droop to produce a graceful habit.

This species is native to the foothills of the western Himalayas of Asia at elevations ranging from 4,000-10,000 ft. It is naturally adapted to cool and wet winters, including snow, where annual precipitation reaches 70 inches. Summers are warm and have periodic rain and high humidity. Some trees also grow at lower elevations in warmer and drier areas, where precipitation is closer to 20 inches. In its native habitat, the deodar cedar grows with species of spruce, fir, and pine.

In western regions, the deodar cedar is one of the most frequently used tree species in all planting zones, from the coast to inland valleys and deserts. This is a very graceful tree with soft textural character, that can reach monumental proportions in large spaces. It is well suited to parks, civic spaces, wide median plantings, and large garden areas. A number of cultivated varieties also exist in the trade that offer different foliage color, growth habits and hardiness to cold. These include *C. d.* 'Aurea', with golden tipped foliage; *C. d.* 'Pendula', a slow growing and weeping form; *C. d.* 'Viridis' that has deeper green foliage; and others. Plates 268 - 270.

270. Cedrus deodara, Sacramento, California

Centaurea

Asteraceae

A large and complex group of annuals, biennials, and perennials that include an estimated 400-500 species. Only a few species are cultivated for use in ornamental gardens. These species are perennials and are appreciated for their flower and foliage character. Several types provide striking grey or white foliage character that make them popular choices as accent plants in mixed gardens and along borders. They tolerate many types of soil, prefer full sun, and need only low to moderate amounts of supplemental water.

Centaurea cineraria

(Centaurea candidissima)

Dusty Miller

A low mounding perennial, growing 12-15 in. high, with striking white foliage character. Leaves grow to 12 in. long, are soft, velvety, and divided into many rounded lobes. Showy yellow flower heads occur in late spring to early summer. This is one of the most popular choices for ornamental use in western regions. It comes from southern Europe, on limestone cliffs, and can be grown as an annual or perennial. Plates 271 - 272.

Centaurea gymnocarpa

Velvet Centaurea

A loosely branched and sprawing plant that grows 2-3 ft. high, 2-4 ft. wide. Leaves are white, felt-like, and divided into narrow segments; numerous clusters of purple flowers occur in mid-spring. This species is considered to be the most drought tolerant once established. Plate 273.

Centranthus ruber

(Valeriana rubra)

Red Valerian, Jupiter's Beard

Valerianaceae

A herbaceous perennial growing 2-3 ft. high. Foliage is blue-green; showy flowers are red to pink and occur for long periods throughout the summer. *C. r.* 'Albus' is a white flowering variety.

This plant is native to the Mediterranean region where it grows on rocky slopes and in disturbed areas. In western gardens, it has proven to be highly adaptable to any type of soil and either moist or dry conditions. It responds quickly to winter rains and starts to flower in spring and summer as temperatures rise and soils dry out. It easily survives drought by shedding its foliage under stress and producing seeds to establish new plants. As a result, it has become naturalized in both moist and dry habitats in western states and should be avoided in natural areas. In urban gardens, this plant is well suited to background borders, in perennial groupings, and on banks and rocky slopes. Flowering can be extended and seed heads avoided if spent flowers are cut off. Plates 274 - 275.

271. **Centaurea cineraria**

272. **Centaurea cineraria**

273. **Centaurea gymnocarpa**

274. **Centranthus ruber**

275. **Centranthus ruber**

Cephalophyllum 'Red Spike'
Red Spike Iceplant
Aizoaceae

A small clumping succulent growing 4-6 in. high, eventually spreading 12-15 in. in diameter. Fleshy leaves are medium green and cylindrical in shape; showy magenta flowers occur in mid-winter through spring.

Red spike iceplant is a perennial succulent that is best adapted to mild coastal and frost free inland regions. There are more than 70 species of *Cephalophyllum*, most come from the Cape region of South Africa. These plants do not like extreme heat or frost and prefer well drained soils and limited summer water. This variety will grow with good character for 3-4 years before some dieback starts to occur. New plants are easily started from cuttings and can be used to replenish a planting. It is most commonly used in small spaces such as rock gardens and narrow planters with other succulents and provides rich winter flower color. Plates 276 - 277.

276. Cephalophyllum 'Red Spike'

277. Cephalophyllum 'Red Spike'

278. Ceratonia siliqua

279. Ceratonia siliqua

Ceratonia siliqua
Carob Tree, St. John's Bread
Fabaceae

A medium to large evergreen tree, 25-50 ft. high and as wide. Foliage is comprised of dark green, leathery leaves that are divided into 4-10 round leaflets. Flowers occur in late spring and are pungent. Long, bean-like fruit develop over summer and mature into dark brown pods, 5-7 in. long. This fruit contains a high percentage of sugar and protein which is a valuable source for food products.

The carob tree is native to the Mediterranean region where it grows to largest sizes and in greatest numbers on rocky soils and in foot-hills near the coast. It is well adapted to warm and dry regions in the west, from the coast to inland valleys and low deserts. It prefers full sun, low amounts of supplemental water, and requires good drainage. With age, it develops a dense and broad canopy that produces deep shade. It is a tough and durable plant that has often been used along highways as a large shrub, or as a shade tree in parking lots and background areas where it is often neglected. In more ornamental landscape settings, the flower odor and leaf and pod litter can become a nuisance. Plates 278 - 280.

280. Ceratonia siliqua

Cercidium

Palo Verde

Fabaceae

A small group of deciduous shrubs and trees that are principally native to the desert regions of the southwest U.S., Mexico, and Central America. Of the 10 species that are known, three are commonly found in landscape use. These plants are well known for their green bark, leafless stems, and showy yellow flowers. They commonly grow along washes and in canyons in deep, sandy soil, where they can develop extensive root systems to draw from groundwater supplies. They produce an abundance of flowers in early spring and then will drop their leaves during periods of heat and drought stress. Branches are armed with spines; flowers and seed are of value to birds.

Species of palo verde are most often used in low and high desert regions as shade trees and courtyard specimens. They are combined with associated desert species such as *Carnegiea gigantea*, *Fouquieria splendens*, *Larrea tridentata*, *Pithecellobium flexicaule*, and *Yucca elata*. Understory shrubs often include *Encelia farinosa*, *Cassia* species, *Dalea greggii*, *Dasylirion* species, *Hesperaloe parviflora*, *Leucophyllum* species, and *Salvia greggii*. They prefer sandy, well drained soils and periodic deep watering. These plants grow faster and to larger sizes when provided with regular water.

281. Cercidium floridum

282. Cercidium floridum

283. Cercidium floridum, Phoenix, Arizona

284. Cercidium microphyllum, The Arizona-Sonora Desert Museum, Tucson, Arizona

285. Cercidium microphyllum

286. Cercidium praecox

287. Cercidium praecox, The Desert Botanical Gardens, Phoenix, Arizona

Cercidium floridum
Blue Palo Verde

A medium deciduous tree, 25-30 ft. high, with an equal spread. Foliage is comprised of bipinnately divided leaves; both stems and leaflets are blue-green. Colorful bright yellow flowers occur in large numbers in March and April.

This species is native to many desert regions of the Southwest, particularly Arizona and Mexico. It is frequently established along washes and on plains where it can establish deep roots to obtain underground moisture. This species is one of the most attractive desert trees and is widely planted in residential and commercial landscapes. It grows fast and can be managed as a single or multi-trunk specimen and canopy tree. Plates 281 - 283.

Cercidium microphyllum
Foothill Palo Verde, Littleleaf Palo Verde

A large shrub to small tree, 15-25 ft. high and as wide. Leaves are pale green and divided into 4-7 pairs of tiny leaflets. Flowers are pale yellow and white and occur in early spring.

Foothill palo verde is another species that is widely established in desert areas of the Southwest. It inhabits slopes, rocky hillsides, alluvial fans, and dry foothills where it tolerates heat, aridity, and extended periods of drought. This species is adapted to drier conditions than *C. floridum* or *C. praecox*. As a result, it is often smaller and more of a shrub when established on slopes and away from washes and canyons where groundwater can be obtained. It is often used as a slope and screen plant, and with age can be pruned to form a small, multi-trunk accent tree. Plates 284 - 285.

Cercidium praecox
Sonoran Palo Verde, Palo Brea

A medium size deciduous tree, 20-25 ft. high and as wide. Trunks and branches are very distinctive and attractive due to their bright chartreuse green bark. Medium green leaves are bipinnately divided into 1-2 pairs of leaflets; very colorful bright yellow flowers occur in early spring.

This species comes from Baja California, central Mexico, and Venezuela to Peru on desert slopes and plains. It grows best in areas where it can obtain deep ground moisture. This is a very handsome plant that provides striking bark and flower character for use in courtyards and as a specimen element and is becoming one of the most popular choices for use in low desert landscapes. Plates 286 - 287.

Cercis

Redbud

Fabaceae

A small group of deciduous shrubs or trees including seven species that come from North America, Europe, and Asia. These attractive plants are characterized by rounded to heart-shaped leaves, showy magenta flowers, and yellow to red foliage color in the fall. Young plants usually develop into many stemmed shrubs, 12-20 feet high and as wide. All species respond easily to pruning to form a single or multiple trunk canopy tree, sometimes attaining a height and spread of 25 feet.

Redbuds typically occur in foothill woodland and forest plant associations in regions having a cool, moist winter season. They grow on slopes in part shade to full sun, often in well developed organic soils. Years of planting experience in western gardens has demonstrated that most species of redbud grow rapidly and are highly adapted to garden conditions. Flowering is more prolific in locations with winter frost, and plants will grow to larger sizes when provided with regular moisture. Most species can be planted with good success in coastal, inland, and valley regions; some tolerate high desert locations. The two species coming from North America are most popular and widespread in landscape use.

Cercis canadensis

Eastern Redbud

A small to medium tree, 25-35 ft. high, 20-25 ft. wide. Leaves are heart-shaped with a pointed tip, medium green, and grow 3-6 in. across. Clusters of showy magenta flowers occur in early spring and are followed by small, bean-type pods.

This species occurs throughout the eastern United States and in southern parts of Ontario, Canada. It frequently grows in hardwood forests as an understory plant in valleys, on slopes, and in sandy loam soils. It is adapted to cold winters, snow, ample moisture, and full sun to partial shade.

Eastern redbud is the largest species of redbud available for landscape use. Its fast growth and tree-like habit make it a good choice for use as a street tree, in patios, and in lawn areas. In western gardens, it performs best in inland and valley regions where winters are longer and cooler. In warmer and more arid zones, it maintains better foliage character when planted within the partial shade of mature landscapes, in well drained loam soils, and with moderate amounts of water. It also tolerates high desert regions if it is protected from extreme heat and high winds. Several cultivated varieties are available that provide other characteristics including *C. c.* 'Forest Pansy' that has deep purple-red foliage, *C. c.* 'Alba' that produces white flowers, and *C. c.* 'Oklahoma' that produces deep red flowers. Plates 288 - 291.

Cercis occidentalis

Western Redbud

A large shrub to small tree, 15-20 ft. high and as wide. Medium green leaves are round, 2-3 in. wide, and heart-shaped at the base. Showy clusters of pea-shaped flowers occur in early spring and range in color from light to deep magenta, or sometimes white. Numerous seed-pods mature through spring and summer and persist while the plant is deciduous in winter.

288. **Cercis canadensis**

289. **Cercis canadensis 'Forest Pansy'**

290. **Cercis canadensis**

291. **Cercis canadensis**

292. **Cercis occidentalis**

293. **Cercis occidentalis, Sierra Nevada**

294. Cercis occidentalis

This species is native to several western states, ranging from coastal foothills of California to inland regions of Arizona and Utah. In California, it is found in woodland and chaparral plant communities of the northern coastal ranges, the Sierra Nevada, and even parts of the desert slopes of the Laguna and Cuyamaca mountains in southern California. Within this range, western redbuds grow under many conditions. Some plants establish on dry slopes with sunny exposures, others grow in canyons and on north facing exposures that are cooler, moister, and shady.

Western redbud is one of the most popular western native species for landscape use. Typically, it develops as a many branched shrub and is often planted in garden locations where it can be featured as a specimen element. It also can be pruned to form a multiple trunk canopy tree or periodically is trained as a single trunk tree for patio and street tree uses. It grows well in many types of soil, including clayey, and in sun to partial shade. With its tolerance of varying moisture conditions, it can be grown near or in lawns with regular moisture, or on slopes and hillsides where it receives low amounts of supplemental water. In warmer and drier environments, this species prefers protection from extreme heat and sun with monthly deep watering in the summer. A number of colorful native shrubs and perennials are often planted as an understory to redbud including *Iris douglasiana* cultivars, *Heuchera* cultivars, *Ribes speciosum*, *Mahonia repens,* and prostrate varieties of *Arctostaphylos* and *Ceanothus*. Plates 292 - 294.

Cereus
Cactaceae

A diverse group of succulents that often reach tree-like sizes, ranging from 10-40 ft. high. Approximately 36 species are known and are native to the West Indies and the eastern parts of South America. They develop thick fleshy stems that often have numerous ribs and spines. Most species produce large, white flowers that open at night; sometimes they are lightly scented. These plants thrive in warm coastal and inland regions, where they are highly adapted to heat and drought but are quite tender to frost. They require good drainage, light soils, and can be grown in containers for many years. Species and varieties of *Cereus* are best available through specialty growers and nurseries.

Cereus peruvianus
Peruvian Apple

This is one of the most popular species that can reach 12-18 ft. high, and develop striking landscape specimen character with age. A cultivar, *C. p.* 'Monstrosus', grows with heavily twisted and knobby stems for unique effects. Plates 295 - 296.

295. Cereus peruvianus

296. Cereus peruvianus

Chamaerops humilis
Mediterranean Fan Palm
Palmae

A clumping fan palm that is the only member of the genus *Chamaerops*. It is native to the Mediterranean region, where it inhabits coastal cliffs and foothills to 3,300 ft. elevation, as well as sandy seashores. In this range, it has adapted to strong winds, salt spray, and even periodic occurrences of snow. Soils are often poor, rocky, and typically well drained. Most rainfall occurs in the winter, ranging from 20-30 in., with extended periods of drought occurring throughout the summer and fall.

The Mediterranean fan palm is perhaps the toughest and most durable of palms. It tolerates cold temperatures below 10° F and summer temperatures above 115° F. It develops numerous trunks from its base and can grow 10-20 ft. high. Leaves are pale green, 2-3 ft. across, and cut in the shape of a fan. The bases of the leaves are covered with many sharp, pointed spines. Flowers are golden yellow and often hidden by the foliage.

This palm is most frequently grown as a specimen plant in raised planters, in containers, and in courtyards. It grows in all regions, from the coast to high deserts. Like most palms, it is capable of absorbing and retaining moisture within its fibrous tissue which it uses to withstand extended periods of heat and drought. Periodic deep watering easily sustains this species. Within its natural habitat, the Mediterranean fan palm grows with *Pinus halepensis, Quercus ilex, Ceratonia siliqua, Cistus* species, *Rosmarinus officinalis*, and *Lavandula* species. Plates 297 - 299.

297. **Chamaerops humilis**

298. **Chamaerops humilis**

299. **Chamaerops humilis, Santa Barbara, California**

300. Chamelaucium uncinatum

301. Chamelaucium uncinatum

302. Cheiranthus 'Bowles Mauve'

303. Cheiranthus 'Bowles Mauve'

304. Cheiranthus 'Bowles Mauve'

Chamelaucium uncinatum
Geraldton Wax Flower
Myrtaceae

A wispy evergreen shrub, 8-10 ft. high, spreading 6-12 ft. wide. Foliage is comprised of small, needle-like leaves; colorful white to rose flowers have five distinct petals and occur during late winter to early spring.

There are 21 species within the genus *Chamelaucium*; all are restricted to the southwestern part of West Australia. Geraldton wax flower comes from coastal and inland areas where it is native to sandy plains, mild temperatures, and extended periods of drought. In western gardens, this species has been planted primarily for its value as a cut flower. These flowers are quite firm and sculptural and develop in loose clusters at the ends of long, flexible branches. It is often planted in background areas and staked or pruned to control the loose foliage habit and stimulate stronger flowering. With age, these plants can develop an interesting multi-branched character. Garden plants need well drained soil, periodic water during the summer, and protection from frost. One variety, *C. u.* 'Vista', has larger, pinker flowers. Plates 300 - 301.

Cheiranthus 'Bowles Mauve'
(Erysimum linifolium 'E. A. Bowles'*)*
Shrubby Wallflower
Brassicaceae

A small, rounded perennial, growing 2-3 ft. high and as wide. Leaves are 1-2 in. long, narrow, and light grey-green. Showy spikes of lavender-purple flowers occur for many weeks through spring.

This colorful perennial has been introduced in recent years to western regions and is becoming a popular flowering accent plant in coastal, inland, and valley gardens. It performs best in full sun, with low to moderate amounts of supplemental water, and can tolerate light frosts. It develops a compact, mounding form and becomes covered with many flower spikes. Light shearing after a flower cycle will help to maintain its shape and renew its flowering. It is often used in perennial gardens with other grey and green foliage plants including *Artemisia* 'Powis Castle', *Achillea taygetea*, *Helianthemum nummularium*, and *Agave attenuata*. Plates 302- 304.

Chilopsis linearis
Desert Willow, Desert Catalpa
Bignoniaceae

A large deciduous shrub to medium tree, ranging in height from 15-40 ft. Leaves are linear, to 5 in. long, and are shed under moisture stress. Colorful trumpet-shaped flowers are white, pink, or purple, with purple markings. These flowers are fragrant, useful for honey production, and occur for several weeks from mid-spring into summer.

Desert willow is native to high and low desert regions, from California to Texas and south into Mexico. It is most commonly found along washes in deep, sandy soil, where it can obtain the greatest benefit from seasonal rainfall. It is deciduous in the winter and in periods of drought stress.

Desert willow is a very adaptable plant for use in desert landscapes. In contrast to many other desert trees, it produces flowers for many weeks in the spring, whereas most species flower for only brief periods. It has a graceful and open foliage habit that is useful for courtyard and lawn settings, where the flowers can be appreciated at close distances. In natural landscapes, it survives with little supplemental water and can be used for habitat and revegetation projects. In garden settings, it performs best and grows to larger sizes when given periodic deep irrigation. It is often used in mini-oasis plantings within courtyards, where its light shade benefits other desert species such as *Ruellia peninsularis, Sphaeralcea ambigua, Justicia spicigera, Penstemon* species, and others. Young plants grow quickly and can benefit from pruning to control their form. Plates 305 - 308.

305. Chilopsis linearis

306. Chilopsis linearis

307. Chilopsis linearis

308. Chilopsis linearis, Palm Desert, California

Chitalpa tashkentensis
Chitalpa
Bignoniaceae

A medium size deciduous tree, growing rapidly 20-30 ft. high, spreading as wide. Foliage is comprised of long, pointed deep green leaves. Leaves grow 4-5 in. long, to 1 in. wide. Trumpet-shaped flowers are pink to white with purple markings and occur in showy clusters in early summer.

Chitalpa is a genus hybrid between *Catalpa bignonioides*, common catalpa, and *Chilopsis linearis*, desert willow. It combines the larger flower size and clusters of the former species, with the linear leaves and desert adaptations of the latter. As a result, this hybrid provides a highly attractive combination of flowers, foliage, and adaptations for landscape gardens. It grows naturally as a large mounding shrub or low branched tree and easily can be shaped into a multi-trunked canopy tree for use in courtyard spaces. It provides a long season of flowers and is briefly deciduous in mild climate regions. It tolerates heavy frost, sun, heat, and does best with moderate amounts of supplemental water. Most landscape specimens are currently being grown in coastal and inland zones, however, it should be well adapted to valley and desert landscapes as well. Two cultivars are currently available including *C. t.* 'Morning Cloud' that produces white flowers with purple markings, and *C. t.* 'Pink Dawn' that produces a soft pink flower cast. Plates 309 - 311.

309. **Chitalpa tashkentensis 'Morning Cloud'**   310. **Chitalpa tashkentensis 'Pink Dawn'**

311. **Chitalpa tashkentensis 'Pink Dawn', Rancho Santa Ana Botanic Garden, Claremont, California**

Cistus
Rockrose
Cistaceae

A diverse group of evergreen shrubs including 17 species that are noted for their bright flower character and tolerance of dry landscape situations. Most species are native to coastlines and inland foothills around the Mediterranean Sea, from southern Spain through the French Riviera, Italy, and into Greece. These habitat conditions are very similar to the coastal sage scrub and coastal chaparral environments of California.

Rockroses exhibit characteristics and adaptations that are typical of plants that have evolved in dry Mediterranean environments. All species respond to winter rains with rapid growth and then flower intensely during early mid-spring through early summer. It is common for these plants to enter a period of inactivity during the dry season of late summer and to shed some leaves while under drought stress. Leaves are heavily textured and often dull green in color. Flowers are bright and colorful and vary from white and pink to purple. Most types have also evolved on poor soils that are low in nutrients and organic humus. They are adapted to calcareous as well as slightly acid soil conditions. Most species are short lived and provide their best value for 5-7 years before they become rank and need replacement.

Numerous species, hybrids, and cultivars of rockrose are in landscape use. Some types are low and spreading, while others are mounding shrubs. Foliage character and flower value are often best in coastal regions where humidity and cooler summer temperatures offset the dry summer season. Some species can tolerate low desert conditions, but should be placed in microclimates that provide relief to extreme heat and aridity. Low to moderate amounts of supplemental water is recommended in most landscape regions; overwatering and poor drainage often lead to rank growth and early deaths. These plants are frequently used on slopes and in mixed shrub plantings. They respond to selective pruning to remove older growth, and can be lightly sheared to maintain their shape and foliage density. Plate 312.

312. **Cistus species and hybrids**

Cistus 'Doris Hibberson'

A medium size mounding shrub, 3-4 ft. tall with an equal spread. Pink to lavender flowers occur in early spring on upright branches that contrast nicely with dull green foliage color. This selection is often used as a background and flowering accent plant on slopes and in mixed garden plantings. It grows well in coastal, inland, and valley regions in full sun and in average soils.

Cistus hybridus
(Cistus corbariensis)
White Rockrose

This selection is a natural hybrid between *C. salviifolius* and *C. populifolius*. It is a mounding shrub, 3-5 ft. high, spreading from 6-8 ft. Numerous clear white flowers with yellow centers cover this plant for several days in mid-spring, receding to intermittent blooms for several weeks.

This hybrid provides some of the most consistent foliage and growth character among rockroses. It also produces a striking show of white flowers in early spring. It is very adaptable to sun; poor soils, including calcareous; low amounts of supplemental water; and periodic frosts. It is very effective on slopes and in mass plantings where it can work as a large scale ground cover. Plate 313.

313. **Cistus hybridus**

314. **Cistus ladanifer**

315. **Cistus purpureus**

316. **Cistus salviifolius**

317. Cistus salviifolius

318. Cistus skanbergii

319. Cistus 'Sunset'

320. Cistus 'Sunset'

Cistus ladanifer
(Cistus ladanifer maculatus)
Crimson-spot Rockrose
This is a tall, upright species, to 5-7 ft. high and as wide. It has long, narrow dark green leaves that are very sticky. Showy white flowers with yellow centers are large to 3 in. across and have a bright crimson spot at the base of the petals. Flowers are of greatest interest when viewed up close.

Crimson-spot rockrose is native to coastal, inland, and foothill environments on thin and slightly acid soils. It often associates with *Lavandula stoechas* and as an understory to *Pinus pinea*. This species is adapted to periods of drought, as well as seasonal frosts. The size and foliage character of this species makes it well suited to slope and background locations. It has proven to be a very tough species when used along roadsides and in neglected areas. Plate 314.

Cistus purpureus
Orchid Rockrose
This hybrid comes from *C. ladanifer* and *C. creticus*. It is a mounding shrub, 3-4 ft. tall and as wide. Leaves are long, dark green, and wrinkled. Flowers are deep orchid purple with a distinctive purple spot at the base of the petals.

Orchid rockrose provides handsome foliage character and a long flowering season. It performs more consistently than most types of *Cistus*, growing with good form, and being relatively long lived. It is often used in commercial and residential landscapes, where it is clipped and can be watered on a regular basis. It accepts many soil conditions, including calcareous, and is tolerant of heat, drought, and aridity. Plate 315.

Cistus salviifolius
Sageleaf Rockrose
A spreading shrub, 18-24 in. high, reaching 5-6 ft. across. Small medium green leaves are heavily textured. Bright white flowers have yellow centers and yellow spots at the base of the petals. These flowers cover the plant for 1-2 weeks in early spring for striking color value.

Sageleaf rockrose is a dense and compact species that can be used as a ground cover and in mixed shrub plantings. This species is well adapted to coastal and inland locations where it provides good character for 3-5 years. It prefers well drained soils and only low amounts of supplemental water. Plates 316 - 317.

Cistus skanbergii
A natural hybrid of *C. parviflorus* and *C. monspeliensis* that develops into a spreading shrub, 18-24 in. high, 3-5 ft. across. Foliage is grey-green and contrasts nicely with its clear pink flowers. Flowers grow to 1 in. across and occur in large numbers in early spring.

This hybrid is known for soft foliage and flower color in landscape plantings. It has a more refined character than other types of rockrose and is better suited to smaller garden spaces. Plate 318.

Cistus 'Sunset'
A low spreading shrub, 12-18 in. high, ranging 3-5 ft. across. Colorful flowers are deep rose with yellow centers. Foliage is dull green and heavily textured.

This hybrid is a popular choice for use as a ground cover and on banks with other drought tolerant plants. It responds well to pruning and maintains good form and foliage character for 4-6 years. Plates 319 - 320.

Cleome isomeris
Bladderpod
Capparaceae

A small to medium evergreen shrub, 3-6 ft. tall and as wide. Foliage is comprised of soft grey-green leaves that are divided into three leaflets. Showy yellow flowers occur in early spring and intermittently during warm months; numerous inflated, green seed pods develop after flowering.

Bladderpod is principally native to the high and low deserts of California and Baja California. It grows to largest sizes in sandy washes where it can receive additional moisture from seasonal rains. In early spring, it adds to the wildflower character of desert regions by becoming completely covered with yellow flowers. In its natural range, it grows in the creosote bush scrub and Joshua tree woodland plant communities and is often found in association with *Larrea tridentata, Chilopsis linearis,* and *Encelia farinosa.* Varieties of bladderpod also grow naturally in coastal and inland foothill regions of southern California and are well adapted to local area slope plantings and restoration projects. Plates 321 - 322.

321. **Cleome isomeris**

322. **Cleome isomeris**

Comarostaphylis diversifolia
Summer Holly
Ericaceae

A medium to large evergreen shrub, slowly growing 6-10 ft. high, 6-8 ft. wide. Leaves are dark green, leathery, have toothed margins, grow 2-3 in. long, and tend to curl to the underside. Showy spikes of urn-shaped flowers are creamy white and occur in mid-spring. Attractive red berries mature in early summer and can persist into fall. Bark on the stems and trunks matures to grey-brown and sheds to reveal reddish new growth.

Summer holly is native to the coastal foothills in San Diego County. It is a member of the chaparral plant community in association with such species as *Quercus dumosa, Ceanothus* species, *Rhamnus crocea, Heteromeles arbutifolia, Trichostema lanatum, Eriogonum fasciculatum*, and *Salvia* species. A larger variety, *C. d.* var. *planifolia* is more widespread and is found on islands off of southern California, and coastal foothills from Santa Barbara to San Diego and to northern Baja California. This variety has leaves that curl under along the margins and is most commonly found in cultivation. It is also a slow growing plant, but it can become a small tree, reaching 12-18 ft. high.

These western natives are often recognized for their attractive foliage, flowers, and fruit characteristics. With age, they can be shaped into a specimen shrub or tree, where the handsome trunk and bark character can be revealed with pruning. They prefer well drained soils, periodic deep watering in the summer, and are well suited to slope and background areas in combination with other natives. Plates 323 - 325.

323. **Comarostaphylis diversifolia**

324. **Comarostaphylis diversifolia**

325. **Comarostaphylis diversifolia var. planifolia**

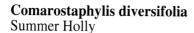

Convolvulus
Convolvulaceae

A large and diverse group of perennials or subshrubs that includes over 225 species. Most types have soft, herbaceous foliage and develop trailing and twining stems. Two species found in landscape use come from the Mediterranean region of Europe and are recognized for their bright flower character and spreading habits. These plants require low to moderate amounts of supplemental water and perform well for 3-4 years before needing replacement.

Convolvulus cneorum
Bush Morning Glory

A small shrub, 2-3 ft. high, spreading 2-4 ft. across. Distinctive silvery foliage is comprised of small, pointed leaves that are covered with numerous soft hairs; showy white flowers with yellow centers occur in early spring and intermittently through summer and fall. This species is native to the Mediterranean region, principally Italy to Greece, where it grows on limestone bluffs near the sea. In western gardens, it does well in full sun and well drained soils in coastal, valley, and low desert regions. Plates 326 - 327.

Convolvulus mauritanicus
Ground Morning Glory

A low growing perennial reaching 1-2 ft. high, spreading 2-3 ft. across. Small dark green leaves are tightly clustered on the stems; colorful light to deep lavender-blue flowers occur from early summer into fall. This species comes from coastal regions of North Africa, and has been widely used in western gardens as a bank, rock garden, and seasonal accent plant. It thrives in coastal and inland zones in full sun and on well drained soils. Plate 328.

Coprosma
Rubiaceae

A large group of evergreen shrubs or small trees, including more than 90 species that are native to New Zealand, Australia, and the Pacific Islands. Most species prefer ample moisture and subtropical temperatures. Several hybrids within this group are used in western regions as spreading ground covers in coastal and adjacent inland areas. They show good tolerance to light or heavy soils, sun to partial shade, and do best with moderate amounts of supplemental water.

Coprosma kirkii

A many branched spreading shrub, 2-3 ft. high, 4-6 ft. across. Foliage is comprised of glossy, medium green leaves that are narrow and grow to 1 in. long. Flowers and fruit are insignificant.

This plant is a natural hybrid between *C. repens* and *C. acerosa*. Both parents come from the North Island of New Zealand, where they grow in sand dune habitats. As a result, this hybrid is well adapted to sandy soils with light salinity, wind, and mild temperatures. In western gardens it grows best in coastal regions and shows sensitivity to frost. It grows with a spreading habit with its branches sweeping outward and upward, and is useful as a ground cover on slopes and banks. A variegated selection also exists, *C. k.* 'Variegata'. Plate 329.

326. Convolvulus cneorum

327. Convolvulus cneorum

328. Convolvulus mauritanicus

329. Coprosma kirkii

330. Coprosma 'Verde Vista'

Coprosma 'Verde Vista'

A low spreading shrub, growing 2-3 ft. high, reaching 6-8 ft. across. Glossy, bright green leaves, are oval, pointed, and grow to 3/4 in. long. Branches mound upward from the center of the plant, then spread outward and lay close to the ground.

This is a natural hybrid that has been introduced from New Zealand. It has proven to be an attractive ground cover that is more cold tolerant than *C. kirkii*, tolerating temperatures to 15°F in the Sacramento valley. It provides rich, glossy green foliage character and is adapted to heat and average soils. Plates 330 - 331.

331. Coprosma 'Verde Vista'

Cordia
Boraginaceae

A large and diverse group of evergreen or deciduous shrubs or trees that contains over 300 species worldwide. Two species come from arid climate regions of the Southwest and Mexico. These are well adapted to low and intermediate desert regions and are used as slope and screen plants and for revegetation projects. These species are noted for their evergreen foliage, colorful white flowers, and tolerance of heat, drought, and aridity. They are most frequently planted with other desert species including *Cercidium, Prosopis, Larrea, Ruellia,* and *Acacia.*

Cordia boissieri
Wild Olive, Anacahuita

A large shrub to small tree, 15-30 ft. high and as wide. Leaves are large, to 5 in. long, medium green above, pale green below, and covered with numerous short hairs. Showy white flowers with yellow centers reach 1 1/2 in. in size and occur in clusters at the ends of branches in early spring.

Wild olive comes from southern parts of New Mexico and Texas extending into Mexico. It frequently grows as a dense, multi-branched shrub along streambanks, on plains, and on gravelly slopes. It tolerates temperatures below 20° F, heat, full sun, and drought. In low and intermediate desert regions, it is often used as a background, slope, and median plant, where it prefers well drained soils, and performs well with low to moderate amounts of supplemental water. It can eventually grow to large sizes and be pruned to form a small canopy tree. Plates 332,334.

Cordia parvifolia

A medium evergreen shrub with twisting branching, 8-12 ft. high and as wide. Dull green leaves are heavily veined and small, to 1/2 in. long; colorful white flowers grow at the ends of branches in spring.

This species comes from desert areas of Baja California. It grows on rocky slopes and plains, as well as in sandy arroyos and silty bottomlands. It is well adapted to sun, heat, aridity, and drought. In recent years, this species has been introduced for landscape use as a slope and background plant along highways and in desert gardens. Plate 333.

332. Cordia boissieri

333. Cordia parvifolia

334. Cordia boissieri

335. Cordyline australis with Phormium tenax in native habitat in New Zealand

Cordyline australis
(Dracaena australis)
Giant Dracaena, Cabbage Palm
Agavaceae

A tall palm-like plant that develops single and multiple trunks. Foliage is comprised of 2-3 ft. long, sword-like leaves that occur in terminal clusters at the top of the trunks. Young plants appear as shrubs and have slender, unbranched trunks; older specimens develop stouter trunks with side branching and can attain heights of 20-30 ft. Large clusters of creamy white flowers occur in early spring and are lightly fragrant.

Giant dracaena is native throughout all parts of New Zealand. This species is commonly found growing in swampy lowland areas, as well as exposed hillsides. It is highly adaptable to many types of climate and soil conditions and is widely grown in western gardens. Contrary to its native habitat, this species is very tolerant of heat and drought stress, as well as tolerating temperatures below 20° F. It is planted in coastal, inland, valley, and desert regions as an accent plant in both tropical and arid planting schemes. It can be grown in sandy or clayey soils, in containers, and can be cut back to cause several trunks to develop. *C. a.* 'Atropurpurea' is an attractive cultivar with purple-bronze foliage that grows slower and to smaller sizes. A variegated form, *C. a.* 'Variegata', also exists in the trade. Plates 335 - 337.

336. Cordyline australis 'Atropurpurea'

337. Cordyline australis

Coreopsis
Asteraceae

A large group of annual and perennial plants that contains over 100 species and numerous cultivars. Most species and cultivars found in western gardens come from the Midwest and southern United States. They produce an abundance of colorful yellow to orange flowers and are widely used in perennial gardens and as border plants. They prefer full sun, well drained soil, and will flower longer and better if supplied with regular moisture during spring and summer. Some perennial species are grown in desert gardens for their seasonal color and are replaced each year. Two species come from coastal foothills of California and Mexico and are adapted to periods of summer drought.

Coreopsis gigantea
Giant Coreopsis

A perennial species that is native to the coastal foothills of southern California and Baja California, where it grows in the coastal sage plant community with species such as *Artemisia, Diplacus, Eriogonum,* and *Rhus integrifolia.* It is the largest species of *Coreopsis,* and can develop stems that reach 10 ft. and higher. It provides unique character value in coastal gardens where its soft, divided foliage grows at the tops of its stems. Numerous bright yellow flowers occur in early spring. In natural areas, this species endures drought stress by shedding its leaves and becoming dormant during late summer and fall. Plate 338.

Coreopsis grandiflora

A colorful perennial growing 1-3 ft. high, 2-3 ft. wide. Narrow, dark green leaves are often divided into 3-5 lobes; orange-yellow flowers

338. Coreopsis gigantea

339. Coreopsis grandiflora

can reach 2-3 in. across. This species is native to many parts of the Midwest and southeastern United States. It is easily cultivated in gardens and can be established from seed or containers. Flowers are large, colorful, and develop on long stems above the foliage. One cultivar, *C. g.* 'Sunburst', provides semi-double flowers. Plate 339.

Coreopsis lanceolata

A clumping perennial, 1-2 ft. high and as wide. Long, linear leaves are deep green and grow mostly from the base. Large, yellow flowers, to 2 1/2 in. across, occur in large numbers in mid-spring to early summer. This species is native to the Midwest, south to Florida, and from Texas to New Mexico. It is one of the most durable and colorful species of coreopsis found in western gardens and easily adapts to coastal, inland, valley, and low desert regions. One cultivar, *C. l.* 'Sunray', produces bright, orange-yellow, double flowers. Plates 340, 342.

Coreopsis maritima
Sea Dahlia

A small, bushy perennial, 1-2 ft. high, 2-3 ft. wide. Foliage is comprised of light green leaves that are finely divided into many narrow segments. Colorful flowers are bright yellow, reach 2-4 in. across, and occur on long, leafless stems above foliage in spring. Sea dahlia is native to coastal bluffs and beach areas of southern California to northern Baja California. It is found in well drained, often sandy, soils and is exposed to wind and salt air. It readily tolerates garden cultivation but should be used in areas that are natural and become dry by late summer to become dormant.

Coreopsis verticillata

A bushy perennial, growing 2-3 ft. high on upright stems. Foliage is finely divided into many linear segments. Flowers are bright yellow and are produced for many months from late spring through summer. This species is open and airy and provides a long season of color. It develops a durable root system that enables it to withstand neglect and seasonal drought. One cultivar, *C. v.* 'Moonbeam', is a smaller variety with light yellow flowers. Plate 341.

Correa
Australian Fuchsia
Rutaceae

A small group of evergreen shrubs, including some 11 species, all being native to coastal edges and inland foothills of Australia. These plants are small to medium shrubs that are principally noted for their hanging, tubular flowers. Flower colors can be solid or mixed, and vary from white, green, and yellow to red.

Australian fuchsias require good drainage, low to moderate amounts of moisture, and prefer full sun to light shade. Established plants tolerate drought and cold but need cooler microclimate locations when used in hotter regions. The best success in western landscapes occurs in coastal areas, particularly northern California. New hybrids continue to be developed that provide different choices of flower color and forms. These plants perform well on banks, in mixed plantings, and provide nectar value to hummingbirds.

340. Coreopsis lanceolata 'Sunray'   341. Coreopsis verticillata 'Moonbeam'

342. Coreopsis lanceolata 'Sunray'

343. Correa alba   344. Correa hybrid pink

345. Correa schlechtendalii

346. Correa schlechtendalii

347. Cortaderia selloana

Correa alba
White Correa

An upright shrub, growing 3-4 ft. high and as wide. Small, round foliage is dull green above, white below. Bright white flowers are star shaped and accent the plant in late spring to summer. This species grows extensively on coastal dunes and cliffs of southern Australia and Tasmania. It is adapted to sandy or calcareous soils, wind, and drought in both coastal and inland areas. Plate 343.

Correa 'Dusky Bells'
(*Correa* 'Carmine Bells')

A spreading plant, growing up to 3-4 ft. high, 5-6 ft. across. Small leaves are dark green above, lighter below; colorful deep pink flowers occur in fall to spring. A hybrid selection closely related to *C. pulchella*. It develops a dense habit that is useful for ground cover situations on banks and in planters.

Correa 'Ivory Bells'

A compact shrub with upright branching, 3-4 ft. tall and as wide. Leaves grow to 1 in., are round to oval, dull, dark green above, pale below. Numerous cream to white, star-shaped flowers occur along upright stems through fall and winter.

Correa pulchella

A low spreading shrub, 1-2 ft. high, 3-4 ft. across. Small, 1/2 in., oval leaves are deep green above; flowers can be pink, orange, or red. This species occurs in well drained calcareous soils and is adapted to extended periods without moisture. It is highly variable in form and flower color, and has been used in hybridizing other cultivars.

Correa schlechtendalii

An upright shrub, 3-4 ft. tall. Medium green leaves are narrow and reach 1 in. long. Long, tubular flowers occur in winter and are red with yellow tips. This species comes from inland locations and rocky places in scrub vegetation of South Australia. It is more tolerant of heat, full sun, and drought in warmer regions than other species. Plates 345 - 346.

Cortaderia selloana
Pampas Grass
Poaceae

A large evergreen grass with a clumping habit, growing 10-12 ft. high, 10-12 ft. in dia. Long, blade-like foliage consists of sharply serrated, dull green leaves. Dramatic flower plumes are creamy white to light pink and occur on tall stems above the foliage in fall through winter.

Pampas grass is a very tough and durable plant. It is native to subtropical regions of Brazil, Argentina, and Chile, but is highly adapted to coastal, inland, valley, and desert regions throughout the west. Established plants require little supplemental water in coastal zones, moderate amounts in drier locations. Unfortunately, this species has become naturalized in coastal foothill areas of southern California and should be used with caution. Another species, *C. jubata*, has also become widely naturalized throughout central and northern California coastal foothills and is highly destructive to natural plant communities. Plate 347.

Cotoneaster

Cotoneaster

Rosaceae

A variable group of plants including about 50 species of deciduous, semi-deciduous, and evergreen shrubs or small trees. Most types are native to cool and moist climate regions of Asia, with the greatest concentration occurring in China. They have been cultivated for years in gardens around the world, where they are appreciated for their rich foliage character and colorful berry-type fruit.

In western gardens, most cotoneasters prefer regions with cool winter conditions, well drained soils, and sunny locations. In warmer and drier regions, they benefit from partial shade, richer soils, and more frequent watering. Otherwise, these are tough and adaptable plants that can grow with little care once established. They range in shape from low and spreading to tall and mounding and are useful on banks, for ground covers, screening, and as transition plants between lawn and shrub areas. Prostrate varieties are often well suited to partial shade under native oaks and other trees, surviving in good character without regular summer water. Both prostrate and shrub varieties have an arching branch habit that should be selectively pruned, rather than sheared. Several of the deciduous species are virtually evergreen in character when they are used in areas with mild winters.

Cotoneaster adpressus

Creeping Cotoneaster

A low spreading deciduous shrub, growing 12-18 in. high, slowly spreading to 6 ft. across. Tiny, dark green leaves are pointed, reach 1/2 in. long, and turn red in the fall before dropping. Colorful red berries last from fall into winter. This prostrate species is useful for understory plantings in light shade and for cascading over walls and banks. It is semi-deciduous in areas having mild temperatures and prefers moderate amounts of supplemental water.

Cotoneaster apiculatus

Cranberry Cotoneaster.

A medium size semi-deciduous shrub, mounding 3-4 ft. high, spreading 5-6 ft. across. Deep green leaves grow to 1/2 in. long, are pointed, and have red tinged edges. Colorful red fruit resemble cranberries in winter. Cranberry cotoneaster develops into a densely mounding shrub for use on banks and adjacent to lawn areas. It tolerates sun or part shade, moderate amounts of supplemental moisture, and can be clipped to form a hedge.

Cotoneaster buxifolius

A stiffly branched evergreen shrub, mounding 3-4 ft. high, spreading 5-6 ft. across. Evergreen foliage is comprised of tiny, grey leaves, heavily covered with fine hairs. Bright red berries provide modest color accent value in fall. Useful as a foliage accent plant, this species can be combined with either grey or green foliage colors. Often used on banks and small planters, it can be clipped into a low hedge or used as a ground cover. Plates 348 - 349.

Cotoneaster congestus

(Cotoneaster microphylla glacialis)

A low mounding evergreen shrub, reaching 2-3 ft. high and 3-4 ft. across. Tiny, deep green leaves grow to 1/3 in. long; bright white flowers accent the foliage in early spring. Colorful red berries occur in fall and winter. This species is useful as a bank and ground cover plant. It can be grown in partial shade with low amounts of supplemental

348. **Cotoneaster buxifolius**

349. **Cotoneaster buxifolius**

350. **Cotoneaster congestus**

351. **Cotoneaster congestus**

352. Cotoneaster lacteus

353. Cotoneaster lacteus

354. Cotoneaster salicifolius 'Repens'

355. Cotoneaster salicifolius 'Repens'

water or in full sun with moderate amounts. Plates 350 - 351.

Cotoneaster dammeri
(Cotoneaster humifusus)

A very prostrate shrub, developing branches that hug the ground, growing 6-9 in. high, spreading 6-10 ft. across. Evergreen leaves reach 3/4 in. long, are medium green, and oval in shape. Clusters of bright red berries produce a showy display in winter. A good ground cover in partial shade or sun. Its prostrate habit works well on banks, around boulders, and cascading over walls. Several cultivars are available including C. d. 'Coral Beauty' that has coral colored fruit; C. d. 'Eichholz' that has red foliage in the fall and scarlet red fruit; C. d. 'Skogsholmen' with a more open growth habit that reaches 12-15 in. high; and C. d. 'Lowfast' that is a fast growing plant to 12 in. high, spreading 12-15 ft. across.

Cotoneaster horizontalis
Rock Cotoneaster

A low spreading shrub with semi-evergreen foliage, growing 2-3 ft. high, spreading as much as 12-15 ft. wide. Small, glossy green leaves are round, grow to 1/2 in. across, and occur on distinctive herringbone branches. Leaves turn red with cool temperatures; colorful red fruit occurs in winter. Rock cotoneaster is a popular bank and rock garden plant in cool climate regions. It prefers protection from intense heat and sun when used in inland and valley locations, and moderate amounts of supplemental water.

Cotoneaster lacteus
(Cotoneaster parneyi)
Parney Cotoneaster, Red Clusterberry

A medium to large evergreen shrub, reaching 8-10 ft. high, spreading 10-12 ft. Foliage is comprised of 1-2 in. size leaves that are dull, medium green above, and whitish below. Noticeable clusters of white flowers occur in spring, followed by showy clusters of red fruit that persist from late summer through fall. This species develops into a large, mounding shrub that is useful on slopes, for screens, and in background areas. It is often used along highways and other difficult areas where it has proven to be one of the best choices of Cotoneaster for use in warm, arid, and dry regions. It grows in full sun or partial shade and tolerates average soils. Established plants require low amounts of supplemental water in coastal areas, moderate amounts are better when used in the hotter inland, valley, and desert regions. Mature plants can be pruned to reveal an interesting branching character. Plates 352 - 353.

Cotoneaster salicifolius
Willowleaf Cotoneaster

A large evergreen shrub, 12-15 ft. high, spreading 12-18 ft. wide. Narrow leaves are dark green above, lighter below, growing 1-3 in. long. Bright red berries develop in twos and threes in late fall. Willowleaf cotoneaster is a vigorous species with a distinctive arching branch habit. It works well on large banks and for background screening, or can be pruned to form a multi-stemmed specimen shrub or small tree. One cultivar, C. s. 'Repens', is a low growing variety that reaches 2 ft. high with weeping branches that spread 5-8 ft. across. It is a good ground cover for large areas in sun or part shade. Plates 354 - 355.

Cotyledon

Crassulaceae

A small group of succulent shrubs, including about 35 species that come primarily from the Cape region of South Africa. Several species are used in mild coastal regions as accent plants in rock gardens, containers, and along borders. They grow best in full sun to partial shade and in well drained soils. Their foliage character varies from round and flat to cylindrical; flowers are typically bell-shaped, orange-red, and hang from upright stems. Cotyledons are easily propagated by cuttings and require little supplemental water. They are most often found in nurseries specializing in succulents.

Cotyledon orbiculata

A small plant, 2-3 ft. high, spreading 1-3 ft. across. This species is distinguished by its attractive grey foliage color, rounded leaves, and orange-red flowers that occur in early summer. Plate 356.

Cotyledon teretifolia

A species that has long, cylindrical leaves, grey-green, and 4-5 in. long. Orange-red flowers occur in early spring. Plate 357.

Cotyledon undulata

One of the most unique species with thick, undulating leaves that have red margins. The foliage and flower stems are covered with white powder that produces a striking contrast to other plants in the garden.

Cowania mexicana

(*Cowania mexicana* var. *stansburiana*)
Cliff Rose
Rosaceae

A small to medium shrub, 2-6 ft. high, with stiff, irregular branching character. Foliage is comprised of tiny, dark green leaves that are divided into many lobes. Showy white or yellow-white flowers occur in spring and are followed by seeds that have an attractive feathery plume.

Cliff rose is native to the high desert and arid basin regions in many southwestern states including, California, Arizona, Nevada, and Utah. It grows on slopes, mesas, and along washes at elevations ranging from 3,500-8,500 ft., and is tolerant of sun, heat, drought, snow, aridity, and wind. This is a tough and durable plant for high desert gardens that grows best on well drained soils with low amounts of supplemental water. It is not highly ornamental in character and is often best suited to background, slope, and restoration uses. Plates 358 - 359.

Crassula

Crassulaceae

A large group of succulent perennials and shrubs that come principally from mild, dry areas of Africa. Many species and cultivars are in landscape use and provide a range of sizes, flower color, and foliage character for garden situations. All do well as container plants; some fit rock gardens; others are suited to border and mixed succulent plantings. Currently, specialty nurseries provide the greatest diversity of choice for some of the more interesting and smaller varieties.

Most types are best adapted to mild coastal regions and frost free inland locations in full sun to part shade on well drained soils. They

356. Cotyledon orbiculata

357. Cotyledon teretifolia

358. Cowania mexicana

359. Cowania mexicana

360. Crassula arborescens

361. Crassula argentea

362. Crassula argentea

363. Crassula argentea 'Variegata'

are sensitive to frost, as well as desert heat and sun, where they need to be planted in protected locations. They are easy to propagate and grow and can survive with little supplemental water once established. Flowering occurs in mid-winter to early spring. The size of plants is easily managed by pruning after the flower cycle. They are often combined with other succulents including *Aloe, Agave, Sedum*, and *Cotyledon*. A few of the species and varieties are discussed below.

Crassula arborescens
Silver Jade Plant
An upright species that grows 4-6 ft. high and has distinctive grey-green foliage. Leaves are 2-3 in. long and have red margins. Showy clusters of white, star-shaped flowers occur in late winter. Plate 360.

Crassula argentea
Jade Plant
A medium to large upright shrub that can reach 6-9 ft. tall. Its foliage is comprised of smooth, emerald green leaves, 1-2 in. long, that are tinged with red. Plants grown in full sun will become covered by showy clusters of whitish pink flowers in mid-winter. This is one of the most popular and widely planted species for both garden and indoor use. Numerous cultivars have been produced to achieve compact selections with smaller leaves, variegated foliage, and deeper pink flower colors. Plates 361 - 363.

Crassula falcata
Sickle Plant
A small to medium trailing species that can reach 2-3 ft. high, 4-5 ft. across. Leaves are grey-green, 3-5 in. long, and sickle shaped. Striking flowers are bright red, providing an intense contrast to the foliage color. Plates 364, 366.

Crassula multicava
A low trailing species that is suited to ground cover and hanging basket uses. Leaves are light green, round, to 2 in. long. Large numbers of light pink flowers occur in mid-winter to provide a pleasant haze of color. Plates 365, 367.

364. Crassula falcata

365. Crassula multicava

366. Crassula falcata

367. Crassula multicava

Cupressus

Cypress

Cupressaceae

A small group of coniferous trees or shrubs that includes 22 species. Several species are native to the western United States where they are quite distinct in character and adaptation. One species has been introduced from Europe, *Cupressus sempervirens*, the Italian cypress, and has become one of the most visible and widely known plants in western gardens.

Cypress species prefer well drained soils and can grow with little or no supplemental water once established. However, most types will tolerate heavy and calcareous soils, as well as regular moisture. Most species are fast growing and perform with good success in coastal, valley, and desert regions where they tolerate sun, heat, wind, and aridity.

Cupressus arizonica

Arizona Cypress

A medium to large evergreen tree, 35-50 ft. tall, eventually reaching heights of 80-90 ft. Foliage is comprised of pale blue-green to yellowish, scale-like leaves; bark of trunks and mature branches is dark red-brown, rough, shredded in character, and persists year to year.

This species is native to gravelly slopes, mountain canyons, and well drained soils throughout the arid basin regions of New Mexico, Arizona, California, and Mexico. It typically grows at elevations ranging from 3,000-8,000 ft. and is tolerant of cold, drought, heat, and wind. This species is sometimes called the rough-barked Arizona cypress in recognition of its persistent bark character. It has proven to be well suited to high desert regions where it is grown as a windbreak and screen tree. It is also used in rural areas where it has proven to perform well with little care and low amounts of supplemental water. Over the years a number of cultivars have been introduced including *C. a.* 'Compacta', a low growing form with a conical shape; *C. a.* 'Glauca', a selection with silvery grey foliage; and *C. a.* 'Pyramidalis', a smaller, symmetrical form.

Cupressus forbesii

Tecate Cypress

An upright tree, growing 20-30 ft. tall, 12-15 ft. wide. Foliage is comprised of tiny, scale-like leaves that are medium to light green; bark on trunks is reddish to mahogany in color and flakes off each year.

This species is native to only a few isolated locations within the coastal and inland foothills of southern California, where it grows on dry slopes within the chaparral plant community at elevations of 1,500-4,000 ft. It is found in rocky, well drained soils, and can tolerate many months of drought. When grown in western gardens, it responds to additional water with faster growth, reaching larger sizes. It can be used for restoration projects, as well as for screen, background, and slope plantings.

Cupressus glabra

(Cupressus arizonica var. glabra)

Smooth Arizona Cypress

A medium tree with an upright habit, 30-40 ft. high. Foliage color is often distinctively grey-

368. **Cupressus glabra**   369. **Cupressus glabra**

370. **Cupressus macrocarpa, Monterey, California**

371. Cupressus sempervirens 'Stricta'

372. Cupressus sempervirens

373. Cupressus sempervirens, Boboli Garden, Florence, Italy

green; bark is reddish brown and will shed from trunks and branches to reveal smooth new bark beneath.

The smooth Arizona cypress is closely related to *C. arizonica* but has different foliage and bark character. It is native to central Arizona in woodland and chaparral plant communities on north facing slopes and in canyons at elevations from 3,000-5,000 ft. This species has become very widely cultivated for windbreaks, screen, and accent plantings in dry, arid regions.   Plates 368 - 369.

Cupressus macrocarpa
Monterey Cypress

A large evergreen tree, growing 30-40 ft. high, with an equal spread. Foliage is comprised of dark green, scale-like leaves; bark is rough, persistent, and dark brown.

This western native is restricted in its natural distribution to only two areas on the Monterey Peninsula. However, due to its popularity, it has been widely planted along the California coastline and in some places has become naturalized. Young trees grow exceptionally fast and develop into angular and pyramidal shapes. Older trees develop massive trunks and a broad canopy. Trees that are planted along the coastline are often shaped by on-shore winds and form dramatic profiles. This species is best suited to northern and central coastal habitats, where it is not exposed to extreme heat or aridity. In coastal zones, established plants can survive without supplemental water. Mature plants can often become monumental specimens that need large spaces to be appreciated. Surprisingly, this species can also be hedged and trimmed into screens and topiary shapes. Several cultivars can be found including *C. m.* 'Golden Pillar', a variety that produces yellow new growth and *C. m.* 'Stricta', a tall, slender, columnar selection. Plate 370.

Cupressus sempervirens
Italian Cypress

A tall, upright tree, reaching 40-60 ft. high. Foliage is deep green; persistent bark is rough and medium to dark brown.

This species comes from southern Europe, including the Mediterranean region, as well as western Asia. It often grows in forest and woodland communities where it develops into many forms, ranging from broad and open, to narrow and columnar. Varieties found in cultivation have been selected from the more upright forms in order to achieve the greatest vertical shape and consistent character.

The Italian cypress has been widely used in ornamental landscapes around the world. In western gardens, it grows well in many types of soils, including clayey and calcareous, and tolerates ample or little amounts of supplemental water. It grows best in coastal, inland, and valley regions but proves to be hardy in high, intermediate, and low desert zones as well. It is often associated with Mediterranean style architecture, yet is used as an accent or colonnade plant in many types of gardens. Several cultivated selections exist in the trade including *C. s.* 'Stricta', a very narrow form; *C. s.* 'Glauca', with rich blue-green foliage; and *C. s.* 'Swanes Golden', a variety with bright yellow new growth. Plates 372 - 373.

Dalea

Indigo Bush

Fabaceae

A diverse group of evergreen and deciduous shrubs or small trees that includes over 200 species. Many are native to arid climates and desert areas of the Southwest; several have now become recognized for landscape use in low and intermediate desert regions. Daleas prefer sunny locations, well drained soils, and low amounts of supplemental water. They are sensitive to frost and excessive summer water. They are often combined with other desert natives including *Fouquieria splendens, Cordia boissieri, Acacia smallii, Cercidium floridum, Prosopis* species, *Encelia farinosa*, and *Larrea tridentata.*

Dalea frutescens

Black Dalea

A small mounding shrub, 1-3 ft. high, equal in spread. Leaves are pinnately compound, having 13-17 leaflets that are grey-green in color. Colorful flowers are purple and occur in round heads in late summer and fall.

Black dalea is native to dry areas on rocky hills and plains in desert regions of Texas, New Mexico, and Mexico. This is an open and delicately branched shrub that is tolerant of heat, aridity, and periods of drought stress. It works well in courtyard plantings and in areas that receive periodic deep watering. In areas of high moisture stress, this species will shed some of its foliage.

Dalea greggii

Trailing Indigo Bush

A low growing evergreen shrub, 12-18 in. high, spreading 5-10 ft. Dense, silvery green foliage is comprised of pinnately divided leaves; numerous heads of purple flowers provide a light color accent in early spring.

This species is native to southern Texas and Mexico where it grows in rocky, limestone soils and in sunny, exposed areas. It is very tolerant of heat, sun, aridity, and drought. It is one of the best low desert ground covers for residential and commercial scale gardens, as well as for highway slopes, landscape medians, and for erosion control. Its grey foliage color makes it suited for use with other desert species to achieve a color scheme which matches the desert region. It grows quickly while retaining a dense foliage character and spreading habit. This species should not be overwatered during summer to avoid overgrowth and root rot difficulties. Plates 374, 376.

Dalea pulchra

Indigo Bush

A small evergreen shrub, 3-5 ft. high and as wide. Leaves are silvery green and divided into 5-7 leaflets; tiny, lavender-purple flowers are grouped together into showy heads at the ends of branches during early spring.

This species comes from the intermediate desert areas of Arizona and Mexico. It grows on rocky slopes and in canyons at elevations from 3,000-5,000 ft. in several plant communities, including the desert grassland. It tolerates sun, heat, and aridity but will shed some foliage during periods of extreme drought stress. Indigo bush is a good foliage and flowering accent plant for desert regions. It can adapt to small scale garden spaces, as well as survive in

374. Dalea greggii

375. Dalea pulchra

376. Dalea greggii with Yucca elata at The Desert Botanical Garden, Phoenix, Arizona

377. Dalea spinosa

378. Dalea spinosa

difficult median and highway landscapes. It is an open and loosely branched shrub that can be pruned to control shape and size and should not be overwatered during the summer. Plate 375.

Dalea spinosa
Smoke Tree

A large shrub to small tree, slowly growing to 20 or 25 ft. high. Much of the visual character of this plant is due to its many silvery blue branches that produce a smoke-like appearance. Leaves develop after winter rains occur; showy indigo purple flowers produce an intense display in late spring and early summer.

The smoke tree is found in sandy and gravelly washes in low desert regions of California, Arizona, Baja California, and Mexico at elevations between 1,000-1,500 ft. It becomes larger and more tree-like in areas where it can receive run-off from rains as well as ground water. Smaller plants will develop on exposed slopes and in drier soils. It is well adapted to heat, sun, wind, and aridity but suffers from frost and temperatures below 25°F. It has sometimes proven to be difficult to establish in landscapes. Mature plants become unique specimens in the garden. In contrast to its soft, billowy appearance, the branchlets are stiff, pointed, and care is required around them. Plates 377 - 380.

379. Dalea spinosa, Living Desert Reserve, Palm Desert, California

380. Dalea spinosa, immature

Dasylirion
Sotol, Desert Spoon
Agavaceae

A small group of evergreen shrubs, including 15 species that are native to the Southwest including Texas, Arizona, and Mexico. These plants are characterized by their rosettes of long, pointed leaves and tall flower spikes, similar to yuccas. Several species are currently found in landscape use in low and intermediate desert regions. They tolerate heat, sun, aridity, and drought and prefer well drained soils with periodic deep irrigation. Sotols are most often used in combination with other desert species such as *Fouquieria splendens, Larrea tridentata, Carnegiea gigantea, Cercidium floridum, Encelia farinosa, Acacia smallii,* and *Agave* species. They provide accent character in contrast to foliage plants.

Dasylirion acrotriche
Green Desert Spoon

A rounded shrub, slow growing, 5-8 ft. high. Leaves are sea-green, 2-3 ft. long, 1/2-1 in. wide, and have small teeth on the margin. This species comes from eastern Mexico and provides green color character in desert landscapes. Plate 381.

Dasylirion longissima
Mexican Grass Tree

A large species with long, narrow foliage that develops a rosette 5-7 ft. across. Leaves lack spines and can reach 3-6 ft. long; trunks develop after many years of growth. Mexican grass tree is native to eastern Mexico and is a striking plant that is currently grown in coastal, inland, valley, and desert regions. Plate 382.

Dasylirion wheeleri
Sotol, Desert Spoon

A medium shrub growing 3-4 ft. high, eventually developing a short trunk with a height of 6-8 ft. Leaves are grey-green, grow to 3 ft. long, and have sharp, upward facing teeth on the margins. Older plants produce a showy stalk of creamy white flowers in late fall. Sotol is native to desert slopes at elevations from 3,000-5,000 ft. in western Texas, Arizona, and New Mexico. It grows on rocky and gravelly soils and is adapted to heat, aridity, and extended periods of drought. It is one of the most commonly planted species in low and intermediate desert gardens throughout the Southwest. Plate 383.

Delosperma 'Alba'
White Trailing Ice Plant
Aizoaceae

A low succulent, 6-12 in. high, which spreads for several feet along stems that root in moist soil. Dull green leaves are triangular, growing to 3 in. long. Showy white flowers are most profuse in mid-spring and occur intermittently all year.

White trailing ice plant is one of the best succulent ground covers for coastal and inland gardens. It tolerates many types of soils, salt spray, and requires low amounts of supplemental water to retain an attractive appearance. It is a fast growing species that does not build up as much heavy thatch as other ice plants. However, like most ice plants, it can be removed from time to time and replanted to revitalize its character. It can be planted from unrooted cuttings at 12-18 in. apart and will usually fill in together in 12-15 months. It can be clipped to fit into small planters, or be planted on large, gentle slopes. Plates 384 - 385.

381. Dasylirion acrotriche

382. Dasylirion longissima

383. Dasylirion wheeleri

384. Delosperma 'Alba'

385. Delosperma 'Alba'

386. Dendromecon harfordii

387. Dendromecon harfordii

388. Dendromecon rigida

389. Dendromecon rigida

Dendromecon
Bush Poppy
Papaveraceae

A small group of evergreen shrubs that are native to California and Baja California. Bush poppies are known for their intense sulphur yellow flowers and blue to grey-green foliage that provide colorful character in landscape plantings. Two species are currently in the trade; unfortunately, both are difficult to propagate and establish from containers. They require well drained soils with no summer water once established and grow best in warm, sunny locations in coastal and inland regions. They slowly develop into large plants that are useful in background areas and on slopes in combination with other natives including *Heteromeles arbutifolia, Eriogonum fasciculatum, Diplacus longiflorus, Romneya coulteri, Trichostema lanatum,* and *Fremontodendron* cultivars. Pruning after the flower cycle will help to maintain size and character.

Dendromecon harfordii
(*Dendromecon rigida* ssp. *harfordii*)
Island Bush Poppy

A medium to large mounding shrub that can eventually reach 15-20 ft. high and as wide. Foliage is comprised of 3-5 in. long leaves that are a rich blue to grey-green; intense sulphur yellow flowers reach 2-3 in. across and are very showy during spring to summer and intermittently all year.

Island bush poppy is native to Santa Cruz and Santa Rosa Islands where it grows on exposed slopes, bluffs, and canyons within the chaparral plant community. It is considered to be the most attractive form of bush poppy due to its rich foliage color and dense growth habit. It should be planted in coarse sandy to gravelly soils, in raised planters, or on slopes to insure good drainage. This species can be a very effective accent and specimen element in natural garden settings. Plates 386 - 387.

Dendromecon rigida
Bush Poppy

A medium to large shrub with many upright branches that reach 5-10 ft. high. Narrow leaves are grey-green, 2-4 in. long; colorful sulphur yellow flowers reach 1-2 in. across and occur in late spring to early summer and intermittently all year.

Bush poppy is widely distributed. It typically grows on warm, dry foothills and slopes, from northern California to the Sierra Nevada, south to the coastal foothills of Baja California. It grows at low elevations, between 1,000-3,000 ft., on sunny, exposed areas within the chaparral plant community. This species requires good drainage with no summer water. It is often valued for revegetation and slope planting situations. Older plants develop long branches and an unkempt character. They can be pruned in late fall to stimulate new growth. Plates 388 - 389.

Dietes
(Moraea)
Fortnight Lily
Iridaceae

A colorful group of clumping perennial plants, including five species that are native to tropical and southern Africa. Two species and several hybrids are widely cultivated in western gardens for their colorful flower character and suitability for many landscape situations. All varieties grow fast; produce flowers at two week intervals throughout spring, summer, and fall; and tolerate many types of soil and moisture conditions. Their best performance and growth occurs in coastal, inland, and valley regions in sunny areas, on rich, well drained soils with regular moisture. Established plants tolerate neglect and infrequent watering but foliage character and flower production will suffer if conditions become too hot and dry. Fortnight lilies are popular choices for accent areas in gardens, around pools, entry walkways, adjacent to lawns, and in containers. They can be mixed into lush, evergreen landscapes, as well as combined in water conserving gardens.

Dietes bicolor

This is a smaller and less aggressive species of *Dietes*, growing to 2 ft. high, and producing bright yellow flowers. Flowers reach 2 in. wide and have a maroon spot at the base of the petals. Remove old flower stems at the ground after flowering to encourage more production; divide old clumps in late fall. Plates 390 - 391.

Dietes vegeta
(Moraea iridioides)

This species is a vigorous grower that reaches 4 ft. high and develops many plants to form a dense clump with age. It produces numerous, 4-5 in., large, white flowers with purple, yellow, and maroon markings that cover the plant for a very showy display of color. Several cultivars have been developed from this species that provide different combinations of flower color. Remove old flowers as they fade, but keep the flower stems for future production; divide old clumps in late fall. Plates 392 - 395.

390. **Dietes bicolor**

391. **Dietes bicolor**

392. **Dietes vegeta**

393. **Dietes 'Lemon Drops'**

394. **Dietes vegeta**

395. **Dietes vegeta**

396. Diplacus longiflorus

397. Diplacus longiflorus

Diplacus
(Mimulus)
Monkey Flower
Scrophulariaceae

A small group of evergreen shrubs, including 7 species that are native to western states from Oregon to Baja California. These plants are known for their colorful tubular flowers that accent the natural landscape during spring and summer. Within their natural range, different species have evolved and adapted to both wet and dry habitats, providing many choices for use in western gardens. Most species and cultivars from dry habitats prefer sunny locations and well drained soils. Flowering occurs from spring through summer; watering should be restricted during this period, otherwise excess foliage growth and disease problems can occur.

Monkey flowers perform well as flowering accent plants on banks and with other natives including *Romneya, Salvia, Artemisia, Eriogonum, Epilobium,* and *Trichostema.* They can be cut back hard in late fall or early spring to control their size and to stimulate greater flowering. Several species are planted by seed for revegetation and naturalizing purposes including *D. longiflorus,* Southern Bush Monkey Flower, that grows 2-3 ft. high and produces pale orange, cream, or red flowers and *D. puniceus,* Red Bush Monkey Flower, that reaches 5 ft. high and has small, dark red flowers. Plates 396 - 397

Diplacus hybrids

In recent years, the genus *Diplacus* has been extensively propagated and hybridized to develop many striking flower color selections. One group, known as the Verity hybrids, have particularly large and colorful flowers and have received widespread attention among native plant growers. These hybrids are quite ornamental in character and are used as perennial plants where they can provide 2-3 years of value before they require replacement. Plates 398 - 402.

398. Diplacus hybrids

399. Diplacus hybrids

400. Diplacus hybrids

401. Diplacus hybrids

402. Diplacus hybrids

Dodonaea viscosa
Hopseed Bush, Hop Bush
Sapindaceae

A large shrub or small tree, growing 12-18 ft. and higher, spreading 6-12 ft. wide. Evergreen foliage is comprised of long, narrow leaves, 3-4 in. in length, to 1/2 in. wide. Flowers are tiny and inconspicuous. Lime green seed capsules are tinged with pink and are modestly showy when young, then turn brown and become conspicuous when mature.

Hopseed bush comes from many different parts of the world including Arizona to South America, the West Indies, and New Zealand. Within its range, different varieties have evolved that provide varying leaf and size characteristics. A popular cultivar, *D. v.* 'Purpurea', Purple Hopseed Bush, is of New Zealand origin and is often preferred for its rich purple-bronze leaf color. The foliage of this cultivar becomes even deeper purple in response to cool weather during the winter months and when planted in shade. Plants native to desert regions in Arizona have smaller, deep green leaves and are considered to be more tolerant of heat, aridity, and drought.

Overall, all varieties of hopseed bush have proven to be highly adaptable throughout the West. They grow in many types of soils including sands, clays, and calcareous, and are easily grown on coastal bluffs to low and intermediate deserts. They grow with lots or little supplemental water; plants given ample water grow faster and to larger sizes.

Hopseed bush is often used as a background screen and slope plant. It can also be clipped to form a hedge or be grown as a small canopy tree for courtyards and patio spaces. As these plants attain larger sizes, they can be pruned to reveal interesting bark and branch character in landscape settings. Experience has shown that these plants can be relatively short lived, 10-15 years in some instances, and that large and small branches can die at even earlier ages. Plates 403 - 408.

403. **Dodonaea viscosa**

404. **Dodonaea viscosa**

405. **Dodonaea viscosa, desert form**

406. **Dodonaea viscosa, desert form**

407. **Dodonaea viscosa, seed capsules**

408. **Dodonaea viscosa 'Purpurea'**

Dracaena draco
Dragon Tree
Agavaceae

A medium to large tree, slowly growing to 25 ft. high. Old, mature plants develop large, smooth trunks with many branches extending outward to form a broad canopy shape. Grey-green foliage is comprised of 2 ft. long, sword-shaped leaves; showy creamy white flowers occur in large spikes above the foliage and are followed by bright orange berries.

The dragon tree is one of the most unusual plants for western gardens. It comes from the Canary Islands where it is fully adapted to mild coastal climates and extended dry periods. It is quite sensitive to cold; even mature plants can be killed by temperatures below 25° F. Young plants are often grown in containers and raised planters to display their character. Well drained soils and periodic watering is preferred. It takes many years to achieve tall and large specimen stature, but it is well worth the effort since few plants provide such unique character. Plates 409 - 410.

409. Dracaena draco

410. Dracaena draco

411. Drosanthemum floribundum

412. Drosanthemum floribundum

413. Drosanthemum hispidum

414. Drosanthemum hispidum

Drosanthemum
Aizoaceae

A large group of succulent shrubs and perennials, including more than 95 species, native to South Africa. The most popular species for western gardens are used as ground covers and are noted for their vibrant pink and purple flower color. These plants are best suited to coastal, inland, and valley regions where they tolerate full sun, heat, and frost.

Drosanthemum floribundum
Rosea Ice Plant

A low growing ground cover, 4-6 in. high, spreading 5-6 ft. and wider on stems that will root in moist soil. Leaves are tiny and glisten with translucent dots; a carpet of fluorescent pink flowers occur in late spring and last for 2-3 weeks.

This species is a popular ground cover for large or small slopes in coastal and inland areas where it is valued for erosion control and its fine textured foliage character. It tolerates many types of soil and drainage conditions and requires low amounts of supplemental water. Plates 411 - 412.

Drosanthemum hispidum

A mounding shrub, 2-3 ft. high and as wide. Leaves are round and grow to 1 in. long; very showy flowers are an intense magenta-purple color and occur in late spring to early summer.

This species has more of a shrub habit that makes it well suited to container, rock garden, and border plantings. It can also be used as a ground cover in small spaces and on banks, or it can be trimmed back each year to maintain size and flower character. Plates 413 - 414.

Dudleya
Crassulaceae

A diverse group of succulent perennials that are native to warm and dry regions of the southwestern United States. These plants frequently grow in rock outcroppings and on cliffs in the coastal sage and chaparral plant communities. All species develop a characteristic rosette form with their foliage that creates an interesting visual character. Flowers vary in color and occur on fleshy stems above the foliage in late spring through fall.

Of the approximately 40 species known to exist, few are in cultivation or available for garden use. Most species are found in botanical gardens and in native plant nurseries. These plants are well suited to small garden spaces in coastal regions where they can be grown in full sun and on well drained soils. They rarely need supplemental water and are quite carefree.

Dudleya brittonii.
Chalk Dudleya

This species comes from the coastal foothills of southern California and northern Baja California. It is one of the most striking varieties due to its large, flat leaves that are heavily coated with white, chalky powder. Pale yellow flowers develop on 2-3 ft. long stems in early summer. Plate 415.

Dudleya virens
Island Live-forever

A species native to the rocky bluffs of San Clemente and Santa Catalina islands. It develops fleshy, dull to medium green, strap-like leaves that reach 10 in. long, and it produces clusters of reddish flowers. Plate 416.

Dudleya viscida

A species that comes from rocky places in coastal foothills near San Juan Capistrano. It has bright green cylindrical leaves and produces attractive pink flowers in mid-summer. Plate 417.

Dymondia margaretae
Asteraceae

A very low growing perennial, 1-3 in. high, slowly spreading 12-24 in. Small narrow leaves grow 2-3 in. long and are dull green above, white below. Yellow daisy-like flowers occur in summer and are quite small and partly hidden by the foliage.

This species comes from South Africa and has been introduced to western gardens as a ground cover for use in small spaces, between paving stones, and for rock garden situations. It tolerates full sun, heat, light frost, and requires low amounts of supplemental water once established. It is a very small plant that can be encouraged to faster growth and greater coverage by providing it with more water. Its best performance is in well drained soils and in coastal regions. Plates 418 - 419.

415. Dudleya brittonii

416. Dudleya virens

417. Dudleya viscida

418. Dymondia margaretae

419. Dymondia margaretae

420. Echeveria crenulata

421. Echeveria imbricata

422. Echeveria imbricata

423. Echium fastuosum

424. Echium fastuosum

Echeveria
Hen-and-chickens
Crassulaceae

A diverse group of succulent plants, native to areas ranging from Texas to Argentina. The vast majority of the 100 or more species known to exist come from dry regions of Mexico. In addition to these species, numerous hybrids have been cultivated and introduced into western gardens.

Echeverias are known for their rosettes of fleshy foliage and bell-shaped flowers. They have been long time favorites for use in succulent gardens and for containers where their symmetrical foliage patterns can be enjoyed. They are easily propagated from unrooted cuttings and require very little care or attention. They thrive in sunny, warm locations, and are quite drought tolerant. The best choice of species and hybrids often comes from specialty nurseries and retail growers.

Echeveria agavoides

A species that develops bright green foliage, 6-8 in. in dia., with reddish brown edges and pointed tips. It produces small red and yellow flowers in summer. A hardy plant for coastal, inland, and valley regions.

Echeveria crenulata

A species that develops large pale green, round leaves with very wavy edges that are purple to red. The leaves are sometimes covered with white powder; flower stalks and flowers are pink to red-orange and are showy. A good coastal plant. Plate 420.

Echeveria imbricata

A low growing species that develops rosettes of grey-green leaves, 4-6 in. across. This species develops many offsets and has colorful orange-red and yellow flowers. This is one of the most popular and widely planted echeverias that tolerates coastal, inland, and valley regions. Plates 421 - 422.

Echium fastuosum
Pride of Madeira
Boraginaceae

A medium to large evergreen shrub, quickly growing 4-6 ft. high and as wide, eventually reaching heights of 10 ft. Foliage is comprised of soft, grey-green leaves that attach to heavy, woody stems. Dramatic spikes of blue to purple flowers cover the plant in early to mid-spring.

This species comes from the Canary Islands where it is well adapted to coastal climates. It grows on rocky slopes in full sun and tolerates wind, humidity, and periods of drought. In western gardens, it is best suited to coastal regions from San Diego to the San Francisco Bay region. In these locations, this species can thrive with low amounts of supplemental water. Plants that are grown in warmer and drier inland conditions need more water and protection from extreme heat, sun, and frost.

Pride of Madeira is often planted on slopes and in background areas where it has space to develop. It is a striking flowering accent element in any location in a garden and is often combined with other bright flowering species such as *Eschscholzia, Fremontia, Coreopsis, and Limonium*. It grows very fast and should be pruned after flowering to maintain its character; some plants will still become quite large and woody in 5-6 years. Plates 423 - 424.

Elaeagnus pungens
Silverberry
Elaeagnaceae

A medium to large evergreen shrub, 6-15 ft. high, spreading as wide. Branches are stiff, angular, and contain some spines. New foliage is bronze in color; mature leaves are stiff, olive green, and lightly flecked with silvery scales on top and heavily covered beneath. Flowers are inconspicuous; fruit is silvery in color.

Silverberry is a hardy plant that comes from China and Japan. It occurs naturally in coastal lowlands and into inland mountain regions that have cool climates and ample moisture. Contrary to its natural habitat conditions, silverberry has been used throughout western gardens in some of the most difficult landscape conditions. It is grown in coastal, as well as inland, valley, and high and low desert regions. In these locations, it is a very rugged plant that can tolerate heat, cold, aridity, wind, and poor soils. Established plants require only low to moderate amounts of supplemental water.

This species is often used in landscapes as a large screen, barrier, and hedge plant. Several cultivated varieties are available in the trade that offer yellow and white variegated foliage character but otherwise are equal in size and durability. Plates 425 - 426.

425. Elaeagnus pungens

426. Elaeagnus pungens

427. Elymus condensatus 'Canyon Prince'

Elymus
Giant Wild Rye
Poaceae

A grouping of annual and perennial grasses that includes some 50 species that are native to many climates and countries of the Northern Hemisphere. Several species are native to western states and are becoming of interest for use in ornamental landscapes. Other species have been introduced from Europe and have proved to be highly aggressive and will naturalize by underground stolons or by seed. Caution must be used when considering plants from this group for use in dry regions, particularly exotic species, since they can aggressively naturalize.

Elymus condensatus 'Canyon Prince'

A large clumping selection taken from *E. condensatus*, a species that is native to California. This perennial variety has striking grey-green foliage and is currently being used in ornamental landscapes. It grows 3-4 ft. high and produces slender flower spikes from early to late summer that can reach 4-6 ft. high. Over time, it develops a 2-3 ft. dia. clump but does not spread or become invasive. It will retain its foliage through the winter months but can be cut back each year to renew its character. Plates 427 - 428.

428. Elymus condensatus 'Canyon Prince'

429. Encelia californica

430. Encelia californica

431. Encelia farinosa

432. Encelia farinosa, Twentynine Palms, California

Encelia
Asteracea

A small group of evergreen shrubs, including about 14 species that are widely distributed throughout the Southwest and Mexico and extend to Chile, Peru, and the Galápagos Islands. Several species are native to warm and dry areas of southern California and Baja California, where they have been recognized for many years for their wildlife and landscape restoration value.

Encelia californica
California Encelia

A small mounding shrub, 3-5 ft. high and as wide. Foliage is comprised of long, deep green leaves that are covered with fine hairs. Showy lemon yellow flowers with dark grey centers occur primarily from winter to spring and intermittently all year.

California encelia is native to several coastal islands, as well as seacoast bluffs and foothills, from Santa Barbara County south to Baja California. It is a member of the coastal sage plant community and will grow in open areas within the chaparral. Its principal use is for slope planting, erosion control, and restoration projects. It is usually planted by seed with other native species including *Eschscholzia, Lupinus, Eriogonum, Artemisia*, and *Diplacus*. Plates 429 - 430.

Encelia farinosa
Desert Encelia, Incienso

A small, rounded shrub, 2-4 ft. high and as wide. Leaves are a distinctive white-grey color and contrast well with the colorful golden yellow flowers that occur in mid-spring.

This species has its widest area of distribution throughout the low and intermediate desert regions of the southwestern United States within the creosote bush scrub plant community. It grows under very difficult conditions, tolerating heat, aridity, wind, and drought. Under extreme moisture stress, it will shed some leaves and become dormant. Plants growing along washes will become larger and flower longer due to the availability of moisture. Desert encelia can be established by seed or be transplanted from containers. It is a highly successful plant for the revegetation of slopes and disturbed areas in both dry inland and desert zones. It is also widely used as a foliage and flowering accent plant in medians, planters, and desert gardens with such species as *Fouquieria, Larrea, Ruellia, Dalea,* and *Cercidium*. Plates 431 - 432.

Epilobium

(*Zauschneria*)
California Fuchsia
Onagraceae

A large and complex group of annuals and perennials, including more than 200 species that come from many parts of the world. Several species are native to California, Arizona, and Baja California that have until recently been classified in the genus *Zauschneria*. These types are best known for their showy tubular flowers that are most often scarlet to orange-red; white and pink forms also exist. Flowering begins in summer and continues to fall, during an important season to provide nectar to birds. Well suited as perennials in coastal and inland gardens, many cultivated varieties and hybrids are currently being introduced by specialty native plant growers.

Epilobium californica
California Fuchsia

A low growing species with linear, grey-green foliage, reaching 12-15 in. high, spreading 3-4 ft. across. Native to coastal and inland foothill locations on dry slopes and exposed areas. Prolific numbers of bright orange-red flowers are produced each summer. *E. c.* ssp. *latifolia* develops into a mounding plant and has broader leaves and a denser habit. *E. c.* 'Solidarity Pink' produces light pink flowers. Plates 433 - 435.

Epilobium cana
Hoary California Fuchsia

A small perennial, to 12 in. high, 2-4 ft. wide. Foliage is comprised of very fine, linear leaves that are grey and covered with many fine hairs. Flowers are bright orange-red.

Erigeron
Fleabane
Asteraceae

A large group of annuals and perennials, mostly native to North America. More than 200 species have been identified; only a few are cultivated for use in western gardens. Known for their profusion of colorful, daisy-like flowers from spring to summer, they are most often used in rock gardens and small mixed plantings.

Erigeron glaucus
Beach Aster, Seaside Daisy

A low mounding species, 10-12 in. high, spreading to 2 ft. across. Colorful flowers are purple with yellow centers and occur in spring. This species is native to coastal sand dunes and bluffs from Oregon to southern California. It is suited to coastal gardens where it grows best for 2-3 years on well drained soils with low amounts of supplemental water. It needs protection from extreme heat and sun and additional water when planted in warm, inland regions. Several cultivars have been introduced into the trade that provide more compact forms. Plate 436.

Erigeron karvinskianus
Mexican Daisy

A species native to Mexico through Venezuela. It is a more widely adapted species than *E. glaucus* that performs well in coastal, inland, and valley regions on well drained soils with

433. **Epilobium californica**

434. **Epilobium californica**

435. **Epilobium c. 'Solidarity Pink'**

436. **Erigeron glaucus**

437. **Erigeron karvinskianus**

438. **Erigeron karvinskianus**

439. Eriogonum arborescens

440. Eriogonum cinereum

441. Eriogonum crocatum

442. Eriogonum fasciculatum

443. Eriogonum fasciculatum

low amounts of supplemental water. It grows 10-18 in. high with an equal spread. It has medium green, linear leaves and produces an abundance of small, white to pinkish flowers, to 1 in. across, from spring into summer and intermittently all year. New varieties are being introduced that have more compact forms and deeper pink to lavender flower color. Plates 437 - 438.

Eriogonum
Wild Buckwheat
Polygonaceae

A diverse group of evergreen annuals, perennials, and shrubs that are found throughout the western states in habitats ranging from coastal to desert to alpine. Over 200 species have been identified; only a handful are propagated for ornamental landscape uses. Flowering character on most species is quite distinct and colorful; colors range from white to pink to sulphur yellow. Many times these flower heads develop into dried seed heads and persist for several months.

Species that are grown in cultivation need well drained conditions in either light or heavy soils. They tolerate heat, wind, and aridity in both coastal and inland zones. Perennial types of buckwheat grow well for 2-3 years and then often need to be replaced. These types are well suited to small scale plantings on banks and in rock gardens. Larger shrub varieties are used on slopes and for naturalizing disturbed areas, are better adapted to periods of drought, and are important pollen plants for bees. All species like full sun and require little or no supplemental water once established.

Eriogonum arborescens
Santa Cruz Island Buckwheat

A mounding evergreen shrub, reaching 3-5 ft. high, 4-6 ft. wide. Small, grey-green leaves are attached in whorl-like clusters at the ends of branches. Soft pink to rose flowers occur from early spring to summer.

This species comes from slopes and canyon walls of the coastal islands of California. It is a member of the coastal sage and chaparral plant communities and is adapted to calcareous soils. This species has attractive foliage character and is used as a filler and background plant. With age, it can be pruned to reveal interesting bark and branch character, and can serve as a small rock garden specimen. Plate 439.

Eriogonum cinereum
Ashyleaf Buckwheat

A dense evergreen shrub, mounding 4-6 ft. high and as wide. Foliage is comprised of small leaves, to 1 in. long, medium green above, white below. Flowers are cream to pink in color and occur in numerous ball-like clusters above the foliage in summer.

Ashyleaf buckwheat is common to foothills and bluffs in the coastal strand and coastal sage scrub communities from Los Angeles to Santa Barbara Counties. It tolerates salt spray, wind, and prefers sandy soils. This species is very useful for slope stabilization with other native species in coastal environments or on banks in ornamental settings. Plate 440.

Eriogonum crocatum
Conejo Buckwheat

A perennial with striking white foliage and sulphur yellow flowers. This is a small plant, growing 12-18 in. high, that produces a very intense flower display in early spring.

Saffron buckwheat is a rare and endangered species that naturally occurs on dry slopes of the Conejo Grade in Ventura County. It is a member of the coastal sage scrub plant community and shows low tolerance for summer water in ornamental gardens. Its small size and striking flower and foliage character make it well suited for accent, border, rock garden, and container plantings. It is short lived, declining after 2-3 years. Plate 441.

Eriogonum fasciculatum
Common Buckwheat

A densely branched shrub, growing 2-3 ft. high, equal in spread. Leaves are small and needle-like. Flowers occur in late spring and are white to light pink when young. They mature to deep copper and russet brown by late fall and persist through winter.

Common buckwheat is one of the most widespread species in California. It is frequently found on dry slopes and plains in coastal and inland habitats and is often an indicator species of coastal sage scrub plant communities. Within its range, it has proven to be adaptable to many types of soils, as well as heat, wind, aridity, and drought. It provides pollen for bees for honey production and produces an abundance of seed for birds. This species has great value in slope stabilization and in the restoration of natural areas, where it is easily established by seed. A number of prostrate varieties have been introduced into the trade which can be used as ground covers in ornamental gardens. These include E. f. 'Theodore Payne', E. f. 'Prostrata', E. f. 'Dana Point', and E. f. 'Wildwood'. Plates 442 - 443.

Eriogonum giganteum
St. Catherine's Lace

A medium shrub with strong branching habit, 5-8 ft. high, up to 6-10 ft. wide. Leaves are white to grey-green. Large, flat clusters of white flowers develop from late spring through summer .

This species comes from coastal environments of Santa Catalina and San Clemente Islands and is a member of the coastal sage and chaparral communities. It is adapted to many soils, including calcareous, and performs well in coastal and inland landscapes. This species is well suited to banks, slopes, and background settings in landscapes. Flowers develop over 2-3 months, turn brown as they age, and are sometimes used in dry arrangements. This species can be selectively pruned to develop interesting branch character. Plates 444 - 445.

Eriogonum grande ssp. rubescens
(Eriogonum latifolium rubescens)
Red Buckwheat

A low growing perennial, 6-10 in. high, spreading 2-3 ft. across. Soft, grey-green foliage contrasts well with rose-red flower heads that develop in early summer.

Red buckwheat is a variety that comes from coastal habitats of San Miguel and Santa Cruz Islands. It is useful for rock gardens, containers, and in bank plantings among other native

444. Eriogonum giganteum, Rancho Santa Ana Botanic Garden, Claremont, California

445. Eriogonum giganteum

446. Eriogonum grande ssp. rubescens

447. Eriogonum grande ssp. rubescens

448. Eriogonum umbellatum, above Mono Lake, California

perennials. It performs best in coastal zones and needs relief from full sun and extended periods of drought when used in inland locations. It shows little tolerance for summer water and performs best for 2-3 years. Plates 446 - 447.

Eriogonum parvifolium
Coastal Buckwheat
A densely branched spreading shrub, growing 1-2 ft. high, spreading 5-6 ft. across. Foliage is comprised of rounded to triangularly shaped leaves, green above, white below. Clusters of white to pink flowers cover the plant in late spring to summer.

Coastal buckwheat is native to coastal flats and bluffs from Monterey County south to San Diego County, where it grows in the coastal strand and coastal sage plant communities. This species is well suited to slopes and banks in both coastal and inland gardens with low amounts of supplemental water.

Eriogonum umbellatum
Sulphur Flower
A low perennial, 6-12 in. high, spreading 1-3 ft. across. Dull green leaves are covered with small, white hairs. Striking sulphur yellow flowers occur in round heads from June to August.

This species is native throughout the Northwest. In California, it grows on dry slopes and rocky places, 8,000-9,000 ft. in elevation, in the yellow pine forest plant community of the Sierra Nevada range and within the Klamath Mountains. It is best suited for cooler garden locations and in well drained soils with periodic summer moisture. One colorful cultivar, *E. u.* var. *polyanthum* 'Shasta Sulphur' is a compact, mounding plant with tightly grouped clusters of flowers. Plates 448 - 450.

449. E. u. var. polyanthum 'Shasta Sulphur'

450. E. u. var. polyanthum 'Shasta Sulphur'

451. Eschscholzia californica

452. Eschscholzia californica

Eschscholzia californica
California Poppy
Papaveraceae
A short-lived perennial, 6-15 in. high. Finely divided, grey-green leaves develop from a basal root crown. Showy flowers range in color from pale yellow to deep orange and occur in early spring to summer.

California poppy grows in many regions of California and Oregon, ranging from coastal sand dunes and bluffs to grassy inland valleys and foothills. As a result, many variations in size, foliage, and flowering characteristics can be observed. It is the state flower of California and is very popular as a color accent plant. It is easily established from seed and can be used in small gardens, as well as in large scale slope plantings and naturalization projects. Poppies live for several years and often reseed to establish new plants. Plates 451 - 452.

Eucalyptus
Myrtaceae

Introduction:
A large genus of evergreen shrubs and trees including more than 750 species. This is one of the most important plant groups native to Australia and is widely noted for its many variations and uses. Species range from sprawling shrubs with large flowers to tall trees that grow 200-300 ft. and higher. Several species are grown and managed through forestry practices to obtain wood that is valued for construction, pulp and paper production, and fuel. Other species are cultivated in warm climate regions around the world for ornamental character in urban and rural landscapes. Oils from the leaves of several species are used for medicines and perfumes; flowers produce abundant nectar that is valued by insects and birds. Foliage and flowers of many types are used in cut arrangements. Interestingly, only 12-15 species of *Eucalyptus* are commonly used in western gardens. Many people are confused by their identity and growth habits, which tends to limit the choices made. Both arboreta and specialty nurseries are growing another 40-50 species that are being introduced into the trade.

Character:
Eucalypts provide many interesting and distinctive features, ranging from their bark, foliage, and flowers to their many sizes and shapes. Flowers are comprised of many linear stamens and range in color from white, cream, or yellow to pink and rose. These occur in many sizes, ranging from 1/8 in. to 2 in. across, and can be very showy. Flowering for most species is greatest in the winter months; otherwise, there is intermittent flowering throughout the year. Flowers evolve into hard woody capsules that contain seeds. These capsules are often unique and striking and are one of the best features to use when identifying eucalypts in the field. Species selected for their ornamental flower character include *E. caesia, E. torquata, E. erythrocorys, E. ficifolia, E. sideroxylon,* and *E. torquata.*

Foliage is comprised of leaves of many shapes, sizes, and colors from round to linear and deep green to ashy grey-green. Leaves on many species have two distinct forms: juvenile and mature. Juvenile foliage is often softer and grey; mature foliage is harder and often longer. When leaves are crushed, oils are released that produce a strong characteristic eucalypt scent. Species selected for their distinctively grey foliage character include *E. cinerea, E. papuana,* and *E. polyanthemos.*

Bark can be smooth and colorful, renewed each year by shedding; or it can be hard and rough and persist from year to year. Colors vary from creamy white to grey to red-brown. Species often selected and used for their ornamental bark character include *E. citriodora, E. polyanthemos,* and *E. sideroxylon.*

It is also important to understand that all species of *Eucalyptus* are propagated by seed; cuttings are rarely possible. Seed propagation can lead to many variable characteristics within the same species. For example, *E. sideroxylon,* red ironbark, can have flowers that range from creamy white to deep rose; its foliage can be medium green or very grey-green; and its bark can be light red-brown or very deep red-brown. *E. ficifolia,* red-flowering gum, is another species that is highly variable in both flower and form due to this method of propagation.

Habitat and Culture:
Species of *Eucalyptus* come from virtually all habitats throughout Australia, from coastal foothills and plains to the arid interior regions. Some types are also native to the wet subtropical forests of the northeast. Within this range, individual species grow in widely varying moisture and soil conditions.

Species selected for landscape use in western gardens have shown wide tolerance of many habitat and planting conditions. Most types are adapted and easily grow in coastal and inland habitats throughout California. Some have greater tolerance of cold and can be successfully grown in interior valleys, such as the San Joaquin Valley, where heavier winter frosts occur. Species selected for desert regions should be adapted to iron poor soils and to extreme heat, aridity, and wind conditions.

Eucalypts have a wide tolerance of soil and moisture conditions. They readily accept regular moisture but are well adapted to the winter rains and summer drought of the Mediterranean climate. In urban landscapes, rich soils and regular moisture stimulate faster growth and larger sizes. This often results in the need to prune them regularly and to remove trees as they grow beyond the limits of their planting spaces. Irrigation management is the key to conserving water and moderating growth. It is also important to note that many plants can be observed growing in unmaintained and rural landscapes in coastal and inland habitats without supplemental water once they are established.

Uses and Considerations:
For many decades, eucalypts have been popular and widely used in various landscape situations. A great deal of this use is due to their fast growth rate and easy tolerance of both garden and natural growing conditions. Plantations were established around the turn of the century with the hope of providing high quality construction timber. Windrows of trees were planted in coastal and agricultural areas. Ease of care and adaptability have made eucalypts highly suited to rural as well as urban areas for parks, open space, and background plantings. Species such as *E. cladocalyx,* the sugar gum, have brought a forested appearance to the grassland landscape of many coastal foothills throughout southern California. Similarly, *E. globulus,* the tasmanian bluegum, was established in foothill areas of the San Francisco Bay area.

453. Damage caused by bark beetle borers.

Eucalypts have also been popular choices in contemporary landscaping as demand increased for immediate character and fast growth.

Several considerations should influence the selection and use of eucalypts. Most species grow to large sizes and are best suited to commercial or community scale spaces. Pruning often becomes necessary as plants outgrow smaller spaces. Eucalypts often do not respond consistently or easily to pruning. Additionally, many trees that are heavily pruned are likely to need careful pruning maintenance each year to manage the suckering regrowth. Unfortunately, many of the larger species of eucalypts are used in residential gardens and small urban spaces with little understanding of their mature sizes and bulk.

Root development in eucalypts occurs quickly. Avoid large plants in small containers that have coiled roots. Plants installed in landscapes from smaller sizes, 5 and 15 gallon containers, often establish better and grow more quickly. Good staking practices are needed for trunk development. Young trees often have flexible and spindly trunks. Under most conditions, these trunks will fill out and be self supporting in 2-3 growing seasons. Smaller tree species, such as *E. caesia, E. erythrocorys* and *E. torquata,* tend to have more problematic trunk and branch development. Care should be taken to monitor tree ties on larger species to avoid girdling problems. Larger species, such as *E. camaldulensis, E. globulus, E. polyanthemos,* and *E. viminalis,* are also subject to limb failure when they are old and mature. The combination of weight, age, and wind can lead to the

454. *Eucalyptus cladocalyx*, Flinders Range, South Australia

breakage of large side branches. An ongoing effort to anticipate branch failure and the need for pruning is recommended.

Eucalypts produce abundant amounts of leaf, bark, and seed capsule litter. Some of this litter is seasonal, but there is usually some form of litter throughout the year. Leaves are hard, contain oils, and do not compost easily. These oils effect the understory soils and often inhibit the growth of understory shrubs and ground covers. Generally, the larger the tree, the greater the litter.

Eucalypts also have the capacity and tendency to use great amounts of water from the soil. This use of moisture is frequently at the expense of other landscape plants, often increasing their drought stress.

In recent years, the eucalyptus longhorn beetle, *Phoracantha semipunctata*, has been brought to western gardens. This beetle is having a serious impact upon several species of eucalyptus. Beetles do not harm healthy trees that produce enough sap to kill the beetle larvae. However, trees occurring in natural areas, where drought stress or old age has reduced their vigor, are being extensively damaged or killed. As a result, eucalypts can no longer be recommended for areas of prolonged drought and climate stress without concern for the effects of this beetle. Currently, it is recom-

mended that existing trees be inspected regularly and good management practices be followed. Trees should receive enough moisture to reduce drought stress; pruning should occur in winter and spring only; infested trees and wood should be removed and chipped immediately. Biological control appears to offer the best method for long term management. An Australian species of wasp, *Syngaster lepidus*, is a natural predator of this longhorn beetle and has been recently introduced as part of this program.

Associated Plantings:

Eucalypts are very successful plants for many landscape situations. When they are used in large spaces and in large groupings, they produce shade and litter that must be taken into consideration. Successful understory plants for these situations include *Acacia* species, *Myoporum laetum*, *Melaleuca nesophila*, *Leptospermum laevigatum*, *Nerium oleander*, and *Jasminum mesnyi*. These are all large shrub species that can grow within filtered sun and survive with the accumulation of litter. When eucalypts are used in courtyards and other small spaces, it is possible to plant many understory plants around them. It is advisable to remove most of the leaf litter to minimize the amount of oils that reach the soil.

Helpful References:

Boland, D. J., M. I. H. Brooker, G. M. Chippendale, N. Hall, B.P.M. Hyland, R. D. Johnston, D. A. Kleinig, J. D. Turner. Forest Trees of Australia. Melbourne: Thomas Nelson Australia, 1985.

Boomsma, C. D., and N. B. Lewis. The Native Forest and Woodland Vegetation of South Australia. Bulletin 25. South Australia: Woods and Forests Department.

Costermans, Leon. Native Trees and Shrubs of Southeastern Australia. Dee Why West, NSW: Rigby Publishers, 1986.

Elliot, W. Rodger, and David L. Jones. Encyclopaedia of Australian Plants. Vol. 4 Melbourne: Lothian Publishing Company, 1982.

National Botanic Gardens. Growing Native Plants. No. 2. Canberra: Australian Government Publishing Service, 1981.

Nicholson, Nan, and Hugh Nicholson. Australian Rainforest Plants. Australia: Terania Rainforest Nursery, 1985.

Williams, Keith A. W. Native Plants: Queensland. North Ipswich, Australia: Keith A. W. Williams, 1984.

Wrigley, John W., and Murray Fagg. Australian Native Plants. Sydney: William Collins Publishers, 1980.

Eucalyptus caesia
Gungurru

A small tree, 15-20 ft. high and as wide that develops an open and weeping character with slender branches. Branches are often pendulous; branchlets and flower pods are typically chalky white. Leaves are distinctively grey-green, curved with a pointed tip, and contrast nicely with the colorful pink-red flowers that occur in large clusters.

Gungurru is a rare and endangered species in its native habitat of southwestern West Australia. It grows on granite outcrops and in moderately well drained, sandy loams, where it has adapted to moderate levels of frost and periods of summer drought.

This can be a striking specimen plant for garden situations. The trunk, bark, foliage, flowers, and seed pods are of ornamental value. However, plants with good trunk structure should be selected as many plants develop irregular character. Good staking and pruning is often necessary to achieve the best results. It prefers a well drained soil, slightly acid to slightly alkaline, and full sun. With age, it tolerates periods of drought but will produce less growth and poorer flower character under prolonged stress. Excessive water and fertilizer promote weak growth. Plate 455.

Eucalyptus camaldulensis
River Red Gum, Red Gum

A medium to large tree, 60-100 ft. high, that develops a full crown, 40-60 ft. wide. Leaves are olive green, narrow, and curved, 7-9 in. long, and hang from small, red colored branches. Bark on stems and trunk is deciduous, leaving a distinctly mottled character that is white, tan, and grey. Large clusters of inconspicuous, creamy white flowers occur in late fall. Flowers and nectar attract bees and birds.

This is the most widely distributed species of eucalypt in Australia, covering the entire continent, where it is adapted to many climate conditions. In arid and semi-arid interior regions, it can survive only along seasonal watercourses. In other locations, it occurs in woodland, open forest landscapes and on floodplains. In its range, it is associated with *Acacia melanoxylon*, *A. stenophylla*, *Eucalyptus viminalis*, and *E. leucoxylon*. It nearly always grows in acidic and sandy alluvial soils. Its habitat ranges in elevation from 75-2,200 ft. Mean maximum temperature reaches 80-104° F; while mean minimum temperature ranges 37-59° F, with periodic frosts occurring in cooler locations. Mean annual rainfall varies from 6-24 in., sometimes reaching 50 in. Plants in drier locations survive off seasonal flooding or the existence of high water tables.

In western gardens, this species adapts particularly well to warm inland valleys and foothills, where it can survive with low amounts of supplemental water. Larger growth occurs in deep alluvial soils and where there is regular moisture. It tolerates moderate frosts and temperatures to 12°-15° F, making it suited to cooler interior valleys. This is a large tree, well suited for groves, open space, and park plantings. Certain faster growing selections of river red gum are planted in valley areas to develop biomass for energy production. Plates 456 - 457.

455. Eucalyptus caesia

456. Eucalyptus camaldulensis

457. Eucalyptus camaldulensis

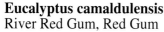

458. Eucalyptus cinerea

Eucalyptus cinerea
Argyle Apple

A medium size tree, 20-40 ft. high, that develops a round crown, 20-30 ft. wide. Persistent bark is red-brown, with deep fissures, and occurs on twisting trunks and branches. Leaves are a distinctive ash grey color. Juvenile leaves are round; adult leaves are elongated and curved. Inconspicuous flowers occur in clusters at the base of stems in late spring and are valuable to bees.

This species comes from foothill locations in eastern Australia, where it is adapted to many types of soils. In western gardens, it shows good adaptation to sun, heat, frost, and low amounts of supplemental water but dislikes iron poor soils. Established plants can survive on rainfall in coastal, inland, and valley zones.

Argyle apple offers special foliage and bark interest value for ornamental use. It can develop upright or crooked trunks with twisting branches to produce many sculptural shapes. The foliage provides a bright contrast to most other plants and is used in cut arrangements. It is well suited to mixed plantings in large parks and commercial spaces and grows well in interior valleys. Plates 458 - 459.

459. Eucalyptus cinerea

460. Eucalyptus citriodora

Eucalyptus citriodora
Lemon-scented Gum

A medium to large tree, 70-100 ft. high, 25-40 ft. wide, with a smooth and elegant trunk character. Deciduous bark drops in the early summer to reveal new, pinkish to white bark beneath. Leaves are 4-7 in. long, curved, and exude a strong lemon scent when crushed. Inconspicuous clusters of white flowers occur in late fall.

This species is native to two principal areas in eastern Australia. Its habitat ranges from near the coast to inland sites on rolling hills and in frost free zones. Annual rainfall varies from 25-60 in., with most moisture coming in summer months. Within its range, it is associated with *Angophora costata.*

Lemon-scented gum has caught the eye and fancy of many people for use in western gardens. It is valued for its upright habit, smooth bark, graceful stance, and fragrant foliage. It is a very fast grower that can easily enframe a 2-3 story building. Good drainage is necessary, and it performs best with moderate amounts of supplemental water. It is not suited to areas having heavy seasonal frosts or extended periods of drought stress. Plates 460 - 462.

461. Eucalyptus citriodora

462. Eucalyptus citriodora

Eucalyptus cladocalyx
Sugar Gum

A medium to large size tree, attaining heights of 45-75 ft. high, developing a spreading crown, 35-50 ft. wide. Foliage is comprised of shiny, medium green leaves, 3-5 in. long; new growth at the tops of trees is coppery red. Inconspicuous creamy white flowers occur in spring and summer. Bark is pale yellow to tan and drops off in patches in late summer and fall.

This species is native to three areas in South Australia, where it grows in coastal and inland foothill habitats. It is found on both slightly acidic soils and alkaline soils. The mean maximum temperature of the hottest month can reach 90° F; periodic winter frosts also occur. Annual rainfall ranges from 15-25 in., with most occurring in the winter. In its range, it often associates with *E. leucoxylon*.

Sugar gum is one of the most popular and naturally adapted species for coastal foothills, from San Diego to Santa Barbara to warm hillsides of the San Francisco Bay area. This species is planted individually or in groves. Mature plants provide striking silhouette character for background and skyline impact. It is quick to establish and can easily survive with low amounts of supplemental water. It is successfully used within freeway landscapes, parks, and open spaces, from the coastal edge to inland foothill and valley locations. Plates 454, 463 - 465.

463. Eucalyptus cladocalyx

464. Eucalyptus cladocalyx

465. Eucalyptus cladocalyx

466. Eucalyptus erythrocorys

Eucalyptus erythrocorys
Red-cap Gum

A small tree, 15-25 ft. high, to 10 ft. wide. This species has an irregular growth habit. It can develop single, upright trunks or become sprawling with multiple trunks. Leaves are 5-10 in. long and pointed. Flowers have a striking red cap that releases and reveals colorful yellow stamens in the fall.

Red-cap gum comes only from the western coast of West Australia. It typically grows on well drained, sandy loams over a limestone subgrade in warm and semi-arid locations. In cultivation, it needs neutral to alkaline soils with good drainage and full sun.

This species is suited to coastal and inland gardens, where it tolerates heat and drought and needs only low amounts of supplemental water. It is a difficult tree to train into an upright habit; most plants need several years of careful staking and pruning. It is a smaller species that enables it to be planted in parking lot planters, small shopping center planters, and in background plantings. Too much water produces unwanted top heavy growth. Plates 466 - 468.

467. Eucalyptus erythrocorys

468. Eucalyptus erythrocorys

469. Eucalyptus ficifolia

Eucalyptus ficifolia
Red Flowering Gum

A medium tree, 25-40 ft. high, with a round crown, 25-40 ft. wide. Leaves are 3-7 in. long, pointed, and deep green. Showy flowers range from white, salmon, pink to red in color and occur in large clusters in mid-summer. Flowers are good for honey production; large urn-shaped pods persist on the tree for many months.

This species comes from a narrow coastal belt in West Australia that is characterized by warm summers and frost free winters. It grows in slightly acidic or gravelly sands that are well drained. Annual rainfall varies from 35-55 in., with most occurring in the winter.

Red flowering gum is widely known for its flowering value. Its finest form and performance occurs in humid, coastal landscapes from San Diego to San Francisco. In these locations, it survives with low amounts of supplemental water. Many flower and form variations of this plant can be seen in western landscapes. Propagation from seed often produces plants of uncertain flower value; try to purchase plants in summer when flowers are visible. Flowering can be diminished if trees get too much water or are located in lawns without good drainage. Plants grown in inland gardens are damaged by frosts and tend to be more inconsistent in performance. Plates 469 - 470.

470. Eucalyptus ficifolia

471. Eucalyptus globulus

Eucalyptus globulus
Blue Gum, Tasmanian Blue Gum

A large tree, 60-120 ft. high, 35-50 ft. wide. Trunks become massive with age and are covered with light brown bark which peels off in large sheets each fall. Foliage is comprised of long, curved leaves which are often sea-green in color; juvenile foliage is very grey-green. Large creamy white flowers are inconspicuous and occur in winter.

Blue gum is native to forest landscapes of southern and eastern parts of Australia and Tasmania. Within its natural range several subspecies have evolved. The species most commonly found in cultivation in western gardens is *E. g.* ssp. *globulus*, known as the tasmanian blue gum. Its natural habitat occurs at elevations from sea level to 1,500 ft. within cool, moist coastal to inland climates. Mean summer maximum temperature ranges 68-74° F; frost is common, 10-30 times per year. Rainfall averages 25-55 in. and is heaviest in winter. The best development of this species occurs in moist valleys on good quality acid to neutral loam soils.

Blue gum shows good adaptation to shallow and sandy soils. Moisture conditions influence tree size and character. It is a species historically planted across the state of California in windrows and plantations. Many occurrences of naturalization and stump regeneration after cutting can be observed. This is a large species that produces an abundance of bark, leaf, and pod litter. A smaller and more densely branched cultivar, *E. globulus* spp. 'Compacta', is frequently used for large scale screening of industrial sites and along freeway setbacks. Plates 471 - 473.

472. Eucalyptus globulus

473. Eucalyptus globulus 'Compacta'

Eucalyptus lehmannii
Lehmann's Mallee

A large shrub to small tree, 20-30 ft. high, with a round shape to 30 ft. wide. Densely clustered foliage is comprised of pale green leaves that grow to 2 in. long and turn brown to red in the fall before dropping. Inconspicuous flowers are apple green and develop from large many segmented pods during summer.

This species comes from coastal areas of West Australia. It generally grows on slightly acidic, well drained sands, and is tolerant of salt spray and coastal winds. Annual rainfall varies from 10-20 in. and extended dry periods are common. In western gardens, this is a popular plant for roadside screening along coastal highways where it can survive with little or no supplemental water. It is widely grown as a shrub until mature, then is pruned to form a handsome single or multi-trunk canopy tree. It can also be grown as a standard tree for use in parking lots and along streets. It is damaged by frost in inland locations and becomes chlorotic in iron poor soils or with poor drainage. Plates 474 - 475.

474. Eucalyptus lehmannii

Eucalyptus leucoxylon
White Ironbark, Yellow Gum

A medium size tree, 30-50 ft. high, 15-40 ft. wide. Trunk and branches often develop irregular to upright shapes and are covered with white bark that is deciduous. Leaves are medium green, slightly curved, and pointed. Creamy white flowers occur in large clusters and are valued for honey production.

White ironbark is widely distributed in southern areas of Australia, where it occurs in humid coastal regions, as well as dry inland habitats. It grows on many soil types, including calcareous to slightly acid sands. The mean annual rainfall ranges from 15-30 in.; inland areas experience 10-15 frosts per year. It is found in association with *E. cladocalyx*. A subspecies, *E. leucoxylon macrocarpa* 'Rosea' (also, *E. leucoxylon* ssp. *megalocarpa*), is native to coastal areas, usually in slightly alkaline soils. This subspecies produces showy, rose colored flowers and develops into a large shrub to small tree, 20-25 ft. high. Both species are popular in coastal regions in the west, and are used for slope, setback, and screen planting situations where they need little supplemental water. They have also been successfully used in low desert regions. Plates 476 - 478.

475. Eucalyptus lehmannii

476. Eucalyptus leucoxylon

477. Eucalyptus leucoxylon 'Rosea'

478. Eucalyptus leucoxylon 'Rosea'

479. Eucalyptus maculata, eastern Australia

480. Eucalyptus maculata

Eucalyptus maculata
Spotted Gum

A tall, upright tree, growing 60-80 ft. high, developing a round crown 30-40 ft. wide. Trunks are covered with yellow, grey, and charcoal colored bark that flakes off each year to create an attractive spotted character. Leaves are 4-7 in. long, dark green, and pointed; inconspicuous clusters of creamy white flowers are fragrant and provide pollen for bees for honey production.

This species comes from coastal areas of New South Wales, Australia, where it grows on foothills and slopes from sea level to 3,000 feet. Mean maximum temperature ranges from 77-86° F; mean minimum 33-46° F, with periodic frosts each year. Annual rainfall ranges from 25-50 in. and occurs throughout the year. This species tolerates a wide range of soils, however, best development occurs in heavy textured soils that are on moist, well drained sites. In its range, it grows in open forests and is found associated with *Tristania conferta*.

Spotted gum is useful in large spaces within parks and commercial landscapes. It is often grown in stands and groves where bark character becomes more distinctive with age. This species is easily mistaken for *E. citriodora* due to the similarities in bark character. However, spotted gum leaves do not have a lemon scent when crushed. Plates 479 - 482.

481. Eucalyptus maculata, eastern Australia

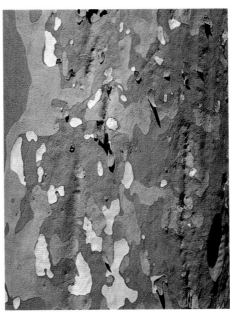

482. Eucalyptus maculata, bark

Eucalyptus microtheca
Coolibah

A medium tree, 30-40 ft. tall, with a rounded crown 20-30 ft. wide. Trunks can be single or multiple and are covered with persistent grey bark. Foliage is comprised of pale green leaves, 3-7 in. long. It produces numerous small and inconspicuous creamy white flowers that are valued for honey production.

Coolibah is widely distributed throughout arid and semi-arid regions of Australia. It tolerates long periods of heat; the mean maximum temperature ranges from 87-105° F, with mean minimum of 39-57° F. Annual precipitation averages from 10-25 in. with long periods between rains. It tolerates a wide range of soils including clays, coarse textured sands, and alkaline conditions. It grows in open forests and along seasonal water courses in association with *E. camaldulensis, Pittosporum phillyraeoides,* and *Cassia nemophila*.

This species has proven to be one of the best eucalypts for low desert regions. It tolerates heat, wind, and iron poor soils. It can develop into many forms, but is most often preferred as a single trunk tree with a dense crown. Plates 483 - 484.

483. Eucalyptus microtheca

484. Eucalyptus microtheca, Phoenix, Arizona

Eucalyptus nicholii
Willow Peppermint,
Nichol's Willow-leaved Peppermint

A medium tree, 30-40 ft. high, 20-30 ft. wide. Foliage is comprised of narrow, pale blue-green leaves, 3-5 in. long, that hang gracefully from branches to create a soft textured appearance. Persistent bark is rough and often a rich red-brown color. Flowers and pods are insignificant.

This species is native to eastern Australia where it grows on well drained slopes and ridges in shallow, clayey soils. It is adapted to wind, frosts, and dry summer conditions. In western regions, this species is valued for its soft, billowy texture and moderate size. It is suited to residential and commercial landscapes, as well as for parks, on slopes, and for screen plantings. It becomes chlorotic in iron poor soils and when given too much water. Young trees vary in growth habit; select strong trunks, and both stake and prune carefully in early years for best development. Plates 485 - 487.

485. Eucalyptus nicholii

486. Eucalyptus nicholii

487. Eucalyptus nicholii

Eucalyptus papuana
Ghost Gum, White Gum

A medium size tree, 30-50 ft. and higher, spreading 25-40 ft. wide. Foliage is comprised of long, grey-green leaves; inconspicuous flowers occur in small clusters and have white to pale green stamens. Trunks are often straight with twisting branches and are covered with very white bark that is deciduous.

Ghost gum is native to many parts of northern and central Australia, where it grows in subtropical and arid climate regions. Rainfall in moister areas reaches 60 in. annually and enables this species to grow faster and to larger sizes. Arid regions receive as little as 10 in. each year which results in trees that are more twisted and smaller in size. Summer temperatures reach as high as 104° F.

In Australia, this species is noted for its striking white bark and handsome trunk and branch character. It has been recently introduced into western regions and is showing good adaptation to low and intermediate desert areas in Arizona. Like other eucalypts, it should be highly adapted to coastal and inland zones, in well drained soils, and with low to moderate amounts of moisture. Plates 488 - 489.

488. Eucalyptus papuana

489. Eucalyptus papuana

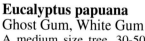

490. Eucalyptus polyanthemos

Eucalyptus polyanthemos
Red Box, Silver Dollar Gum

A large tree, 45-60 ft. tall, with a dense, full crown, 30-45 ft. wide. Trunks are covered with rough, grey bark that peels off in flakes and strips. Distinctive foliage is comprised of grey-green leaves. Juvenile leaves are round; mature leaves are long and pointed. Noticeable clusters of creamy white flowers occur in winter.

Red box comes from foothills and ranges of eastern Australia at altitudes varying from 400 to 2,500 ft. It is best adapted to warm, inland areas and is tolerant of numerous frosts each year. Mean maximum temperature ranges from 78-90° F; mean minimum ranges from 32-39° F. Annual rainfall ranges from 20-30 in., often with maximum distribution in winter. It is tolerant of many soils, and is often found on dry, stony or gravelly soils to heavy, poor soils. It grows in open forest and savanna woodlands in association with *E. leucoxylon* and *E. sideroxylon*.

This species is popular as a foliage accent tree for large spaces such as parks and commercial spaces. Specimens with rounded foliage are preferred for their silver dollar-like character. Provide careful staking in early stages to assist trunk development. Plates 490 - 491.

491. Eucalyptus polyanthemos

492. Eucalyptus rudis

Eucalyptus rudis
Flooded Gum

A medium to large size tree, 30-50 ft. high, 25-40 ft. wide. Leaves are deep green, broad at the base, pointed at the tip. Inconspicuous clusters of creamy white flowers occur in early spring. Bark on trunk is grey, rough, and persistent.

Flooded gum is native to Western Australia, where it grows near the coast and adjacent inland foothills. It grows on river plains and along stream banks in regions that have hot, dry summers with temperatures that reach 96° F. Winters are mild, have periodic frosts and receive an average 16-39 inches of precipitation. This species is best adapted to heavier silts and loams but will also grow on sandy and clayey soils.

Flooded gum is a tough and adaptable species. It will grow in areas that receive lots or little water and endure heat, drought, and aridity. In western gardens, it has been a successful species for low and intermediate desert regions, where it has been used in both residential and commercial landscapes. It is also widely adapted to coastal, inland, and valley zones and will grow well in lawns or in places that receive periodic deep watering. Plates 492 - 494.

493. Eucalyptus rudis

494. Eucalyptus rudis

Eucalyptus sideroxylon
Red Ironbark

A medium to large tree 35-70 ft. tall with an upright crown. Bark on trunks is persistent and often a rich red-brown color. Foliage occurs on pendulous branchlets and is comprised of long, pointed leaves that vary in color from grey-green to medium green. Flowers occur in winter and range from creamy white to deep rose. Rose colored varieties often provide moderate flower accent value.

This species occurs principally in inland areas of southeastern Australia on low plains to foothills above 3,500 ft. elevation. It is often found on poor, shallow soils comprised of sand, gravel, or clay and in association with *E. leucoxylon* and *E. polyanthemos*. The mean maximum temperature ranges from 77-92° F; mean minimum ranges from 32-42° F with numerous winter frosts at higher elevations. Annual rainfall ranges from 20-40 in. with uniform to summer maximum distribution.

Red ironbark is a popular species that is noted for distinctive bark, foliage, and flower character. It is well suited to large landscape spaces in commercial, industrial, and park settings. Flower color in this species is highly variable; select plants when flowers are visible. Red flowering forms are often known as *E. s.* 'Rosea' and are available and the most popular. Varieties with very grey foliage and dark, red-brown bark are also common. Chlorosis can occur in iron poor soils and from excessive watering. Plates 495 - 498.

495. Eucalyptus sideroxylon

496. Eucalyptus sideroxylon

497. Eucalyptus sideroxylon 'Rosea'

498. Eucalyptus sideroxylon

Eucalyptus spathulata
Narrow-leaved Gimlet, Swamp Gimlet

A large shrub to small tree developing many trunks, growing 15-25 ft. high, 15-20 ft. wide. Foliage is comprised of very narrow, dull green leaves that have a pointed tip. Bark is persistent, grey to brown in color; white flowers are insignificant.

This species is native to low basin areas in Western Australia, often in association with saline lakes. It grows in sandy loams or clay loams that can have varying levels of salinity. It is adapted to periods of heat, cold, drought, and aridity, as well as short spells of flooding.

Narrow-leaved gimlet is well suited to coastal, inland, valley, and low desert regions. It can be used as a screen, slope, and windbreak plant or be pruned into a small scale canopy tree for use in courtyards. Its small size and versatility as a shrub or tree enable it to be used in both commercial and residential landscapes. Plates 499 - 500.

499. Eucalyptus spathulata

500. Eucalyptus spathulata, Palm Springs

Eucalyptus torquata
Coral Gum

A small to medium tree with a round crown, 15-25 ft. high, spreading as wide. Trunks are covered with persistent bark that is rough textured and deep brown in color. Leaves are 2-6 in. long, pointed, and pale green. Colorful pink to rose flowers occur in large numbers in summer and create a distinctive flowering accent quality. Large amounts of nectar are produced by these flowers for bees and insects to harvest.

Coral gum is found in limited areas of West Australia, where it is native to low elevations on stony slopes and hills. Soils are often well drained loams that are slightly alkaline. In cultivation, this species has shown good tolerance of sandy and clayey soils as well. This is one of the smaller and more ornamental species for use in smaller spaces. It can be used as a patio, parking lot, or street tree but needs careful staking and pruning when young to produce a good shape. It is well suited to semi-arid and warm inland regions, where it tolerates heat, wind, and moderate frost. It can easily grow with low amounts of supplemental water; excessive water leads to top heavy growth and chlorosis. Plates 501 - 503.

Eucalyptus viminalis
Manna Gum, Ribbon Gum

A medium to large tree, 40-120 ft. high, with an open branching habit and spread to 50 ft. wide. Branches are covered by deciduous bark that becomes tan with age and peels in large strips to reveal white bark beneath. Trunks are covered by persistent brown bark. Foliage is comprised of 4-6 in. long, dark green, pointed leaves. Inconspicuous flowers are creamy white and occur in large clusters in winter.

This species is widely distributed throughout the southeastern parts of Australia and Tasmania. Its habitat is highly varied, including both moist and dry sites, cool to warm climate conditions. The mean maximum temperature ranges from 68-89° F; mean minimum ranges from 24-46° F. Plants in cooler parts of this range experience periodic snow and up to 100 frosts per year. Rainfall ranges from 20-80 in. and occurs throughout the year. Larger plants develop on moist, well drained alluvial soils in valley locations. It grows in forest associations in combination with other eucalypts and *Acacia dealbata and Acacia melanoxylon*. In western regions, manna gum is often used in large areas for windbreaks, screens, and groves. It is tolerant of heat, aridity, and low to moderate amounts of supplemental water. Plates 504 - 506.

501. **Eucalyptus torquata**

502. **Eucalyptus torquata**

503. **Eucalyptus torquata**

504. **Eucalyptus viminalis**

505. **Eucalyptus viminalis, southern Australia**

506. **Eucalyptus viminalis**

Euphorbia

Spurge

Euphorbiaceae

A very large genus of plants that includes annuals, perennials, herbs, succulents, shrubs, and trees. More than 1,600 species have been found growing throughout the world and are extremely diverse in character. One species, *Euphorbia pulcherrima*, Poinsettia, is widely known as a commercial flower plant for the winter holiday season in many countries. Most plants in landscape use are succulent in character and contain an acrid, white, milky sap that can cause skin irritation and, in some species, is poisonous. Many species exist with the widest selection coming from specialty nurseries. Most tolerate heat and drought stress. They are planted as special interest and accent plants in rock gardens, with succulents, and in containers.

Euphorbia characias

Large Mediterranean Spurge

A small to medium evergreen perennial, 3-4 ft. high and as wide. Foliage and branches are blue-green; leaves are long and narrow to 4 in. Showy clusters of chartreuse flower bracts reach 3-5 in. dia. and occur in early spring. This species is native to the Mediterranean region where it grows on dry, rocky ground and exposed areas, from coastal to inland foothills. In western regions, it is grown from the Pacific Northwest to the high and low desert landscapes of California and Arizona. It prefers well drained soils, moderate amounts of supplemental water, and tolerates heat, frost, and short periods of drought stress. Old stems die after flowering and should be cut off at the base to stimulate new growth. One subspecies, *E. c.* ssp. *wulfenii*, is the most widely planted form, producing large clusters of flower bracts that reach 5-6 in. dia. Plate 507.

Euphorbia ingens

Candelabra Tree

A large tree-like species, slowly growing 15-25 ft. high, and developing a rounded crown comprised of many heavy branches. Small clusters of yellow-green flowers accent the branches in spring. Candelabra tree is native to inland and coastal parts of South Africa where it grows in dry, rocky regions. With age, it becomes a massive specimen plant in coastal and inland gardens; younger plants are often used in containers. It prefers well drained soils, periodic deep watering, and is tender to frost. Plate 508.

Euphorbia milii

(Euphorbia splendens)

Crown of Thorns

A low mounding subshrub, 1-4 ft. high, 3-4 ft. across. Woody stems have multiple 1 in. long stems. Leaves are bright green, grow 1-2 in. long, and are dropped during periods of moisture stress. Colorful pairs of red flower bracts cover the plant in early spring and intermittently all year. This species comes from subtropical regions of Madagascar and is well suited to coastal or frost free inland and low desert regions. Plate 511.

Euphorbia rigida

(Euphorbia biglandulosa)

Narrow-leaved Glaucus Spurge

A small to medium succulent shrub, 3-4 ft. high, 4-5 ft. wide. Foliage and stems are striking blue-green; leaves are pointed and arranged around the stems in opposite pairs. Showy clusters of char-treuse flower bracts develop in early spring. This

507. **Euphorbia characias ssp. wulfenii**

508. **Euphorbia ingens**

509. **Euphorbia rigida**

510. **Euphorbia rigida**

511. **Euphorbia milii**

512. **Euphorbia tirucalli, Palm Springs**

513. Euryops pectinatus

514. Euryops pectinatus 'Viridis'

515. Euryops pectinatus 'Viridis'

516. Fallugia paradoxa

517. Fallugia paradoxa

species is native to dry, rocky places around the Mediterranean region. This species has proven to be tolerant of heat, sun, cold, and drought. It prefers well drained soils and requires only low amounts of supplemental water whether in coastal, valley, or desert regions. Old stems die after plants flower and should be removed. Plates 509 - 510.

Euphorbia tirucalli
Milkbush, Pencilbush

A large mounding shrub with intricate branching, 12-18 ft. and higher. Numerous green stems develop in billowy masses and create a striking pattern of lines. This species is native to frost free coastal and inland zones in tropical and South Africa, where it becomes a tree with stout trunks growing to 30 ft. high. It can be used as a container and accent plant in courtyards in coastal, inland, and low desert regions where it is protected from temperatures below 25 F. Plate 512.

Euryops pectinatus
Gray-leaved Euryops
Compositae

A medium to large evergreen perennial, 3-6 ft. high and as wide. Foliage is comprised of grey-green leaves that are deeply divided; bright yellow, daisy-like flowers cover the plant during early spring and intermittently through fall.

This species comes from the Cape region of South Africa, where is it highly adapted to coastal habitats with wind, salt spray, sandy soils, and mild levels of drought stress. This is a very popular flowering shrub for western gardens and is grown throughout the coastal, inland, and valley regions. It tolerates many types of soils, including calcareous, but does require good drainage, moderate levels of water, and sun in order to perform best. A popular cultivar, *E. p.* 'Viridis', grows to similar sizes but has deep green foliage. These plants are used in containers, along borders, and as flowering accents around entries and pools. Cut off old flowers to extend the flowering season. Plates 513 - 515.

Fallugia paradoxa
Apache Plume
Rosaceae

A medium to large shrub, growing 3-8 ft. high, 6-10 ft. wide. Tiny dark green leaves are divided into 3-7 lobes and occur on small, twiggy branches. They are deciduous under drought stress and through winter. Moderately showy flowers have white petals and occur during early to mid-spring. Seeds develop in late spring with clusters of feathery tails that turn pink and are showy.

Apache plume is native to high desert and interior plateau regions from California and Arizona to New Mexico, Colorado, and into Mexico. It grows on dry hillsides, gravelly slopes, and sandy plains at elevations ranging from 3,500 to 7,500 ft. in association with such desert species as *Larrea tridentata* and *Artemisia tridentata*. It tolerates heat, aridity, wind, frost, and extended periods of drought. It is considered to be a valuable browse plant, as well as being useful for restoration and soil erosion control projects. It is not widely used in ornamental gardens but is most appropriate for landscape use within its natural range. Plates 516 - 517.

Feijoa sellowiana
Pineapple Guava
Myrtaceae

A large evergreen shrub to small tree, 15-25 ft. high and as wide. Foliage is comprised of oval leaves, 2-3 in. long, that are deep, glossy green above and distinctively white beneath. Showy red and white flowers develop in late spring and are comprised of thick, edible petals. Edible, grey-green fruit matures by end of summer or fall and can reach 2-4 in. long. Fruit has a thick skin and seedy pulp that tastes like pineapple.

Pineapple guava is one of two species within the genus *Feijoa*. It is native to subtropical regions of South America, including Brazil, Paraguay, Uruguay, and northern Argentina. It has been widely cultivated in warm climate regions around the world for both its ornamental character and fruit value. Fruit can be eaten fresh or made into jellies; numerous cultivated varieties have been developed to provide different qualities of fruit. Fruiting is best when plants are grown in deep soils, sunny and warm locations, and with regular moisture. In western gardens, this species is frequently used as a courtyard specimen, background, or screen plant. It grows well in coastal, inland, valley, and, with protection, in low desert regions. Established plants require only low amounts of supplemental water to retain good visual character. As plants mature, they can be pruned to reveal interesting multiple branching and bark character. They can also be clipped to form a hedge when used for background and screen plants. Plates 518 - 520.

518. Feijoa sellowiana

519. Feijoa sellowiana

520. Feijoa sellowiana

Festuca ovina glauca
Blue Fescue
Poaceae

A small, clumping, perennial grass, to 1 ft. high. Distinctive foliage is comprised of bluish grey-green leaves that are tightly rolled into a cylindrical shape. Attractive wheat colored flower plumes occur in spring to summer.

Blue fescue is the most popular variety of ornamental grass for dry landscape situations. It shows good tolerance of heat, aridity, and drought stress and is widely planted in coastal, inland, valley, and desert regions. It prefers full sun, well drained soils, and performs best with moderate amounts of moisture in hot, dry locations. Established plants in coastal and inland areas need only low amounts of supplemental water. This species provides a soft texture and mounding shape that is highly attractive when contrasted with other foliage plants and when used around pools and garden sculptures. It is often used in rock gardens, along borders, and for creating patterns of clumping plants around shrubs and trees. This variety can be clipped or divided in late fall to maintain size and character. Plate 521.

521. Festuca ovina glauca

522. Ficus carica

Ficus carica
Common Fig, Edible Fig
Moraceae

A large deciduous shrub to multi-branched tree, 20-40 ft. high, with an equal spread. Medium green leaves are large, papery, and divided into 3-5 deep lobes; edible fruit develops in early spring and matures in summer.

The common fig is native to the Mediterranean region where its precise area of origin is unknown. It is one of the earliest plants to be cultivated for its fruit which is rich in sugar and protein. Over the years a number of cultivated varieties have been developed that provide many variations in fruit color, size, and taste.

This species is only one of the estimated 800 species of *Ficus* believed to exist. Most species are evergreen, adapted to tropical and subtropical climates, and do not have edible fruit. The common fig is deciduous during the winter and very adaptable to Mediterranean climates. It grows on many types of soil, including clays, responds well to heat and sun, yet tolerates frost. Fruit production occurs on both old and new growth and is sustained by maintaining moderate amounts of supplemental moisture.

The common fig is widely planted in coastal, inland, valley, and desert regions. It likes warm locations in coastal gardens and protected areas in desert landscapes. It is often used as a garden tree, a specimen in courtyards, espaliered along walls, and grown in containers. Trunks and branches are smooth and become thick and twisted with age. They can be pruned to reveal interesting character. When used as a garden tree for fruit production, it is often combined with plants such as, *Laurus nobilis, Punica granatum, Rosmarinus officinalis, Salvia officinalis*, and other culinary species. Birds and insects like the fruit. Local growers should be consulted to select varieties that suit the needs and conditions of specific gardens. Plates 522 - 524.

523. Ficus carica

524. Ficus carica

Fouquieria splendens
Ocotillo
Fouquieriaceae

A unique desert shrub with numerous, long, spiny branches, growing 15-20 ft. high. Deciduous foliage is comprised of oval, bright green leaves, to 1 in. long, occurring only when plants receive adequate moisture. Colorful clusters of red flowers occur at the tips of branches from early to late spring after seasonal rains.

Ocotillo is native to intermediate and low desert regions from California, Nevada, and Arizona to Texas, Mexico, and Baja California. It is commonly found on dry, rocky slopes, flats, and edges of seasonal washes. It has been widely cultivated as an ornamental plant in low desert landscapes from Palm Springs to Phoenix and Tucson for many years. It grows best in sandy, well drained soils, in full sun, and with little or no supplemental water. It is often used as an accent plant in courtyards, entry planters, and in plantings with other desert species such as, *Carnegiea gigantea, Dasylirion* species, *Larrea tridentata, Encelia farinosa, Simmondsia chinensis*, and *Acacia smallii*. Plates 525 - 526.

525. Fouquieria splendens

526. Fouquieria splendens

Fremontodendron
(Fremontia)
Flannel Bush
Bombacaceae

A small group of evergreen shrubs that includes only two species that are native to warm and dry foothills throughout California, Baja California, and parts of Arizona. These plants are widely known for their intensely colorful yellow flowers that occur in large numbers in spring. Branching is dense and stiff; leaves are hard and variable in size and shape, dark green above, lighter below. Both leaves and stems are covered with fuzzy hair that is highly irritating to the skin. Several subspecies and hybrid selections exist in the trade that provide a number of different forms and flowering characteristics for landscape use.

Fremontodendrons typically grow in sunny locations on slightly acid, well drained soils. In western gardens, they are considered among the most colorful native flowering shrubs, as well as some of the most difficult plants to grow due to their sensitivity to summer water. When used in cultivation, good drainage is essential. Summer water is rarely tolerated and not advised for established plants.

Most *fremontodendrons* found in cultivation are hybrids that have been selected for their flower character and variation in form. Larger types are used as flowering accent features in large garden spaces in coastal, inland, and valley regions. Lower growing hybrids and subspecies selections are useful on banks, slopes, and as background plantings. All types grow fast and should be considered short-lived, perhaps 10-12 years in garden settings.

Fremontodendron californicum
California Flannel Bush

A medium to large mounding shrub, 10-20 ft. high and as wide. Leaves are often small, from 1/2-2 in. long, and vary in shape from oval to lobed. Colorful clear yellow flowers occur in large numbers for an intense but short-term display in early spring.

California flannel bush is native to dry foothill slopes at elevations ranging from 3,000-6,000 ft. from northern to southern California. Some populations also occur along the western edge of the Mojave Desert. It grows within the chaparral, foothill woodland, and pinon-juniper woodland plant communities. Due to its wide range of distribution, many leaf and flower variations and subspecies exist. One subspecies, *F. c.* ssp. *decumbens*, develops into a mounding shrub, 3-5 ft. high, 6-10 ft. across, producing red-orange flowers that are largely hidden by its foliage. Plate 527.

Fremontodendron mexicanum
Southern Flannel Bush, Mexican Fremontia

A large shrub with upright branching, reaching 15-25 ft. high, spreading 20-25 ft. across. Leaves and flowers are larger than *F. californicum*. Leaves grow 2-3 in. long and are deeply lobed. Flowers are golden yellow on top, orange tinted below, tulip-shaped, and 2-3 in. wide.

Southern flannel bush is quite rare and restricted in its natural range. It is native to coastal foothills from San Diego County into upper Baja California, where it is a member of

527. **Fremontodendron californicum**

528. **Fremontodendron 'California Glory'**

529. **Fremontodendron 'California Glory', Santa Barbara Botanic Garden, California**

530. **Fremontodendron 'Pacific Sunset'**

531. **Fremontodendron 'San Gabriel'**

the chaparral and oak woodland communities. This species develops an upright branching habit and produces large numbers of flowers for several weeks in early spring for very showy character.

Fremontodendron hybrids

Several hybrid selections of flannel bush have been produced from the crossing of *F. californicum* and *F. mexicanum*. These include:

Fremontodendron 'California Glory'

A hybrid with small leaves, 1-2 in. across, and partially lobed. Flowers are clear yellow above, rusty below, and partially cup-shaped. It develops an upright form when young and becomes more mounding with age. Plates 528 - 529.

Fremontodendron 'Pacific Sunset'

A hybrid with medium size leaves, 2-3 in. across, moderately lobed. Flowers are rich yellow above and below, and open rather flat to produce a rounded shape. It develops an upright form with long, arching branches. Plate 530.

Fremontodendron 'San Gabriel'

A hybrid with large, deeply lobed leaves, 3-4 in. across. Flowers are bright yellow above, orange below, and are quite cupped and tulip-like. This variety has long ascending branches that develop a sharp, angular silhouette profile. Plates 531 - 532.

Fremontodendron 'Ken Taylor'

A selection that has been produced through the crossing of *F. c.* ssp. *decumbens* and *F.* 'California Glory'. This is a low, mounding plant, 3-4 ft. high, that spreads 6-8 ft. Flowers range from yellow to orange and are partly hidden by foliage. Plates 533 - 534.

532. Fremontodendron 'San Gabriel'

533. Fremontodendron 'Ken Taylor'

534. Fremontodendron 'Ken Taylor'

Gaillardia grandiflora
Blanket Flower
Asteraceae

Blanket flower is a clumping perennial plant resulting from the hybridization of two North American natives, *G. aristata* and *G. pulchella*. It grows 2-3 ft. high and produces an abundance of flowers from late June into fall. Many variations of this hybrid exist; therefore, flowers can be single or double and are often bright red and yellow, with orange to maroon markings on the petals.

This hybrid has proven to be well adapted to many landscape and garden conditions throughout the West. It is often planted by seed for erosion control and in slope planting projects where it can become established on poor soils, in full sun, and with inconsistent irrigation practices. It is also popular for use in perennial gardens, where its warm colors mix well with plants such as, *Romneya coulteri, Achillea filipendulina, Helianthemum nummularium,* and *Cistus* species. It grows best in well drained soils with low to moderate amounts of supplemental water. Spent flower heads should be removed to extend its flowering season; small numbers of seeds will germinate in garden areas to develop new plants. Plates 535 - 536.

535. **Gaillardia grandiflora**

536. **Gaillardia grandiflora**

537. **Galvezia speciosa**

Galvezia speciosa
Island Bush-snapdragon
Scrophulariaceae

An evergreen mounding shrub with long, vining stems, growing 6-8 ft. high, spreading 8-12 ft. across. Stems and leaves are bright green. Colorful red, tubular flowers attract hummingbirds and occur from spring through mid-summer.

Island bush-snapdragon is native to bluffs and rocky canyons of Santa Catalina, San Clemente, and Guadalupe islands off the southern California coastal region. It is best adapted to coastal and inland areas in partial shade and with low to moderate amounts of supplemental water until established. It tolerates light or heavy soils but needs well drained conditions. It is often used on banks and slopes for erosion control, and under the canopy of established trees. Due to its long, vining branches, it also can be trained onto fences or trellises and be treated as a vine. A more compact and colorful selection, *G. s.* 'Firecracker', is available and can be used in smaller spaces. Plates 537 - 538.

538. **Galvezia speciosa**

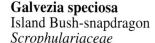

Garrya

Silktassel

Garryaceae

A small group of evergreen shrubs, including about 15 species that come from the western United States, Mexico, and the West Indies. Several species are native to California, where they grow in coastal and inland foothill regions within the chaparral and mixed evergreen plant communities. These plants have tough, leathery foliage, and attractive flower tassels that occur from late winter to early spring. Several species and selections are available from nurseries specializing in native plants. Most types perform best in well drained soils, are tolerant of heat and drought, and require only low amounts of supplemental water once established.

Garrya elliptica

Coast Silktassel

A medium to large shrub, 8-12 ft. high, eventually reaching tree-like proportions. Stiff, dark green leaves have heavily undulated margins. Showy creamy white flowers hang in long, pendulous strands in late winter; clusters of fleshy berries mature in summer and are eaten by birds.

Coast silktassel is native to coastal ranges of California from Ventura County to Oregon, where it grows on dry ridges and slopes, on well drained soils, and at elevations below 2,000 ft. It has been used in coastal and inland gardens as a background and slope plant and for revegetation of disturbed areas within the chaparral. One selection, *G. e.* 'James Roof', develops 8-10 in. long flower catkins that are particularly showy. Plates 539 - 540.

539. Garrya elliptica 'James Roof'

540. Garrya elliptica 'James Roof'

541. Gaura lindheimeri

Gaura lindheimeri

Gaura

Onagraceae

Gaura is a large clumping perennial that produces numerous slender stems that reach 3-4 ft. high. Leaves often occur only at the base of stems, while showy white flowers occur along the stems and at the tips for many months from spring to summer.

This southwestern native comes from arid regions of Texas and Mexico. It can be grown in coastal, inland, valley, and desert regions where it prefers full sun and well drained soils. It can survive short periods of drought and be sustained with low amounts of supplemental water but is more attractive and colorful with additional moisture. Plants can be rejuvenated each year by cutting all stems off at ground level in late fall. Gaura has proven to be a popular flowering accent plant in perennial gardens where its delicate flower character and long blooming season is appreciated. Plates 541 - 542.

542. Gaura lindheimeri

Gazania

Asteraceae

A diverse group of South African perennials that includes about 16 species. Gazanias are one of the best known and most widely planted ground covers in coastal, inland, valley, and desert gardens throughout the West. They are known for their brightly colored daisy-like flowers and prolific flowering habits. The best flowering occurs in late spring through summer and during warm spells through fall and winter. All varieties found in landscape use are now hybrids that have been developed for improved flower character and longer life span. Flowers can be a single color or mixed and include cream, rose, red, orange, and yellow. Foliage can be dark green or grey-green.

Two forms of gazania are available for landscape use: clumping and trailing. Clumping varieties grow 6-12 in. high and spread 12-18 in. in diameter. Some clumping varieties are easily established by seed for slope and erosion control. These varieties, often hybrids of *Gazania splendens*, come in mixed and blended colors, and often produce large, conspicuous seed heads in the fall. Other clumping varieties are carefully developed hybrids that must be planted from rooted cuttings to maintain their exact flower color type and patterns. These varieties are often planted 15-18 in. apart and can quickly fill in to cover small to medium size planting spaces. Popular types include *G.* 'Aztec Queen', *G.* 'Burgundy', *G.* 'Copper King', *G.* 'Fiesta', *G.* 'Gold Rush', *G.* 'Moonglow', and *G.* 'Pink'.

The trailing forms of gazania offer fewer flower and foliage color variations but are often longer lived and better suited to slope plantings. One common variety, *G. rigens leucolaena*, has distinctive grey-green foliage and clear yellow flowers. It has proven to be a very successful slope and bank plant that can last 10 years and longer with good character. Newer trailing hybrids are being introduced into the trade which offer green foliage and larger orange, yellow, and white flowers. Some of these hybrids include *G.* 'Mitsuwa Orange', *G.* 'Mitsuwa Yellow', and *G.* 'White'.

Gazanias prefer well drained soils, full sun, and low to moderate amounts of supplemental water. They are naturally adapted to coastal climates but are widely grown everywhere that stays above 25°F. In desert landscapes and cold regions, they are often grown as annuals. They are well suited to small garden spaces, as well as large, expansive slope areas. After several years, the combination of age and overcrowding can lead to dieback and bare spots in ground cover plantings. This is remedied by clearing out overgrowth and replanting the bare areas. Plates 543 - 546.

543. Gazania species

544. Gazania species

545. Gazania rigens leucolaena

546. Gazania 'Mitsuwa Yellow'

Geijera parviflora
Australian Willow, Wilga
Rutaceae

A small to medium size evergreen tree, 20-35 ft. high, with a short trunk, and oval to broad dome crown, 20-30 ft. wide. Pale green leaves are very long, 4-6 in., and narrow, to 1/2 in. wide. Leaves hang from branches to create a drooping character. Inconspicuous clusters of small, creamy white flowers occur in late fall to early winter.

Australian willow is native throughout the interior regions of Australia where it naturally occurs in semi-arid inland plains and foothill habitats. Within this range, it occurs in woodland and open forest communities in association with *Pittosporum phillyraeoides*, *Eucalyptus microtheca*, and other eucalyptus species. Annual rainfall varies from 6-15 in. It is one of seven known species of *Geijera*; the other members of the genus are adapted to subtropical and tropical habitats and are not found in cultivation. This tree typically grows in deep, well drained, heavy to sandy loams, and has shown a tolerance for alkaline conditions. It often develops a deep rooting habit and tolerates high temperatures and long periods of drought.

Australian willow is a graceful tree that has an upright habit in youth and becomes more rounded with age. Young plants often develop a low branching habit that can be pruned to achieve tree-like proportions. It is commonly used in background and mixed plantings where its foliage color and character contrasts with other ornamental tree species. It grows rapidly and is adapted to coastal, inland, valley, and desert environments and will tolerate heat, aridity, and frost. Low to moderate amounts of supplemental water are preferred after it has become established. Plates 547 - 549.

547. Geijera parviflora, plains of central Australia

548. Geijera parviflora

549. Geijera parviflora

Grevillea

Proteaceae

A diverse group of evergreen shrubs and trees comprised of more than 250 species, mostly from Australia. These plants are noted for their striking flower character and many leaf and form variations. Flowers come in many bright colors, including cream, red, pink, purple, to yellow and gold. Many types provide nectar for birds, others do well in cut arrangements. Leaves range from small, needle-like, and prickly, to large and deeply divided. Species vary in habit from prostrate ground covers to upright shrubs; a few grow as trees.

Grevilleas have evolved and adapted to many different climates and regions throughout Australia. Species selected for landscape use come from coastal, rainforest, and alpine habitats. They grow in a variety of soils, from clay loams to sands, and usually prefer acid to neutral pH. As with other plants in the *Proteaceae* family, grevilleas do not like too much phosphorous; care should be taken when adding fertilizers with phosphorous. The best growth occurs in sunny locations with good drainage, particularly in heavier soils. Young plants are fast growing and are often susceptible to damage during moderate frosts. Established plants can survive quite well with low to moderate amounts of supplemental water; periodic deep soakings are best. Many of the species in cultivation are shrubs that perform well as screens, barrier plants, and ground covers on large slopes.

Grevillea banksii
Red Silky Oak

An upright shrub or small tree, reaching 12-20 ft. high, 10-12 ft. wide, often with twisting branches. Leaves are large, 6-10 in. long, and cut into many lobes. Showy, deep red flowers, 3-6 in. long, occur in large clusters in spring. This species is native to coastal regions and frost free areas in sandy soils of eastern Australia. In western landscapes, it grows best in coastal, inland, and valley areas and is often used as a specimen plant in courtyards and raised planters to display its foliage and striking flowers. Plate 550.

Grevillea 'Canberra Gem'

A mounding shrub, 5-10 ft. high, 6-12 ft. wide. Needle-like leaves grow to 1 in. long, are bright green above, whitish below. Bright red flowers provide accent color throughout the spring and summer. This vigorous cultivar has rich flower character, arching branches, and stiff, prickly foliage. It can be used to control traffic, for erosion control, and screening. It also takes shearing to perform as a hedge. It is adapted to coastal and foothill locations and shows tolerance to heat, cold, and dryness. Plate 551.

Grevillea lanigera
Woolly Grevillea

A spreading to mounding shrub, 3-5 ft. high, 5-10 ft. wide. Needle-like leaves to 3/4 in. long, and are pale green above, white below. Clusters of attractive cream and pink flowers are rich in nectar and occur in summer. Woolly grevillea grows as an understory plant in eucalypt forests in foothill areas, as well as coastal heath habitats. It grows in acid and slightly alkaline soils and tolerates long dry spells and semi-arid conditions. It performs well in sun or partial shade, prefers good drainage, and tolerates moderate frost. Plate 552.

550. Grevillea banksii

551. Grevillea 'Canberra Gem'

552. Grevillea lanigera

553. Grevillea 'Noellii'

554. Grevillea 'Poorinda Constance'

555. Grevillea robusta

556. Grevillea thelemanniana

557. Grevillea victoriae

558. Grevillea robusta

Grevillea 'Noellii'

A mounding shrub, 3-6 ft. high, 6-10 ft. wide, with bright green, needle-like foliage. Flowers are pink and cream and provide accent value spring to summer. This cultivar originated in California and for many years has been the most common choice of *Grevilleas* for slope, screen, and median plantings. It is grown in coastal, inland, and low desert areas with good success. It prefers slightly acid, well drained soils, and moderate amounts of supplemental water in hotter regions. Plate 553.

Grevillea 'Poorinda Constance'

A dense, blocky shrub, 5-7 ft. high, 5-10 ft. wide. Needle-like leaves grow to 1 in. long, are pale green above, white below. Flowers are orange and red, rich in nectar, and develop in colorful clusters at the tips of branches. This cultivar grows well in sunny, frost free areas, in well drained soils, and with low amounts of supplemental water. It shows tolerance to slightly alkaline conditions and responds well to shearing and pruning. Plate 554.

Grevillea robusta
Silky Oak

A large evergreen tree, 40-75 ft. high, 25-30 ft. wide. Leaves are 6-12 in. long, deeply divided, dark green above, white below, and create a soft, fern-like texture. Large clusters of deep orange flowers occur in spring while many trees are briefly deciduous. Flowers are very striking and also produce heavy amounts of nectar for birds.

Silky oak is the largest species of *Grevillea* in landscape use. It is native to subtropical rainforests and along seasonal streams in moist, fertile soils in eastern Australia. Rainfall averages 40-60 in. per year, mean maximum temperature ranges from 82-86°F; winter frosts occur occasionally.

Experience in western landscapes has shown that this species can tolerate much more frost and drier conditions than is indicated by its natural habitat. It thrives best in deep soils with regular water, but can be used in coastal, inland, and low desert regions under many stressful conditions. It is very fast growing and produces an abundance of leaf litter. It is best used in large spaces, such as parks and wide medians, where its eventual size and character can be appreciated. Plates 555, 558.

Grevillea thelemanniana
Hummingbird Bush

A small to medium upright shrub, 4-6 ft. high and as wide. Light green leaves are divided into fine segments and create a soft, delicate appearance. Numerous red-pink flowers occur in early spring and attract hummingbirds. This species comes from Western Australia and is more tolerant of alkaline conditions than other grevilleas. It prefers well drained soils, sun to partial shade, and is often selected to provide accent color value in small gardens and spaces. Plate 556.

Grevillea victoriae
Royal Grevillea

A small to medium shrub, 3-6 ft. high, 5-12 ft. wide. Leaves are medium green above, whitish below and vary from needle-like to lanceolate, 1-3 in. long, to 1/2 in. wide. Orange to red flowers are showy and nectar-rich. Royal grevillea comes from rocky sites in mountain habitats above 3,000 ft. in elevation where it tolerates heavy frost. It prefers well drained conditions, lightly acid soils, and moderate amounts of supplemental water. Plate 557.

Hakea suaveolens
Sweet-scented Hakea
Proteaceae

An upright shrub, growing 10-18 ft. tall, 8-12 ft. wide. Foliage color is medium to dark green and produces a fine textured appearance. However, leaves are needle-like, dense, stiff, and sharply pointed. Inconspicuous white flowers occur in late fall and winter and are sweetly fragrant.

Sweet-scented hakea belongs to a large group of plants that includes 150 species, all native to Australia. This species comes from coastal habitats of southern Western Australia where it grows in granitic soils. It tolerates wind, salt spray, and shows adaptation to many soils including those with some alkalinity, if they are well drained. Young plants and new growth can be damaged by frost. As with other species in the family *Proteaceae*, this species is harmed by phosphorous fertilizers. This species is fast growing and often used as a screen, barrier, or background plant in coastal and inland landscapes. It can be clipped into a hedge, or as it matures, be pruned to form a small tree. Plates 559 - 560.

Hardenbergia
Fabaceae

A small group of plants that includes 3 species, all native to Australia. Two species are flowering vines that are popular in western landscapes. One species, *H. violacea*, has shown good adaptation to dry conditions in coastal and inland locations. The second vine species, *H. comptoniana*, develops best on moist, slightly acid soils and is not considered drought tolerant. Both vines are easy to manage and have handsome deep green, leathery foliage. Several varieties of these species are also available and produce clusters of purple, rose to pink flowers in early spring.

Hardenbergia vines need support and are often used on small trellises or fences where they can easily be maintained with periodic pruning. These plants have also been used as ground covers to cascade over banks and slopes. They prefer slightly acid, well drained soils. They are damaged by light to moderate frosts, but mature foliage is tough and capable of enduring wind, sun, and aridity.

Hardenbergia violacea
(Hardenbergia monophylla)
False Sarsaparilla

This is a shrubby vine with climbing branches that reach 10-12 ft. long. Its handsome foliage is deep green; showy clusters of purple, pea-shaped flowers occur in early spring.

False sarsaparilla comes from many parts of eastern and southern Australia. Within this range, it grows along the coast and into inland foothills on a diverse range of soil and exposure conditions. It grows in many well drained soils, from stony, rocky clay, to sand and decomposed granite.

This is a versatile vine or bank plant for western gardens. It does best in coastal and frost free inland areas and needs only low amounts of supplemental water after established. Two cultivated varieties can be found. *H. v.* 'Alba' has white flowers; *H. v.* 'Happy Wanderer' is a robust selection that has deep purple flowers. Plates 561 - 562.

559. Hakea suaveolens

560. Hakea suaveolens

561. Hardenbergia violacea

562. Hardenbergia violacea

563. Helianthemum nummularium

564. Helianthemum nummularium

565. Helianthemum nummularium

566. Helianthemum nummularium

567. Helictotrichon sempervirens

Helianthemum nummularium
Sunrose
Cistaceae

A low growing subshrub, 6-8 in. high, spreading 2-3 ft. across. Foliage is comprised of small leaves that are often grey-green and covered with fine hairs. Flowers are rose-like with five petals and a yellow center. Flower colors include white, yellow, peach, red, and orange and occur from spring into early summer.

Some 110 species of sunrose have been identified in many parts of the world. This species is the most popular choice for ornamental use in western gardens. It is native to areas across Europe, from the low foothills in the Mediterranean region into mountain grasslands, where it grows on rocky slopes, in limestone soils, and exposed areas. Most flowering selections from this species are hybrids and are valued for their colorful spring character. They are easily grown in all regions of the West, particularly coastal and inland zones, where they perform best in full sun on light, well drained soils, and with low amounts of supplemental water.

Sunroses are often used in borders, on banks, rock gardens, and perennial plantings in combination with species such as, *Lavandula, Achillea, Rosmarinus, Phlomis,* and *Helictotrichon.* Avoid overwatering, and cut plants back after flowering to maintain good character. Plates 563 - 566.

Helictotrichon sempervirens
(Avena sempervirens)
Blue Oat Grass
Poaceae

Blue oat grass is a striking evergreen perennial with distinctive blue-grey foliage and a clumping habit that can reach 2-3 ft. high. With the growing interest in ornamental grasses for western gardens, it has quickly become a favorite. Its size, color, and texture is well suited as a contrasting element in mixed plantings along with such plants as, *Agave, Aloe, Romneya, Achillea, Helianthemum,* and *Perovskia.*

This species is native to Europe but is easily adapted to all regions of the West, from coastal to desert. It does not show a tendency to naturalize and prefers sunny locations, well drained soils, and low amounts of supplemental water once established. Plate 567.

Hesperaloe parviflora
Red Yucca
Agavaceae

A clumping perennial with long, grey-green leaves. With age, several plants develop together into a yucca-like clump; leaves reach 3-4 ft. long. Each plant produces a long spike of showy flowers for several weeks in late spring. Flowers range in color from pink to coral and red.

Red yucca is one of three species within the genus *Hesperaloe*. This species is native to southern Texas and adjacent areas of Mexico where it grows in arid, dry habitats. It has become a popular flowering accent plant in all desert regions, where it is often combined with cactus and species such as *Larrea tridentata, Leucophyllum frutescens, Calliandra eriophylla, Cercidium floridum*, and *Fouquieria splendens*. It prefers well drained soils, full sun, and requires only low amounts of supplemental water once established. It is also grown in coastal, inland, and valley areas in rock gardens and containers with good success. Plates 568 - 569.

568. Hesperaloe parviflora

569. Hesperaloe parviflora

Heteromeles arbutifolia
Toyon, California Holly
Rosaceae

A large evergreen shrub to small tree, 12-18 ft. high, eventually reaching 25 ft. with age. Dense foliage is comprised of dark green, leathery leaves that have small teeth on the margins. Flowers are creamy white and not very showy even though they develop into large clusters during mid-spring to early summer. Showy clusters of orange to red berries mature in late fall through winter, and are a significant source of food for birds and other wildlife.

Toyon is the only species of the genus *Heteromeles*. However, it is one of the most common and widely distributed members of the chaparral plant community throughout California and northern Baja California. It develops deep roots and grows on dry slopes, ridges, and in canyons from sea level to over 3,500 ft. in elevation. It prefers well drained soils, full sun, and can tolerate long periods of drought.

Toyon has for many years been one of the most widely cultivated western natives. It offers both attractive foliage and fruiting character and has shown a wide tolerance for different types of soils, exposure, and moisture conditions. As a result, it is used for revegetation and habitat restoration, on slopes for erosion control, and for screening and background uses. This species is often retained on slopes and hillsides in areas that are cleared for fire safety purposes. Pruning will expose its multiple branching habit, which can be performed to achieve specimen and sculptural qualities in both ornamental and natural landscapes. Its best performance is in coastal, inland, and valley habitats; protection from extreme wind, heat, and aridity is advised when used in desert landscapes. Two varieties can sometimes be found at native plant nurseries: *H. a.* var. *cerina* has yellow berries and *H. a.* var. *macrocarpa* has larger and showier red fruit. Plates 570 - 572.

570. Heteromeles arbutifolia

571. Heteromeles arbutifolia

572. Heteromeles arbutifolia

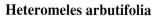

573. Heuchera maxima

574. Heuchera hybrids

575. Heuchera hybrids

576. Hibiscus syriacus

577. Hibiscus syriacus

Heuchera
Alum Root, Coral Bells
Saxifragaceae

A group of clumping perennials, including as many as 50 species that are native to North America and Mexico. Some species grow on coastal bluffs, others are found in canyon, foothill, and alpine areas. Within these habitats, this group often establishes in shaded spots and locations that have moisture seepage occurring through late spring into summer.

Coral bells develop tall, slender spikes of bell-shaped flowers that vary in color from white to deep pink and red. This group is quite popular as a flowering accent element in both native and ornamental gardens. Most types do best in partial shade, well drained soils, and with moderate amounts of supplemental water. A number of hybrids have been cultivated, particularly from *H. sanguinea* and *H. maxima*. This has led to variations in flower colors and moisture needs. Some of these can do well with low amounts of summer water and are used under the canopy of native oaks.

Heuchera maxima
Island Alum Root

The largest species of coral bells, growing 12-18 in. high, with leaves that reach 3-4 in. across. It is native to coastal islands off California where it grows in wooded canyons and on cliff faces. Numerous spikes to 3 ft. high develop in early spring with showy white to light pink flowers. This species has vigorous underground rhizomes that enable it to survive in shaded areas during the dry summer season. For this reason, it is often selected for use under native oaks. Plate 573.

Heuchera sanguinea
Coral Bells

A small species, growing 8-12 in. high and producing bright red to coral pink flowers. This is a very popular garden species that is native to Arizona, New Mexico, and Mexico. It performs best in rich, moist soils, and is not considered reliably drought resistant. Several cultivated varieties of this species provide white and pink flower color.

Hibiscus syriacus
Rose of Sharon, Althaea
Malvaceae

A medium to large deciduous shrub, 8-12 ft. high, with many upright stems, or a single-trunk tree, eventually to 15 ft. high. Dark green leaves are 3-4 in. long and divided into three distinctly notched lobes. Showy flowers occur from summer into fall and are 2-3 in. across. Many varieties are available that offer different flower character. Flowers can be single or double, varying in color from white to magenta and purple, often with a crimson spot at the base of the petals.

Rose of sharon is native to temperate regions throughout central China. It is a very durable species of *Hibiscus* that is grown in many parts of the world where it tolerates frost, average soils, and neglect. In western gardens, it is well suited to inland and valley regions that have cold winters and summer heat. It performs best with moderate amounts of supplemental water but once established needs little care. It provides several months of flowering during the summer and is often used as a screen or patio tree. All plants need pruning to improve shape and flower size. Plates 576 - 577.

Iris douglasiana
Douglas Iris, Pacific Coast Iris
Iridaceae

A small clumping perennial with strap-like leaves, growing 12-18 in. high, spreading 1-2 ft. across. Flowers are most commonly blue-purple, can reach 4 in. across, and produce a showy display for several weeks in early spring.

Douglas iris is one of three species of *Iris* that are native to the west coast of North America. It is a vigorous plant that naturally occurs in moist, shaded canyons and slopes within the coastal ranges from mid-Oregon to Santa Barbara County. Contrary to these conditions, this species is able to tolerate dry summer conditions in partial shade and has often been used as an understory flowering accent plant below native oaks. In recent years, this species has been hybridized to provide a number of colorful selections that offer white, yellow, rose, and purple. These selections are available principally from native plant nurseries and botanical garden plant sales. They grow best in part sun, rich soils, and with low to moderate amounts of supplemental water. They are very good for mass plantings under trees, along borders, and in rock gardens adjacent to streams. Plates 578 - 580.

Iva hayesiana
Hayes Iva, Poverty Weed
Asteraceae

A low growing shrub, 2-3 ft. high, 4-5 ft. across. Foliage is comprised of aromatic, pale green leaves, growing 2-3 in. long. Flowers and fruit are inconspicuous.

Hayes iva is native to the foothills of San Diego County and into northwestern Baja California. It grows within a wide range of conditions, including full sun, clay, and alkaline soils and with varying amounts of seasonal moisture. It is a very tough plant that survives long periods of drought by shedding some of its leaves and becoming dormant.

Hayes iva is grown principally in native plant nurseries and is most frequently used on slopes for erosion control and revegetation of disturbed areas in natural landscapes. It is fully adaptable to coastal and inland regions where it can survive with natural levels of rainfall once established. In more ornamental settings, it will look better if longer stems are clipped off in late fall, and with low to moderate amounts of supplemental water. This plant also can be clipped 12-18 in. high to achieve a more regular ground cover appearance. Plates 581 - 582.

Jasminum
Jasmine, Jessamine
Oleaceae

A large, complex group of evergreen or deciduous shrubs or vines, including about 200 species coming from Asia, Africa, and Australia. More than a dozen species are grown in western gardens as border, hedge, slope, and background plants. Most species produce colorful flowers in spring; some are highly fragrant as well.

Several of the larger vining and shrub type species of *Jasminum* have proven to be well adapted to tough landscape situations, including heat, frost, wind, and drought. These varieties develop many trailing stems and are

578. Iris douglasiana

579. Iris douglasiana cultivar

580. Iris douglasiana cultivar

581. Iva hayesiana

582. Iva hayesiana

583. Jasminum humile

584. Jasminum humile

585. Jasminum mesnyi

586. Jasminum mesnyi

587. Jasminum officinale

588. Jasminum officinale

often grown on slopes for erosion control, along highways, and in background areas for screening. With age, they develop a woody interior that can be removed by cutting stems back to the ground. They are adapted to coastal and inland valley areas throughout the West. Only low amounts of supplemental water are required once established. They will shed some foliage during periods of prolonged drought stress but quickly regrow when watered.

Jasminum grandiflorum
(*Jasminum officinale grandiflorum*)
Spanish Jasmine

A large evergreen to semi-deciduous vine with twisting branching that can reach 10-15 ft. long. Branches and foliage are deep green. Leaves grow 2-3 in. long and are divided into 5-7 leaflets; the upper 3-5 leaflets are joined together at the base. Colorful white flowers accent the plant from spring through fall. Spanish jasmine comes from Asia but has been widely planted throughout the Mediterranean region to obtain scent oils for perfumes, hence its common name. This species is a strong, twining vine that does well on trellises, providing a long season of flower and sweet fragrance.

Jasminum humile
Italian Jasmine

A large evergreen shrub with long, willowy branches. Plants eventually mound 10-12 ft. high, 8-12 ft. across. Bright green leaves are divided into 3-7 leaflets; colorful yellow flowers occur summer through fall and are fragrant. Italian jasmine is native to dry forest foothills of the Himalayas of western China. This species shows very good tolerance of warm, dry climates in western gardens and is often planted on banks and slopes where it receives little care or attention. In more ornamental settings, it can be pruned to form a hedge or screen and responds well to moderate amounts of supplemental water. Plates 583 - 584.

Jasminum mesnyi
(*Jasminum primulinum*)
Primrose Jasmine

A large evergreen shrub with long, arching branches, mounding 6-10 ft. high, spreading 10-12 ft. across. Colorful bright yellow flowers occur from early to late spring and are often double but unscented. Primrose jasmine is native to western China in forest regions that receive ample winter moisture and some winter frost. This species is a very effective erosion control plant on large slopes and for use along walls and roadsides. Plates 585 - 586.

Jasminum officinale
Common White Jasmine, Poet's Jasmine

A large evergreen to deciduous vine with long, twining branches that can reach 25-30 ft. and longer. Green stems and divided leaves are very similar to *J. grandiflorum*, however, all 3-7 leaflets are separated. Very fragrant, white flowers occur in summer and have been widely used in making perfumes. This species comes from the Himalayas of western China. In western gardens, it is used on trellises and fences for its foliage and fragrance value. Established plants require little water; pruning is needed periodically to control growth. Plates 587 - 588.

Juglans californica
Southern California Black Walnut
Juglandaceae

A large deciduous shrub to medium tree, often developing many trunks. This species grows quickly when young, then more slowly to eventually reach mature heights of more than 20-35 ft. Leaves are deep green and pinnately divided into 9-19 leaflets. Flower catkins occur in early spring and are followed by small, round walnuts that mature by late fall.

This species of walnut is native to coastal and inland foothill slopes from San Luis Obispo County, south to San Bernardino County, where it is a member of the southern oak woodland plant association. The largest stands of this species have evolved on calcareous soils of coastal and inland foothills. In addition, it is most numerous and grows to larger sizes on north and east facing slopes. This slope aspect extends the availability of moisture from winter rains before the summer drought cycle occurs.

Juglans californica is one of the few tree species that is native to the low elevation foothills and slopes of southern California. A great deal of attention is given to other tree species, including oaks such as *Quercus agrifolia* and *Q. engelmannii*. Unfortunately, the walnut has not been regarded as highly and few measures have been taken to preserve and protect its existence as urban development continues. This species offers both habitat value to wildlife, as well as aesthetic character to natural hillsides. Mature trees on natural slopes often develop an extensive and far reaching root system to obtain seasonal moisture. Grading and construction activities can severely impact older plants by removing the spreading roots that occur beyond the canopy line of the tree. Fortunately, this species can be established from seed and container stock and is becoming more widely used in restoration and revegetation projects. Native plant nurseries are often the best source to contact regarding container stock. Seeds should be collected from trees on the site where restoration is planned in an effort to preserve the local species characteristics. Plates 589 - 592.

589. Juglans californica

590. Juglans californica, San Dimas, California

591, 592. Juglans californica, natural hillside plantings, San Dimas, California

593. **Juniperus californica at Joshua Tree National Monument, California**

594. **Juniperus californica**

595. **Juniperus chinensis 'Alba'**

596. **Juniperus chinensis 'Alba' with Juniperus sabina 'Tamariscifolia'**

Juniperus
Juniper
Cupressaceae

Junipers comprise a diverse group of evergreen trees and shrubs, that includes about 70 species. They come from many climate and habitat regions of the Northern Hemisphere from dry and arid to cool and moist. These plants are characterized by coniferous foliage that is often formed of tiny, needle-like and scale-like leaves.

Overall, this is a remarkably adaptable and hardy group of plants that is highly popular and widely used in all regions of the world. The greatest variety for landscape use occurs in cool climate areas where many named varieties can be found in cultivation. However, many of these species and various cultivars are well suited to the West due to the many climate variations. In warm and dry zones, the foliage of junipers is well adapted to aridity and moisture stress by being hard, rigid, having a low surface to volume ratio, and protected stomates. They also tolerate most types of soils, including calcareous, but do not tolerate boggy conditions.

Only 5-7 different species are used in western gardens but many cultivated varieties of these species have been developed and provide a wide range of ground cover, shrub, and small tree choices for landscape use. Junipers are propagated by cuttings or grafted onto rootstock which results in a high amount of uniformity in their character. The most popular species of junipers originate in cool climate regions where they have developed tolerances to low temperatures and seasonal rainy periods. These plants also experience moisture stress when cold temperatures reduce the movement of soil moisture during the winter, as well as during periods of drought that can occur in summer or fall. These adaptations, in combination with their foliage character, enable junipers to be widely tolerant of many temperature and moisture variations.

Several species of juniper are native to arid climates of the Southwest and have evolved within conditions of extreme heat and drought. These species are not as widely used in ornamental landscapes, instead, they are considered valuable habitat and watershed species that should be protected in their natural settings.

Juniperus californica
California Juniper

A large shrub to small tree, mounding 5-15 ft. high as a shrub, reaching 25-40 ft. as a tree. Dark green foliage is comprised of scale-like leaves; colorful fruit is blue-grey in early spring and matures to red-brown.

California juniper is native to dry climate regions from the interior basins of southern Oregon and northern California, south to Mexico. Throughout this range it occurs in great abundance on desert slopes, including those from Palmdale to Joshua Tree National Monument. It grows to large sizes in sandy soils where it can develop deep roots, or matures at smaller sizes when established on dry hillsides in rocky and compacted soils.

This species is tolerant of heat, aridity, frost, and drought. However, it is not often found in cultivation and is valued principally as a habitat plant where it stabilizes soils and provides berries and shelter to wildlife. Unfortunately, development occurring in desert regions often removes established plants. Plates 593 - 594.

Juniperus chinensis

This is a highly variable juniper species. It is native to Asia, with particular significance in the central to northern portions of China at elevations ranging from 5,000-10,000 ft. The climate within central regions is often cool and moist; annual rainfall varies between 40-70 inches. Northern latitudes and higher elevations have very cold winters with periods of physiological drought when temperatures freeze the ground. Summers are warm with average temperatures reaching 75-80°F.

Throughout this range, this species grows principally as a tree to 60 ft. high. However, it also occurs as a small to medium size shrub and sometimes develops a trailing branching habit. These variations have led to the selection and cultivation of many specific forms for landscape use, particularly ground covers and shrubs. Overall, this is one of the most diverse and popular groups of junipers. Some of the available types are listed below.

Ground cover types:

J. c. 'Alba', Variegated Prostrata Juniper - Grows 1 1/2 ft. high, 4-5 ft. across. Foliage contains patches of creamy yellow markings.

J. c. procumbens, Japanese Garden Juniper - To 3 ft. high, spreading 12-20 ft. Blue-green needle foliage, vigorous spreading branches.

J. c. procumbens 'Nana' - To 1 ft. high, 4-5 ft. across. Blue-green foliage, slow growth. Plate 597.

J. c. 'San Jose' - Grows 2 ft. high, spreads 6-8 ft. across. Dense needle and scale-like foliage, deep sage green.

Shrub and tree types:

J. c. 'Armstrongii', Armstrong Juniper - Small shrub, to 4 ft. high with upright branches and medium green, needle-like leaves.

J. c. 'Corymbosa Variegata', Variegated Hollywood Juniper - Upright shrub, 8-12 ft. high, developing some twisting branch habit with age. Scale-like foliage is variegated, creamy yellow. Plate 597.

J. c. 'Columnaris', Japanese Blue Column Juniper - A narrow, columnar form, blue-green foliage, reaching 12-15 ft. high.

J. c. 'Gold Coast' - Medium spreading shrub, 4 ft. high, 4-6 ft. across. Medium green, scale-like foliage has golden foliage at tips of branches. Plate 548.

J. c. 'Hetzii', Hetz Blue Juniper - Large fountain shaped shrub, 12-18 ft. high. Distinctive blue-grey foliage and arching branches.

J. c. 'Mint Julep' - Upright shrub with vase-like shape, 5-8 ft. high and as wide. Deep mint green foliage, arching branches. Plate 600.

J. c. 'Pfitzerana', Pfitzer Juniper - Large shrub, 5-6 ft. high, spreading 12-20 ft. Distinctive grey-green, needle-type leaves occur on broadly arching branches.

J. c. 'Pfitzerana Glauca' - Large spreading shrub, 5-6 ft. high, spreading 12-25 ft. Stiff, grey-green, needle-type leaves occur on horizontal branches. Plate 599.

J. c. 'Sea Green' - Arching branches, developing 4-5 ft. high and as wide. Dark green foliage.

J. c. 'Torulosa', Hollywood Juniper - Large shrub to small tree, with twisting, upright branches, 15-25 ft. high. Deep green, scale-like foliage. Plate 601.

597. Juniperus chinensis 'Corymbosa Variegata'

598. Juniperus chinensis 'Gold Coast'

Plate 599. Juniperus chinensis 'Pfitzerana Glauca'

600. Juniperus chinensis 'Mint Julep'

601. Juniperus chinensis 'Torulosa'

602. Juniperus conferta

603. Juniperus horizontalis 'Bar Harbor'

604. Juniperus horizontalis 'Wiltonii'

Juniperus conferta
Shore Juniper

A low growing shrub, reaching 1 ft. high, spreading 6-8 ft. Foliage is comprised of medium green, needle-like leaves that have a distinct white strip on the underside.

Shore juniper is native to coastal dunes and bluffs along the shorelines of southern and eastern Japan. It is naturally adapted to sandy soils, tolerates salt spray, and grows in full sun to partial shade. In western gardens, this species has proven to be highly adaptable to coastal, inland, valley, and protected areas in low desert regions. It prefers cooler and moister conditions but can be sustained in warmer and drier locations with moderate amounts of water on a regular basis.

This is a very handsome and relatively fast growing species. It is widely used in residential and commercial landscapes in planters, on banks, and in mixed conifer plantings. Several cultivated forms are available in the trade, including *J. c.* 'Pacific Blue', which has a blue color cast and is more heat tolerant, and *J. c.* 'Emerald Sea', which is a brighter green selection. Plate 602.

Juniperus horizontalis
Creeping Juniper

A low growing shrub that rarely exceeds 1 ft. high and spreads for many feet across. Foliage is comprised of blue-green, scale-like leaves that grow on long trailing branches.

This species is native to temperate regions of North America from Alaska to Nova Scotia, south to New Jersey, Minnesota, and Montana. It is highly adapted to cold winters and short summer growing seasons. Many varieties have been introduced into cultivation, several are suited to warmer climates. In warmer and drier regions of the West, the cultivars have proven to be highly adaptable to heat and aridity, as long as they are provided with moderate amounts of water on a regular basis. They grow best in soils that are slightly acid, light, and well drained. They prefer full sun in coastal, inland, and valley zones and partial shade in desert landscapes.

Creeping juniper and its many cultivars are popular for ground cover use on slopes and in planters. They are slow to moderate in their growth habit and often will develop a purple cast to their foliage during the cool months. Several cultivars are listed below.

J. h. 'Bar Harbor', Bar Harbor Juniper - A low growing selection with fast growth to 1 ft. high, 8-10 ft. spread. Foliage is distinctive blue-grey and develops a plum cast in winter. Plate 603.

J. h. 'Emerald Spreader' - Low growing, 6-9 in. high, spreading several feet across. Deep emerald green foliage produces a dense, feathery effect.

J. h. 'Hughs' - A low growing plant to 1 ft. high, 4-5 ft. across, with a distinctive radial branching pattern. Foliage is silver-blue.

J. h. 'Huntington Blue' - Intense blue-grey color, growing to 1 ft. high, 6-7 ft. across.

J. h. 'Prince of Wales' - A selection with medium green foliage, growing to 8 in. high, spreading 4-5 ft. across.

J. h. 'Turquoise Spreader' - Low growing, to 6 in. high, with dense, turquoise foliage color.

J. h. 'Wiltonii', Blue Carpet Juniper - A very low ground cover, growing 4 in. high, slowly spreading 8-10 ft. Foliage is dense, rich silver-blue. Plate 604.

Juniperus sabina
Savin Juniper

A spreading shrub, growing 3-5 ft. high, reaching as much as 10-15 ft. across. Foliage is dark green and comprised largely of scale-like leaves. Leaves contain a poisonous oil that is highly pungent when crushed.

This species is native to central Europe and Siberia, where it grows in alpine meadows and rocky mountain slopes. It is well adapted to cold climate regions where it has been cultivated for ornamental use. Several varieties are grown in western gardens and are used as ground covers and screens in residential and commercial landscapes.

Savin juniper and its cultivated varieties provide a range of deep green foliage color and perform best in well drained soils that are neutral to slightly alkaline in pH. Established plants are quite heat and drought tolerant, although periodic deep watering is recommended. They are grown in all regions, from the coast to inland valleys and deserts. Several popular varieties are listed below.

J. s. 'Arcadia' - A low mounding form, 1-3 ft. high, spreading 10 ft. across. Deep sea-green foliage is soft and billowy in appearance.

J. s. 'Broadmoor' - A dense and spreading form, 12 in. high, over 10 ft. across. Scale-like foliage is dense, medium green. Plate 605.

J. s. 'Buffalo' - A spreading form, 8-12 in. high, 6-8 ft. across. Bright green foliage lays horizontal and is feathery in character.

J. s. 'Tamariscifolia', Tamarix Juniper - A large spreading selection, growing 1 1/2 ft. high, reaching 10-15 ft. across and more. This is a highly popular selection with arching branches and feathery, medium green foliage. Plates 596, 606.

Juniperus scopulorum
Rocky Mountain Juniper

A large shrub to small tree, growing upright to 30-40 ft. high, 10-15 ft. wide. Foliage is comprised of heavy, scale-like leaves, light green to grey-green in color.

This species is native to western North America from British Columbia, south to Arizona and Texas. Within this range, its greatest development occurs in mountain regions on slopes, along canyon bottoms, and along streams and lakes. It grows to largest sizes in moist, well drained, loam type soils but tolerates drier and rockier conditions.

Several cultivars of this species can be found in the trade, ranging from large spreading shrubs, to tall columnar trees. Most of these varieties have grey-green foliage character that is thicker and heavier than other juniper species. This group is also relatively slow growing.

J. s. 'Blue Haven' - A tall pyramidal selection, slowly growing 15-20 ft. high. Rich, blue foliage character.

J. s. 'Cologreen' - A handsome green foliage selection that develops a narrow pyramidal form, 15-20 ft.

J. s. 'Pathfinder' - A tall columnar selection with distinctive grey-blue foliage. Considered one of the best, reaching 20-25 ft. high. Plate 609.

J. s. 'Table Top Blue' - A large, spreading selection, growing 5-6 ft. high, reaching 8-10 ft. across. Foliage is silvery blue and develops on many arching branches. Plate 607.

605. **Juniperus sabina 'Broadmoor'**

606. **Juniperus sabina 'Tamariscifolia'**

607. **Juniperus scopulorum 'Table Top Blue'**

608. Juniperus scopulorum 'Tolleson's Weeping'

J. s. 'Tolleson's Weeping' - A grafted variety that provides a unique weeping foliage character. Both grey and green foliage colors are available and develop 20-25 ft. high, 10-12 ft. wide. This is a relatively fast growing selection. Plate 608.

Juniperus virginiana
Eastern Redcedar

A tall columnar tree growing 40-70 ft. and higher. Deep green foliage is comprised of finely divided branchlets and tiny, scale-like leaves.

Eastern redcedar is native to eastern North America from Ontario, Canada, south to Florida, west to Ohio and Tennessee. It grows in forested regions on plains and low, rolling foothills and develops best in moist, loam soils with good drainage. Within its natural range, it is often used as a specimen, hedge, and windbreak plant.

This species is best suited to cool climate regions and is seldom planted in the warmer and drier locations of the Southwest. Cultivated varieties are considered to be better than the true species; several can be found for use in western gardens, including:

J. v. 'Manhattan Blue' - A dense, compact pyramidal selection, with blue-green foliage, growing 10-15 ft. high.

J. v. 'Skyrocket' - A very narrow, columnar selection, growing 10-15 ft. high. Foliage is pale blue-green and grows on thin branches. Plate 610.

609. Juniperus scopulorum 'Pathfinder'

610. Juniperus virginiana, Nashville, Tennessee

Justicia
Acanthaceae

A large group of perennials and shrubs, including about 300 species, most of which come from tropical and subtropical climates. A few species, however, are native to the southwestern deserts and are valuable in both ornamental and natural landscapes. These plants are characterized by long, tubular flowers that are very colorful during spring.

Justicia californica
Chuparosa, California Beloperone

A low mounding shrub with a dense branching habit, 3-5 ft. high, spreading 6-8 ft across. Leaves are 1/2 in. long and drop during periods of moisture stress. Intense red flowers cover the plant in early spring.

Chuparosa is native to low desert regions of California, Arizona, and Mexico. It grows most frequently in sandy soils along seasonal washes and ravines where plants can receive runoff from rainfall. It provides important wildlife value, and between March and May it becomes one of the most colorful plants in the desert. Plates 611-612.

Justicia spicigera
Mexican Honeysuckle

An upright shrub with many branches, growing 2-3 ft. high and as wide. Branches and soft leaves are pale green. Clusters of bright orange flowers occur in spring through summer and are attractive to hummingbirds.

This species is native to arid and subtropical climates from Mexico to Columbia. In drier regions, it is confined to sandy soils near seasonal streams and washes. It is quite lush and vibrant in late spring, then becomes sparse during drought stress. Pruning in late fall will improve appearance; periodic deep watering and planting in part shade increases foliage and flower character. Plate 613.

Kalanchoe
Crassulaceae

A diverse group of succulent perennials or shrubs. Only a few of the estimated 125 species are found in landscape use; most of these come from subtropical and coastal climates of South Africa and Madagascar. Kalanchoes are quite different in character and easily hybridize. Several species and hybrids are available for use in western gardens and are often found at specialty nurseries. Most types provide colorful foliage and flowering character and are well suited to rock gardens, borders, and containers in frost free zones along the coast and adjacent inland areas.

Kalanchoe beharensis
Felt Plant

One of the largest species in cultivation, growing with several thick, knobby stems, 5-7 ft. high. Large, fuzzy leaves have wavy margins and heavy, felt-like surfaces. This is a unique plant that is well suited as a specialty accent element in containers and raised planters in courtyards. Plate 614.

Kalanchoe blossfeldiana

A small species, growing 12-15 in. high and developing many stems from the base. Succulent, deep green leaves are rounded with lightly lobed, red margins. This species is very popular as an indoor and outdoor flowering plant that is widely sold by retail nurseries and florists. Many hybrids exist to provide flower colors from red, orange, yellow, and salmon. Plate 615.

611. Justicia californica

612. Justicia californica

613. Justicia spicigera

614. Kalanchoe beharensis

615. Kalanchoe blossfeldiana

616. Keckiella hybrid, cross between K. antirrhinoides and K. cordifolia

617. Keckiella hybrid

618. Kniphofia uvaria

619. Kniphofia uvaria

620. Kniphofia 'Little Maid'

Keckiella
Scrophulariaceae

A small group of only five species all native to California and northern Baja California. These plants are closely related to penstemons and develop similar tubular flowers that are of value to birds. In natural environments, most types grow best in semi-shaded locations, north exposures, and where soil moisture from rainfall is greater. Several species and hybrids are used in coastal and inland regions for revegetation and restoration projects. They are adapted to sun or partial shade and do well around the perimeter of native oaks with little summer water.

Keckiella antirrhinoides
Yellow Penstemon

A large mounding shrub, 6-8 ft. high, developing arching stems and spreading 6-10 ft. across. Leaves are small, to 1 in. long, and toothed on the margins. Rich yellow flowers occur at the tips of stems in spring.

This species is native to the chaparral plant community in foothill areas throughout southern California and adjacent Baja California. It is a vigorous plant with colorful flowers and erosion control value.

Keckiella cordifolia
Heart-leaved Penstemon

A mounding shrub with long, vining branches, growing 5-6 ft. high, spreading 8-10 ft. across. Foliage is comprised of medium green, heart-shaped leaves, 1-2 in. long. Deep red flowers occur in spring to summer.

Heart-leaved penstemon is native to coastal and inland foothills and canyons from San Luis Obispo County to northern Baja California. This species is a good slope or bank plant and does well in the shade of native oaks. It will often hybridize with *K. antirrhinoides* and produce plants with yellow and red flowers. Plates 616 - 617.

Kniphofia uvaria
(Tritoma uvaria)
Red-hot Poker, Torch Lily, Poker Plant
Liliaceae

Red-hot poker is a clumping perennial that develops long, grass-like foliage to 3 ft. high and striking stalks of brightly colored flowers. It is native to the Cape Region of South Africa, where it grows on slopes and in grassy meadows in moist, rich soils. In western gardens, this species has proven to be quite tolerant of many conditions including heat, aridity, frost, and drought. This capacity is due largely to its thick, succulent root system that can renew foliage after drought stress and frost.

Many hybrids and varieties are available in the trade that offer different sizes and flower colors. The larger varieties are the most durable and once established, require low amounts of supplemental water. These plants are naturally suited to subtropical and coastal regions but perform quite well in warm inland and valley areas if given some protection from extreme heat and sun. Ragged foliage can be cut back in fall and let regrow again in spring.

Red-hot poker is often used along borders, in perennial gardens, and in containers. It is often combined with other grass-like plants, as well as succulent and broad-leaf species such as *Agave attenuata*, *Aloe arborescens*, *Euphorbia rigida*, *Cereus peruvianus*, *Gazania hybrids*, and *Cortaderia selloana*. Plates 618 - 620.

Lagerstroemia indica
Crape Myrtle
Lythraceae

A large deciduous shrub to small tree, growing slowly to 15-20 ft., eventually reaching 25 ft. Trunks and branches are covered with thin bark that is shed each year to reveal smooth, pale pink bark below. Medium green leaves are oval, 2-3 in. long; large clusters of colorful flowers occur at the ends of branches during mid-summer.

Crape myrtle is one of 55 species known within the genus *Lagerstroemia*. It is by far the most popular species and is widely cultivated in warm regions around the world. It is native to central and eastern China where it grows in mixed forest landscapes below 2,000 ft. in elevation. It is adapted to wet winters with regular frost and warm, humid summers. In western landscapes, it is widely grown in inland, valley, and low desert regions with good success. Unfortunately, it is very prone to mildew problems when grown in coastal areas and during periods of high humidity. Most types grow best with moderate amounts of water on a regular basis, however, established plants are easily sustained with little supplemental water.

Crape myrtles are popular flowering accent plants used for many purposes. They grow to sizes that fit residential and small scale commercial spaces where they provide bright flower color during the warm months of summer. Many types work well as multi-branched specimen plants or can be pruned to form single trunk canopy trees. They can be used as lawn trees, street trees, and in entry and courtyard spaces.

621. Lagerstroemia indica 'Glendora White'

622. Lagerstroemia indica

623. Lagerstroemia 'Muskogee'

624. Lagerstroemia 'Tuscarora'

Over the years, numerous hybrids and named varieties have been developed that offer a wide selection of size and flower color for garden use. When matching colors are needed, such as for street trees, it is best to purchase named varieties and to select plants while they are in flower. Flower colors are principally white, pink, red, lavender, and purple. Colors available for standard size tree selections that grow 15-20 ft. include *L.* 'Glendora White', *L.* 'Shell Pink', *L.* 'Rosea', *L.* 'Rubra', *L.* 'Watermelon Red', *L.* 'Watermelon Red Improved', *L.* 'Peppermint Lace', *L.* 'Lavender', *L.* 'Majestic Orchid', and *L.* 'Select Purple'. Smaller selections, known as petite varieties that grow as large, multi-stemmed shrubs, 8-15 ft. high, include *L.* 'Petite Embers', *L.* 'Red Imp', *L.* 'Petite Pinkie', *L.* 'Petite Plum', and *L.* 'Petite Snow'.

In addition to these selections, several hybrid cultivars have been developed from the crossing of *L. indica* with *L. fauriei*. This effort has led to plants that develop many stems, a rounded form, grow 9-10 ft. high, and are more resistant to powdery mildew. Some of the named hybrids include *L.* 'Acoma', white flowers; *L.* '*Hopi*', pink flowers; *L.* 'Pecos', clear medium pink flowers; and *L.* 'Zuni', rich lavender flowers. Other hybrids from this parentage grow to larger sizes, 15-25 ft. high, have many trunks, and very large leaves. These types include *L.* 'Muskogee', light lavender flowers; *L.* 'Natchez', bright white flowers; and *L.* 'Tuscarora', deep pink to red flowers. These hybrids often develop long flower clusters at the tips of their branches and sometimes produce a drooping effect. Plates 621 - 625.

625. Lagerstroemia 'Nachez', left, Lagerstroemia 'Muskogee', right

Lampranthus
Ice Plant
Aizoaceae

A large group of succulent ground covers and shrubs that are native to the coastal regions of South Africa. Only a small number of the 160 known species are currently available for use in western gardens. However, these few species and their many cultivars can be easily identified by their vibrant flowers that occur in early spring. Flower colors range from purple, red, and orange to white and rose. Lampranthus ice plants grow best in mild coastal and warm, frost free zones. They need well drained soils, a sunny location, and only periodic watering.

Lampranthus aurantiacus
A mounding species, 12-18 in. high, with grey-green leaves, and bright orange flowers. *L. a.* 'Glaucus' has intense yellow flowers, and *L. a.* 'Sunman' produces gold-yellow flowers. Plates 626 - 627.

Lampranthus productus
A mounding species, 12-15 in. high, with bright purple flowers. Plate 626.

Lampranthus spectabilis
A trailing species, 10-12 in. high, spreading 18-24 in. across. Several shocking flower colors are available including pink, rose, red, and purple. Plate 628.

Lantana
Verbenaceae

A large group of shrubs and perennials that come from subtropical and tropical climates of North and South America. More than 155 species exist, but only two are popular in western gardens. These plants are known for their long flowering season that often lasts from summer through fall. They have been widely planted in coastal, inland, and low desert regions as flowering accent plants in containers, on slopes, and background planters in both residential and commercial landscapes. In cold climate regions, they are often planted as summer annuals to provide flower color until frosts kill them. A large number of hybrids and named varieties have been cultivated to provide different sizes and flower colors. All types do best in sunny locations and require only low amounts of supplemental water.

Lantana camara
Yellow Sage
A medium to large shrub with long, rambling branches that reach 4-6 ft. high. Leaves are deep green and pungent when crushed; flower heads are comprised of red, white, yellow, and orange flowers.

This species is native to tropical America and has become a widely naturalized pest in subtropical and tropical regions around the world. It does not escape as readily in dry climate regions where it is often used as a slope and background plant. This species is hybridized with *L. montevidensis* to produce many excellent shrub and ground cover varieties. Plate 629.

626. Lampranthus aurantiacus 'Glaucus', Lampranthus a. 'Sunman', Lampranthus productus

627. Lampranthus aurantiacus 'Sunman'   628. Lampranthus spectabilis

629. Lantana camara, Scottsdale, Arizona

630. **Lantana montevidensis**

631. **Lantana montevidensis**

Lantana montevidensis
(Lantana sellowiana)
Trailing Lantana

A low and spreading shrub, 12-18 in. high, spreading 5-10 feet. Foliage is dark green with toothed margins; showy purple and white flowers develop in mid-spring and intermittently all year.

Trailing lantana is native to subtropical regions of South America. It has been widely used in western gardens as a slope and erosion control plant on dry hillsides. Once established, it is highly tolerant of drought stress. Plants will shed their leaves during moisture stress but will quickly regrow them when irrigated. This species is often planted within other ground covers such as English ivy and Hall's Japanese honeysuckle to add color and fill in dry, bare spots. Plates 630 - 635.

Selected varieties:

L. 'Confetti' - Yellow, pink and purple flowers, 2-3 ft. high, 6-8 ft. across.

L. 'Cream Carpet' - Soft, cream flowers with yellow throats, spreading 5-7 ft. across.

L. 'Dwarf Orange' - Bright orange flowers, mounding 2-3 ft. high, 3-4 ft. across.

L. 'Dwarf Pink' - Light pink flowers, mounding 2-3 ft. high, 3-4 ft. across.

L. 'Dwarf White' - White flowers, mounding 2-4 ft. high and as wide.

L. 'Dwarf Yellow' - Clear yellow flowers, 2-4 ft. high and as wide.

L. 'Gold Mound' - Deep yellow flowers, 3-4 ft. high, 5-6 ft. across.

L. 'Lemon Swirl' - Clear yellow flowers, variegated foliage, 18-24 in. high, 3-4 ft. across.

L. 'Pink Frolic' - Dark pink and yellow flowers, 3-4 ft. high, 5-6 ft. across.

L. 'Radiation' - Intense orange-red flowers, 4-5 ft. high, 6-8 ft. across.

L. 'Spreading Sunset' - Shocking orange-red flowers, 15-18 in. high, 4-6 ft. across.

L. 'Spreading Sunshine' - Bright yellow flowers, 15-18 in. high, 4-6 ft. across.

632. **Lantana 'Cream Carpet'**

633. **Lantana 'Spreading Sunset'**

634. **Lantana 'Spreading Sunshine'**

635. **Lantana 'Dwarf Yellow' front, Lantana 'Pink Frolic' behind**

Larrea tridentata
Creosote Bush
Zygophyllaceae

A medium to large evergreen shrub, developing a mounding shape, 5-10 ft. high and as wide. Tiny, dark green leaves reach 1/4-1/2 in. across, have a resinous surface, and a distinctive creosote pungence. Numerous yellow flowers accent the plant in early spring, followed by white, fuzzy seed balls.

Creosote bush is one of the most common plant species found in both high and low deserts throughout the Southwest from sea level to over 4,000 ft. It is a member of many plant communities including, the pinyon-juniper woodland, Joshua tree woodland, and the creosote bush scrub. In comparison to most desert plant species, the creosote bush is considered to be one of the toughest evergreen shrubs capable of enduring some of the hottest and driest conditions. Its best growth and largest sizes occur when it grows in sandy soils along washes and seasonal water channels where it obtains additional seasonal moisture. Some leaves are dropped during periods of extreme drought stress. Otherwise, it grows in many soils, including clayey and calcareous, and is able to develop an extensive surface and tap root system to survive the desert elements.

This species is used primarily for revegetation and restoration projects in desert regions where it is valued for erosion control and wildlife habitat value. It is also used along highways, in median islands, and in residential communities designed to retain the natural desert landscape. Larger specimens occurring in landscape settings can be pruned to enhance their branching character. Plates 636 - 639.

636. Larrea tridentata, Valley of Fire State Park, Nevada

637. Larrea tridentata

638. Larrea tridentata

639. Larrea tridentata

640. Laurus nobilis

641. Laurus nobilis

Laurus nobilis
Sweet Bay, Grecian Laurel
Lauraceae

A large evergreen shrub to medium tree, growing 15-25 ft. high, eventually reaching as high as 40 ft. Foliage is comprised of leathery, dark green leaves, 2-4 in. long. These leaves contain oils that are both aromatic and valued for culinary uses. Small, yellow flowers and round; fruits are inconspicuous.

Sweet bay is native to the Mediterranean region where it most frequently occurs in ravines and on semi-shaded slopes within coastal foothills at elevations below 2,000 ft. In these locations, it often develops into dense thickets on moist, well drained soils. In western gardens, this species has proven to be tolerant of many soils and climate conditions. Established plants can become quite self-reliant and require only low to moderate amounts of supplemental water. It is planted in coastal, inland, valley, and low desert regions where its tough foliage resists heat, wind, aridity, and frost. It will grow faster and to larger sizes when planted in well drained, composted soils, with regular moisture.

Sweet bay is a slow growing plant that develops a dense foliage character and a rounded shape. It can be maintained as a shrub and clipped for hedge and topiary use. It can also be pruned as a canopy tree and used as a lawn or street tree. Frequently, it is planted in containers, courtyards, and around vegetable gardens. Leaves can be used fresh or dry for seasoning food. One variety, *L. n.* 'Saratoga', is more tree-like in habit and has broader leaves. Plates 640 - 642.

642. Laurus nobilis

Lavandula
Lavender
Laminaceae

A small group of evergreen subshrubs and shrubs that are widely noted for their colorful flowers and fragrant foliage. Some 25 species of lavender are known, most coming from coastal and inland hillsides throughout the Mediterranean region. Many types grow within open pine woods and scrub plant communities in areas receiving 15-20 inches of annual rainfall. These plants are well adapted to sunny locations, light frost, and prefer light, well drained soils. In western gardens, they are grown in coastal, inland, valley, and protected areas in desert regions. Young plants do best with moderate amounts of supplemental water, once established they grow well with low amounts.

Lavenders are very popular in landscapes due to their small size, ease of care, and colorful character. Flowers are predominantly blue to purple, develop on slender stalks above the foliage, and attract bees. Different species and cultivars produce flowers from early spring to late summer. Diligent removal of spent flower heads will often encourage flowering to continue for many months. These plants perform well in small garden spaces, including borders, perennial gardens, containers, and herb gardens. Dried flowers and foliage are frequently used in potpourri. Most types can be kept handsome and compact for many years with light pruning. Currently, a number of new hybrids and selections are being cultivated and added to the trade.

Lavandula angustifolia
(Lavandula officinalis, L. spica, L. vera)
English Lavender

A round shrub, 2-3 ft. high and as wide. Smooth, bluish grey-green leaves reach 1 in. long, are narrow and held upright. Flowers are light to medium purple and grow on long, unbranched stalks, 24-36 in. above the foliage, in late spring to mid-summer.

English lavender is one of the most popular species for landscape use. It comes from northeast Spain and maintains very good form as a foliage plant, as well as for having flowering accent value. It is the most cold tolerant species, surviving temperatures to 20 F. Fragrant oils from flowers are used in perfumes. Numerous hybrids have been developed from this species that are often more compact and vary in flower color. *L. a.* 'Hidcote' is slower growing, 1-2 ft. high, with silver-grey foliage, and deep purple flowers. *L. a.* 'Munstead' has leaves arranged in opposite pairs, grows to 18 in. high, and produces lavender-blue flowers in early spring. *L. a.* 'Nana' and 'Compacta' seldom grow larger than 6-8 in. high and have smaller, deep blue flower heads. Plates 643 - 644.

Lavandula dentata
French Lavender

A firm, rounded shrub, 2-3 ft. high and as wide. Narrow, bluish grey-green leaves are heavily textured; flowers are light to medium blue and develop on stalks 3-5 in. above the foliage. Flowering begins in winter and continues into summer.

This species provides the longest period of flower display among the lavenders. Flower-

643. **Lavandula angustifolia**

644. **Lavandula angustifolia**

645. **Lavandula dentata**

646. **Lavandula dentata**

647. **Lavandula intermedia 'Provence', deep blue selection**

648. Lavandula pinnata var. buchii

649. Lavandula pinnata var. buchii

650. Lavandula stoechas 'Otto Quast'

651. Lavandula stoechas 'Otto Quast'

ing is greatest in early spring but occurs intermittently all year in warm areas, particularly if old flower heads are removed. This species comes from southern and eastern Spain, Greece, North Africa, and the Canary Islands where it grows along coastal edges and in inland hills. It is highly adapted to warm, dry locations and tolerates both slightly acid and calcareous soils. One cultivar, *L. d.* var. *candicans*, is a more robust grower that has greyer foliage color. Plates 645 - 646.

Lavandula intermedia
(Lavandula burnati, L. hortensis, L. spica-latifolia)
Lavandin
A low mounding plant, 1-2 ft. high, 2-3 ft. across. Linear, grey-green leaves reach 1 in. long; flower color varies from light blue to purple and occurs on 12-18 in. high spikes in summer to fall.

This cultivar is a hybrid between *L. angustifolia* and *L. latifolia* that has resulted in various combinations of flower color and growth habit between the two. One selection, *L. i.* 'Provence', has been recently introduced with both light and dark blue flower characteristics and a compact foliage habit. Plate 647.

Lavandula latifolia
Spike Lavender
An open, rounded shrub, 2-3 ft. high. Leaves are narrow and grey-green; fragrant, lavender-blue flowers typically occur on branched stalks 18-24 in. above the foliage in early summer.

Spike lavender is native to low elevation foothills and slopes from Spain to the Balkan Peninsula region. It is quite similar to *L. angustifolia* but has branched flower spikes, wider leaves, and is more sensitive to temperatures below 25 F. It produces colorful and fragrant flowers for border, container, and cut flower uses.

Lavandula pinnata
A small shrub with an open and light habit, growing 3-4 ft. high. Delicate, grey foliage is bipinnately divided; flowers are deep violet-blue and occur in multiple groups of twos and threes on long slender stems from spring to fall.

This species comes from the western Mediterranean region and provides a different appearance to other lavenders. Its open habit, greener foliage, and unusual flower character are quite distinctive. It is not as hardy as other species, being damaged by temperatures in the mid-20's. One selection, *L. p.* var. *buchii*, is a recent introduction into the trade. Removal of flowers extends the blooming cycle; light pruning can help to maintain size and shape. Plates 648 - 649.

Lavandula stoechas
Spanish Lavender, Italian Lavender
A rounded shrub, 2-3 ft. high and as wide. Foliage is grey-green, narrow and linear; flowers feature a large, deep purple bract, and occur on stems 4-6 in. above the foliage.

Spanish lavender comes from warm, dry areas of Spain and Portugal on thin, non-calcareous soils. This species produces the most unique and striking flower character of the lavenders due to its pairs of large purple bracts that grow out of the top of its flower heads. This species has also been used for making perfumes. *L. s.* 'Otto Quast' (*L. s.* 'Quasti') is a more prostrate and spreading selection, 18-24 in. high, 2-3 ft. across, that produces a carpet of purple color in early spring. Plates 650 - 651.

Lavatera
Tree Mallow
Malvaceae

A small group of annuals, perennials, and evergreen shrubs including between 20-25 species. Many come from Mediterranean climates where they are adapted to moist winters without frost and with warm, dry summers. Species grown in western gardens are best suited to full sun in coastal regions, partial shade with periodic deep watering in warmer inland areas. They tolerate drought but accept regular water and respond with rapid growth to larger sizes. They are well suited to background, hillside, and screen planting purposes.

Lavatera assurgentiflora
California Tree Mallow

A large evergreen shrub that develops a mounding form, 8-12 ft. high and as wide. Large, dull green leaves reach 3-5 in. across, are palmately lobed, and will drop under drought stress. Colorful rose-purple to light purple flowers occur from spring through fall and intermittently all year. The visibility of the flowers is often hidden within foliage.

This species is native to Santa Barbara and Santa Catalina Islands, where it grows on sandy soils and bluffs within the coastal sage plant community. With age, it develops stout trunks and branches that can be pruned to form a small tree and achieve interesting structural character. Plates 652 - 653.

Lavatera bicolor

A colorful species from coastal areas of southern France. It develops into a large mounding shrub, 6-8 ft. high, 8-12 ft. wide. Foliage is comprised of light grey-green leaves, 2-3 in. across, palmately lobed; showy flowers are white with rose-purple centers and purple veins. The flowers on this species are more visible and occur over a very long flowering season, from early spring into late fall in coastal regions. Both foliage and flower character is attractive in background and screen planting situations. Plate 654.

Leonotis leonurus
Lion's Tail, Wild Dagga
Laminaceae

An evergreen shrub growing to 5-6 ft. high and as wide. Striking flowers are vibrant orange and produced from late spring into summer. Foliage is comprised of deep green leaves that are long and narrow.

This plant comes from subtropical climate habitats of South Africa, where it grows on hillsides and slopes that receive intermittent wet and dry spells throughout the year. In western gardens, it grows well in coastal, inland, valley, and low desert regions. It is subject to frost damage below 25° F and is best treated as a perennial that is cut back in late winter to maintain good foliage character and flower development. It prefers full sun, well drained soils, and low amounts of supplemental water.

Lion's tail is used as a colorful accent plant in background and perennial plantings. It combines well with subtropical succulents such as *Agave attenuata, Dracaena draco, Aloe* species, and with flowering perennials in water conserving gardens, such as *Romneya coulteri, Salvia clevelandii,* and *Trichostema lanatum.* Plates 655 - 656.

652. Lavatera assurgentiflora

653. Lavatera assurgentiflora

654. Lavatera bicolor

655. Leonotis leonurus

656. Leonotis leonurus

657. **Leptospermum laevigatum**

Leptospermum
Tea Tree
Myrtaceae

A small group of evergreen shrubs and trees that includes some 50 species. Two species have become the most popular for ornamental landscapes in western gardens, one coming from Australia and the other from New Zealand. Both of these species are native to coastal habitats and are well adapted to wind, sea spray, and sandy soils. Tea trees are often used as accent and specimen plants in both residential and commercial landscapes. Some types provide colorful flowers, others develop twisting branches and interesting forms.

Leptospermum laevigatum
Australian Tea Tree

A large evergreen shrub or small tree, growing 15-25 ft. high, with an equal spread. Small round leaves are light grey-green; numerous white flowers occur in spring and provide modest color value. Trunks and branches twist as they develop and are covered with shredding bark, lending a natural sculptural quality to older plants.

This species comes from coastal sand dunes and headlands of southern Australia and is part of the mallee plant association, which is similar to the coastal chaparral of California. It is highly adapted to sea coast conditions, including salt spray and slightly saline soils. It prefers slightly acid, sandy, well drained soils, and protection from temperatures below 25° F. In western gardens, it has proven to be a tough and durable species that also can be used in inland, valley, and microclimate locations in low desert regions.

Australian tea tree is very popular as a specimen plant in containers, raised planters, and in courtyard spaces. It can also be used for sand dune stabilization, clipped into hedges, and grown on banks to control erosion. Two compact selections are available: *L. l.* 'Compactum' which grows 5-8 ft. high, and *L. l.* 'Reevesii' which has denser, rounder foliage and a compact form to 4-5 ft. high. Both of these cultivars can be planted closely together and be maintained as clipped or informal hedges and screens. Plates 657 - 659.

659. **Leptospermum laevigatum**

658. **Leptospermum laevigatum, Wilson's Promontory, southern Australia**

Leptospermum scoparium
New Zealand Tea Tree

Evergreen shrubs or small trees with fine, prickly foliage and small, colorful flowers. Flowers of the true species are white; numerous cultivars have been developed to provide flowers that vary in color from white to pink and red. Blossoms occur from mid-winter to early spring.

The New Zealand tea tree is commonly found throughout New Zealand in many different habitats, ranging from lowland bogs and sandy coastal headlands, to forest and high mountain scrublands over 3500 ft. in elevation. This true species is highly variable in form and is not considered to be of value for ornamental landscapes. Instead, active hybridization has led to the development of many attractive cultivars. These cultivars range from prostrate and dwarf forms, to upright shrubs and small trees. More than 85 cultivars have been registered; local nurseries should be contacted for available forms and flower colors.

These cultivars grow best in cooler, coastal environments, as evidenced by how well they perform in the San Francisco Bay area and other northern coastal communities. However, they also grow well in warmer inland and valley locations when they get some relief from intense heat and sun. They need good drainage, part to full sun, and dislike iron poor soils. They are only moderately tolerant of drought conditions and prefer low to moderate amounts of supplemental water. Some of the cultivated varieties are described below.

L. s. 'Apple Blossom' - Mounding shrub, 5-7 ft. high, double flowers, light rose-pink.

L. s. 'Helene Strybing' - Large shrub, 6-10 ft. high, single flowers with light pink edges, deep pink centers. Plates 660 - 661.

L. s. 'Keatleyi' - Large open shrub, 6-12 ft. high, large single flowers with pink edges, red centers, can reach 1 in. across.

L. s. 'Pink Cascade' - Low spreading shrub, 12 in. high, 4-6 ft. across, single pink flowers.

L. s. 'Ruby Glow' - Medium to large shrub, 6-10 ft. high, double flowers are deep red. Plates 662, 664.

L. s. 'Red Damask' - Medium to large shrub, 6-10 ft. high, red-tinged foliage, double red flowers.

L. s. 'Snow White' - Mounding shrub, 3-5 ft. high, double white flowers. Plate 663.

660. Leptospermum scoparium 'Helene Strybing'

661. Leptospermum scoparium 'Helene Strybing'

662. Leptospermum scoparium 'Ruby Glow'

663. Leptospermum scoparium 'Snow White'

664. Leptospermum scoparium 'Ruby Glow'

665. Leptospermum scoparium, North Island, New Zealand

666. Leucophyllum candidum 'Silver Cloud'

667. Leucophyllum candidum 'Silver Cloud'

668. Leucophyllum frutescens 'Green Cloud'

669. Leucophyllum frutescens 'Green Cloud'

670. Leucophyllum frutescens 'White Cloud'

671. Leucophyllum laevigatum

Leucophyllum
Cenizo, Purple Sage
Scrophulariaceae

A small group of evergreen shrubs, including about 12 species that are native to deserts of the Southwest and Mexico. These plants are noted for bright flowers, durable foliage, and tolerance of heat, cold, aridity, and extended periods of drought. They often have several flowering periods each year in response to cycles of high humidity or rains.

Most species of *Leucophyllum* grow in limestone soils and can also tolerate alkaline conditions. In cultivation, they prefer good drainage and suffer under heavy, wet conditions. Research and field studies being conducted in Texas and Arizona are leading to new hybrids and to the introduction of other species and improved cultivars. These plants are excellent choices for use in all desert regions as foliage and flowering accent elements. They fit residential as well as commercial spaces, where they are frequently used in combination with other desert species such as *Encelia farinosa, Fouquieria splendens, Simmondsia chinensis, Cercidium floridum, Cassia phyllodenia*, and *Agave* species. Some species are also grown in coastal and inland regions, where they perform best in warm and sunny locations.

Leucophyllum candidum
Violet Silverleaf

A small shrub, reaching 4-5 ft. in size, that is native to the gravelly hillsides in southern Texas into northern Mexico. Leaves are small, to 1/2 in., and silvery; flowers are deep violet-purple. This species is a smaller and more compact form of *Leucophyllum* that has intense silver foliage. *L. c.* 'Silver Cloud' provides improved flowering character; *L. c.* 'Thundercloud' is a smaller form with strong flowering habits, 3-4 ft. high. Plates 666 - 667.

Leucophyllum frutescens
(Leucophyllum texanum)
Texas Silverleaf, Cenizo

A medium to large shrub, mounding to 6-8 ft. high and as wide. Distinctive foliage is comprised of silver-white leaves; showy flowers are violet to purple. Texas silverleaf grows in arid regions of New Mexico, Texas, and northern Mexico on well drained, limestone soils. This species is currently the most widely known and popular for landscape use. Several cultivars are currently available in the trade that provide variations in foliage and flower character. *L. f.* 'Compactum' has violet flowers, tightly clustered leaves, and grows into a dense mound 3-4 ft. in size. *L. f.* 'Green Cloud' has deep violet flowers and distinctive green foliage. Plates 668 - 669. *L. f.* 'White Cloud' has silvery color foliage and white flowers. Plate 670.

Leucophyllum laevigatum
Chihuahuan Sage

A medium shrub with upright branching, 3-4 ft. high, 4-5 ft. wide. Foliage and stems are medium green; leaves are tiny, 1/4-3/8 in. long. Colorful flowers are blue-purple. Chihuahuan sage is another species with green foliage color which produces frequent cycles of flowers. Plate 671.

Limonium perezii
(Statice perezii)
Sea Lavender
Plumbaginaceae

A small clumping perennial with large, deep green leaves and intense purple flowers. Plants grow 12-18 in. high, with flower stalks reaching over 2 ft.

This species comes from the Canary Islands and is fully adapted to mild and dry coastal climates. In western regions, it has proven to be one of the best perennials for seaside gardens, where it needs little care or attention once established. However, it has also become naturalized on dunes and bluffs in coastal areas and should be used with care. It is also widely grown in frost free inland and valley zones. In warmer and drier locations, it needs low amounts of supplemental water and protection from extreme sun and heat.

Sea lavender is one of the longest flowering perennial plants for ornamental gardens. Its lush foliage character and striking flower color make it useful as an accent element, either individually or in mass plantings. It is commonly used in rock gardens, containers, and small planter spaces along with such species as *Eschscholzia californica*, *Agave attenuata*, *Drosanthemum hispidum*, *Gazania* species, and *Echium fastuosum*. Another species, *L. sinuatum*, is a short-lived perennial that is often planted by seed on slopes for erosion control. It has rose, lavender, and blue flowers and is very colorful during early spring. Plate 672.

672. **Limonium perezii**

Lobelia laxiflora
Mexican Bush Lobelia
Lobeliaceae

A sprawling perennial shrub, 2-3 ft. high, spreading by underground rootstocks to 4-6 ft. across. Colorful tubular flowers are orange and red and accent the plant from late spring into summer.

Mexican bush lobelia is native to warm and dry regions throughout southern Arizona, Mexico, and Central America. It grows in areas of partial shade around rocks, by washes, and under trees to receive protection from full sun and heat. This species can be easily grown in coastal and inland regions but is appreciated most in low desert landscapes. It can be grouped with *Chilopsis linearis*, *Cercidium floridum*, *Ruellia* species, *Penstemon* species, and *Calliandra californica* as part of a mini-oasis that is given periodic summer water. Plates 673 - 674.

673. **Lobelia laxiflora**

674. **Lobelia laxiflora**

Lonicera
Honeysuckle
Caprifoliaceae

A large group of deciduous and evergreen vines and climbing shrubs. More than 150 species exist and are native to many climate regions of the world. Honeysuckles are widely known and appreciated for their fragrant, colorful flowers, and are used on trellises, fences, and as ground covers throughout the West. Most species perform best when provided with regular moisture, however, several types are quite tough and grow well on difficult sites with only low to moderate amounts of supplemental water.

Lonicera japonica 'Halliana'
Hall's Japanese Honeysuckle

An aggressive evergreen vine with medium to dark green leaves and fragrant white and yellow-

675. **Lonicera japonica 'Halliana'**

676. Lonicera japonica 'Purpurea'

677. Lonicera japonica 'Halliana'

orange flowers. This variety of honeysuckle has become widely used as a ground cover on slopes and banks in many parts of the West, particularly throughout southern California. It tolerates heat, cold, sun or partial shade, and many types of soils, including clay and calcareous. Once established, it needs only low amounts of supplemental water in coastal, inland, and valley regions.

Hall's honeysuckle has proven to be one of the most durable and attractive ground covers for erosion control on large slope areas. It is sometimes used on slopes adjacent to natural landscapes within fuel modification zones to reduce fire risk. All plantings need a regular winter pruning to keep it from climbing into shrubs and trees and to remove woody thatch that can become a fire hazard. It can also escape and become naturalized in moist ravines and woodland areas, particularly in northern California, therefore, it should be managed with additional care. *L. j.* 'Purpurea' is a less vigorous variety that has purplish foliage and purple-red flowers. Plates 675 - 677.

678. Lupinus albifrons

679. Lupinus albifrons, Sierra Nevada

Lupinus
Lupine
Fabaceae

A large group of annuals, perennials, and small shrubs that are particularly common throughout the western states. More than 200 species are known and are widely recognized by their colorful spikes of pea-shaped flowers. Both native species and hybrid varieties are available for cultivation. Many hybrid varieties are popular flowering accent plants that do best in rich, well drained soils, with regular moisture, and are not considered drought tolerant. Flower colors range from white, rose, and yellow to blue and purple.

Native lupines occur in many habitats, including coastal, desert, forest, and alpine, and are among the favorite spring wildflowers in many parts of the West. Most species are annuals that flower from early to late spring. These plants provide nectar and pollen for wildlife and contribute to the fertility of the soil through nitrogen fixation. Seeds from annual species can be collected and used for restoration and revegetation projects. A few native species are shrubs that can be used in ornamental gardens as perennials; two are described below.

Lupinus albifrons
Silver Lupine

A rounded shrub to 5 ft. high, with silky, grey-green leaves. Colorful blue to purple flower spikes grow 8-12 in. long in mid-summer. This species comes from dry hillsides in the southern coastal foothills and from parts of the Sierra Nevada. It is well suited to heat and drought in inland and valley gardens. Plates 678 - 680.

Lupinus arboreus
Coastal Bush Lupine

A shrubby species, growing 3-6 ft. high, that usually develops tall spikes of lemon yellow flowers in mid-spring. This species is native to sandy bluffs and plains along the coastline from Ventura to northern California. It is a handsome flowering accent plant in coastal regions, where it requires little or no supplemental water once established.

680. Annual lupines with Encelia farinosa in Mojave Desert, Nevada

Lyonothamnus floribundus
Catalina Ironwood
Rosaceae

A medium to large evergreen tree, growing slender and upright to 30-60 ft. high, 25-35 ft. wide. Foliage is comprised of deep, glossy green leaves that are narrow, 5-6 in. long, and have lobed margins. Numerous tiny white flowers develop in large, flat-topped clusters, and are showy in late spring to early summer.

Catalina ironwood is native to Catalina Island, where it grows to its largest sizes in canyon habitats. It also becomes established on exposed slopes within the chaparral plant community, where it tolerates persistent winds and long periods of drought. A related subspecies, *L. f.* ssp. *asplenifolius*, Fernleaf Catalina Ironwood, is found under similar conditions on San Clemente, Santa Rosa, and Santa Cruz islands. This subspecies develops more attractive foliage character because of deeply divided leaves and heavily lobed leaflets.

Ironwood trees are well adapted to coastal habitats throughout California. In valley and inland regions, they perform best when planted in areas that are partially shaded from late afternoon sun and heat in the summer. They tolerate many types of soils, including calcareous, but require periodic deep watering in the summer. These plants provide good overstory protection and visual character in gardens in combination with other natives including *Ceanothus* species, *Arctostaphylos* species, *Mahonia* species, *Ribes viburnifolium*, *Iris douglasiana*, and *Heuchera* hybrids. The bark develops an interesting shredding character, however, flowers, leaves, and bark generate ample litter. Plates 681 - 684.

681. Lyonothamnus floribundus

682. Lyonothamnus f. var. asplenifolius

683. Lyonothamnus f. var. asplenifolius

684. Lyonothamnus floribundus var. asplenifolius

Lysiloma microphylla var. Thornberi
Feather Bush, Desert Fern
Fabaceae

A large shrub to small tree with soft foliage character, growing 12-15 ft. high. Deep green leaves are bipinnately divided into many tiny leaflets and are briefly deciduous in cold areas. Numerous white flower balls occur in spring and create a soft accent character.

Feather bush is native to intermediate and upper desert foothills in Arizona where it grows in loose, well drained soils. Plants occurring near seasonal washes grow to larger sizes and retain their foliage for longer periods of time. This species is most commonly planted in low and intermediate desert regions where it is adapted to heat, aridity, and periods of drought. Plants are damaged by temperatures below 25° F but quickly regrow. It has a short deciduous habit during cold spells and will also shed some foliage during periods of high drought stress. Most plants look best when planted in areas, such as courtyards, that provide protection from intense sun and heat and when provided with moderate amounts of supplemental water. This plant can become a handsome canopy tree that provides a green, lush appearance in both residential and commercial landscapes. Plates 685 - 686.

685. Lysiloma microphylla var. Thornberi, University of Arizona, Tucson

686. Lysiloma microphylla var. Thornberi

687. Macfadyena unguis-cati

Macfadyena unguis-cati
(Bignonia tweediana, Doxantha unguis-cati)
Cat's Claw, Yellow Trumpet Vine
Bignoniaceae

A large and aggressive vine that has unique claw-like tendrils and colorful yellow, trumpet-shaped flowers. The foliage of this species is partly evergreen in warm, coastal regions, and deciduous in cooler climates that have frost. Large numbers of bright yellow flowers provide a striking display for 1-2 weeks in early spring.

Cat's claw is one of four known species within this genus group. It comes from subtropical climates of the Yucatan in Mexico and from Guatemala and Argentina. In contrast to its native habitat, this species grows well in both warm and cool regions, from coastal foothills, to high and low deserts. It thrives with heat and periodic deep watering, and easily grows 30-40 ft. and longer. Established plants develop strong root systems that help to obtain the moisture plants need. Stems cling to rough surfaces by sharp tendrils and will twine their way around posts and beams, as well as on overheads and trellises.

Cat's claw is a popular plant for both residential and commercial spaces. It is a large vine, but with pruning, it can be contained to many sizes. It is also very adaptable to harsh urban conditions and can be planted in tight spaces to cover large, exposed walls and fences. Plates 687 - 688.

688. Macfadyena unguis-cati, University of Arizona, Tucson

Mahonia

Berberidaceae

A large group of evergreen shrubs including over 100 species that come from Asia, and North and Central America. Most types in landscape use come from western states and are widely appreciated for their yellow flowers, colorful fruit, and adaptability to a wide range of sun, soil, and moisture conditions.

Flowers are typically deep yellow and occur in terminal clusters from early winter to mid-spring. Deep purple-blue berries will follow and are both colorful as well as valuable to wildlife. Foliage is pinnately divided into leathery leaflets that have spines on the margins. In areas having frost, some foliage will turn purple to red and remain colorful through winter.

Most mahonias are naturally suited to moist areas in rich, organic soils, located in partial shade to full sun. However, they have proved to be a widely adapted group of plants that are used in warmer, drier regions of the West, where their leathery foliage helps them resist heat, aridity, and full sun. They grow best with moderate amounts of supplemental water but often become quite drought resistant as they mature. In harsher climate areas, they should be placed in areas that receive some protection from extreme sun, heat, and wind. They are used as slope, screen, and flowering accent plants in both commercial and residential spaces. They are also widely used around native oaks where they tolerate variations in sun and shade and low amounts of summer water. In other landscape settings, they can be combined with *Cercis occidentalis, Ribes speciosum, Iris douglasiana, Ceanothus* species, and *Heuchera* hybrids.

Mahonia aquifolium

(Berberis aquifolium)
Oregon Grape

An evergreen shrub with many upright branches, 5-6 ft. high, 4-5 ft. wide. Showy clusters of bright yellow flowers occur in early to mid-spring. Large clusters of showy purple fruit occur in late spring. Fruit is of value to wildlife, is also edible, and can be used in making jelly. Dark, glossy green leaves have spiny margins, are 5-10 in. long, and are most often divided into 5-9 leaflets.

Oregon grape is native to foothills and mountains from Vancouver Island, British Columbia, south to Trinity and Humboldt counties in northern California. It grows at many elevations and as an understory shrub within forest communities in moist, shaded sites. It grows best in cool, northern regions of the West but tolerates inland, valley, and desert regions, where it performs best in partial shade with moderate amounts of supplemental moisture. A lower growing form is also available. *M. a.* 'Compacta', matures to 18-24 in. high and is an excellent ground cover choice for shaded areas and on small banks. Plates 689 - 691.

Mahonia 'Golden Abundance'

An upright evergreen shrub, 5-6 ft. high and as wide. Heavy, leathery foliage is dull medium green and divided into 7-9 leaflets. Large clusters of showy yellow flowers occur in spring, followed by colorful purple fruit.

689. Mahonia aquifolium

690. Mahonia aquifolium

691. Mahonia aquifolium 'Compacta'

692. Mahonia 'Golden Abundance'

693. Mahonia 'Golden Abundance'

694. Mahonia 'Golden Abundance'

695. Mahonia nevinii

696. Mahonia nevinii

697. Mahonia pinnata 'Ken Hartman'

698. Mahonia pinnata 'Ken Hartman'

699. Mahonia repens

This cultivar is a seedling hybrid involving several species: *M. piperiana*, *M. aquifolium*, and *M. amplectans*. The result is a plant that has handsome foliage character, striking flowers, and good tolerance of heat, sun, and aridity. It is better suited to drier, warmer conditions than *M. aquifolium* and is widely planted throughout southern California as a screen, background, and flowering accent plant. Plates 692 - 694.

Mahonia nevinii
Nevin Mahonia

A medium shrub, 8-12 ft. high and as wide. Distinctive foliage is comprised of blue-green leaves that are divided into 3-5 leaflets. Loose clusters of showy, clear yellow flowers occur in spring; colorful fruit is yellow to red and of value to wildlife.

This species comes from dry wash areas in southern California where it is a member of the coastal sage scrub plant community. It is naturally adapted to well drained, sandy soils, full sun, and extended periods of drought. In western gardens, it grows well with low amounts of supplemental water but can also accept regular watering. It has shown good adaptability to clayey soils. Currently, this species is most widely used as a background and screen plant and combines well with other natives including *Yucca whipplei*, *Rhus ovata*, *Trichostema lanatum*, *Eriogonum* species, and *Artemisia californica*. Plates 695 - 696.

Mahonia pinnata
California Grape

A medium shrub, 4-5 ft. high and as wide. Foliage is comprised of thin, shiny green leaves that are most often divided into 5-11 leaflets. Margins of leaflets are wavy and covered with many spines. Bright yellow flowers are showy in early spring; modest amounts of blue-purple berries follow.

California grape is native to many parts of the northern coastal ranges of California and northern Baja California. It often occurs in sunny locations on well drained slopes. It is used in coastal, inland, valley, and low desert regions as a barrier, hedge, and flowering accent plant in both native and ornamental landscapes. It is considered more sun, heat, and drought tolerant than *M. aquifolium*, and has a stiffer, more prickly texture. *M. p.* 'Ken Hartman' is a cultivar that has a dense, compact shape, and grows 4-5 ft. high. Plates 697 - 698.

Mahonia repens
Creeping Mahonia

A low spreading shrub, 8-12 in. high, 2-3 ft. across. Foliage is dull green and divided into 5 leaflets. Small clusters of yellow flowers are showy in early spring; small numbers of blue-purple fruit follow.

Creeping mahonia occurs in several northwestern states and Canada. In California, it grows in pine woods on well drained soils, usually in partial shade. In cultivation, it grows best in rich soils with moderate moisture and will spread by underground stems. It is widely adapted to garden conditions in coastal, inland, valley, and microclimate areas in desert regions. It is used as a ground cover around native oaks, on banks, and in small planter areas. Plate 699.

Maleophora

Ice Plant

Aizoaceae

A small group of succulent shrubs and ground covers native to South Africa, including about 15 species. Two species are cultivated in western gardens and are used principally as ground covers on slopes and banks in residential landscapes. These species are well suited to coastal and inland regions, in sunny locations, and with low amounts of supplemental water. They produce a showy display of flowers in early to mid-spring and intermittently all year.

Maleophora crocea

A low spreading plant to 6 in. high, growing several feet across. Succulent foliage is grey-green and cylindrical; colorful purple-red flowers occur with greatest intensity in spring. This is the most widely used species of *Maleophora* due to its spreading habit and greater tolerance of heat and cold. It is used for erosion control on small and large slopes alike, and can grow in protected areas in valley and desert regions. Plates 700 - 701.

Maleophora luteola

A clumping species, mounding 12-15 in. high, 1-2 ft. across. Grey-green, cylindrical foliage contrasts well with bright yellow flowers in spring. It is not as vigorous or cold tolerant as *M. crocea* and is better suited for small banks, raised planters, and containers. Plate 702.

Malosma laurina

(Rhus laurina)

Laurel Sumac

Anacardiaceae

A large evergreen shrub, mounding 12-20 ft. high, and spreading as wide. Foliage is comprised of 3-4 in. long, dark green leaves that contain pungent, resinous oils. Plumes of creamy white flowers are showy for a brief period when they occur between spring to early summer.

Laurel sumac is native to coastal and inland foothills of California from Santa Barbara County into northern Baja California. It is a member of the coastal sage scrub and chaparral plant communities where it is often limited to areas that do not experience regular frost. It grows on many types of soil, and tolerates heat, wind, and extended periods of drought. Within its natural range, it helps to stabilize slopes with its deep root system and also produces berries eaten by birds. However, it is considered to be quite flammable during wildfires and can increase the fire risk when it occurs in large populations. As a result, it is often removed from fuel modification zones around developments in an effort to increase fire safety. Otherwise, it can be grown with good results along highways and is used for revegetation of large slope areas. Plate 703.

700. **Maleophora crocea**

701. **Maleophora crocea**

702. **Maleophora luteola**

703. **Malosma laurina**

704. Melaleuca armillaris

705. Melaleuca armillaris

706. Melaleuca linariifolia

707. Melaleuca linariifolia

Melaleuca
Honey Myrtle
Myrtaceae

A diverse group of evergreen trees and shrubs. Of the 150 estimated species believed to exist, most come from Australia where they inhabit the edges of coastal swamps and estuaries that become seasonally inundated with run-off. Some species are noted for their interesting papery bark, others for striking flowers or branching character.

Several species of *Melaleuca* are popular in western gardens. They are best suited to frost free coastal landscapes but are frequently used in inland, valley, and low desert regions. The mature foliage character of many types is hard and leathery which helps them adapt to warm and arid regions. However, plants used in drier climates do best with moderate amounts of supplemental moisture. These plants are also valued for their tolerance of poorly drained and shallow soils as well as light amounts of salinity. Some plants show iron deficiency in calcareous soils.

Melaleuca armillaris
Drooping Melaleuca, Bracelet Honey Myrtle

A large shrub or small tree with flexible branching and fine foliage character. This species provides rich green color and soft, billowy texture; noticeable white flowers occur in 1-2 in. long brushes in early spring. As a shrub, this species grows 12-15 ft. high, while spreading 15-30 ft. wide. Plants grown as trees reach 15-25 ft. high.

This species is native to sand dunes, coastal escarpments, and granite outcrops of eastern Australia. It occurs in association with *Leptospermum laevigatum, Casuarina stricta,* and *Acacia retinodes.* In western landscapes, drooping melaleuca is often used along freeways and large scale slopes as a screen and filler plant. It is highly adapted to wind, salt spray, and calcareous soils. It requires little care and performs well in large shrub masses or as a small tree that is appreciated for its soft texture and weeping branch habit. Once established, it can survive in coastal regions with little or no supplemental water. Plates 704 - 705.

Melaleuca linariifolia
Flaxleaf Paperbark

A small to medium tree, 20-30 ft. high, that develops a dense, rounded shape, 20-25 ft. wide. Medium green leaves are narrow, needle-like and create a soft, billowy textural quality. Masses of showy white flowers occur in late spring to mid-summer on the upper tips of branches creating an effect of snow for 2-3 weeks. Bark is papery in character, white to tan in color.

Flaxleaf paperbark is found in swampy gullies and along the banks of streams and low lying coastal zones throughout eastern Australia. In cultivation, it becomes a handsome canopy tree that is used as a street tree, for yard specimens, and in park landscapes. In warm inland and low desert locations, it performs best with moderate amounts of supplemental water on a regular basis. Plates 706 - 707.

Melaleuca nesophila
Pink Melaleuca

A large shrub to small tree, 10-18 ft. high, 15-20 ft. wide. Branching often develops an interesting twisted character. Leaves are round, to 1 in. long; showy white to pink flowers occur in clusters during early summer.

Pink melaleuca is found on the islands off Western Australia on sandy soils and in areas exposed to salt spray and wind. In western gardens, it has proven to be tolerant of many soils and grows well with low to moderate amounts of moisture. It is a versatile plant that is useful for beach plantings, on slopes, banks, and for screens. It also shows tolerance for the aridity and heat of low desert regions. This species can be sheared into a hedge, but it is highly suited as a special interest plant in gardens when selective pruning reveals its twisting branches and thick bark character. Plates 708 - 709.

Melaleuca quinquenervia
(Melaleuca leucadendra)
Cajeput Tree, Paperbark

A medium to large tree, 25-40 ft. high, 15-25 ft. wide. Firm, leathery leaves are 2-3 in. long, pale green, and pointed; noticeable creamy white flowers occur in large, brush-like clusters at the ends of branches in fall. Attractive bark is white to tan, developing in thick, spongy layers that can be peeled off like paper.

This species is native to coastal habitats in eastern Australia. It occurs along stream banks and within estuaries and marshes that are subject to extended periods of flooding. It is sensitive to cold; temperatures below 25°F will damage new growth and can kill young plants. It tolerates a wide range of soils including silts, clays, loams, and salinity.

The cajeput tree is a very popular species for western gardens due to its upright form and distinctive, white bark. It is highly adapted to coastal regions where it grows well with low to moderate amounts of supplemental moisture. Its leathery leaf character enables it to withstand heat and aridity in inland and low desert regions, but regular moisture is recommended. It grows fast and performs well in narrow spaces between buildings, as well as in lawn situations. It is also useful as a street tree or as a multi-trunk specimen in courtyards and residential gardens. Iron deficiency in calcareous soils can cause chlorosis and damaged foliage growth. Plates 710 - 711.

708. Melaleuca nesophila

709. Melaleuca nesophila

710. Melaleuca quinquenervia

711. Melaleuca quinquenervia

712. Melampodium leucanthum

713. Melampodium leucanthum

714. Melia azedarach 'Umbraculiformis'

715. Melia azedarach

716. Melia azedarach 'Umbraculiformis'

Melampodium leucanthum
Blackfoot Daisy
Asteraceae

A low growing perennial, 12-15 in. high, spreading 2-3 ft. across. Narrow grey-green leaves reach 1 in. long. Intensive display of white, daisy-type flowers occurs in spring and intermittently through summer and fall.

Blackfoot daisy is native to a wide area from Kansas to Texas, Arizona, and into Mexico. Throughout the Southwest, it is common to desert regions where it typically grows in limestone soils on dry mesas and rocky slopes. In these arid zones, it responds to seasonal rains with fast growth and prolific flowering. It will die back during drought cycles and from late fall to winter.

This is a colorful and easy to grow perennial that is popular for use in desert landscapes. It can be planted from seed or container, and works well in small spaces such as, raised planters, banks, and courtyard gardens. It can survive in natural landscapes with little water but maintains better foliage and flower character when provided with low to moderate amounts of water during the spring. Plates 712 - 713.

Melia azedarach
Chinaberry
Meliaceae

A medium to large deciduous tree, 30-50 ft. high, developing a wide canopy 40-50 ft. across. Dark green leaves grow 2-3 ft. long and are pinnately divided into many 1-2 in. long leaflets. Tiny lilac to purple flowers grow in large clusters in spring. Flowers are replaced by large clusters of poisonous fruit in late summer. Fruit is round and golden in color and persists on trees through fall and winter.

Chinaberry is native to central China where it is a member of the deciduous oak forest plant community. This habitat is characterized by cold, moist winters and short, mild summers. In western gardens, this species has proven to be highly tolerant of heat, cold, and drought and has been planted in all regions. It develops a strong root system and is capable of surviving on seasonal rainfall or will accept regular moisture. As a result, it has often been used in tough and difficult landscape areas such as rural communities and farming areas, where it often receives little attention or care and where it is appreciated for its deep summer shade. It can be cut back hard in late fall to control its size and will quickly regrow to a canopy shape each year. One cultivar, *M. a.* 'Umbraculiformis', Texas Umbrella Tree, grows to 30 ft. high and wide, and achieves a very dense, regular dome shape. Plates 714 - 716.

Metrosideros excelsus
(Metrosideros tomentosus)
New Zealand Christmas Tree,
Pohutukawa
Myrtaceae

A large shrub to medium size evergreen tree, growing 15-30 ft. and higher, with an equal spread. Foliage is comprised of deep green leaves that have white fuzz on the edges and undersides. Colorful red flowers have many stamens and occur in spring to early summer.

This species is native to coastal edges and forests on the North Island of New Zealand. It grows in sand dunes and on cliffs within range of salt spray and persistent onshore winds. The maritime climate of this region keeps summer temperatures mild. Rainstorms are frequent throughout the year; there is seldom frost.

In western gardens, this species is best suited to coastal zones ranging from the Pacific Northwest to San Diego. These plants grow faster and to larger sizes with regular water, however, established plants do fine with little supplemental water. This is a popular plant for use as a street, residential patio, or courtyard tree. It can be clipped as well and be used for screens and hedges. Large specimens with handsome trunk character can be seen in parks and residential gardens. They often have aerial roots in areas of frequent fog and high humidity. *M. e.* 'Aurea' is a cultivar that produces yellow flowers; *M. e.* 'Variegata' has yellow color markings on the leaves. Plates 717 - 719.

717. **Metrosideros excelsus**

718. **Metrosideros excelsus**

719. **Metrosideros excelsus, North Cape, New Zealand**

720. Morus alba

Morus alba
White Mulberry
Moraceae

A medium to large deciduous tree, 30-60 ft. high, spreading 30-50 ft. across. Medium green leaves grow 8-10 in. across and are deeply lobed. Flowers are insignificant; large quantities of raspberry-type fruit are produced in mid-spring to early summer. Fruit is edible but is also messy and causes stains to paving and clothing.

White mulberry is native to central China and is a member of the mixed deciduous forest plant community where it grows on hills and alluvial plains at elevations above 1,500 ft. elevation. The climate is cold and moist during winter with annual rainfall ranging 40-60 in.; summers are short and warm. This species is widely known for its role in silk worm cultivation.

In western gardens, the fruiting species is seldom grown. Instead, several fruitless and weeping varieties have been planted for their ornamental character and tolerance of difficult landscape conditions. Standard fruitless forms include *M. a.* 'Fruitless', *M. a.* 'Kingan', and *M. a.* 'Stribling'. These varieties have proven to be highly tolerant of heat and cold and have been widely planted in rural communities where they survive with little care. They are fast growing and appreciated for their broad canopy and deep shade during summer months. Mulberries typically develop a strong surface root system that is capable of obtaining any available moisture and causing problems for lawns, shrubs, and paving. They can use high amounts of water, but trees in neglected areas indicate their adaptability to seasonal rain and periodic watering. They can be cut back hard in late fall to control their size and will quickly regrow each year. Weeping cultivars are smaller, grow more slowly, and include *M. a.* 'Pendula', *M. a.* 'Teas' Weeping', and *M. a.* 'Chaparral'. Plates 720 - 721.

721. Morus alba

722. Muhlenbergia rigens

723. Muhlenbergia rigens

Muhlenbergia rigens
Deer Grass
Poaceae

Deer grass is a member of a small group of clumping perennial grasses that are native to many parts of the Southwest. This species grows 24-30 in. high and has long, light grey-green foliage. Insignificant flower stalks are tan in color.

Deer grass naturally occurs in sandy and gravelly washes of southern California, Arizona, Texas, and northern Mexico. It is a durable plant that has been recently introduced into cultivation for slope and bank planting uses in commercial scale spaces where it provides a distinctive clumping form. It grows in coastal, inland, valley, and desert regions and tolerates heat, aridity, and low amounts of supplemental water. Several other species of *Muhlenbergia* are currently being introduced into the trade that provide other foliage and flowering characteristics. Plates 722 - 723.

Myoporum
Myoporaceae

A small group of evergreen shrubs and trees that includes 30 species from many parts of the world. Several species and varieties are grown in western regions where they are noted for their fast growth and rich, deep green foliage character. Some types are better suited to coastal regions, others are adapted to arid zones. They grow fastest and to larger sizes with regular moisture, but all perform quite well with far less. Most types are tolerant of calcareous soils, as well as heat, wind, and sun. Established plants show good resistance to drought stress. In recent years, several new seedling hybrids that grow as large, spreading shrubs have been introduced into the trade and are useful as ground covers on large slopes and roadside setbacks.

Myoporum 'Davis'

A low spreading shrub, 8-12 in. high, growing 12-15 ft. across. Small linear leaves become 1 in. long, to 1/8 in. wide and have distinctly toothed margins. Noticeable clusters of white flowers occur near the tips of branches in spring.

This selection is from seeds collected from plants within interior regions of South Australia. It is very similar in character to *M. parvifolium* due to its foliage size and low growing habit. It is well adapted to coastal, inland, and valley regions, where it tolerates heat and frost to 22°F. Low amounts of supplemental water are needed throughout summer.

Myoporum laetum

A large mounding shrub to small canopy tree, 20-30 ft. high, 15-25 ft. wide. Leaves are deep green, 3-4 in. long, and covered with numerous translucent dots. Small flowers are white with purple dots and occur in inconspicuous clusters in summer; small purple fruits follow and are poisonous.

This species of *Myoporum* is native to coastal edges of the North and South Islands of New Zealand. It grows on sandy soils and bluffs within a maritime climate zone that includes regular onshore winds, salt spray, and monthly rainstorms. It has been widely planted in coastal gardens in California, from San Francisco to San Diego, where it is often used as a screen along highways and on banks and beachfronts. This is a fast growing plant that develops dense, lush, foliage character that can be pruned into a handsome canopy tree as it matures. It requires little care or attention in coastal areas, but should be given low to moderate amounts of supplemental water when planted in warmer and drier inland areas. Unfortunately, it has also escaped and become naturalized in coastal foothills. One cultivar, *M. l.* 'Carsonii', has larger and darker green leaves and is quite popular in the trade. Plates 724 - 725.

Myoporum 'Pacificum'

A large spreading shrub, 2-3 ft. high, reaching as much as 15-30 ft. across. Deep green leaves reach 3 in. long, to 1/2 in. wide and have lightly toothed margins. Small white flowers develop along stems during spring and summer.

This seedling hybrid is very fast growing and will root along its stems and spread for many feet in diameter. It is a popular slope plant in coastal areas that grows well in calcareous

724. Myoporum laetum, North Island, New Zealand

725. Myoporum laetum

726. Myoporum 'Pacificum'

727. Myoporum 'Pacificum'

728. Myoporum parvifolium, Palm Desert, California

729. Myoporum parvifolium

730. Myrica californica

731. Myrica californica

soils, full sun, and with low to moderate amounts of supplemental water. Heavy pruning can manage size and help renew foliage character. Plates 726 - 727.

Myoporum parvifolium

A very prostrate shrub, 6-8 in. high, spreading 12-15 ft. across and more. Foliage is comprised of small, medium green leaves, to 1/2 in. long, 1/8 in. wide, and have small teeth around their margins. Numerous white flowers occur in clusters along branches in early spring and intermittently all year.

This species is native to hot, dry, interior plains of southern Australia. In western gardens, it has proven to be an excellent ornamental ground cover for use in low and intermediate desert regions in wide planters, on slopes, and along highways. It tolerates heat, frost, and can be sustained with low amounts of supplemental water. It is also adapted to coastal, inland, and valley areas where it does best in warm, sunny locations. Sometimes this species is short-lived and can lose foliage or die in as little as 5-6 years. Several varieties with larger leaves are now in cultivation, including *M. p.* 'Putah Creek', which has larger leaves, to 1 1/2 in., produces vigorous growth, and has proven to be successful in the San Joaquin Valley. Plates 728 - 729.

Myoporum 'South Coast'

A large spreading shrub, to 3 ft. high, growing 10-15 ft. across. Slender leaves are shiny, medium green, grow to 2 in. long, 1/2 in. wide and have mostly smooth margins. Numerous showy white flowers occur in clusters of 3-5 along the tops of branches in spring.

This seedling hybrid offers another low growing choice for use as a ground cover and bank plant in coastal, inland, and valley regions. It is an aggressive selection, growing quickly with low to moderate amounts of supplemental water, and adapted to sun and cold temperatures to 22°F.

Myrica californica
Pacific Wax Myrtle
Myricaceae

A large evergreen shrub to small tree, 15-25 ft. high, 15 ft. spread. Dark green leaves are linear, grow to 5 in. long. Flowers are inconspicuous; fruit matures in summer and is eaten by birds.

The pacific wax myrtle is native to canyons and slopes within coastal ranges from Los Angeles northward to Washington. It can also be found growing on sand dunes in more northerly regions. Within this range, it is found within the coastal sage scrub and chaparral plant communities. It reaches tree-like sizes with lush foliage character when established in canyons and is typically a shrub when it occurs on exposed hillsides. This is a very attractive foliage plant that can be clipped and used for screens and hedges or be pruned as a small patio tree. It grows best in northern coastal regions where it requires little or no supplemental water once established. In warmer locations and inland zones, it should be protected from extreme heat and sun, and be provided with low to moderate amounts of water. It can be planted with many other natives including *Arctostaphylos*, *Ceanothus*, *Cercis*, and *Mahonia* species. Plates 730 - 731.

Myrtus communis
Greek Myrtle, True Myrtle
Myrtaceae

A medium size evergreen shrub to small tree. When grown as a shrub, plants reach 8-10 ft. high; with age and pruning, multiple trunk specimen shrubs and small scale trees, 15 to 20 ft. high, can be attained. Foliage is comprised of pointed leaves that are bright, glossy green and have a spicy fragrance when clipped or crushed. Noticeable clusters of small, white flowers are pleasantly fragrant and occur in early summer. Deep purple to black berries mature by fall.

The Greek myrtle is one of 16 known species within the genus *Myrtus*. It is the only species native to Europe where it occurs in coastal and inland habitats around the Mediterranean region. It has been cultivated in gardens for centuries for the scented oils contained within its foliage, flowers, and bark. These oils are widely used in the production of perfumes. In natural settings, it is often found in moist places such as ravines or on poor soils in pine woods and scrub vegetation. In western gardens, this plant has shown wide adaptability to many types of soils, including calcareous. It needs low to moderate amounts of supplemental water and grows best in full sun on well drained soils. It is planted in coastal, inland, valley, and low desert regions and is tolerant of frost, heat, and wind.

The Greek myrtle has a tight branching habit with dense foliage character that makes it one of the best choices as a clipped hedge. Older plants can be pruned to reveal twisting trunks that have an interesting bark character for specimen value in raised planters. Several cultivars are available that provide varying character. *M. c.* 'Compacta', Dwarf Myrtle, can grow 5-8 ft. high and is a highly popular plant for clipped hedges and topiary uses. *M. c.* 'Boetica' grows 5-8 ft. and provides unusually stiff and dark green foliage. *M. c.* 'Variegata' reaches standard sizes and has yellow and green coloration. Plates 732 - 734.

732. **Myrtus communis 'Compacta'**

733. **Myrtus communis 'Compacta'**

734. **Myrtus communis 'Variegata'**

Nerium oleander
Oleander
Apocynaceae

A medium to large evergreen shrub, growing 8-12 ft. high and as wide. Foliage is comprised of long, pointed leaves that are medium green and attached to flexible stems and branches. Very showy flowers occur in mid-spring through summer and vary in color from white to pink, red, salmon, and yellow. All parts of this plant contain a milky juice that is highly poisonous if eaten.

Oleanders come from many parts of the Mediterranean region, from Spain and North Africa to Greece and further east to the Persian Gulf. It has proven to be widely adapted, including very dry sections of Spain and Portugal where it inhabits seasonal water courses and ravines in order to capture winter moisture. It tolerates heat, aridity, sun, wind, and extended periods of drought.

In western gardens, oleander is highly respected for its adaptability to coastal, inland, valley, and desert regions. It does best in

735. **Nerium oleander 'Sister Agnes'**

736. Nerium oleander 'Mrs. Roeding'

737. Nerium oleander 'Mrs. Roeding'

warm, frost free locations with low to moderate amounts of supplemental moisture. It tolerates most soils, including calcareous, sandy, and lightly saline, and can withstand short periods of wetness in poorly drained areas. Oleanders are among the most widely used flowering shrubs in the western states. They develop into uniform mounding shrubs or can be clipped and pruned for use as formal hedges and screens. They are often planted on slopes, in background areas, and are highly successful in roadside plantings. Larger varieties can also can be pruned as single or multiple trunk trees for use in patios, courtyards, and parking lot planters. Many cultivars are now available that provide single or double flowers, compact or intermediate sizes. Some are described below.

N. o. 'Algiers' - Large mounding shrub or standard tree, 10-12 ft. high, single deep red flowers.

N. o. 'Casablanca' - Intermediate size mounding shrub, 4-6 ft. high, single clear white flowers.

N. o. 'Hawaii' - Large mounding shrub, 5-7 ft. high, single salmon-pink flowers. Frost sensitive.

N.o. 'Isle of Capri' - Large mounding shrub, 5-7 ft. high, single light yellow flowers.

N. o. 'Petite Pink' - Dwarf mounding shrub, 4-5 ft. high, single clear pink flowers. Plates 738 - 739.

N. o. 'Petite Salmon' - Dwarf mounding shrub, 4-5 ft. high, single salmon flowers. Plate 740.

N. o. 'Mrs. Roeding' - Large mounding shrub, 6-8 ft. high, double salmon-pink flowers. Plates 736 - 737.

N. o. 'Sister Agnes' - Large mounding shrub or standard tree, 12-15 ft. high, single white flowers. Plate 735.

N. o. 'Tangier' - Intermediate size shrub, 4-6 ft. high, single light pink flowers.

738. Nerium oleander 'Petite Pink'

739. Nerium oleander 'Petite Pink'

740. Nerium oleander 'Petite Salmon'

741. Nerium oleander red

Nolina

Bear Grass

Agavaceae

A small group of yucca-like shrubs that develop long, grass-like foliage. About 25 species exist and are native to desert regions of the southwestern United States and Mexico. These plants need well drained soils and are well adapted to heat, aridity, and drought. Mature plants often have short, stout trunks, and produce tall flower stalks that are quite showy and dramatic in desert settings. Unlike agaves, these species will not die after flowering.

Nolina bigelovii

Bigelow Nolina

A large species, reaching 5-8 ft. in dia. and producing long, narrow leaves without teeth on the margins. This species is found in many desert areas from California and Arizona into Baja California, at elevations ranging from 500-3,500 ft. It grows within the creosote bush scrub plant community on dry, rocky slopes, and bajadas. Plate 742.

Nolina parryi

Parry's Nolina

A medium size species with flexible grey-green leaves, toothed margins, growing 4-5 ft. high. It is native to inland foothills within the chaparral plant community at elevations from 3,000-7,000 ft. and on hillsides around the Mojave and Colorado deserts in California and Arizona. A larger subspecies, *N. p.* ssp. *wolfii*, Wolf's Bear-grass, can have 3-6 ft. trunks and grow 8-10 ft. high. It produces striking flower stalks in late spring. Plates 743 - 744.

Oenothera

Evening Primrose, Sundrops

Onagraceae

A large group of annuals and perennials, containing more than 80 species, many of which are native to North America and the Southwest. These plants are widely known for their colorful flowers and adaptability to small spaces, borders, and rock gardens. They prefer well drained soils, full sun, and require little care once established. Species from moist climates prefer regular water; types native to desert regions of the West are well adapted to drought and are easily planted from seed or container.

Oenothera berlandieri

Mexican Evening Primrose

A spreading perennial, 12-18 in. high, 2-3 ft. across. Remarkable quantities of pink flowers occur from early spring through fall. Native to Mexico and Texas, it will grow with much or little water in all regions and can become invasive. Plates 745 - 746.

Oenothera caespitosa

Tufted Evening Primrose

A clumping perennial, 15-18 in. high. Large white flowers are pleasantly scented, open in the evening during spring and fall. A striking accent plant well adapted to low and intermediate desert regions on well drained soils.

Oenothera stubbii

Baja Evening Primrose

A spreading perennial with deep green leaves to 5 in. long, growing to 1 ft. across. Large yellow flowers occur on raised stems during the spring. A desert species from Baja California well suited to low desert gardens.

742. Nolina bigelovii

743. Nolina parryi ssp. wolfii

744. Nolina parryi

745. Oenothera berlandieri

746. Oenothera berlandieri

Olea europaea
Olive
Oleaceae

A medium size evergreen tree, growing upright to 35 ft. high, spreading 20-30 ft. Distinctive grey-green foliage is comprised of 1-2 in. long leaves; creamy yellow flowers occur in great numbers in mid-spring. Numerous olive-type fruit develop green and mature to black by winter.

The olive is one of the most widely recognized trees around the world. It has a rich and varied history since the earliest days of civilization and continues to be one of the most symbolic and characteristic garden plants in Mediterranean regions.

The genus *Olea* contains a total of 20 species of evergreen trees and shrubs that come from Europe and Asia. This species is native throughout the Mediterranean region where it is widely adapted to many types of soil, including calcareous, as well as sun, heat, cold, and drought. It has been cultivated for hundreds of years to obtain the oils from its fruit; it has also been widely used in western gardens as an ornamental tree. The olive is grown extensively in coastal, inland, valley, and desert regions, where it is often used as a specimen plant in courtyards, lawns, entry planters, and on slopes. Established plants require only low amounts of supplemental water; young plants grow more quickly if watered regularly. Periodic deep watering is recommended to encourage deeper roots and increase drought tolerance.

Olive trees that are used in ornamental landscapes present several difficulties. Pollen from flowers is highly allergenic to many people; large quantities of fruit ripen and fall each year and can stain pavement. Newer varieties have been introduced that produce far less pollen, and commercial sprays can be applied to the flowers in order to reduce the amount of fruit production. Other varieties grow to smaller sizes and with lighter foliage color. Some types are briefly described below. Plates 747 - 749.

O. e. 'Fruitless' - A standard form that produces less fruit.

O. e. 'Little Ollie' - Dwarf fruitless form to 3 ft. high with dense branching and tiny leaves.

O. e. 'Majestic Beauty' - A lighter green variety, standard size, no mature fruit.

O. e. 'Manzanillo' - Standard form, large fruit, useful for ornamental and commercial growth.

O. e. 'Mission' - Standard form, small fruit with good taste, also useful as an ornamental.

O. e. 'Skylark Dwarf' - Small, compact, fruiting variety that grows into a large, dense shrub.

O. e. 'Swan Hill' - A proven fruiting cultivar with less than 1% of normal pollen production for ornamental gardens.

747. Olea europaea, Santa Barbara, California   **748. Olea europaea**

749. Olea europaea, Tucson, Arizona

Olneya tesota
Desert Ironwood
Fabaceae

A medium size evergreen tree, slowly growing 25-30 ft. high, spreading 20-25 ft. Foliage is grey-green and comprised of pinnately divided leaves. Large clusters of white and lavender pea-shaped flowers occur in mid-spring and are modestly showy; numerous bean-like seed pods are produced and contain edible seeds. Both stems and branches are heavily armed with sharp thorns. Wood from this tree is extremely hard and dense and will not float in water.

Desert ironwood is native to low and intermediate desert regions throughout California, Arizona, and northern Mexico. It commonly grows on rocky foothills, sandy mesas, and along washes in association with species including *Cercidium floridum, C. microphyllum, Larrea tridentata*, and *Prosopis* species. It is the only species within the genus *Olneya* and is a very durable tree that is adapted to heat, aridity, and drought. Cold temperatures below 20° F will cause the foliage to drop, but it quickly regrows.

Desert ironwood is an excellent specimen and shade tree for all but the coldest desert regions. It can be used in courtyard, patio, and background spaces in both commercial and residential landscapes. It prefers deep, well drained soils, and periodic watering to enable it to establish a strong root system for greater drought endurance. It is slow growing and needs many years before good specimen sizes are reached. Care should be taken to place away from walkways or to prune lower branches to prevent harm from the sharp thorns. Plates 750 - 752.

750. Olneya tesota

751. Olneya tesota

752. Olneya tesota, Scottsdale, Arizona

753. Opuntia ficus-indica

754. Opuntia ficus-indica fruit

Opuntia
Prickly Pear, Cholla
Cactaceae

A large and diverse group of succulent plants, including over 300 species that are native to a wide geographic area across North and South America. Throughout this range, species of *Opuntia* are found within temperate, Mediterranean, subtropical, and arid climate types. The greatest diversity and concentration occurs within the arid regions of the Southwest and Mexico where they are highly adapted to heat, aridity, and drought. Most types do not have leaves, instead they produce fleshy stems and pads that can be cylindrical or flattened in shape. They are typically armed with sharp spines and can be low and prostrate in form or become tree-like to 20 ft. high. These plants use a unique method of conserving water by closing the stomates on their pads during the heat of the day, and completing the process of photosynthesis at night when temperatures are cooler.

The diversity of sizes, shapes, and spines has led to the classification of this group of cactus into several subgenera and sections. Local sources can be helpful in describing the types and characteristics of species suited for landscape use in specific project situations. A few types are discussed below.

Opuntia basilaris
Beaver-tail Cactus

A low growing species, 2-4 ft. high, spreading several feet across. Flattened pads are grey-green or purplish, elongated to 12 in. long, and have tiny spines across the surface and margins. Colorful magenta, pink, or sometimes yellow flowers produce a showy display in early spring. This species comes from all desert regions from Nevada, Colorado, California, Arizona, and Mexico.

Opuntia ficus-indica
Indian Fig

A tall growing species, 10-18 ft. high and as wide. Flattened pads are medium green, reach 12-18 in. long, and lack spines but have small bristles. Clusters of pale yellow to white flowers occur in spring and are followed by large, edible fruit, either red or yellow in color. This species is widely grown in tropical and subtropical regions for its fruit and in western regions as an ornamental accent plant. Plates 753 - 754.

Opuntia lindheimeri var. linguiformis
Cow's Tongue

A unique species with very spiny and elongated pads that can reach 2-3 ft. long. It slowly grows into a large plant, 6-10 ft. high with a greater spread. Cow's tongue is native to southern Texas. The shape and character of its pads provide unusual character and silhouette value in arid gardens. Plates 755 - 756.

Opuntia robusta

A large species with distinctive round, grey pads. Plants can eventually reach 12-15 ft. high. Circular pads can reach 18 in. in dia. and have small numbers of long, sharp spines. This species is native to Mexico and is used as a sculptural accent plant in coastal, inland, and desert gardens. Plate 757.

755. Opuntia lindheimeri var. linguiformis

756. Opuntia lindheimeri var. linguiformis

757. Opuntia robusta

Parkinsonia aculeata
Mexican Palo Verde, Jerusalem Thorn
Fabaceae

A small to medium size deciduous tree with distinctive yellow-green bark and lacy foliage character. This species is one of two known plants within the genus *Parkinsonia*. It grows quickly to 20-30 ft. high and as wide, but yearly pruning is needed in order to develop good branching character and a broad canopy shape. Foliage is comprised of very long, hanging leaves that have numerous tiny leaflets. Leaves drop under drought and cold stress. Showy flowers are bright yellow with red, occurring in greatest profusion in spring but intermittently all year. Sharp thorns cover stems and smaller branches.

Mexican palo verde is native to both tropical and arid regions from the West Indies and Florida, to California, Mexico, and South America. In the warmer and drier parts of this range, it is often found growing on gravelly or sandy soils along desert washes, bajadas, and foothills up to 4,500 ft. elevation. It is tolerant of heat, aridity, drought, as well as alkaline soils.

This species is most often used in desert landscapes as an accent and shade tree in courtyards, in raised planters, and for parking lots. Except for staking and pruning, it requires little or no assistance and only periodic deep watering. It is also grown in coastal and inland zones where it provides unique bark and foliage contrast to other ornamentals. Use of this species in low desert regions is being discouraged due to its tendency to reseed and naturalize; instead, varieties of *Cercidium* and *Prosopis* are recommended. Plates 758 - 759.

758. Parkinsonia aculeata

759. Parkinsonia aculeata

760. Pennisetum setaceum

Pennisetum setaceum
Fountain Grass
Poaceae

A small clumping perennial grass, growing 2-3 ft. high. Leaves are light to medium green; numerous, showy flower stalks grow above the foliage in summer through fall and have mixed colors of white, pink, and purple.

Fountain grass is one of 80 known species within the genus *Pennisetum*. This species is native to Africa and has been introduced to western gardens as an ornamental plant for use in rock gardens, small planters, and on banks and slopes. It is widely adapted to many conditions including heat, sun, drought, cold, and poor soils. Unfortunately, it produces a highly viable supply of seed and has escaped cultivation to become widely naturalized in many regions from the coast to the desert. This species is not recommended for landscape use, instead *P. s.* 'Cupreum', Purple Fountain Grass, which produces predominantly sterile seeds can be used. This variety grows 3-4 ft. high, has striking purple foliage, rose to purple flowers, and is useful as an accent plant. Plates 760 - 762.

761. Pennisetum setaceum 'Cupreum'

762. Pennisetum setaceum 'Cupreum'

763. Penstemon centranthifolius

764. Penstemon centranthifolius

765. Penstemon heterophyllus (lower), Penstemon spectabilis (taller)

766. Penstemon spectabilis

767. Penstemon superbus

Penstemon
Penstemon, Beard Tongue
Scrophulariaceae

A large group of perennials and small shrubs that are widely known for their colorful tubular flowers. This is one of the most colorful and diverse perennial plant groups of the western states, where the great majority of the 250 known species can be found. Penstemons are native to many habitats and plant communities, from coastal foothills to mountains and deserts, where conditions vary from warm and dry, to cool and moist. Due to their popularity as color accent plants and nectar value to birds and butterflies, many species and varieties of penstemon are available for landscape use. Flower colors vary from white, pink, red, to yellow and blue, and occur in mid-spring.

Species native to dry climates do best in sunny locations on well drained soil. Once established, they can be sustained by natural rainfall or low amounts of supplemental water. These types will die back and become dormant in summer months under drought stress. Local native plant nurseries are the best sources for species and varieties suited to different landscape regions. Several species are briefly described below.

Penstemon centranthifolius
Scarlet Bugler

An upright species, 2-3 ft. high, with distinctive grey foliage and scarlet flowers. It is native to dry foothill environments and desert edges that makes it suited for coastal, inland, and low desert landscapes. Plates 763 - 764.

Penstemon eatoni
Firecracker Penstemon

An upright species, 3-4 ft. high, developing long stalks of bright red flowers. A colorful accent plant from desert regions that prefers having some summer water.

Penstemon heterophyllus
Foothill Penstemon

A spreading variety, 1-2 ft. high, developing deep purple flowers. It comes from coastal and inland foothills of central to southern California where it is popular in native plant gardens. Plate 765.

Penstemon palmeri

A tall, upright species with several stalks reaching 5 ft. high, producing very large white to pink flowers. A native of desert habitats in California and Arizona unusually large, fragrant flowers.

Penstemon parryi

A native to southern Arizona, developing tall, upright stems to 4 ft. high and colorful rose-magenta flowers. Good for low and intermediate desert landscapes.

Penstemon spectabilis
Showy Penstemon

A tall species, with stems to 4 ft., produces light lavender to blue flowers. It is found within dry coastal and inland foothills of southern California where it is suited to native landscape plantings. Plates 765 - 766.

Penstemon superbus

A vigorous grower with clear grey foliage, producing tall stems, 3-4 ft. high, with deep red to rose flowers. A desert species, native to California and Arizona. Plate 767.

Perovskia atriplicifolia
Russian Sage
Laminaceae

An upright perennial with many branches growing from the base, reaching 3-4 ft. high. Distinctive foliage is comprised of finely divided grey-green leaves that produce a light, delicate effect. Small lavender-blue flowers grow in large numbers on branched stems during the summer.

Russian sage comes from west Pakistan and can be planted in all zones of the western region. It is popular as a color accent plant in perennial gardens where it can be mixed with species such as *Coreopsis lanceolatus, Penstemon heterophyllus, Lavandula angustifolia,* and *Phlomis fruticosa.* Both foliage and flowers produce an open, light effect that contrasts nicely with other plants. Old flowers should be removed to extend the flowering season; stems should be cut back to the ground in late fall to renew character. Established plants need low amounts of supplemental water in coastal gardens; moderate moisture is needed in warmer regions. Plates 768 - 769.

Phlomis
Laminaceae

A diverse group of perennials and small shrubs numbering about 100 species. Two species native to the Mediterranean region are currently grown as perennials throughout the West. They are particularly well suited to sunny locations in coastal regions and require only low amounts of supplemental water. However, they easily grow in many hotter and drier climates where they should be planted in areas that provide some protection from intense heat and sun and be given more regular watering. They prefer light, well drained soils but are also adapted to calcareous conditions.

These plants produce colorful yellow flowers in spring and summer. They can be combined with other bold flowering perennials including *Asteriscus maritimus* and *Kniphofia uvaria,* as well as with grey foliage plants such as *Artemisia* 'Powis Castle' and *Helianthemum nummularium.* Heavy pruning after flowering will help control the shape of these plants and to produce good foliage and flower character each season.

Phlomis fruticosa
Jerusalem Sage

A large shrubby perennial, growing 3-4 ft. high and as wide. Heavily textured leaves reach 2-3 inches, are yellowish grey-green above, white and woolly beneath. Bright yellow flowers occur in large whorls on tall stems from mid-spring into early summer. This species produces the largest flower size, boldest color value, and is the most widely used in western gardens. It is native to dry, rocky cliffs and slopes in coastal and inland areas of the Mediterranean region. Plates 770, 772.

Phlomis lanata

A low growing species 2-3 ft. high, with a 3-4 ft. spread. Small leaves grow on yellowish stems, reach 1 in. in size, are grey-green above, woolly below. Numerous yellow flowers grow in whorls on short stems above the foliage in mid-spring to early summer. This species is from islands and coastal slopes on limestone soils in the Mediterranean region. It provides unique foliage color and texture for use in rock gardens and in mixed plantings. Plate 771.

768. Perovskia atriplicifolia

769. Perovskia atriplicifolia

770. Phlomis fruticosa

771. Phlomis lanata

772. Phlomis fruticosa

773. Phoenix canariensis

774. Phoenix dactylifera

775. Phoenix canariensis

Phoenix
Date Palm
Palmae

A small group of palms with long, feathery fronds, including 17 or 18 species that are native to tropical, subtropical, and semi-arid regions of Africa and Asia. Most species develop into large, stately trees and have been widely planted for ornamental use in warm regions around the world.

In western landscapes, all species of date palm do best in sandy, well drained soils, in sunny locations. However, a distinction can be made between types based upon their tolerance for heat, cold, and drought. Species such as *P. reclinata*, Senegal Date Palm, and *P. roebelenii*, Pygmy Date Palm, prefer warm, subtropical zones and perform best with ample moisture. Others, such as *P. canariensis*, Canary Island Date Palm, and *P. dactylifera*, Date Palm, are more tolerant of heat and cold. These hardier types can resist long periods of drought as long as they obtain adequate moisture from time to time to replenish their tissues. Large species are popular as focal elements around entries, in raised planters, and for colonnades along roads and garden walls. Smaller species work well in containers, in atrium courts, and in smaller residential and commercial spaces.

Phoenix canariensis
Canary Island Date Palm

A large, bold tree that develops a massive trunk and large, gracefully arching fronds. Mature trees can reach 50-60 ft. high with a 40-50 ft. spread. Old fronds eventually detach from the trunk and leave a distinct basal scar.

This species comes from protected canyons and ravines of the Canary Islands where soils are deep and moist. It is one of the most widely used species in coastal, inland, and valley landscapes as a specimen in large spaces, ranging from parks and plazas, to medians and slopes. As with most other species of palms, large, mature specimens can be transplanted during the warm season of the year and be used to provide an instant landscape effect. It can also be grown from seed but will take 12-15 years to attain a 10 ft. trunk. This species is hardy to 20°F and can be grown in low desert regions where it needs periodic deep watering. Plates 773, 775.

Phoenix dactylifera
Date Palm

A tall tree, growing 50-60 ft. high, 30-40 ft. wide. Leaves are grey-green, 15-20 ft. long, and are held stiffly upward and outward. Fruit develops on female trees; mature dates are table-ready or can be steamed to obtain their sugar and food value.

The date palm is native to arid regions of North Africa in sandy soils around oases and seasonal water courses. This species and its several improved fruiting varieties have been cultivated for centuries and are an important food and economic resource in the Middle East and Africa. It was introduced into cultivation in the Coachella Valley of California around 1900 and has become significant as a crop plant, as well as an ornamental tree. It is now widely used in low desert landscapes as an accent and specimen element. It accepts regular water when grown in turf, or can easily survive with periodic deep watering. Fruit from this tree is often a problem around paving and in commercial spaces. This species is now becoming planted in coastal and inland communities of southern California. Plate 774.

Phormium

New Zealand Flax, Flax Lily

Agavaceae

A small group of perennial plants that includes only two species, both from New Zealand. These plants produce striking visual character due to their long, blade-like foliage and clumping habit that contrasts greatly with other types of foliage plants. In their native habitat, they are adapted to cool, moist zones within maritime climates. In western landscapes, they have proven to be widely adapted to many types of soils, as well as sun, heat, and low amounts of supplemental water. They are most naturally adapted to coastal gardens but are often planted in inland, valley, and desert regions. Poor drainage and excessive water can lead to crown rot in warmer and drier locations.

These plants are frequently used in containers, around pools, and in shrub planting schemes where their bold texture and line patterns can be appreciated. Flowers occur in summer to fall on tall, woody stems above the foliage. Numerous hybrids have been introduced in recent years that provide many different sizes and variations in foliage color. Plates 776 - 781. See also plate 337, page 141.

Phormium colensoi

(Phormium cookianum)

Mountain Flax

A species native to hillsides and along streams, from coastal bluffs to inland foothills near 5,000 ft. elevation on the North and South Islands of New Zealand. This species grows 3-4 ft. high, producing yellow and red-brown flowers that twist and hang from tall stalks. Mountain flax is smaller and provides a softer, more weeping foliage character than *P. tenax*.

Phormium tenax

New Zealand Flax

A large and robust plant, growing in upright clumps reaching 7-10 ft. high. Leaves are medium green and can grow to 9 ft. long. Tall flower spikes develop in summer that prominently display dull red flowers. This species is very common throughout New Zealand in swampy areas of coastal zones and on exposed, windy grassland hillsides. Plates 778 - 779.

Some of the popular hybrids and varieties are listed below:

P. colensoi 'Cream Delight' - Graceful, weeping habit, to 24 in. high. Leaves have many stripes, with cream in the middle, red at the margins.

P. colensoi 'Tricolor' - Rich green leaves, weeping habit, to 3 ft. high, with red-brown and yellow flowers. Plates 776 - 777.

P. 'Duet' - Dwarf form, to 24 in., deep green foliage with cream margins.

P. 'Jack Sprat' - One of the smallest, to 18 in., twisting deep red-bronze foliage.

P. 'Tom Thumb' - Dwarf form, to 24 in., has narrow green leaves with red-bronze margins.

P. 'Maori Queen' - Upright form, to 4 ft., olive green and variegated leaves, rose margins. Plate 781.

P. 'Maori Maiden' - Graceful, weeping form, to 30 in., rose-red foliage with olive margins.

P. 'Maori Sunrise' - Soft, weeping form, 3-4 ft. high, light pink and bronze foliage.

P. tenax 'Atropurpureum' - Upright form, 4-5 ft. high, deep purple-red foliage.

P. tenax 'Variegatum' - Tall, upright form, 4-5 ft., olive green leaves with yellow stripes and margins. Plate 780.

776. Phormium colensoi 'Tricolor'

777. Phormium colensoi 'Tricolor'

778. Phormium tenax

779. Phormium tenax, New Zealand

780. Phormium tenax 'Variegatum'

781. Phormium 'Maori Queen'

Pinus
Pine
Pinaceae

Introduction:
A diverse group of coniferous trees and shrubs including more than 90 species that are found throughout the Northern Hemisphere. A large number of these, some 55 species, are native to North America with over half of these being native to the western states. Pines are well known by their needle-like foliage and characteristic woody cones. Needles occur singly or in bundles of two to eight and, along with cones, provide a key basis for species identification.

Pines are the largest and most important group of conifers, particularly when viewed for the commercial value of their wood. They are also widely used as ornamental plants around the world in many climate regions. Both native and exotic species of pines are popular for landscape use in the West.

Character:
Pines can be divided into two broad subgroups known as soft or white pines, and hard pines. White pines commonly have needles in bundles of 5, produce comparatively soft wood, and develop smooth bark, particularly on young trees. Hard pines typically produce denser wood, have needles in bundles of 2's and 3's, and develop coarse, rough bark.

Species of pine vary from tall and upright, to dense and rounded, or even irregular. Needles vary greatly in length and number per bundle. There appears to be a correlation between climate and needle length. Species with short needles often come from cooler and more temperate climates; longer needle species come from subtropical and warmer climates. Needles often live for 3-4 years and usually are shed most heavily from summer through fall.

Cones are prominent features that are unique to each species and are often the best means to identify them. They range in length from 2-3 in. to over 18 in., and in weight from a few ounces to several pounds. Cones can mature and persist on some species for many years, while others drop on a seasonal basis.

Habitat and Culture:
Over the millennia, species of pine have evolved in many habitats from coastal bluffs to alpine forests. It is interesting to note that they have not naturally migrated past the warm, tropical belt of the equator into the Southern Hemisphere. However, it has been discovered that many species can be very successfully introduced to southern regions.

Most species of pine occur in habitats that experience some form of drought. Plants in northern latitudes and at higher elevations experience physiological drought when cold winter temperatures stop the movement of moisture in the soil. Species in warmer regions often have moist winters but typically must survive dry summers. The development of needles as a type of foliage is a response to these conditions. Needles resist moisture loss by being hard, having sunken stomata, being covered with waxy coatings, and having a small surface to area ratio. These adaptations enable most species of pine to grow and

survive on low to moderate amounts of supplemental water in western landscapes. However, species that are native to colder and more alpine habitats often perform poorly in subtropical zones that lack distinct winters or in desert regions where heat and aridity lasts for many months.

Species that are best suited to warm and dry climates principally come from western states and the Mediterranean region. Those native to California and adjacent states show distinct preferences for the region of their natural origin; desert species prefer the desert, coastal species grow best near the coast. Types native to the Mediterranean region show far more tolerance and adaptation to coastal, inland, and desert environments.

Most pine species prefer light, well drained soils, and the opportunity to develop both deep and lateral rooting habits. Deep root development is particularly important when they are young. Studies regarding the ecology of pines have discovered the importance of mycorrhizal fungi in helping them obtain necessary nutrients from the soil. Western natives in particular rely upon these fungi to survive in nutrient poor soils. Container grown plants should be checked for coiled roots that can limit the future health and stability of the plant. Well established trees can often survive with natural rainfall and periodic deep watering. On the other hand, some species do have a high level of tolerance to frequent irrigations when planted in lawn areas, as long as drainage is good and soil texture is light. Pines do not survive well in heavy, poorly drained soils.

Uses and Considerations:
Pines are highly suited to many landscape situations. Large species are valued for street trees, in parks, and large commercial and institutional spaces. They live for many years and often become monumental in size. Types that develop more irregular shapes are often slower growing and can be pruned to achieve interesting sculptural character for use in courtyards and raised planters.

Several species found in cultivation have a strong central growth leader such as, *P. canariensis, P. radiata*, and *P. torreyana*. If these leaders are pruned, a new leader emerges from the lower branches resulting in an unpredictable shape. Pines also produce significant amounts of litter as they mature. Their needle litter can be used as a surface cover over bare soil, but it does not compost or decompose well and often should be removed.

A wide number of pines have been grown in desert regions over the years. Many types become chlorotic in the iron-poor soils and are often highly stressed under prolonged cycles of

782. Pinus brutia, Palm Desert, California

heat and aridity. A few of these have shown successful adaptation to desert conditions including *P. brutia, P. eldarica*, and *P. halepensis*. These species do well with moderate amounts of supplemental water, but are often highly inconsistent in character with the surrounding natural landscape.

There is growing evidence that pines are harmed by urban air pollution. Both gaseous and particulate pollutants combine to diminish the functioning of needles. This impact is further compounded when trees are under heat and drought stress. Trees appear to remain healthier when planted in landscapes where they receive moderate amounts of supplemental water and when winter rainfall is heavy enough to provide a good annual cleansing.

Helpful References:
Fowells, H. A., ed. Silvics of Forest Trees of the United States. Agriculture Handbook No. 271. Washington, D.C.: United States Department of Agriculture, Forest Service, 1965.

Mirov, Nicholas T., and Jean Hasbrouck. The Story of Pines. Bloomington: Indiana University Press, 1976.

Schopmeyer, C. S., ed. Seeds of Woody Plants in the United States. Agriculture Handbook No. 450. Washington, D.C.: United States Department of Agriculture, Forest Service, 1974.

Pinus brutia
Calabrian Pine

A large upright tree, quickly growing 30-60 ft. high and more. Needles are dark green, occur in bundles of 2, grow 5-6 in. long, and create a dense foliage appearance. This species is considered by some to be a variety of *P. halepensis* but is quite different in needle color and form.

Calabrian pine is native to the eastern Mediterranean, from the islands of Crete and Cypress, through the Middle East from Lebanon into Turkey. It grows in semi-arid climates that are cold in the winter and hot and dry during the summer. In western regions, this species has proven to be highly tolerant of low, intermediate, and high desert conditions, where it grows well in iron poor soils and with moderate amounts of supplemental water. It is also adapted to coastal, inland, and valley regions and develops a symmetrical pine tree profile. Plates 782 - 783.

783. **Pinus brutia left, Pinus halepensis right**   784. **Pinus canariensis**

Pinus canariensis
Canary Island Pine

A tall vertical tree, growing quickly to 40-60 ft. high, eventually reaching 100 ft. Needles are deep green, occur in bundles of 3, grow 9-12 in. long, and create a soft-textured foliage appearance.

This species comes from steep, rocky slopes of the Canary Islands. Annual rainfall is limited to less than 10 in., however, coastal clouds bring fog and mists that reduce summer temperatures and moisture stress. Soils are often neutral to slightly acidic.

Canary Island pine is very well suited to coastal, inland, and valley landscapes throughout California. Its best performance occurs in deep, well drained soils, with periodic deep irrigation during the summer in warmer, arid regions. This species has been introduced into low desert regions where regular water is needed and its tolerance for aridity and alkalinity in soils is less. This plant is often used as a vertical accent tree for tall buildings and in narrow spaces. Mature specimens become quite large and are suited to parks, medians, and large public spaces. Plates 784 - 785.

785. **Pinus canariensis, Pasadena, California**

786. Pinus coulteri

787. Pinus coulteri

Pinus coulteri
Coulter Pine

A medium to large tree with a rounded crown, 30-60 ft. high, 25-40 ft. wide. Needles are dull blue-green, occur in 3's and grow 5-12 in. long. Cones are very large and distinctive; mature sizes reach 9-12 in. long and have hard, sharp scales.

Coulter pine is native to dry, rocky foothills and mountains in southern California between 4,000-7,000 ft. within the yellow pine forest and foothill woodland plant communities. Annual rainfall varies from 25-35 in. with most coming in the winter. Some precipitation comes as snow that slowly releases moisture into the soil through early spring.

Coulter pine is seldom planted in ornamental landscapes. Instead, it is more frequently used for reforestation projects in natural foothill locations above 2,500 ft. elevation. Seedlings can be planted prior to winter rains and become established in these areas with little care or assistance. Plates 786 - 787.

Pinus eldarica
Afghan Pine

A medium to large tree, reaching 30-60 ft. and taller, 25-40 ft. in spread. Dark green foliage is comprised of 5-6 in. long needles that occur in bundles of 2. Young plants develop a dense, upright shape that becomes wider and more open with age.

Afghan pine is a very fast growing species that comes from the semi-arid regions of Iran, Pakistan, and parts of Afghanistan along the Caspian Sea and central Europe. Within this range, it tolerates heat, wind, and alkaline soils. Annual rainfall varies between 8-16 in.

Pinus eldarica is a relatively recent introduction to western landscapes. Some sources consider it to be very closely related to *P. brutia* and *P. halepensis*. It first received attention for its tolerance of desert conditions, including alkaline soils, wind, heat, and cold. In these regions, it needs low to moderate amounts of supplemental water to maintain good health and vigor. It is also frequently planted in coastal, inland, and valley regions, where it can become established and requires only low amounts of supplemental water. Plates 788 - 789.

788. Pinus eldarica, Palm Desert, California

789. Pinus eldarica, immature

243

Pinus halepensis
Aleppo Pine

A fast growing species with an open habit, 30-60 ft. high, 20-40 ft. wide. Light green needles are short, 2-4 in., occur in bundles of 2. Young plants have very wispy branches and tend to lean or be influenced by wind; mature plants develop a strong trunk and rounded crown.

Aleppo pine is native to coastal and inland foothills throughout the Mediterranean region. It grows in soils that vary from sandy and slightly acidic to calcareous. Annual rainfall varies between 10-20 in. with long periods of summer drought.

This species has been widely used in landscapes throughout the West, from coastal zones to high and low desert regions. It shows a wide tolerance for heat, wind, aridity, and poor soils with average drainage. Extreme heat and drought stress can cause periodic dieback, otherwise this species is one of the most adaptable types for warm climate regions. This is a highly variable species in terms of its growth habit; many different forms can be seen in the landscape. It is often used as a large background screen, as a roadside tree, and in rural areas where it tolerates neglect. Mature aleppo pines achieve monumental sizes and are quite handsome in parks and open spaces. Plates 783, 790.

790. Pinus halepensis, Glendora, California

Pinus monophylla
Single-leaf Pinon Pine

A small shrubby tree with a rounded crown, 10-25 ft. tall. Short, pale green needles are slightly curved, grow 1-2 in. long. Young plants appear stiff and upright; a more rounded habit develops with maturity.

This species is native to arid and desert habitats throughout the Southwest. It frequently occurs on dry, rocky slopes at elevations between 3,500-9,000 ft. and is adapted to high temperatures and drought, as well as winter cold and snow. It is an important member of the pinon-juniper and foothill woodland plant communities where its seeds are highly important to wildlife. It is also the state tree of Nevada.

Single-leaf pinon is well adapted to high, intermediate, and low desert conditions. It is not widely cultivated as an ornamental plant outside its natural range and is sometimes being destroyed in areas of expanding urban development. Efforts should be taken to preserve and protect this pine as a landscape feature wherever possible. It can be successfully combined with other desert natives including *Larrea tridentata, Yucca brevifolia, Encelia farinosa*, and *Juniperus californica*. Plates 791 - 792.

791, 792. Pinus monophylla, Joshua Tree National Monument, California

Pinus pinea
Italian Stone Pine

A large species with a broad crown, growing 40-80 ft. and taller, 30-50 ft. wide. Dark green needles are 5-8 in. long and occur in bundles of 2. Young trees are distinctly round in shape; mature plants have a striking umbrella shape when lower branches are removed. Rich red-brown bark is common on older plants.

Italian stone pine comes from coastal habitats of the Mediterranean region where it shows a preference for sandy, well drained, slightly acid soils. Annual rainfall varies from 15-30 in., with long dry summers.

This species is a popular choice for large landscape and garden spaces, particularly in coastal and valley regions from the San Francisco Bay area to southern California. In central valley cities, it reaches monumental sizes when planted in deep soils, with conditions of summer heat and humidity. Mature trees are among the most massive and striking landscape features. Performance in arid and desert landscapes is best when trees are young. However, in general, heat, aridity, and alkaline conditions are very hard on this species. Plates 793 - 796.

793. Pinus pinea

794. Pinus pinea, immature

795. Pinus pinea, Florence, Italy

796. Pinus pinea, Florence, Italy

Pinus radiata
Monterey Pine

A medium to large species with a dense habit, quickly growing 60-80 ft. tall, 20-35 ft. wide. Dark green needles, 3-7 in. long, occur in bundles of 2 or 3. Young trees appear stiff and pyramidal; mature trees develop a high canopy as lower branches drop off.

Monterey pine comes from the central coast region of California where it is adapted to modest winter rains and extended periods of drought in the summer. Drought stress, however, is often mitigated by humidity, fog, and cool summer temperatures. Soils are slightly acid and fast draining.

Monterey pine is a popular choice for landscapes due to its fast growth and traditional pine tree character. It is best suited to coastal regions to avoid excessive heat and aridity. When used in warmer inland locations, these trees are often overwatered, develop shallow roots, and become susceptible to cankers and water molds. This leads to very fast growth, but plants can die in as little as 15-20 years. These trees are suited to background and mass plantings, or as specimen trees in large spaces. Plates 797 - 798.

797. Pinus radiata, Morro Bay, California

798. Pinus radiata

799. Pinus sabiniana

Pinus sabiniana
Digger Pine

An upright tree with an open habit, 30-50 ft. tall, 25-40 ft. wide. Needles are pale grey-green, grow 8-13 in. long, and occur in bundles of 3. Young trees are open and lanky; mature trees often have forked trunks and an open branching habit.

Digger pine is found in the dry foothills of the central coast ranges and foothills of the Sierra Nevada where it is a member of the foothill woodland and southern oak woodland plant communities. It is a deeply rooted species, well adapted to drought and poor soils, including serpentine. Its seeds are important to wildlife.

This species of pine is seldom planted in ornamental landscapes. Instead, it is most often appreciated within its natural habitat where it adds diversity and character to the native landscape. Mature specimens provide distinctive silhouette character, light grey foliage color, and stand out above the lower scrub vegetation. Plates 799 - 801.

800, 801. Pinus sabiniana, in native foothill settings in California

Pinus torreyana
Torrey Pine

A tall, upright tree, growing 40-60 ft. tall, 25-40 ft. wide. Distinctive grey-green needles, 8-13 in. long, occur in bundles of 5. Young trees grow with a straight, upright habit; mature trees eventually develop a broad crown.

The torrey pine is rare in nature, found only in a very restricted area of San Diego County and on Santa Rosa Island. It is established on coastal bluffs and hillsides in sandy, well draining soils. Annual rainfall is less than 10 inches. It tolerates salt air and wind, and prefers cool temperatures and fog.

This species has been planted with good success in ornamental landscapes throughout coastal areas from southern California, north to the Bay area. It is also adapted to warmer and drier inland locations, where it survives with low to moderate amounts of supplemental water to offset the increased heat and aridity. It grows quickly and needs large spaces to accommodate its mature size. Plates 802 - 805.

802, 803. Pinus torreyana, Torrey Pines State Reserve, Del Mar, California

804. Pinus torreyana, University of California, Santa Barbara, California

805. Pinus torreyana

Pithecellobium flexicaule
Texas Ebony
Fabaceae

A small to medium evergreen shrub or tree, slowly growing 20-25 ft., eventually reaching 35 ft. and more. Foliage is comprised of bipinnately divided leaves that are deep, glossy green; branches are heavily armed with spines. Clusters of creamy yellow flowers occur briefly in late spring and intermittently throughout summer. Large seed pods, growing 4-6 in. long, become dark brown and persist through winter.

Texas ebony is native to lowland areas along the Gulf of Mexico from southern Texas into Mexico. In these regions, it grows in dry chaparral woodlands and along desert washes where it experiences heat, cold, and drought. The climate varies from arid to subtropical; rainfall ranges from 15-30 in. annually. It is a popular shade tree and street tree within Texas and has also been successfully planted in high and low desert regions in Arizona and California. Mature plants are valued for their deep green foliage character. It prefers well drained soils with periodic, deep watering. Established plants are very drought tolerant and hardy to 10°F. Another species, *P. mexicanum*, has grey foliage and is not as common in nurseries. It is native to Baja California and other parts of Mexico along arroyos, bajadas, and seasonal washes. Plates 806 - 808.

Pittosporum
Pittosporaceae

A large group of evergreen shrubs and trees that come from many different climates in Africa, Asia, Australia, and New Zealand. This genus includes about 150 species with some 10 species and numerous varieties being cultivated in western gardens. Most species and cultivars found in landscape use are best adapted to moist climates and rich soils. They grow best in coastal, inland, and valley areas, with protection from heavy frost and with moderate amounts of regular moisture. Many types will become tolerant of drier conditions as they mature, particularly when planted in areas where they are protected from hot sun, high temperatures, and aridity. One species is particularly well adapted to dry climate regions.

Pittosporum phillyraeoides
Willow Pittosporum

A small to medium tree, growing upright 15-25 ft. high. Foliage is light green and hangs from branches in a weeping manner; leaves are narrow to 4 in. long. Flowering intensity varies from plant to plant; bright yellow flowers are fragrant and can be quite showy during late spring. Colorful yellow fruit occurs in summer.

Willow pittosporum is native to coastal and interior regions of central Australia in warm, dry climates. It grows on many soils including, rocky, clayey, alkaline, and loam. In interior areas, it survives on 10-12 in. of annual rainfall by becoming established along seasonal water courses and gullies. In western gardens, this species is planted in coastal, inland, valley, and desert zones where it grows well with periodic deep watering. It tolerates heat, aridity, drought, and cold to 20°F. It has a light, open foliage habit and pleasant flowering character that makes it useful in planters, around pools, and in background areas. Plates 809 - 811.

806. Pithecellobium flexicaule

807. Pithecellobium flexicaule

808. Pithecellobium flexicaule

809. Pittosporum phillyraeoides

810. Pittosporum phillyraeoides

811. Pittosporum phillyraeoides

Platanus
Plane Tree, Sycamore
Platanaceae

A small group of deciduous trees, consisting of 6-7 species, native to North America, Europe, and Asia. These plants are characterized by large, maple-like leaves and striking branch and bark character. All types prefer moist conditions and mature as stately specimens. Species native to western states survive in dry climate regions by growing along streams and washes. With moisture, these species are highly tolerant of heat, cold, wind, and aridity.

Platanus racemosa
Western Sycamore

A large tree, growing 50-90 ft. high, 30-50 ft. wide. Foliage is comprised of large, papery leaves, with deeply cut lobes resembling the shape of a hand, that turn pale brown by the end of the summer. Bark peels and flakes off to reveal interesting mottled colors of white, tan, and brown beneath.

Western sycamore grows in riparian habitats of the coast ranges from central California south to Baja California, as well as within the foothills of the Sierra Nevada. It often develops into one of the most identifiable and characteristic native trees within grassland and oak woodland plant communities. Within this range, it survives with varying amounts of moisture; plants that develop in drier areas are typically smaller in size.

To many, this tree is a signature species of western landscapes. Young plants often develop angular branching character; older specimens can attain a graceful and elegant stature. Best growth occurs with moderate to high amounts of supplemental water. It performs well in coastal, inland, and valley landscapes but can tolerate desert regions when planted in microclimate spaces. It is widely used in large spaces such as parks, greenbelts, and in lawns. And is often planted with other western natives including *Cercis occidentalis, Mahonia* species, *Ribes speciosum, Heuchera* hybrids, and *Iris douglasiana*. All benefit from partial shade and periodic deep watering during the dry summer months. Plates 812 -815.

812. **Platanus racemosa**

813. **Platanus racemosa**

814. **Platanus racemosa, Pomona College, Claremont, California**

815. **Platanus racemosa, fall color**

Plecostachys serpyllifolia
Asteraceae

A low spreading shrub, 1-3 ft. high, spreading 3-4 ft. across. Distinctive silvery white branches and foliage create a dense and compact appearance. Tiny leaves are attached to upright stems; inconspicuous flowers occur in late spring to summer.

This species is native to the Cape region of South Africa where it is adapted to both coastal and inland conditions. In western gardens, it grows best in sun to light shade, in well drained soils, and with low to moderate amounts of supplemental water. Established plants can survive periods of drought in coastal areas.

Plectostachys provides striking color contrast to other plants in perennial and mixed shrub plantings. It develops a spreading form that hugs the ground, making it useful on banks and around large rocks. This species is also known as *Helichrysum orbiculare* and *H. petiolatum* 'Microphyllum' but has been recently reidentified. Plates 816 - 817.

816. Plecostachys serpyllifolia, behind; Erigeron karvinskianus, front

817. Plecostachys serpyllifolia

818. Plumbago auriculata

Plumbago auriculata
(Plumbago capensis)
Cape Plumbago
Plumbaginaceae

A large mounding shrub with long, vining branches, growing 6-8 ft. high, spreading 8-12 ft. and more. Foliage is comprised of thin, medium green leaves, to 2 in. long. Showy white to light blue flowers grow in large 3-4 in. dia. clusters for many months from early spring through fall.

Cape plumbago comes from subtropical regions of South Africa where it grows in bush and scrub thickets on dry slopes. Natural rainfall reaches 36 in. annually, with a distinct dry season in the summer. In western landscapes, this species is well suited to coastal and inland zones in sunny areas on well drained soils. It is also grown in valley and low to intermediate desert regions, but should be protected from frost below 25°F and from hot desert sun.

This species is often used as a mounding and sprawling ground cover on large slopes in parks and open spaces where it can grow in areas of sun and part shade. It also can be planted and maintained as a clipped hedge in residential gardens for screening purposes and flower color. It easily accepts regular moisture and can become quite large and aggressive; often, some of the vining branches will grow into taller shrubs and trees. Established plants are quite tolerant of heat and drought stress but become sparse and rangy if periodic deep water isn't provided. A white flowering variety, *P. A. 'Alba'*, is also available in the trade. Plates 818 - 820.

819. Plumbago auriculata

820. Plumbago auriculata

Polygonum aubertii
Silver Lace Vine
Polygonaceae

A large and aggressive vine, reaching 30-40 ft. and longer. Medium green leaves are heart-shaped, grow 2-3 in. long, and are evergreen in frost free regions. Large clusters of tiny, white flowers occur in summer and create a soft, billowy appearance.

Silver lace vine comes from cold climate regions of western China and Tibet. It is widely adapted throughout western regions and is grown from the coast to the deserts. It does well in most soils and tolerates heat, sun, and heavy frost. Established plants require little care or attention and perform well with periodic deep watering during the summer. This vine is seldom noticed until the flowering begins in summer. It is most often used to grow on fences as a screen plant or on slopes and banks as a twining ground cover. It is also suited to trellises and arbors and can be cut back during late fall to control its size. Plates 821 - 822.

821. Polygonum aubertii

822. Polygonum aubertii

823. Portulacaria afra

824. Portulacaria afra

Portulacaria afra
Elephant's Food
Portulacaceae

An upright succulent growing 6-8 ft. and higher. Stems and trunks are heavy, fleshy, and deep purple in color. Leaves are medium green, nearly round, and occur in pairs on opposite sides of the stems; clusters of tiny purple flowers occur in summer and are modestly showy.

Elephant's food is native to coastal and inland parts of South Africa and is the only plant within the genus *Portulacaria*. Within its natural habitat it becomes a large shrub or small tree to 12 ft. high where it is an excellent source of food for range animals. It is well adapted to heat, sun, and drought, but is sensitive to frost. In western gardens, this plant is used in containers, rock gardens, on banks, and as a hedge. The combination of rounded leaves and purplish stems make this a unique succulent plant for accent uses. Plates 823 - 824.

Prosopis

Mesquite

Fabaceae

A complex group of deciduous and evergreen trees and shrubs that includes about 25 species. Several species comprise one of the most characteristic and widely distributed plant groups of the arid Southwest, particularly in Texas, Arizona, California, and Mexico. Other species are adapted to subtropical climates of South America. Southwestern species cover many acres of dry land where they provide habitat and food value for wildlife and range animals as well as pollen for honey. Smaller plants will grow and survive in areas with as little as 12 in. of annual rainfall; plants growing near washes and floodplains can attain tree sizes to 40 ft. Most species show evergreen foliage tendencies in mild areas, but will become partially deciduous during cold winters. Leaves are finely divided and feathery; flowers are creamy yellow and modestly showy. Most types have long, sharp thorns and are hazardous where people walk or gather. Pruning is needed when plants are small to develop good trunk and branching habits.

Species from both South America and the Southwest are used for landscaping in desert regions. All types easily interbreed and there now exists many confusing forms and variations within the landscape industry. Varieties that show greater tolerance to cold and that have an evergreen habit are preferred, particularly in intermediate and high desert regions.

Mesquites are often used as shade trees in both residential and commercial landscapes. They are well suited for use in courtyards, parking lots, and as street trees, where they tolerate heat, wind, aridity, and drought. They grow best in well drained soils with periodic deep watering. Regular watering will stimulate faster growth and larger sizes. However, growth that occurs in the fall is more susceptible to frost. These trees are often planted with other desert natives including *Larrea tridentata, Encelia californica, Buddleia marrubiifolia,* and *Ruellia peninsularis.*

Prosopis alba

Argentine Mesquite

A medium size evergreen tree with upward branching, 25-30 ft. high and as wide. This species develops a straight trunk, has long white thorns, and large bipinnate leaves with blue-green leaflets. It grows very fast and is briefly deciduous in mid-spring. One cultivated form, *P. alba* var. 'Colorado', has very few thorns, is more cold tolerant, and is grown from cuttings to achieve more consistent shape and hardiness for landscape use. Plate 825.

Prosopis chilensis

Chilean Mesquite

A small to medium evergreen tree, 20-25 ft. high, with an open habit and twisting branches. It has few or no thorns but is more heavily damaged by frost than *P. alba.* This species is often hybridized with *P. alba* to create many variations known as 'South American Hybrids' that are very difficult to accurately identify in the landscape. Plate 829.

Prosopis glandulosa

Texas Mesquite

A medium size deciduous tree with a broad crown, 25-30 ft. high and as wide. Foliage is

825. Prosopis alba

826. Prosopis juliflora

827. Prosopis glandulosa

828. Prosopis pubescens

829. Prosopis chilensis hybrid

830. Prosopis glandulosa

831. Prosopis juliflora

comprised of light to pale green leaves that have very long leaflets; numerous short thorns arm branches. Leaves are similar to *Schinus molle*, California Pepper, and hang from branches to produce a weeping effect. This is one of the best species for patio and courtyard spaces where its broad canopy can provide light shade. Plates 827, 830.

Prosopis juliflora
Mesquite
One of the most common species in the Southwest. It is a large species, often reaching 40-50 ft. high. Throughout its natural range, it has evolved into many varieties that have varying foliage and form characteristics. Many of these varieties are grown for ornamental use and provide variations in leaflet size, foliage color, and number of thorns. Mature plants have broad canopies and rough, dark brown bark on branches and trunks. Plate 826, 831.

Prosopis pubescens
Screw Bean
A large deciduous shrub to small tree, 10-25 ft. high and as wide. Foliage is comprised of bipinnately divided leaves that have tiny blue-green leaflets. Stems are armed with many thorns; conspicuous yellow flowers occur in spring and are followed by a unique spiral-shaped bean pod. This species is native to bottomlands and water courses throughout the Southwest. It can be used as a background shrub, barrier plant, or be pruned as it matures into a many branched specimen element. Plate 828.

832. Prosopis species, The Arizona-Sonora Desert Museum, Tucson, Arizona

Prunus

Rosaceae

A large group of evergreen and deciduous shrubs and trees, comprised of more than 400 species. Most types come from cool, moist climate regions of North America, Europe, and Asia. Deciduous varieties have very colorful flowers and include those that produce edible fruits and nuts such as almonds, cherries, peaches, apricots, plums, and nectarines. These varieties are most productive in regions that have enough winter cold to instill dormancy and enough spring and summer heat to mature the fruit. Good productivity is also attained through careful pruning and watering practices.

In addition to deciduous species, many evergreen varieties are cultivated in ornamental landscapes where they are valued for their rich foliage character and usefulness as shrubs and trees. Some of these species are naturally adapted to heat and drought stress, others become more tolerant after they mature.

Prunus caroliniana
Carolina Laurel Cherry

A large evergreen shrub to medium tree, growing 15-20 ft. high, eventually reaching 35 ft. Foliage is comprised of glossy, deep green leaves, 2-4 in. long; large, brush-like clusters of creamy white flowers are colorful during late winter and early spring. Large, messy, purple-black berries mature in summer.

This species comes from cool, moist climates from North Carolina west into Texas where it grows as an understory plant in woods and scrublands. It is highly adaptable to western gardens and is grown in coastal, inland, valley, and desert regions as a large hedge plant or shade tree. Young plants grow faster with regular water; mature plants require low amounts of supplemental water except in hot valley and desert regions. This species is often planted as a foundation plant or garden shrub but eventually grows into trees up to 35 ft. high. Dwarf selections that grow 8-12 ft. are available and include *P. c.* 'Compacta' and *P. c.* 'Bright 'n Tight'. Plates 833 - 835.

Prunus ilicifolia
Hollyleaf Cherry

A medium to large evergreen shrub, 15-20 ft. high and as wide. With age, this species can eventually reach tree-like sizes up to 30 ft. Medium to deep green leaves are rigid, twisted, and have many spines on the margins. Showy clusters of creamy white flowers on long spikes cover the plant in early to mid-spring.

Hollyleaf cherry is native to dry foothills and valleys from Napa County in northern California, south to Baja California. It is frequently a member of the chaparral, coastal sage scrub, and oak woodland plant communities. It grows on well drained soils and in areas that receive a wide range of precipitation, from 10-25 in. annually. Smaller plants are found in hotter and drier regions; larger specimens grow adjacent to streams in rich, organic soils.

This species is well suited for erosion control on slopes, habitat restoration, and in ornamental gardens as background shrubs or small trees. It is also one of the best choices for a clipped hedge where it provides handsome foliage character and can be maintained at

833. Prunus caroliniana

834. Prunus caroliniana 'Bright 'n Tight'

835. Prunus caroliniana

836. Prunus ilicifolia

837. Prunus ilicifolia

838. Prunus lyonii

839. Prunus lyonii

many sizes. It is well adapted to heat and drought and prefers fast drainage in areas that receive regular water. Plates 836 - 837.

Prunus lyonii
(Prunus integrifolia)
Catalina Cherry

A large evergreen shrub to medium tree, 30-45 ft. high, spreading 20-30 ft. Dark green leaves reach 3-5 in. long; creamy white flowers grow on long spikes that are showy in late spring. Numerous black, berry-type fruits are produced in mid-summer.

Catalina cherry is native to Santa Catalina, San Clemente, Santa Rosa, and Santa Cruz islands off the coast of southern California. It grows in the chaparral plant community and reaches its largest size in canyons and protected areas where greater moisture and deeper soils occur.

This species is naturally adapted to coastal regions where, once established, it can grow with little care or supplemental water. It is also planted in inland, valley, and low desert regions where periodic deep watering is recommended, particularly in hot, sunny locations. It can be used as a tall screen plant or small tree in parks, on slopes, and in natural open spaces. This species often hybridizes with *P. ilicifolia* to produce seedling plants with characteristics from both species. Plates 838 - 840.

840. Prunus lyonii, Rancho Santa Ana Botanic Garden, Claremont, California

Punica granatum
Pomegranate
Punicaceae

A medium to large deciduous shrub or small tree, growing 12-18 ft. high and as wide. Foliage is comprised of bright green leaves to 2 in. long. Many hybrids exist in cultivation that provide dwarf forms, as well as improved flowering and fruiting varieties. Flowers can be single or double and range in color from orange to white or coral. Fruiting varieties produce large, red fruit, 5-6 in. in diameter; dwarf varieties often have colorful miniature fruit.

Pomegranate is native to the eastern Mediterranean region where its greatest area of natural occurrence is in coastal habitats and on alkaline soils. It has been in cultivation in warm climate areas for many centuries and is considered one of the premium plants for fruit and jellies. Fruit production is best when grown in moist, deep soils with summer heat to ripen fruit by mid-fall. In western regions, it is widely grown in coastal, inland, valley, and protected areas within desert zones. It is used in raised planters, courtyards, near lawns, and in edible gardens. With age, standard varieties develop into handsome multi-branched specimen plants. Dwarf varieties show good drought tolerance once established and can be grown in containers. Standard varieties provide good foliage and flower character with low amounts of supplemental water, but fruit production is reduced. Plates 841 - 844.

Selected varieties include:

P. g. 'Chico' - A dwarf form, to 1 1/2 ft. high, produces colorful, double orange-red flowers and no fruit.

P. g. 'Legrellei' - Compact shrub form, 6-8 ft. high, double flowers, cream and coral-red.

P. g. 'Nana' - Dwarf form, to 3 ft. high, single red flowers and tiny, red fruit. Plate 842.

P. g. 'Wonderful' - Medium shrub form, to 10 ft. high. A popular fruiting variety with single orange-red flowers and large fruit.

841. **Punica granatum**

842. **Punica granatum 'Nana'**

843. **Punica granatum, double flower**

844. **Punica granatum, Huntington Gardens, San Marino, California**

845. Pyracantha coccinea

846. Pyracantha coccinea 'Lalandei'

847. Pyracantha 'Ruby Mound'

848. Pyracantha 'Santa Cruz'

849. Pyracantha 'Santa Cruz'

Pyracantha
Firethorn
Rosaceae

A small group of evergreen shrubs, including about 6 species coming from Mediterranean and temperate climates in Europe and Asia. These plants are best known for their colorful orange to red berries that mature from late fall through winter. Most species produce masses of small, white flowers in early spring that are both fragrant and showy. Foliage is glossy; branches are often heavily armed with sharp thorns.

Firethorns are tough, durable plants that are grown in all regions of the West. They prefer well drained soils, no alkalinity, and periodic deep watering. They are highly tolerant of heat, cold, and neglect. It is common to see established plants growing with little care or water in rural areas and on hillsides where they have been planted for screening and erosion control. However, these plants can show difficulties with a number of pests and diseases particularly when under stress. These include, fireblight, scale, and woolly aphids. Most plants develop dense and angular branching habits but can easily be sheared or pruned to maintain the desired shape. Taller varieties can grow into tree-like sizes; medium size varieties are popular as hedges and as espaliered plants along fences and walls. Spreading types are often used on banks and for ground covers. Several species and many similar hybrid varieties are cultivated for the trade. A few are described below. Plates 844 - 848.

Pyracantha coccinea

A medium to large shrub, growing 10-12 ft. high. This is a very dense, thorny species that comes from scrublands throughout the Mediterranean region in both coastal and inland zones. Numerous hybrids of this species exist. These vary in size from low and prostrate to upright, and provide large clusters of orange to red berries. All are very tolerant of heat and cold. Plates 845 - 846.

Pyracantha 'Mohave'

A widely popular hybrid between *P. koidsumii* and *P. coccinea* 'Wyattii'. This is a vigorous form that grows 8-12 ft. high, equally wide, and produces large clusters of orange to deep red berries. Frequently espaliered, considered highly resistant to fireblight.

Pyracantha 'Red Elf'

A compact mounding form with dark green foliage and bright red berries. Good container plant and for small garden spaces.

Pyracantha 'Ruby Mound'

A mounding form with arching branches, 4-5 ft. high, 5-7 ft. across. Deep glossy green foliage and dense clusters of red berries. Plate 847.

Pyracantha 'Santa Cruz'

A prostrate and spreading form, 3-4 ft. high, 4-6 ft. wide. Rich, glossy green foliage and large clusters of orange berries. This variety is planted as a ground cover on banks and in planters. Plates 848 - 849.

Pyracantha 'Teton'

A tall upright variety, growing 8-12 ft. high. This cultivar is more resistant to fireblight and produces yellow-orange berries.

Pyracantha 'Tiny Tim'

A small and compact variety to 3 ft. high. Tiny, dark green leaves, small red berries, few thorns on branches. This variety is suited to containers, on banks, and for clipped hedges.

Quercus
Oak
Fagaceae

Introduction:
The genus *Quercus* includes both evergreen and deciduous shrubs and trees that are most often noted for their monumental character and prominence in many landscape regions. Over 300 species and varieties are known; 70 species are native to the United States. They are considered to be the most important commercial hardwood trees found on the North American continent. Some 16 species are native to California and are dominant members of the oak woodland and oak grassland plant communities. In these communities, they play critical roles in soil development, food for wildlife, and microclimate modification.

Mature oaks are among the most widely recognized and valued trees within ornamental and natural landscape settings. In spite of this, many native trees have been, and continue to be, removed in the process of urban growth and development. Efforts to protect these species are occurring through protective planning ordinances and revegetation programs. Newly planted trees can grow to monumental sizes and become a long term investment for the future.

Character:
Oaks can be deciduous or evergreen. With the exception of *Q. lobata* and *Q. douglasii*, species that are best adapted to warm and dry landscapes are principally evergreen. Deciduous species more often come from cooler and wetter climates.

Evergreen oaks often develop an upright habit when young and with age mature with massive trunks and a broad spreading canopy shape. Most species have a moderate growth rate and begin to develop attractive sizes and shapes after 15-20 years. Leaves are typically hard and leathery; flowers occur in spring and are not showy but produce pollen that can be allergenic to people. Fruit are acorns that are unique to each oak species and serve as an accurate means to identify species, varieties, and hybrids.

Habitat and culture:
Evergreen oak species suited to dry landscape regions come from California and the Mediterranean region of Europe. They grow in habitats that range from coastal foothills to interior valleys. Seedlings become established during winter rains and develop a long tap root to obtain as much soil moisture as possible. In many areas, these deep roots eventually come into contact with ground water sources that can provide ongoing moisture during the long, dry summer season. Trees that grow adjacent to seasonal water channels or in areas with greater ground moisture often will grow faster and to larger sizes. Smaller trees indicate greater moisture stress and poorer soils.

Oaks occurring in natural landscapes are in balance with seasonal cycles of winter rain and summer drought. In addition to deep roots, most trees develop a network of feeder roots throughout the dripline area that are closer to the surface where they obtain nutrients and moisture. Their hard leaves are well suited to resist sun, aridity, and heat.

Culture for established trees:
Oaks in natural areas often are sensitive to disturbance associated with nearby construction and landscaping activities. Species such as *Quercus lobata*, *Q. douglasii*, *Q. engelmannii*, and *Q. agrifolia* often are encountered in the course of urban development in the West. These trees can be critically disturbed by changing grades, removing surface feeder roots, lowering ground water tables through pumping, and by adding summer water that incites fungal growth. This disturbance appears to particularly affect older plants that have grown on a natural site, where the seasonal cycles of moisture, heat, and wind have been repeated for a number of years. Fortunately, oaks have become widely appreciated and there are many guidelines that can help preserve and protect these plants. The most essential checklist of considerations include:

1. Work with a specialist who has experience with the ecology and cultural needs of oaks.

2. Protect the natural condition of oak tree(s) through planning and design that avoids disturbance. Think of creating a small natural oasis around the plant that can remain natural and dry. Impacts to established trees are most critical within the canopy dripline area.

3. Do not disturb the root crown at the base. Avoid trenching, compacting, or lowering grades to expose and damage surface feeder roots. For young trees with a narrow, upright form, plan to protect as much of the area within the potential canopy spread as possible. Raising the grade is possible with proper protection of the tree trunk, but consider the impact to feeder roots that are no longer just below the soil surface.

4. Avoid summer irrigation or exotic plantings under trees that require regular watering and fertilizing practices. In locations where ground water tables have been lowered, resulting in weak growth and declining vigor, a periodic deep watering program is desirable.

Landscape uses and establishment guidelines:
Oaks are widely used in parks, greenbelts, and as street trees. They are often a climax species used in restoration projects. These trees are also one of the best choices for institutional landscapes, such as universities and civic spaces, where their long life span and monumental scale provide many years of value.

Oaks can be planted by seed or from containers. Due to quick development of a tap root, careful selection and planting of container grown trees is needed. Roots should not be coiled and where possible small branches and foliage should be left on the trunk to encourage stronger caliper growth. Some nurseries grow oaks in deeper plant containers that help ad-

850. Quercus agrifolia

dress this concern. Newly planted trees, whether native or exotic, grow faster with regular moisture. After 3-4 years, these trees should be established and the supplemental watering schedule can be reduced to periodic deep watering to maintain vigor and health.

A number of native and Mediterranean plant species are well suited to grow in association with oaks. The most difficult area to address is the deep shade within the canopy. This zone is often best treated with natural leaf mulch from the tree itself or part of this understory area can be covered with loosely fitted stones in an effort to add design character and to enable natural moisture to reach the soil. Recommended companion plants can be found in Section 3 within the plant association checklists.

Helpful References:
Faber, Phyllis M., ed. "Year of the Oak." Fremontia 18 (July 1990). Sacramento: California Native Plant Society, 1990.

Heritage Oaks Committee. Native Oaks—Our Valley Heritage. Sacramento: Sacramento County Office of Education, 1976.

Pavlik, Bruce M., Pamela C. Muick, Sharon Johnson, Marjorie Popper. Oaks of California. Olivos, CA: Cachuma Press and the California Oak Foundation, 1991.

"Saving Our Oaks." Sunset Magazine, October 1990, 75.

Plumb, Timothy R., tech. coordinator. Proceedings of the Symposium on the Ecology, Management, and Utilization of California Oaks. Gen. Tech. Rep. psw-44. Berkeley: Pacific Southwest Forest and Range Experiment Station, U.S. Department of Agriculture, Forest Service, 1979.

Quercus agrifolia
Coast Live Oak

A medium to large tree, growing 30-60 ft. high, and spreading broadly 40-70 ft. wide. Leaves are dark green, rounded, and have a spiny edge; acorns are 1-2 in. long and narrow.

This species is common to coastal foothills and plains from Mendocino County to Baja California. It also grows within inland foothills and valleys including the San Joaquin valley on dry slopes and in canyons to 3,000 ft. in elevation. In this range, the coast live oak is most often associated with southern oak woodland and foothill woodland plant communities. In drier locations, it is also commonly found adjacent to seasonal streams and in the broadleaf chaparral community.

Coast live oaks are one of the most widely known and used western native trees. It often becomes a monumental scale specimen and works well in large scale settings such as parks, open spaces, and as a street tree. Plates 850 - 853.

851. Quercus agrifolia

852. Quercus agrifolia

853. Quercus agrifolia, Wilderness Gardens Preserve, Pala, California

Quercus douglasii
Blue Oak

A medium to large deciduous tree, growing 25-50 ft. high, with an equal spread. Leaves grow 2-3 in. long, have lobed margins, and mature to a resinous blue color during the summer. Bark on the trunks is greyish and heavily textured; acorns are globe-shaped and held by a small thin base.

Blue oak comes primarily from foothills around the central valley region of California where it is a dominant plant in the foothill woodland community. It grows on dry, rocky slopes and plains, usually below 3,500 ft.

The broad, rounded form of this tree provides a great deal of character to the foothill landscapes throughout the Central Valley of California. As a result, it contributes to the romantic images of "Old California". Unfortunately, it has been heavily impacted by decades of cattle grazing. This species is used in restoration programs and is now being protected in many park and open space areas. When used in ornamental landscapes, it shows a slow to moderate growth rate and tolerance to drought. Plates 854 - 856.

854. Quercus douglasii

855. Quercus douglasii

856. Quercus douglasii, Sacramento Valley, California

857. Quercus engelmannii

Quercus engelmannii
Engelmann Oak, Mesa Oak

A medium evergreen tree, 20-50 ft. tall, equal in width. Leaves are long and rounded, pale blue-green; acorns are many lengths but cylindrical in shape and held by thick cups.

Engelmann oak comes from elevated mesas and foothill slopes from the San Gabriel Mountains in Los Angeles County, south to San Diego and into Baja California. In its range, this species was occasionally a dominant tree in the southern oak woodland association or occurred in combination with the coast live oak. It has been so extensively removed by urban development that relatively few specimens or stands have been preserved. Efforts to protect and replant this species are increasing. It prefers rich, well drained soils and develops a moderate growth rate with periodic deep watering during the summer. Plates 857 - 859.

858. Quercus engelmannii, Los Angeles County Arboretum, California

859. Quercus engelmannii

Quercus ilex
Holly Oak, Holm Oak

A medium evergreen tree, 40-50 ft. tall, equal in spread. Dense foliage is comprised of leaves that are dull green above, white below. Acorns are round and pointed at the tip, with the base often covering half the nut. Trees develop an upright habit for the first 15-20 years that eventually broadens into a rounded shape.

Holly oak comes from the Mediterranean region where it is widely adapted to coastal and inland environments. It is well adapted to heat, cold, and drought and grows equally well on calcareous and slightly acidic soils. It is a member of the oak woodland and maquis plant associations that are very similar to the woodland and chaparral environments in California. This species is a popular choice for street tree, lawn, background, and specimen plantings. In Europe, this tree is often clipped as a large hedge to enclose garden spaces. Plates 860 - 862.

860. Quercus ilex

861. Quercus ilex

862. Quercus ilex, Cal Poly University, Pomona

863. Quercus lobata

Quercus lobata
Valley Oak

A large deciduous tree, 50-70 ft. high, 50-70 ft. wide. Leaves are deeply lobed and medium green; acorns range from 1-2 in. long and are held by a hard, rough base. Trunks and branches become massive in size and are covered by heavily fissured bark.

Valley oak grows primarily in the warm interior locations of the central valley of California and southern coastal foothill regions. It often establishes in lowland areas that have the deepest and richest soils. It is well adapted to long summer seasons of drought and heat since its rooting habit extends deeply into areas of subsoil moisture. This species is highly sensitive to construction and urban landscaping activities that have disturbed soil grades, microclimates, and natural moisture conditions around established specimens. As with other native oaks, this species is being more fully protected and new trees are being planted in parks, open spaces, and in large landscape spaces. Plates 863 - 865.

864. Quercus lobata, Sacramento, California

865. Quercus lobata

Quercus suber
Cork Oak

A medium to large evergreen tree, 60-80 ft. high, 40-50 ft. wide. Dull green leaves are heavily serrated; acorns grow to 1 in. long and are held by a coarse, hard base. Trunks and branches are covered by thick bark that is the source of cork for commercial uses.

Cork oak is another species from the Mediterranean region that comes from coastal and inland environments. Within its natural range, it often grows with *Pinus halepensis* and *Quercus ilex*. It is well adapted to heat, cold, aridity, and drought and prefers rocky and slightly acidic soils. This species is most often used for street tree, background, and specimen plantings. It thrives in deep soils and in warm valley regions and tolerates low and intermediate desert conditions. Its unique bark character is always a feature of interest. Plates 866 - 867.

866. Quercus suber

867. Quercus suber, University of California, Davis

868. Rhamnus alaternus

869. Rhamnus alaternus

870. Rhamnus californica

871. Rhamnus crocea

872. Rhamnus californica

Rhamnus
Buckthorn
Rhamnaceae

Evergreen and deciduous shrubs and small trees, including over 150 species. Several types come from Mediterranean climates and are used in western gardens and are typically evergreen. They are widely used as foliage plants for screen and slope plantings and show good adaptation to many types of soils with low to moderate amounts of supplemental water.

Rhamnus alaternus
Italian Buckthorn

An evergreen shrub with an upright branching habit, quickly growing 12-15 ft. high, with an equal spread. Foliage is comprised of shiny, dark green leaves. Flowers and fruit are inconspicuous.

This species comes from the Mediterranean region where it grows in coastal and inland habitats on rocky and calcareous soils. It is a member of the maquis, an evergreen scrub community similar to the chaparral. It is suited to coastal, inland, and valley regions where it is often used for highway, screen, and background plantings. It tolerates clipping and pruning to form hedges and small trees. *R. a.* 'Variegata' has leaves with distinctive creamy white margins. Plates 868 - 869.

Rhamnus californica
California Coffeeberry

A large evergreen shrub, mounding 8-10 ft. and higher, and spreading as wide. Leaves grow 1-3 in. long, to 1 in. wide; tiny, inconspicuous flowers are yellow-green. Showy berries mature to red or black in fall.

California coffeeberry is a member of the coastal sage and chaparral plant communities within the coastal foothills from northern California to Baja California. It grows on both moist slopes or dry ridges and in light or heavy soils. Throughout its range, several subspecies have developed and can be found in the trade. *R. c.* 'Sea View' and *R. c.* 'Little Sur' are low growing, 1-2 ft. high, and spreading several feet across. *R. c.* 'Eve Case' is a selection with dense foliage, colorful berries, and a mounding habit, 3-8 ft. high. Taller forms are used as background and screen plants; lower types are good for borders and on banks. Plates 870, 872.

Rhamnus crocea
Redberry

A medium size evergreen shrub developing a mounding form 6-8 ft. high and equally wide. Tiny leaves, 1/4 to 1/2 in. across, are glossy, dark green with distinctly serrated margins. Branching is intricate and wiry. Flowers are insignificant, however, numerous red berries in late spring are valuable to wildlife.

This species inhabits canyons and washes throughout southern California below 3,000 ft. in the coastal sage and chaparral plant communities. It prefers well drained soils and needs no supplemental water once established. A subspecies, *R. c.* ssp. *ilicifolia*, Holly-leaf Redberry, produces a similar abundance of red berries late in spring but has larger leaves, to 1 1/4 in. long. These plants are often used in revegetation projects and native plant gardens. Plate 871.

Rhaphiolepis

(Raphiolepis)
Rosaceae

A small group of evergreen shrubs, consisting of 14 species that are native to moist and subtropical regions of Asia. Two species and numerous cultivars are widely grown in western gardens and are among the most popular flowering accent plants for both residential and commercial landscapes. Flower colors are most often pink to rose and white and cover the plants for several weeks in early spring. Foliage is typically rich, dark green and leathery.

Rhaphiolepis have proven to be widely adapted to many soil and climatic conditions and are grown in coastal, inland, valley, and protected desert regions. Based upon their natural origin, it can be observed that they grow best in sunny locations, with regular moisture, and in areas that are not extremely arid and dry. Yet, their handsome foliage is tough and durable, and they will grow in difficult places with little care, as well as survive winter frosts to 20° F. Established plants require only low amounts of supplemental water for good character and performance. These are among the favorite plants for use along borders, in raised planters, in entry courts, and on slopes. Small and medium varieties can be clipped as hedges; larger varieties can be trained into small, single trunk patio trees.

Rhaphiolepis indica

India Hawthorn

A medium size mounding shrub, growing 6-8 ft. high and as wide. Dark green leaves grow 2-3 in. long and are distinctly toothed on the margins. Flowers are white to light pink and are very showy in early spring; clusters of purple-black berries develop and persist for many months.

India hawthorn is native to southern China, Taiwan, and Indonesia, where it grows from sea level to above 4,000 ft. in elevation in open evergreen forests. The climate of its native range is subtropical with warm winters and high summer humidity; annual rainfall varies from 40-70 in.

This species and its many varieties are the most widely cultivated types in western gardens. Many different sizes and flower colors are available for landscape use. Confusion often occurs among the different named varieties; some choices include:

R. i. 'Ballerina' - Compact, low growing, 2-3 ft. high, with deep rosy pink flowers. Plates 873 - 874.

R. i. 'Clara' - Medium, rounded form, 3-5 ft. high, white flowers, reddish new growth. Plate 875.

R. i. 'Coates Crimson' - Medium, rounded form, 4-5 ft. high, large clusters of medium pink flowers.

R. i. 'Dancer' - Compact, dense form, 2-4 ft. high, clear pink flowers. Plate 878.

R. i. 'Jack Evans' - Compact habit, to 4 ft. high, bright pink flowers. Plate 876.

R. i. 'Pinkie' - Medium form, 4-5 ft. high, many small clusters of deep pink flowers. Plate 877.

R. i. 'Springtime' - Large form, robust growth, 5-8 ft. high, abundant medium to deep pink flowers. Plates 879 - 880.

873. Rhaphiolepis indica 'Ballerina'

874. Rhaphiolepis indica 'Ballerina'

875. Rhaphiolepis indica 'Clara'

876. Rhaphiolepis indica 'Jack Evans'

877. Rhaphiolepis indica 'Pinkie'

878. Rhaphiolepis indica 'Dancer'

879. Rhaphiolepis indica 'Springtime'

Rhaphiolepis 'Majestic Beauty'

This variety is a vigorous growing hybrid that has larger leaves and grows to larger sizes than other species of *Rhaphiolepis*. Leaves grow 3-4 in. long, are leathery, deep green, and have coarsely toothed margins. Large clusters of bright pink flowers cover the plant in early spring.

Rhaphiolepis 'Majestic Beauty' can be grown as a mounding shrub and will reach 6-10 ft. high or be grown as a small patio tree, eventually reaching 8-12 ft. in size. Some consider the origin of this plant to be from crossing *Rhaphiolepis* with *Eriobotrya* to achieve its size and flower color. Plate 881.

Rhaphiolepis umbellata
(*Rhaphiolepis ovata*)
Yedda Hawthorn

A medium to large rounded shrub, 5-8 ft. high. Leaves are oval, dark green, leathery, grow 2-3 in. long, and are lightly toothed on the margins. Showy flowers are white; noticeable berries are purple-black.

Yedda hawthorn comes from China and Japan. In Japan, it grows near seashores on cliffs and in evergreen woodlands. The maritime climate of this region is humid and moist, with rainfall throughout the year. In western gardens, this species has proven to be as adaptable as *R. indica* to many types of soils, exposure, and moisture variations. It is a larger species that has very handsome foliage character and distinctive white flowers. A dwarf variety, *R. u.* 'Minor', has smaller leaves, to 2 in. long, and slowly grows to 2-3 ft. and higher. New foliage is coppery red; clear white flowers occur in late spring and are lightly scented. Plates 882 - 883.

880. Rhaphiolepis indica 'Springtime'

881. Rhaphiolepis indica 'Majestic Beauty'

882. Rhaphiolepis umbellata

883. Rhaphiolepis umbellata 'Minor'

Rhus
Sumac
Anacardiaceae

A diverse group of evergreen and deciduous shrubs, trees, or even vines, including more than 150 species. Deciduous species are mostly native to cool, moist climate regions and are recognized for their colorful fall foliage color that ranges from bright red to orange to yellow. Evergreen species are often native to Mediterranean and subtropical regions and are noted for their deep green foliage and adaptation to heat and drought.

Several species of *Rhus* are native to western regions including Arizona, California, and Baja California. These varieties are often used for screen plantings, slope stabilization, revegetation, and habitat plantings in combination with other natives.

Rhus integrifolia
Lemonade Berry

A large evergreen shrub, growing 6-15 ft. high and as wide. Thick, leathery leaves grow 1-2 in. long, are deep green, and round with teeth on the margins. Inconspicuous clusters of white with rose flowers occur in late winter to early spring and are followed by colorful fruit with a coating tasting of bitter lemon.

This species is native to coastal bluffs, foothills, and offshore islands from Santa Barbara County to northern Baja California. It grows in sunny locations on well drained soils within the coastal sage scrub and chaparral plant communities. Annual rainfall occurs between December and April and ranges from 12-18 in. Plants growing on coastal bluffs are exposed to daily onshore winds and often grow only 3-4 ft. high and 12-15 ft. across. Plants growing in protected canyons and foothills can become small trees, to 25 ft. high.

Lemonade berry is a tough evergreen plant that is most often used on slopes and in background areas in combination with other California native species for habitat value and naturalizing purposes. Young plants develop long, rambling branching habits that gradually fill in with age. This species is highly adapted to summer drought conditions but also accepts regular water when established in fast draining soils. It also can be pruned into a multi-branched shrub, small tree, or be clipped into a formal hedge. Plates 884 - 886.

Rhus lancea
African Sumac

A small to medium evergreen tree, growing 20-30 ft. high with a round canopy of equal or greater width. Dark green leaves are palmately divided into 3 narrow leaflets, each to 5 in. long. Inconspicuous flowers are yellow-green and occur in late winter.

African sumac is native to the central and northern Cape regions of South Africa where it becomes a dominant plant along streambanks. This species was first introduced into western landscapes in Tucson, Arizona, where it has demonstrated very good adaptability to heat, aridity, poor soils, and drought. However, it grows fastest and to largest sizes when established in sandy, well drained soils with regular moisture. It is now widely planted in low and intermediate desert regions throughout the Southwest, as well as

884. Rhus integrifolia, coastal foothills, Ventura, California

885. Rhus integrifolia

886. Rhus integrifolia

887. Rhus lancea, Tucson, Arizona

all valley, inland, and coastal regions of California. It is valued mostly for its round form and dense shade. As a result, it is often used as a tree for parking lots, medians, lawns, and background plantings. Plates 887 - 889.

Rhus laurina, Laurel Sumac
(See *Malosma laurina*, pg. 222.)

Rhus ovata
Sugar Bush

A large evergreen shrub or small tree, growing 15-20 ft. and higher, spreading 20-25 ft. across. Foliage is comprised of rich, glossy, green leaves that reach 2-4 in. long and are thick, leathery, and pointed. Clusters of cream with pink flowers are showy during early spring and are followed by clusters of large berries.

This species is principally native to inland foothills away from the immediate coast, from Santa Barbara County south to Baja California. However, small occurrences also exist on offshore islands and within arid foothill regions of central Arizona. In California, it is a member of the chaparral and coastal sage scrub plant communities and is highly adapted to sunny areas, well drained soils, and many months of summer drought.

Sugar bush is a handsome foliage and flowering species that is well suited to restoration and revegetation projects. It is often used on slopes for erosion control and screening where it develops into a large mounding shrub. Mature plants can be pruned to reveal interesting bark and trunk character and can eventually become small trees. Plates 890 - 892.

888. Rhus lancea

889. Rhus lancea

890. Rhus ovata

891. Rhus ovata

892. Rhus ovata

Ribes

Currant, Gooseberry

Saxifragaceae

A diverse group of deciduous and evergreen shrubs that includes between 120-150 species mostly native to North America. A distinction can be made between species that do not have spines, which are called currants, and those that do, which are known as gooseberries. Many species have colorful flowers or fruit that have both ornamental and wildlife value.

Most species of *Ribes* are naturally adapted to cooler climate regions where they grow in sunny locations in moist, rich soils with little drought stress. Species that are native to the drier climate areas found in California and the Southwest are often found as understory plants in partially shaded wooded areas, in locations near streams, and on shaded slopes that retain more winter moisture. Some of these types show good tolerance to heat and summer drought once established and have been introduced into the trade for landscape use. These are mostly deciduous shrub varieties and are planted with other natives on slopes, in background plantings, and for naturalizing hillsides. They grow well in combination with species such as *Mahonia aquifolium*, *Iris douglasiana*, and *Heuchera* cultivars. They are adapted to many types of soils, including clays, and perform best with moderate amounts of supplemental moisture.

Ribes aureum

Golden Currant

A semi-deciduous shrub developing many branches from the base, growing 4-6 ft. high and as wide. Bright green leaves are distinctly lobed; colorful yellow flowers occur in early spring and are followed by clusters of orange, red, and black berries.

Golden currant is native to many parts of the Northwest, where it is commonly found in moist areas of foothills within many plant communities. Part of its natural range extends into warmer and drier parts of central and southern California. In these locations, a variety known as *R. a.* var. *gracillimum* occurs on dry alluvial soils within the southern oak woodland plant community. This variety has showy yellow with red flowers and is available from native plant nurseries. It is often used for revegetation and naturalizing purposes. Plates 893 - 895.

Ribes indecorum

White-flowered Currant

An upright deciduous shrub, growing 5-6 ft. high. Foliage is comprised of medium green leaves, 3/4 - 1 1/2 in. across, that are palmately lobed and have a rough texture. Attractive white flowers occur in short, pendulous clusters from late fall into winter.

This species is one of the most heat and drought adapted. It grows within coastal sage scrub and chaparral plant communities in dry washes, canyons, and foothills from Santa Barbara County to Baja California. It becomes deciduous in late fall under drought stress but quickly produces leaves and flowers with the onset of winter rains. Plants grown in ornamental gardens that receive more water will retain their foliage through fall. Plates 896 - 897.

893. Ribes aureum

894. Ribes aureum

895. Ribes aureum

896. Ribes indecorum

897. Ribes indecorum

898. Ribes speciosum

899. Ribes speciosum

900. Ribes viburnifolium

901. Ribes viburnifolium

Ribes malvaceum
Chaparral Currant

A medium to large deciduous shrub, developing upright branches 6-8 ft. high. Dull green leaves vary from 1-3 in. wide, have distinct lobes, and a rough texture. Colorful pink to white flowers occur in 2-4 in. long, drooping clusters from late winter to early spring.

This species is native to coastal and inland foothills throughout northern and southern California, where it is found in the chaparral, foothill woodland, and closed-cone pine forest plant communities. It grows in sunny locations, on well drained soils, and is tolerant of many months of drought stress. It becomes deciduous by late fall under drought conditions and produces new foliage and flowers after the first winter rains. This species provides good flower and fruit character for use in naturalizing slopes and for wildlife benefit.

Ribes speciosum
Fuchsia-flowering Gooseberry

A small to medium deciduous shrub, 4-8 ft. high, with arching branches that are covered with many sharp spines. Leaves are glossy, deep green, and distinctly lobed. Colorful fuchsia-type flowers are bright red, hang individually from branches during early spring, and attract hummingbirds. Numerous spiny berries develop and persist into summer.

This species is one of the most colorful western native shrubs. It comes from coastal foothills throughout northern California, south into Baja California, where it grows in the coastal sage scrub and chaparral plant communities. It is a very adaptable species that accepts sun or shade, as well as moist or dry conditions. Its best character occurs in partial shade with periodic deep watering during the summer. It is often used on banks and in understory plantings, where people can appreciate the flowers but not be harmed by the spines. Plates 898 - 899.

Ribes viburnifolium
Evergreen Currant, Catalina Perfume Currant

A low spreading shrub with arching branches, 2-3 ft. high. Handsome foliage is comprised of glossy, deep green leaves; tiny, maroon flowers are noticeable during early spring.

This species comes from shaded slopes, banks, and canyons on Santa Catalina Island from near sea level to 1,500 ft. elevation, where it grows among species of the chaparral plant community. Everything from its growth habit to its foliage and flowers is very different from most other species of currant. It is widely appreciated for erosion control uses on gentle slopes and is one of the best understory ground covers beneath native oaks and walnuts, surviving in moderate shade with low amounts of supplemental water. It performs best in partial shade and tolerates many soils, including calcareous. It develops long, arching branches that can root along the ground in moist soils and is adapted to coastal, inland, and valley regions. Plates 900 - 901.

Robinia

Locust

Fabaceae

A small group of deciduous trees and shrubs, including about 20 species that are native to cool, moist climate regions of North America. Several types are widely cultivated as ornamental trees in residential and commercial landscapes in all regions of the West, particularly in valley and foothill environments that experience summer heat and regular winter frosts. Unfortunately, one species, *Robinia pseudoacacia*, has become widely naturalized in foothill and canyon habitats from northern to southern California.

Locust trees are valued for their fast growth, colorful clusters of pea-shaped flowers, and open foliage character. These are durable plants that tolerate poor soils and are also well adapted to heat and drought.

Robinia ambigua

A deciduous tree of hybrid origin, coming from *R. pseudoacacia* and *R. viscosa*. Several hybrids have resulted from the crossing of these species, which provide the greatest ornamental flower character of all locusts ranging from light pink to deep purple. Common cultivars include:

R. a. 'Decaisneana' - A tall, upright variety, 40-50 ft. high, to 20 ft. wide, with pale pink flowers.

R. a. 'Idahoensis', Idaho Locust - A medium tree with graceful habit, 30-40 ft. high, 20 ft. wide, pink to lavender flowers. Plate 902.

R. a. 'Purple Robe' - A medium tree with deep pink to purple flowers, red tinged new growth.

Robinia pseudoacacia

Black Locust

A medium to large tree with an upright habit, growing 40-70 ft. high, 30-40 ft. wide. Deep green leaves are pinnately divided into 7-19 leaflets; branches are armed with sharp spines. White flowers are fragrant, showy, and hang in 4-8 in. long clusters during mid-spring. Conspicuous brown bean-like pods develop and persist through winter.

Black locust is native to the eastern and central United States. It is a very tenacious and durable species that tolerates heat, cold, drought, and neglect. In California, it has been widely planted in rural communities and around farmlands. It also has become naturalized in areas such as the foothills of the Sierra Nevada and upper canyons of the San Gabriel Mountains, where the climate is similar to its native habitat. Naturalizing does not occur as frequently when planted in warmer and drier regions.

Black locust grows best in coarse, well drained soils with periodic deep watering. The combination of deep green foliage color and hanging flower clusters produce a graceful appearance. It can be used in parks, lawn areas, or as a street and shade tree. Plates 903 - 904. Several cultivars are available that provide many form and foliage variations, including:

R. p. 'Frisia' - A variety with golden yellow foliage, bright red spines.

R. p. 'Inermis' - A thornless variety with good flower value.

R. p. 'Pyramidalis' - A very narrow and upright variety, producing few flowers.

R. p. 'Umbraculifera' - A broad canopy variety, with a dense crown, thornless branches, few flowers.

902. Robinia ambigua 'Idahoensis'

903. Robinia pseudoacacia

904. Robinia pseudoacacia

905. Romneya coulteri

906. Romneya coulteri 'White Cloud'

907. Romneya coulteri

908. Romneya coulteri

Romneya
Matilija Poppy
Papaveraceae

A small plant group comprised of only two perennial species, both native to dry climate regions of southern California and northern Baja California. These are unusual plants that develop tall stems and produce striking white flowers with yellow centers. The two species are easily confused and have been hybridized for use in cultivation. One species, *Romneya coulteri*, is among the most widely known of all western natives and is grown in perennial gardens around the world for its colorful flowers and distinctive foliage.

Romneya coulteri
Matilija Poppy

A large perennial shrub with many basal stems, growing 5-8 ft. high. Flowers can reach 9 in. wide and are comprised of 5-6 large, white, crepe-like petals with a center containing numerous yellow stamens. These flowers are fragrant and occur in large groups at the top of the stems in late spring through early summer. Both stems and foliage are bluish grey-green and provide good contrast with the flower color.

Matilija poppy is found within the coastal sage scrub and chaparral plant communities in Orange, Riverside, and San Diego counties. It occurs in sunny places on rocky soils in dry washes, along gullies, and in canyon habitats, where it develops a tenacious root base that enables it to obtain moisture, produce abundant growth, and withstand long periods of summer drought. Stem and foliage growth occurs from late fall through winter, concurrent with seasonal rains. Flowering occurs from spring into summer as soils dry out and temperatures increase. By late summer, most parts of the plant die back under drought stress to form a clump of persistent woody stems.

Matilija poppy is among the best high impact accent plants for use in gardens in coastal, inland, and valley regions. It is often combined with other native and Mediterranean perennial species including *Eschscholzia californica*, *Penstemon spectabilis*, *Achillea taygetea*, *Diplacus longiflorus*, *Salvia 'Allen Chickering'*, and *Salvia greggii*. Mature plants are quite large and will often become aggressive and spread many feet across by underground stems. They grow best in sunny locations, on light, well drained soils, and with periodic deep watering. New plants need to be carefully planted to avoid disturbance to the roots. However, once established many people learn of their large size and spreading habits. In ornamental settings, old stems should be cut to the ground in late summer to renew the plant for the next season. Some nurseries offer additional cultivars including, *R. c.* 'White Cloud' that has larger flowers, and *R. c.* 'Ray Hartman' that is a smaller variety with finer leaves and smaller flowers. Plates 905 - 908.

Rosa banksiae

Lady Banks' Rose, Banksia Rose

Rosaceae

A large evergreen shrub developing long, vining branches that reach 20-25 ft. and more. Leaves are divided into 3-5 leaflets, are a rich glossy green, and grow on stems that are relatively free of thorns. Showy flowers are yellow or white in color and occur in late spring to early summer.

Lady Banks' rose comes from central and southern China in habitats ranging from cliffs and crags to gorges and streamsides. It grows within a warm temperate climate region that experiences regular moisture and periodic winter frost. The true species is not often cultivated, instead, two colorful varieties with double flowers have become popular for use in landscapes around the world. *R. b.* 'Alba Plena' produces fragrant white flowers; *R. b.* 'Lutea' produces yellow flowers that lack fragrance. In western gardens, these varieties are highly adapted to coastal, inland, valley, and desert regions where they tolerate heat, frost, and variable moisture conditions. These plants are easily trained onto fences and arbors and can be pruned to control size and shape. They perform well as large, spreading shrubs on hillsides and terraced slopes to control erosion or as an understory to tall trees. They can be irrigated with drip systems and are able to survive with low to moderate amounts of supplemental water once established. Plates 909 - 911.

909. Rosa banksiae 'Alba Plena'

910. Rosa banksiae 'Lutea'

911. Rosa banksiae 'Lutea'

Rosmarinus officinalis

Rosemary

Laminaceae

A medium to large evergreen shrub, 4-7 ft. high, spreading as wide. Foliage is comprised of narrow, needle-like leaves that are deep green above and whitish below. Showy masses of small, blue to lavender flowers occur in winter and intermittently throughout the year. Foliage is valued as a food seasoning and contains oils that are used in perfumes, lotions, and soaps; flowers attract birds and bees.

Rosemary is native to coastal foothills and islands in the Mediterranean region, ranging from Portugal, northwestern Spain, and North Africa, east to Greece and Turkey. It grows on dry hills and rocky soils within a heath-type vegetation. It is a very adaptable plant that endures heat, drought, and poor soils. It has been in cultivation for years for its oils, medicinal, and culinary values.

Rosemary is a widely popular plant for use in western gardens, ranging from the coast to all desert regions. It prefers well drained soils, full sun, and low amounts of supplemental water. It tolerates frost to 15°F, aridity, wind, and calcareous or sandy soils. It is often used in garden spaces with plants designed for edible and culinary herbs including *Laurus nobilis, Ficus carica, Salvia officinalis, Thymus vulgaris,* and *Citrus* species. As an ornamental plant, it is used as a background or screen plant, and as an unclipped hedge. Several cultivated varieties exist in the trade that offer prostrate forms and deeper flower color. *R. o.* 'Collingwood

912. Rosmarinus officinalis 'Tuscan Blue'

913. Rosmarinus officinalis 'Tuscan Blue'

914. **Rosmarinus officinalis 'Prostratus'**

Ingram' grows 24-30 in. high, spreads 4-6 ft. across, with upturned stems and intense purple-blue flowers. *R. o.* 'Ken Taylor' is a cultivar derived from 'Collingwood Ingram', but is lower growing and has trailing branches. *R. o.* 'Prostratus' grows 12-18 in. high and has pale blue flowers and a spreading, cascading habit. *R. o.* 'Lockwood de Forest' is similar to 'Prostratus' but has deeper blue flowers. These varieties are excellent for slope stabilization and ground cover uses. Confusion often exists among growers over the names and characteristics of the many cultivated selections. Plates 912 - 915.

Ruellia
Acanthaceae

A diverse group of perennial herbs or shrubs comprised of over 250 species. Most species are native to tropical regions and need ample moisture. However, four species come from dry regions of Baja California and Sonora, Mexico and are adapted to heat, aridity, and drought. Flowers occur in spring and summer after rains; leaves are dropped during periods of extended drought or from cold spells. These types are best suited to low and intermediate desert regions in well drained soils where they are used as flowering accent shrubs in combination with *Encelia farinosa, Cassia* species, *Fouquieria splendens, Agave vilmoriniana*, and *Larrea tridentata*.

Ruellia californica

A small evergreen shrub, mounding 2-4 ft. high, with showy, deep purple, trumpet-like flowers that occur in spring. This species is native to dry hillsides, arroyos, and rocky canyons throughout the Cape region of Baja California, Sonora, and islands in the Gulf of California. Plate 916.

Ruellia peninsularis

A desert species that comes from the same habitat regions as *R. californica* but is distinguished by having larger purple flowers and is more tolerant of winter cold in intermediate desert zones. Plate 917.

915. **Rosmarinus officinalis 'Collingwood Ingram'**

916. **Ruellia californica, Palm Desert, California**

917. **Ruellia peninsularis**

Salvia
Sage
Laminaceae

A large and complex group of annuals, perennials, subshrubs, and shrubs. More than 750 species are known from around the world with many types being cultivated for their ornamental, culinary, and medicinal values. Leaves are often wrinkled and aromatic; flowers are bright and range in color from white to scarlet, pink, blue, and deep purple. Several types provide flower value during the summer and fall months.

Sage species are adapted to many types of climates and growing conditions. Within this group, a large number have evolved within Mediterranean and arid climate regions, including Europe, the Southwest, and Mexico. These plants are often subshrubs and require only low amounts of supplemental water. In natural environments, they survive drought stress by shedding some of their leaves and becoming dormant. These types typically prefer well drained soils and full sun.

Many exotic types of sage are used in perennial gardens and in mixed shrub plantings where they provide colorful flowering character for long periods of time. Species from the arid west are valued in native gardens, for revegetation, and for naturalizing slopes in coastal and inland gardens. These western natives have excellent wildlife benefit by providing nectar to birds and butterflies and pollen for bees. In the natural garden, they mix well with plants such as *Diplacus* species, *Romneya coulteri*, *Trichostema lanatum*, *Eschscholzia californica*, and *Eriogonum* species.

Most sage species benefit from hard pruning after their flowering cycle is complete. They frequently develop a woody base and semi-herbaceous growth on the upper stems where flowering occurs. Similar to other perennials and subshrubs, this top growth can be removed each year to maintain size and foliage character and to stimulate better flowering habits.

Salvia 'Allen Chickering'
Allen Chickering Sage

A mounding subshrub that grows 3-4 ft. high and as wide. Foliage is grey-green and pleasingly aromatic; colorful blue-purple flowers occur in early spring.

This is a hybrid from two California native species, *S. clevelandii* and *S. leucophylla*. It provides striking flower color and foliage contrast in native garden settings in coastal and inland regions. Its foliage also produces a very noteworthy garden fragrance. It prefers full sun, good drainage, and needs little or no supplemental water after it is established. Plates 918 - 919.

Salvia apiana
White Sage

An upright subshrub that reaches 3-5 ft. tall and as wide. Distinctive foliage is white to grey-green; flowers are white and occur on tall ascending stalks that reach 4-5 ft. high.

White sage is a member of the coastal sage scrub plant community and is commonly found from Santa Barbara County to Baja California in foothills and in washes. It can be

918. Salvia 'Allen Chickering'

919. Salvia 'Allen Chickering'

920. Salvia apiana

921. Salvia apiana

922. Salvia chamaedryoides

923. Salvia clevelandii 'Winifred Gilman'

924. Salvia greggii

925. Salvia greggii 'Alba'

926. Salvia greggii

established from seed or containers and is mainly used in native plantings and for revegetation of slopes and disturbed areas. It is also noted for its value as a honey plant. It can be used for backgrounds and as a flowering accent element in dry garden areas. Plates 920 - 921.

Salvia chamaedryoides

A small spreading subshrub, 2-3 ft. high, 3-4 ft. wide. Small leaves are very grey; colorful purple-blue flowers occur on small stems above the foliage from spring into fall.

This species is native to arid regions in central Mexico. It is a small plant that is suited to borders, perennial gardens, and raised planters where its foliage and flowers can contrast with other species. It tolerates sun or light shade and prefers well drained soils with low amounts of supplemental water. Plates 922 - 923.

Salvia clevelandii
Cleveland Sage

A mounding shrub to 4 ft. high, 4-5 ft. wide. Leaves are heavily wrinkled and pale grey; colorful rich blue flowers occur in mid-spring. Its leaves and flowers are among the most fragrant and pleasing of the salvias.

This species comes from inland foothills and slopes from San Diego County to Baja California. It grows in the coastal sage and chaparral plant communities in full sun on slopes and in well drained soils. Cleveland sage is one of the most popular types of sage due to its bright flowering character and foliage fragrance. As a result, several selections have been introduced into the trade through specialty growers and native plant nurseries. S. c. 'Winifred Gilman' has large, intense violet-blue flowers. S. c. 'Aromas' is lower growing, more compact, and 3-4 ft. high. These plants are highly suited to native gardens in coastal and inland regions with little or no supplemental water once established.

Salvia greggii
Autumn Sage

A woody subshrub that grows 2-3 ft. high, equal in spread. Leaves are small, to 1 in. long, and deep green. Colorful flowers are most often cardinal red and attractive to hummingbirds. Flowering occurs spring, fall, and intermittently all year in coastal and inland gardens and is heaviest in fall through winter in deserts. Cultivated selections are also available that provide white and salmon flowers.

Autumn sage has become one of the most popular salvias for use as a flowering accent plant in many garden settings. It comes from arid climate regions of the Southwest including Mexico, Texas, and New Mexico, where it grows in sandy washes and plains. It is easy to grow and is one of the most widely adapted species that is planted in coastal, inland, valley, and desert regions. It is very tolerant of heat, sun, and aridity and requires only low to moderate amounts of supplemental water. Flowers occur during most of the summer months and pruning is needed in the winter to maintain best character. Several cultivated forms are available. S. g. 'Alba' has white flowers. S. g. 'Sierra Linda' has magenta flowers and is highly suited to desert zones. S. g. 'Salmon' has salmon-orange flowers. Plates 924 - 926.

Salvia leucantha
Mexican Bush Sage

A mounding shrub, growing 3-5 ft. high and as wide. Foliage is comprised of 2 1/2 in. long leaves, pale green above, white below. Long, colorful flower spikes consist of fuzzy, purple bracts and white flowers and occur for many months from late summer into fall.

Mexican bush sage has become a favorite flowering accent plant for coastal and inland gardens. It comes from warm, subtropical regions in Mexico and will do well in all frost free areas including the protected areas in low deserts. This species needs heavy pruning each year to maintain dense form and better flower value. It accepts regular watering as well as short periods of drought. *S. l.* 'Midnight' is a striking selection with purple bracts and purple flowers. Plates 927 - 928.

Salvia leucophylla
Purple Sage

A woody subshrub with upright branching, growing 5-6 ft. tall and as wide. Silvery grey-green leaves reach 2-3 in. long, are wrinkled, and fragrant when crushed. Colorful whorls of light violet flowers occur in early to late spring.

Purple sage is native to the coastal sage plant community in foothills from San Luis Obispo County to Orange County. This species provides colorful flowers and contrasting foliage color in native gardens. One cultivar, *S. l.* 'Point Sal', is a prostrate plant, growing 18-30 in. and spreading up to 10 ft. across. It produces an abundance of rose-pink flowers in the spring and becomes dormant in late fall. Plates 929 - 930.

Salvia mellifera
Black Sage

A woody subshrub, growing 4-5 ft. tall and as wide. Dark green leaves are wrinkled and pungent when crushed; noticeable flowers are pale blue to white and occur in early summer.

Black sage is a dominant member of the coastal sage plant community and is considered one of the best western native honey plants. It grows in habitats from coastal bluffs to inland foothills, from northern to southern California and Baja California, where it is very tolerant of heat and drought stress. This species is seldom used in ornamental gardens, instead it is used in restoration of natural slopes. A prostrate selection, *S. m.* 'Terra Seca', grows only 1-2 ft. high and spreads to 6 ft. This plant was discovered along the coast in Monterey County and is useful on dry banks and slopes where it can cascade and help reduce soil erosion problems. Plates 931 - 932.

Salvia munzii
San Miguel Mountain Sage

A woody subshrub, 2-3 ft. high and as wide. Foliage is dull grey-green and aromatic when crushed. Colorful clear blue flowers occur in whorls in spring.

This species comes from San Diego County and adjacent parts of Baja California where it is native to the coastal sage plant community. It is often used in restoration projects, as well as in native gardens, where it provides flower character and wildlife value.

Salvia officinalis
Garden Sage

A perennial herb, 18-24 in. high, 2-3 ft. wide. Pale grey-green leaves grow 3-4 in. long and

927. Salvia leucantha

928. Salvia leucantha

929. Salvia leucophylla

930. Salvia leucophylla

931. Salvia mellifera 'Prostrata'

are aromatic when crushed; colorful spikes of blue flowers occur in early spring.

Garden sage is principally known for its culinary value as a food seasoning. It is easily grown in herb and perennial gardens throughout the Southwest where it prefers full sun and well drained soils. It needs little care and low amounts of supplemental water once established. Flowers are lightly fragrant; foliage can be used fresh or dried for seasoning. Plate 936.

Salvia sonomensis
Creeping Sage

A prostrate perennial, 8-12 in. high, spreading 3-4 ft. across. Leaves are medium green; violet-blue flowers occur on 4-6 in. tall spikes in spring and summer.

This species is native to coastal and inland foothills throughout California in chaparral and yellow pine forest plant communities. It grows best in full sun on well drained soils. A hybrid seedling from this species, *S. s.* 'Dara's Choice', grows higher, 2-3 ft., and provides darker foliage and blue-purple flower color. Both plants are used on banks and in rock gardens. They grow well for several years and can be maintained to good form with light pruning. Plate 934.

Salvia spathacea
Hummingbird Sage, Pitcher Sage

A small clumping perennial, growing 12-18 in. high and as wide. Large deep green leaves grow 4-6 in. long; vigorous spikes with colorful deep red flowers occur in early spring.

Hummingbird sage is native to foothill regions from Orange County to central California. It frequently grows as an understory plant to native oaks and on grassy slopes in the southern oak woodland plant community. It develops strong rhizomes below the ground that enable it to survive summer drought and to spread to develop several upright stems each spring. Foliage and flowers develop after the winter rains and last into summer. Leaves and stems die back under drought stress. This species is a unique flowering and foliage accent plant that can be used along natural borders, under trees, and in native plant gardens. Plate 935.

932. Salvia mellifera 'Prostrata'

933. Salvia officinalis

934. Salvia sonomensis 'Dara's Choice'

935. Salvia spathacea

Sambucus

Elderberry

Caprifoliaceae

A small group of deciduous shrubs or trees, including about 20 species that are mostly native to cool and moist climate regions of North America and Asia. The natural range of one species, however, extends into warmer and drier areas of the West where it is adapted to long periods of drought. These plants are noted for their large clusters of creamy yellow to white flowers and colorful blue to black berries. The berries on some species are poisonous; others are edible and provide significant wildlife value.

Sambucus caerulea

(Sambucus glauca)

Blue Elderberry

A large mounding shrub to small tree, growing 15-30 ft. high and larger, with an equal spread. Foliage is comprised of celery green leaves that are pinnately divided into 7-9 leaflets. Large clusters of tiny, creamy yellow flowers occur in spring and summer; colorful clusters of blue-purple berries mature by fall. Berries are used in jellies, pies, and for making wine. They are also valued by wildlife.

This species is native to a very broad portion of western North America from British Columbia south to California, Arizona, and northern Baja California. Throughout this vast range, a number of varieties within this species have evolved that are recognized by subtle differences in foliage character and tolerance of different climate conditions. Plants that grow naturally throughout southern California, Arizona, and northern Baja California are identified as *S. c.* var. *neomexicana* or as *S. mexicana*, the Mexican elderberry. This variety is native to many plant communities, including the coastal sage scrub, southern oak woodland, and chaparral. It often grows in canyons, near seasonal washes, and on exposed slopes. It tolerates many types of soils, including calcareous, and survives extended periods of drought by shedding its leaves by late summer and fall. Plants that become established in deeper soils and receive greater moisture will grow to larger sizes and produce a greater abundance of flowers and berries.

Blue elderberry is an important wildlife and habitat species in dry climate regions. It is seldom planted for ornamental purposes but is important in revegetation and open space plantings in natural areas. It is often combined with species such as *Juglans californica*, *Quercus agrifolia*, and *Q. engelmannii*. Plates 936 - 939.

936. Sambucus caerulea var. neomexicana

937. Sambucus caerulea var. neomexicana

938. Sambucus caerulea var. neomexicana

939. Sambucus caerulea var. neomexicana, San Joaquin Hills, Orange County, California

940. Santolina chamaecyparissus

941. Santolina chamaecyparissus

942. Santolina virens

943. Santolina virens

944. Scaevola 'Mauve Clusters'

945. Scaevola 'Mauve Clusters'

Santolina
Asteraceae

A small group of herbs and subshrubs, comprised of about 8 species. These plants are native to the Mediterranean region of Europe and are well suited to warm climate conditions throughout the West. Two species are the most popular for cultivation and are widely used as border and rock garden plants. They have distinctive and colorful foliage character, as well as bright flower heads from late spring to summer that are very showy.

Santolinas grow in all climate regions, from the coast to the deserts. They perform best in sunny locations, on well drained soils, and with low amounts of supplemental water. They are fast growing but become rangy after 2-3 years and should be cut back each spring to maintain best character. They are often replaced as they become overgrown and woody.

Santolina chamaecyparissus
Lavender Cotton

A low spreading shrub, 1-2 ft. high, reaching 2-3 ft. across. This species has distinctive grey foliage that is complemented by its bright yellow flower heads. It can be planted near large rocks or bold plants such as *Agave*. It naturally spreads low to the ground or can be clipped into a border hedge around perennial gardens. This species is often planted in low desert landscapes. Plates 940 - 941.

Santolina virens

A small mounding shrub to 2 ft. high, with deep emerald green leaves. Flowers are chartreuse and stand out distinctly from the foliage. This species is a much deeper green than *S. chamaecyparissus* and more billowy in habit. Plates 942 - 943.

Scaevola 'Mauve Clusters'
Goodeniaceae

A low growing perennial, 4-6 in. high, eventually spreading 3-4 ft. across. Leaves are deep green, to 1 in. dia., and contrast with colorful lilac-purple flowers that occur from spring through summer.

Scaevola 'Mauve Clusters' is a hybrid from *S. humilis* and an unknown species. *S. humilis* is native to Mediterranean climates of Western Australia where it grows on sandy soils in coastal regions. This hybrid has been introduced into western gardens as a low growing ground cover that is valued for its long flowering season. It is well suited to banks and small planters, where it provides a very dense and lush appearance. It performs best in full sun in coastal climates and in partial shade when planted in warmer inland and valley landscapes. With good drainage, it accepts much or little water; established plants need only low amounts of supplemental water and can endure short periods of drought. The foliage character can be renewed by periodic mowing or clipping. Plates 944 - 945.

Schinus

Pepper Tree

Anacardiaceae

A small group of evergreen trees, comprised of about 28 species that are native to many regions throughout South America. Several species are planted in western gardens as street and shade trees in both residential and commercial landscapes. All three species are very different in terms of foliage character and adaptation to moisture and cold.

Schinus molle

Pepper Tree, California Pepper Tree

A medium to large evergreen tree, growing 25-40 ft. high, with a large, broad canopy to 40 ft. across. Foliage is comprised of light green leaves, pinnately divided into many narrow leaflets that hang gracefully from branches. Tiny, yellow flowers are insignificant; clusters of rose color berries are noticeable in fall and winter.

This species is native principally to western Peru and is the most widely known of the genus. It commonly grows along water courses in valley regions at elevations near 2,500 ft. but extends into higher elevations in drier and warmer climate zones within the Andes to as much as 10,000 ft. In contrast to its native habitat conditions, the pepper tree is highly adapted to subtropical and Mediterranean regions around the world. It was first introduced into California at the San Luis Rey Mission in San Diego County in the 1830's, and has since become one of the most distinctive tree species throughout the state and other

946. **Schinus molle**

947. **Schinus molle**

948. **Schinus molle, San Juan Capistrano Mission, California**

949. Schinus polygamus

950. Schinus polygamus

951. Schinus terebinthifolius

952. Schinus terebinthifolius

parts of the arid Southwest. It grows best on well drained soils and can survive in coastal, inland, and valley areas with little or no supplemental water; many plants can be observed in rural and neglected areas where they receive only rainfall to sustain them. In low and intermediate desert regions, this species needs regular deep watering for best performance.

The pepper tree is often used as a large shrub along highways and on slopes where it grows quickly and provides handsome foliage character under difficult conditions. It is also planted as a shade tree in large courtyards, along entry drives, and in parks. With age, it develops massive trunks and branches, as well as monumental scale and character. Experience has shown that older and larger trees should not be over watered, as they will produce excessive foliage that can lead to branch failure. Root systems often become large and invasive and can lift pavement, damage drain lines, and out compete smaller plants for moisture. This species also produces an abundance of litter and deep shade that can overwhelm understory plants and ground covers. Plates 946 - 948.

Schinus polygamus
(Schinus dependens)
Peruvian Pepper

A medium size tree, 20-30 ft. high and as wide. Linear leaves are deep green, grow to 1 in. long; inconspicuous clusters of yellow-green flowers occur in summer and are followed by numerous purple-black berries.

The Peruvian pepper is native to western South America. In western gardens, it has been planted in inland zones of southern California with good success. It develops a broad canopy shape and is often used as a shade tree in lawns, along streets, and in parking lots. It is well adapted to heat, aridity, and drought. Plates 949 - 950.

Schinus terebinthifolius
Brazilian Pepper

A large shrub to medium tree, 20-30 ft. high, and as wide. Dark green leaves are pinnately divided into many rounded leaflets. Flowers are creamy yellow, occurring in large clusters in late summer; showy red berries mature in fall and winter.

This species is native to moist, subtropical climates of Brazil. It is damaged by frost and performs best in coastal and inland landscapes throughout the West where temperatures stay above 25° F. It is also planted in low desert regions where it can tolerate high temperatures and aridity if provided with regular moisture.

Brazilian pepper is not considered as drought tolerant as the other cultivated species. It prefers moderate amounts of moisture and is often planted as a residential tree in lawns or in courtyards and raised planters in commercial spaces. However, it has been planted along highways as a screen plant where it survives under difficult conditions with low amounts of supplemental water. It is also used as a street tree, in parking lots, and as a multi-trunk specimen element. Too much water can lead to fast growth and weak branching that can be heavily damaged during winds. This species, along with *Melaleuca quinquenervia*, have become widely naturalized pests in tropical regions such as Florida. Plates 951 - 952.

Sedum

Stonecrop
Crassulaceae

A large and diverse group of succulents, perennials, and subshrubs that includes an estimated 600 or more species. This group of plants is native to many regions of the world, ranging from coastal bluffs to alpine slopes, where climate conditions range from arid and dry, to cool and moist. Many species and hybrids are found in cultivation in western gardens and are widely available from specialty nurseries and retail growers. Most of these are small succulent types that provide a variety of sizes, foliage types, and flower colors for use in small garden spaces.

Stonecrops grow best in sunny locations in well drained soils. Most types in cultivation are adapted to heat, and able to survive dry spells by absorbing moisture into their fleshy stems and leaves. They are popular in rock gardens, containers, along borders, and as ground covers on banks and in planters. A great deal of confusion exists among the species and hybrids available in the trade. A few varieties are described below.

Sedum anglicum

A very low creeping ground cover form, 2-4 in. high. Native to western Europe. Tiny, dark green foliage contrasts sharply with pink to white flowers.

Sedum brevifolium

A miniature form, 2-3 in. high, with distinctive grey-white leaves that are tightly clustered together; tiny flowers are pink to white. Native from southwest Europe to northwest Africa.

Sedum confusum

A low spreading ground cover form, 6-12 in. high. Light green leaves reach 1 1/2 in. long, colorful clusters of bright yellow flowers. Native to Mexico, suited to small banks and planters. Plates 953 - 954.

Sedum dendroideum praealtum

A spreading ground cover variety, 12-18 in. high. Light green leaves reach 2 in. long; colorful clusters of showy yellow flowers cover the plant. Good for larger borders and bank areas. Plate 955.

Sedum moranense

A miniature spreading form, 2-3 in. high. Grey-green foliage contrasts with tiny white flowers. Native to Mexico.

Sedum morganianum

Donkey Tail, Burro Tail

A trailing form with grey-green foliage and stems that can reach 3-4 ft. long when grown in hanging pots. A popular container plant for protected spaces. Plate 956.

Sedum pachyphyllum

Jelly-bean

A low growing form, 6-12 in. high. Cylindrical, grey leaves are tipped with red; bright yellow flowers occur in winter. From southern Mexico.

Sedum rubrotinctum

(Sedum guatemalense)
Pork and Beans

A garden hybrid that grows 6-8 in. high. Colorful foliage is green with red tips; showy yellow flowers occur in winter. Plate 957.

953. Sedum confusum

954. Sedum confusum

955. Sedum dendroideum praealtum

956. Sedum morganianum

957. Sedum rubrotinctum

958. Sedum sediforme

959. Sedum spectabile

960. Senecio cineraria

961. Senecio mandraliscae

962. Senecio mandraliscae

Sedum sediforme
(Sedum altissimum)
A low spreading plant, 8-16 in. high. Deep green leaves, showy creamy white flowers in summer. Native to the Mediterranean region, North Africa, and Asia Minor. Plate 958.

Sedum spathulifolium
A small clumping form, often with three branches to 6 in. high. Leaves are blue-green, tinged with purple; colorful yellow flowers occur in late spring. Native to western North America, from California to British Columbia. Several varieties with foliage variations are available.

Sedum spectabile
A clumping form 12-24 in. high with large, round, blue-green leaves that are lightly toothed on the margins. Colorful clusters of pink to rose flowers occur in fall. Native to China and Korea. Several varieties are available with deeper foliage and flower colors. Plate 959.

Senecio
Groundsel
Asteraceae
Groundsels comprise one of the largest and richly diverse genera of flowering plants in the world, containing an estimated 2,000-3,000 species. Species include annuals, perennials, and shrubs and range in character from foliage plants to succulents. They are native to many types of climate and habitat conditions; many adapt easily to cultivation. Currently however, only a few species are available for ornamental use in western landscapes. Some of these are adapted to warm, dry conditions and are useful for water conservation.

Senecio cineraria
Dusty Miller
A clumping perennial with striking white, woolly foliage. Mature plants reach 2-3 ft. high; producing clusters of colorful yellow flower heads during spring and intermittently all year. Leaves are pinnately divided into many linear lobes.

This variety of dusty miller is native to sandy and rocky habitats of the Mediterranean region. It is adapted to all landscape zones of the West, from the coast to deserts, where it is often used as a foliage and flowering accent plant in containers and perennial plantings. It does best in sunny locations, in well drained soils, and with low amounts of supplemental water. Plate 960.

Senecio mandraliscae
(Kleinia mandraliscae)
A low growing succulent with distinctive blue foliage color. Upward growing stems reach 12-15 in. high and spread for several feet across. Leaves are cylindrical and reach 3-4 in. long; conspicuous white flowers occur in summer.

This species is native to South Africa and is best suited to coastal and frost free inland regions of the west, in full sun, and with fast drainage. Its blue foliage brings unique color to landscapes where it is often used as a ground cover and border plant. It is easy to propagate from unrooted cuttings and leaves and requires low amounts of supplemental water during the summer months. Plates 961 - 962.

Simmondsia chinensis
Jojoba, Goatnut
Buxaceae

A medium to large evergreen shrub, mounding 8-10 ft. high, spreading 10-12 ft. across. This is a slow growing species with a dense foliage habit comprised of stiff, pale grey-green leaves. Inconspicuous flowers are yellow-green and occur principally in late spring. Female plants produce a small fruit capsule with several seeds that mature in late fall. These seeds contain an oil that is valued in the production of penicillin, soaps, and food products.

Jojoba is native to arid climates throughout the Southwest, from southern California and Arizona to Baja California and Sonora, Mexico. It grows on rocky and other well drained soils, on exposed hillsides and bajadas, and in areas where rainfall ranges from as little as 6-10 in. annually. It grows at elevations ranging from sea level to over 4,000 ft. and is a member of the Joshua tree woodland, creosote bush scrub, and chaparral plant communities.

This southwestern native offers both ornamental and commercial value in western landscapes. It is naturally associated with desert habitats and can be used in residential and commercial projects as a background and screen plant with other native species. It tolerates clipping and can be used as a hedge or for slope plantings along highways where it tolerates heat, sun, aridity, and drought. Young plants are tender to frost below 25° F and grow faster with moderate amounts of supplemental water. Established plants require little or no irrigation to maintain good visual character. Jojoba is also planted in coastal, valley, and arid climate regions as a commercial crop plant for its nuts. Plates 963 - 964.

963. Simmondsia chinensis

964. Simmondsia chinensis

965. Sisyrinchium bellum

Sisyrinchium bellum
Blue-eyed Grass
Iridaceae

A small clumping perennial that reaches 12-18 in. high. Blue-eyed grass is one of about 75 species within the genus *Sisyrinchium* that are found throughout the Western Hemisphere. This species is native to grassy fields and slopes in coastal habitats from northern to southern California. In cultivation, it prefers sunny locations, well drained soils, and regular moisture during winter and spring until flowering begins. It produces colorful purple-blue flowers for several weeks in early spring and reseeds and naturalizes easily in ornamental gardens. It is often combined with *Eschscholzia californica*, *Penstemon* species, and *Lupinus* species to achieve natural meadow and wildflower displays on slopes and along borders of natural pathways. In dry garden areas, the foliage dies back to the ground each year under drought stress but will regrow with the winter rains. A recent introduction, *S. b.* 'Rocky Point' stays below 9 in. high, and develops as a tight clumping plant with large, colorful flowers. Plates 965 - 967.

966. Sisyrinchium bellum

967. Sisyrinchium bellum 'Rocky Point'

968. Sollya heterophylla

969. Sollya heterophylla

970. Sophora secundiflora

971. Sophora secundiflora

Sollya heterophylla
(Sollya fusiformis)
Australian Bluebell Creeper
Pittosporaceae

A small to medium size evergreen shrub or sprawling vine with a twining and creeping habit, 2-3 ft. high, spreading 6-8 ft. across. Bright green leaves are shiny, 1-2 in. long, and occur on twisting stems. Flowers are a clear purple-blue and occur in modestly showy clusters at the ends of branches from late spring through summer. A white flowering form also exists.

Bluebell creeper comes from coastal and inland habitats of southwestern Australia. It is very adaptable to both sun and shade conditions, as well as to heavy or light soils that are slightly acidic and well drained. It prefers regular irrigation but has shown adaptation to dry periods when established in areas of partial shade. This species performs well in raised planters and as an understory plant on banks and below trees including *Eucalyptus*. Stems lying on the ground will often root in moist soils. *S. h.* 'Alba' is a white flowering variety that is occasionally available. Plates 968 - 969.

Sophora secundiflora
Mescal Bean, Texas Mountain Laurel
Fabaceae

A large evergreen shrub or sometimes a small tree, slowly growing 25-35 ft. high. Foliage is comprised of shiny, dark green leaves that are pinnately divided into rounded leaflets, 1-2 in. long. Colorful clusters of violet, pea-shaped flowers are fragrant and occur in early spring. Numerous silver-grey bean-like pods grow 2-5 in. long, persist for several months, and contain highly poisonous seeds.

This species is native to arid climate regions of the Southwest, from New Mexico and Texas to northern Mexico. It grows typically on limestone soils, from bottomland habitats near sea level to inland foothills up to elevations of 5,000 ft.

Mescal bean is well suited to all types of desert environments where it tolerates alkalinity, sun, heat, aridity, and drought. It performs best on well drained soils and can be encouraged to faster growth with periodic deep watering. It is used in background, raised planter, and courtyard spaces, where its deep green foliage and fragrant flowers are appreciated. It is also adapted to coastal and inland regions but needs heat and sun to stimulate growth. Plates 970 - 971.

Sphaeralcea ambigua
Desert Mallow, Desert Hollyhock
Malvaceae

A many branched perennial, growing with an upright habit, 3-4 ft. high and as wide. Foliage is comprised of small, pale green leaves covered with fine, greyish hairs and palmately lobed margins. Colorful flowers develop along the full length of the stems in early to mid-spring and intermittently all year.

This species is native to arid regions throughout the Southwest, from California to Utah and south into Mexico. It grows on hillsides, along washes, in disturbed areas, in full sun, and with long periods of drought. Leaves will shrivel and drop under high drought stress but will regrow with seasonal rains.

Desert mallow is a very durable and tenacious perennial and is one of the most colorful natives in desert landscapes. Throughout its range, several pleasing flower colors have evolved from red and pink to orange and salmon. It is well suited as a color accent plant in desert gardens and in combination with other colorful desert perennials such as *Penstemon palmeri, Baileya multiradiata,* and *Melampodium leucanthum.* It grows best on well drained soils, in sunny locations, and with periodic deep watering. Plates 972 - 974.

972. Sphaeralcea ambigua

973. Sphaeralcea ambigua

974. Sphaeralcea ambigua

Stachys byzantina
(Stachys lanata)
Lamb's Ear
Laminaceae

A low growing perennial with distinctive foliage character. Plants reach 6-12 in. high and spread 2-3 ft. across. Grey leaves reach 4 in. long and are soft, thick, and woolly. Noticeable flower stalks develop in early summer and contain numerous whorls of small, purple flowers.

Lamb's ear is native to Turkey and southwest Asia. It is a popular border plant that is grown in warm climate regions as a perennial and as an annual in cool climate zones. It grows best on well drained soils, with regular moisture, and in sunny locations. Established plants tolerate heat, short periods of drought, and can be sustained with low amounts of supplemental water. This species is often used along borders, around paving stones, in raised planters, and in perennial gardens where it provides unique foliage character and color contrast to other plants. Plates 975 - 976.

975. Stachys byzantina

976. Stachys byzantina

977. Tagetes lemmonii

978. Tagetes lemmonii

979. Tamarix aphylla

980. Tamarix aphylla

Tagetes lemmonii
Mountain Marigold
Asteraceae

A medium to large woody perennial, 3-5 ft. high, spreading 8-12 ft. across. Foliage is comprised of deep green, pinnately divided leaves that have a strongly pungent marigold scent. Intense, yellow-orange, daisy-type flowers occur in large quantities from late fall through winter.

This shrubby perennial is native to foothills of southeastern Arizona and extends further south into Mexico within oak woodland areas. It is adapted to arid climates, with cool winters and light frost, and hot summers with long periods of drought. It grows best in sandy, well drained soils, with periodic deep watering.

Mountain marigold grows well in coastal, in-land, valley, and desert regions throughout the Southwest. It is a highly colorful plant that provides many weeks of flowering, beginning in mid-winter in mild climate areas. It is a good background, slope, and flowering accent plant in both commercial and residential landscapes. In desert regions, it combines well with species such as *Cercidium floridum, Prosopis glandulosa, Agave species, Acacia stenophylla,* and *Leucophyllum frutescens.* This species should be heavily pruned in mid-spring after flowering is completed. Plates 977 - 978.

Tamarix
Tamarisk, Salt Cedar
Tamaricaceae

A small group of shrubs or trees, comprised of about 54 species, many of which are adapted to dry desert regions of Europe, Africa, and Asia. Several species have been introduced into western regions over the years and have become naturalized in many habitats. Their greatest use has been for providing windbreaks, erosion control, and stabilizing sand in coastal, valley, and desert communities. They are highly tolerant of poor soils, particularly saline and alkaline conditions, and develop aggressive root systems that enable them to withstand long periods of drought. Unfortunately, these plants produce highly viable seeds, which has led to widespread naturalization in washes, marshes, and along rivers.

Tamarix aphylla
(Tamarix articulata)
Athel Tree

A large shrub to medium tree, 20-35 ft. high, spreading 20-30 ft. wide. Foliage is comprised of thin, cylindrical branchlets with tiny, scale-like leaves; clusters of white to pink flowers are noticeable in summer.

Athel tree is native to arid climates of North Africa and the eastern Mediterranean region. It is highly adapted to desert heat, aridity, wind, and drought, as well as soils heavy with salinity and alkalinity. It is the largest species of *Tamarix* introduced into cultivation in the Southwest where it is most widely used for windbreaks, sand stabilization, and for creating shade around structures in desert and valley regions and in rural communities. It develops a strong, aggressive root system that sustains it in dryer and poorer sites but will respond with faster growth and achieve larger sizes under improved soil and moisture conditions. Plates 979 - 980.

Tecoma stans var. angustata
Hardy Yellow Trumpet Flower
Bignoniaceae

A large shrub to small tree, 12-18 ft. high, eventually reaching as high as 25 ft. Bright green foliage is comprised of pinnately divided leaves with leaflets having distinctly toothed margins. Showy bright yellow trumpet-shaped flowers reach 2 in. long and occur in large clusters at the ends of branches during mid-spring. Long, cylindrical seed pods mature in summer.

This species is native to arid regions of the Southwest, from Arizona, Texas, and New Mexico south to the states of Sonora and Chihuahua, Mexico. It grows in sunny locations in well drained soils, on rocky slopes, and along seasonal runoff tributaries in many plant communities. It grows to larger sizes in places that concentrate moisture from rainfall, particularly edges of slopes and washes. During periods of drought stress in late fall, it will shed many of its leaves and become dormant until moisture returns.

Hardy yellow trumpet flower is a tough and colorful plant for use in low and intermediate desert landscapes. The true species, *T. stans*, yellow trumpet flower, is native throughout many parts of Central and South America, where it is adapted to more moist conditions and subtropical climates. This variety, however, has adapted to the difficulties of desert climates and has a greater tolerance of frost. In ornamental landscapes, it combines well with species such as *Chilopsis linearis, Cercidium praecox, Ruellia peninsularis,* and *Calliandra californica.* All of these plants grow well in sandy soils and require only periodic deep watering to maintain their best foliage character during the long summer months. Plates 981 - 982.

Tecomaria capensis
(Tecoma capensis)
Cape Honeysuckle
Bignoniaceae

A large evergreen vine growing 15-25 ft. or many branched shrub reaching 6-8 ft. high with a sprawling habit. Foliage is comprised of glossy, deep green leaves that are pinnately divided into numerous rounded and toothed leaflets. Showy clusters of bright orange to red, trumpet shaped flowers occur in late summer through early winter and intermittently during warm spells.

Cape honeysuckle comes from the eastern side of South Africa, where it grows as a climbing shrub that can become a small tree. It is native to coastal regions and adjacent frost free zones along the edges of forests, in scrub communities, and next to stream banks. In western gardens, this species shows very good adaptation to similar conditions, as well as good success in low desert regions. It prefers sunny, frost free locations and with regular water; it grows quite fast into large sizes. It tolerates many soils, including calcareous, and needs only periodic deep watering once established. It is often used as a clipped or sprawling shrub on large slopes, or can be espaliered or trained onto a trellis. One variety, *T. c.* 'Aurea' has clear yellow flowers and is less robust. Plates 983 - 986.

981. Tecoma stans var. angustata

982. Tecoma stans var. angustata

983. Tecomaria capensis

984. Tecomaria capensis

985. Tecomaria capensis

986. Tecomaria capensis 'Aurea'

987. Teucrium chamaedrys

988. Teucrium chamaedrys 'Prostratum'

989. Teucrium cossonii

990. Teucrium fruticans

991. Teucrium fruticans

Teucrium
Germander
Laminaceae

A large group of perennial herbs and shrubs, including over 300 species, with many coming from the Mediterranean region of Europe. Only a few species are found in cultivation in ornamental landscapes. In western regions, two species are perennials, the other is a woody shrub.

Teucrium chamaedrys

A low growing perennial subshrub, 12-15 in. high, spreading 1-2 ft. across. Small, deep green leaves are distinctly toothed; colorful spikes of lavender to purple flowers develop above the foliage in early summer.

This species is native to dry hillsides and open woods, particularly in limestone soils around the Mediterranean region. It is a popular border plant in western gardens that can be maintained in a natural form or clipped to develop a low hedge. It is best suited to coastal and inland gardens where it prefers low to moderate amounts of supplemental water. It is also grown in valley and desert regions where it tolerates frost, as well as heat, but should be located in protected areas and given additional water. Pruning in late winter helps to revitalize the foliage and maintain good shape. *T. c.* 'Prostratum' is a lower growing form, to 6 in. high, spreading 2-3 ft. in dia. Plates 987 - 988.

Teucrium cossonii
(*Teucrium majoricum*)

A low growing perennial, 4-6 in. high, spreading as much as 2 ft. across. Foliage is comprised of small, pale green leaves that are fragrant when crushed. Large quantities of deep purple flowers cover the plant for 5-6 months from spring through summer.

This petite perennial is a recent introduction from the Mediterranean region. It is proving to be very successful in both coastal and inland regions when planted on well drained soils in sunny locations. Drip irrigation is recommended; low amounts of supplemental water are needed for good performance. Plate 989.

Teucrium fruticans
Bush Germander

A large evergreen shrub, 4-8 ft. high, spreading 8-10 ft. across. Distinctive foliage is grey-green above; silvery white hairs occur beneath. Colorful pale lavender flowers accent the plant in late winter to early spring.

Bush germander comes from rocky slopes of coastal foothill habitats in the western Mediterranean region, particularly Spain and North Africa. It is tolerant of heat, frost, wind, and extended periods of drought. It is adapted to coastal, inland, valley, and desert habitats in western states, where it requires little care and low amounts of supplemental watering once established. It can be pruned to create a hedge or planted in background areas to provide an informal screen. Its grey foliage character makes it well suited to contrast with darker green colors in the landscape. Plates 990 - 991.

Thymus
Thyme
Laminaceae

A large group of perennial herbs and small aromatic shrubs numbering some 300-400 species. These plants are most commonly known for their culinary value in flavoring foods and are widely planted in herb gardens throughout the West. Several species come from the Mediterranean region of Europe and do well in sunny locations, on well drained soils, and with low amounts of water once established. These species should be cut back in late fall or early spring to rejuvenate their appearance and foliage character.

Thymus praecox
(Thymus serpyllum)
Mother-of-thyme

A low growing perennial ground cover, 3-6 in. high, spreading 18 in. across. Showy white to rose colored flowers cover the plant during spring. This species comes from many parts of Europe, where it grows on dry slopes, sandy dunes, and in grassland habitats. Foliage is deep green, to 1/4 in. long, and is used as a seasoning. It is good for use as a border plant and between stepping stones where it will tolerate light foot traffic. Plate 992.

Thymus vulgaris
Common Thyme

A small perennial subshrub, mounding 6-12 in. high, spreading 12-18 in. across. Flowers are usually white and showy in late spring. Grey foliage is comprised of tiny 1/4 in. long leaves that are strongly aromatic and valued for cooking, as well as for making perfumes and medicines. This species is native to the Mediterranean region where it always grows in limestone or clay soils, on dry slopes, within scrub vegetation. It is used as a border, small hedge, and herb garden plant. Plate 993.

Trachycarpus fortunei
(Chamaerops fortunei, Chamaerops excelsa)
Windmill Palm, Chinese Windmill Palm
Palmae

A medium size fan palm developing a solitary trunk to heights of 20-30 ft. and higher. Fronds reach 2-3 ft. across, grow on lightly toothed stalks, persisting on the trunk until cut off. Trunks are covered by distinctive, deep brown, matted fiber.

The windmill palm is native to cool, moist climates in Asia below 2,000 ft., from northern Burma, throughout central and eastern China, and possibly into Japan. It is one of the most cold tolerant palms, withstanding temperatures to 0° F but is also tolerant of heat and aridity. As a result, it is widely planted in western gardens from the coast to deserts. In desert regions, it grows best in microclimates with protection from extreme heat and sun. As with other species of palms, it can absorb enough moisture from periodic deep watering to resist drought for long periods of time. It tolerates many types of soils but prefers good drainage.

Windmill palm is a very popular species for both residential and commercial landscapes. It is often used as a sentry element, in containers, or combined with other palms to form a tropical accent. Plate 994.

992. Thymus praecox 993. Thymus vulgaris

994. Trachycarpus fortunei, Balboa Park, San Diego

Trichostema lanatum
Woolly Blue Curls
Laminaceae

A small evergreen shrub, growing 2-3 ft. high, spreading 3-4 ft. across. Foliage is comprised of rich, glossy green leaves that are narrow and 2-3 in. long. Striking stalks of white to deep purple flowers occur with greatest intensity in early spring and intermittently all year.

Woolly blue curls is native to California. It grows in sunny areas on dry slopes, from the northern coast ranges in Monterey County south to San Diego County, where it is a member of the chaparral plant community. It is a popular native plant due to its long flowering season, which can be extended by removing older flowers. This species must have well drained soils and maintains good appearance with low amounts of supplemental water. It can be planted around the perimeters of established trees, such as *Quercus agrifolia*, and in combination with other flowering natives including *Penstemon heterophyllus*, *Ceanothus* 'Concha', *Heuchera* hybrids, and drifts of *Eschscholzia californica*. Several named varieties can be found in the trade that offer different foliage, form, and flowering characteristics. These varieties have been selected from the natural variations that occur among these plants throughout their habitat range. Plates 995 - 996.

995. Trichostema lanatum

996. Trichostema lanatum

997. Tristania conferta

998. Tristania conferta

999. Tristania conferta 'Variegata'

Tristania conferta
Brisbane Box, Pink Box
Myrtaceae

A medium to large evergreen tree, growing 40-70 ft. high and 25-35 ft. wide, having distinctive red-brown bark on trunks and branches. Foliage is comprised of large leathery leaves, deep green above, pale green beneath. Inconspicuous clusters of creamy white flowers occur in summer.

Brisbane box is native to moist coastal and inland habitats of eastern Australia, from sea level to 2,500 ft. elevation. It grows best in fertile soils in valleys and on slopes, where annual rainfall ranges 35-70 in. It often grows in transitional areas between coastal rainforests and adjacent eucalypt forests in areas that are frost free.

This species is best suited to coastal and subtropical regions in western states. Young plants are sensitive to frost and prefer regular water that helps to stimulate faster growth. Older trees survive periodic frost and need little or no supplemental water in coastal gardens. Periodic deep watering is needed by plants in warmer inland locations to maintain health and character. Brisbane box is often used in parks, medians, and for street tree and lawn plantings. Leaves, bark, and seed pods produce much litter; chlorosis occurs in iron poor soils. A variegated hybrid, *T. c.* 'Variegata', is heavily marked with bright yellow color. Plates 997 - 999.

Tulbaghia
Amaryllidaceae

A small group of clumping perennials, comprised of about 24 species that are native to tropical and subtropical climate regions. Two species are commonly grown in western gardens, where they are valued for their easy cultural needs and long flowering season. These species come from South Africa and are best suited to frost free zones within coastal, inland, and low desert regions. They prefer sunny locations, accept light or heavy soils, and require low to moderate amounts of supplemental water. When used in low desert landscapes, they should be planted in microclimates that reduce the intensity of extreme heat and sun.

Tulbaghia fragrans

This species grows 12-15 in. high with strap-like leaves that reach 12-14 in. long. Foliage is medium green and not pungent when crushed. Colorful lavender-pink flowers are pleasantly fragrant and occur in winter. This species can be used for border and perennial plantings, as well as for cut flowers. It has a shorter flowering season than *T. violacea* but does not have a strong garlic odor.

Tulbaghia violacea
Society Garlic

This clumping perennial grows 15-18 in. high and as wide. Strap-like leaves are medium green, grow to 12 in. long, and have a strong garlic-like odor. Tall flower stalks display colorful pale lavender to rose flowers for most of the year, with greatest intensity occurring in spring through summer. This species is an excellent color accent plant for borders and small median spaces where it never seems to stop flowering. Odor from foliage should be considered when using around patios, entries, and other frequently used areas. *T. v.* 'Silver Lace' is a variegated form that has distinctive white stripes on the leaves. Plates 1000 - 1001.

Verbena
Verbenaceae

A large and diverse group of perennials with colorful flowers, including about 200 species. These plants are native to many climate types throughout North and South America and are easily hybridized to provide many selections for cultivation.

Several species of verbena are native to arid climates in the Southwest, where they are popular as temporary ground covers and flowering accent plants in both residential and commercial landscapes. They grow best in sunny locations, in well drained soils, and with low amounts of supplemental water. They provide colorful flower value from early spring through summer; most types accept regular watering that will prolong flowering. Most species are short-lived and need frequent replacement. Heavy pruning in late fall or winter will often revitalize their shape and flower productivity. Some of the popular choices for dry landscapes are described below.

Verbena gooddingii

A short-lived perennial that is native to dry slopes and mesas throughout the desert regions of the Southwest. It grows 18-24 in. high, 3-4 ft. wide. Colorful lavender to pink

1000. Tulbaghia violacea

1001. Tulbaghia violacea 'Silver Lace'

1002. Verbena peruviana

1003. Verbena peruviana

1004. Verbena rigida

1005. Verbena tenuisecta, Tucson, Arizona

1006. Verbena tenuisecta

1007. Vitex agnus-castus

1008. Vitex agnus-castus

flowers reach 1 1/2 in. in dia. An excellent spring flowering perennial for low desert regions that often reseeds where moisture occurs in the landscape.

Verbena peruviana
(Verbena chamaedryfolia)

A low growing perennial, 6-8 in. high, spreading more than 2-3 ft. across. Leaves are medium green with toothed margins; very showy scarlet flowers cover the plant in midspring. The true species with scarlet flowers is native to Argentina through southern Brazil. A number of named varieties can be found at local nurseries that provide other flower colors including rose, pink, purple, and white. This species is highly popular as a border and ground cover plant in warm coastal, inland, and low desert gardens. It grows best for 3-4 years before many plants need to be replaced. Plates 1002 - 1003.

Verbena rigida
Vervain

A low spreading species with unique flattened stems. Mature plants reach 8-12 in. high, 3-4 ft. across, and are covered with deep rose colored flowers in spring. This species is native to South America but has become widely planted and naturalized in the southeastern U.S. It is well suited to the heat and aridity of low desert landscapes with low amounts of water. Plate 1004.

Verbena tenuisecta
Moss Verbena

A spreading perennial, growing 12-15 in. high, 2-3 ft. across. Leaves are bipinnately divided into tiny leaflets; colorful purple flowers occur from spring through summer. This species is native to South America but has been widely planted throughout southwestern and southeastern states. It provides an abundance of color during the spring and is highly successful in both Mediterranean and arid climates. Plates 1005 - 1006.

Vitex agnus-castus
Chaste Tree, Hemp Tree
Verbenaceae

A large deciduous shrub to small tree, growing 15-25 ft. high, 15-20 ft. wide. Medium green leaves are palmately divided into 5-7 leaflets; long, colorful spikes of lavender-purple flowers reach 7-8 in. long and occur in summer.

Chaste tree is native throughout the Mediterranean region of Europe, where it usually grows along stream banks and moist places, particularly in coastal habitats. In western gardens, this species has shown a wide range of tolerance to heat, cold, average soils, and varying amounts of moisture. It grows faster and to larger sizes with regular water but is easily sustained with low amounts of supplemental water once established. Chaste tree is frequently used as a summer flowering accent shrub or tree in small courtyards, containers, and raised planters. It often develops with multiple trunks that can be pruned for structural interest and specimen value. Several varieties can be found in the trade: *V. a.* 'Alba' has white flowers; *V. a.* ' Latifolia' is a vigorous purple flowering selection with broader leaves and greater cold tolerance; and *V. a.* 'Rosea' produces light pink flowers. Plates 1007 - 1008.

Washingtonia

Palmae

A small group of palms with fan-like fronds, containing only two species that are native to the arid climate regions of the southwestern United States and Mexico. Both species grow in rocky ravines, canyons, and sandy oases near permanent springs or high seasonal water tables. These habitats provide needed sources of moisture to offset the heat, aridity, wind, and scant rainfall of the surrounding desert. Soils and ground water often contain high levels of alkalinity.

Washingtonia palms are tall, monumental trees. With age, they become striking specimen and accent elements. They require adequate space and viewing distance to be appreciated. They are often combined with other species of palms such as *Phoenix canariensis*, *Phoenix dactylifera*, *Brahea edulis*, and *Butia capitata* to achieve Mediterranean, or even subtropical landscape themes in western gardens.

These palms grow best in sandy, well drained soils with periodic deep watering. They are capable of absorbing a great deal of water when it is available, then resisting heat and drought for many months. They suffer in areas of poor drainage and saturated soils. Both species take many years to attain large sizes in landscapes. As a result, older plants are often transplanted for use in projects. Transplanting is most successful when done during the warm months of the year to enable plants to regenerate new roots during their natural growing season. The large fronds and leaf bases persist for many years, forming 'skirts' that can be removed to reveal relatively smooth trunks. The long stems of the fronds are edged with numerous, sharp thorns that can be hazardous in pedestrian spaces.

Washingtonia filifera
California Fan Palm

A large tree developing a massive trunk, reaching 60-75 ft. high when mature. Fan-shaped leaves are dull green, reach 3-6 ft. across, have many folds, and are deeply cut. Clusters of tiny, creamy white flowers occur on large, 8-10 ft. long inflorescences in spring; numerous black berries ripen in late summer and sometimes germinate to start new trees.

This species comes from southern California, southwestern Arizona, Sonora, and Baja California in Mexico. It is a heavy, stout tree with trunks that can reach 3 ft. in diameter. It is often used along streets, in medians, and as accents for locations adjacent to tall buildings. It has a larger foliage crown, duller green leaves, and does not grow as tall and slender as *W. robusta*. Plates 1009, 1011.

Washingtonia robusta
Mexican Fan Palm

A tall, slender tree with a tapering trunk, growing 60-100 ft. and higher. Leaves are deep glossy green, fan-shaped, and reach 3-4 ft. across. Long flower inflorescences occur in late spring, followed by heavy seed production that often leads to many seedlings in surrounding landscapes.

This species is native to northwestern Mexico in the states of Sonora and Baja California. It develops into an extremely tall, but graceful tree, that can be seen over long distances. This species can also be used for special effects by planting the trunk at an angle to the ground. Such trees eventually produce sweeping trunk shapes as the crown strives to grow upright. Plate 1010.

1009. **Washingtonia filifera, Palm Springs**   1010. **Washingtonia robusta**

1011. **Washingtonia filifera, Living Desert Reserve, Palm Desert**

1012. Westringia fruticosa

1013. Westringia fruticosa

1014. Westringia fruticosa

1015. Westringia longifolia

1016. Westringia 'Wynyabbie Gem'

Westringia
Laminaceae

A small group of evergreen shrubs that includes about 20 species. These plants are all native to Australia where they have been popular in ornamental gardens for many years. Several types have now been introduced into western gardens and are useful for screen, background, and slope plantings in sun or partial shade. They provide pale grey foliage character and modest flowering value and are often planted with shrubs such as *Cistus* species, *Euphorbia rigida*, and *Agave attenuata*. They also perform well within the understory of *Eucalyptus* in areas of sun and partial shade. They are highly adapted to coastal or inland regions as well as in valley and low desert zones with protection from full sun.

Westringia fruticosa
(Westringia rosmariniformis)
Coast Rosemary

A medium size evergreen shrub, 5-7 ft. high, spreading 6-12 ft. across. Small linear leaves grow to 1/2 in. long, are pale green above, white below, and occur in whorls on whitish stems. Small white flowers occur in small clusters and provide accent character during spring and intermittently during warm periods throughout the year.

Coast rosemary comes from southeast Australia where it is native to sand dunes and adjacent bluffs in both sandy and alkaline soils, with wind and salt spray. This is the most commonly used species in western gardens. It develops a dense, mounding shape for use on slopes, in mixed shrub plantings, and for screening. Its foliage character resembles common rosemary, and it has proven to be a reliable shrub with few pests or problems. Plates 1012 - 1014.

Westringia longifolia

A tall and upright shrub, 5-6 ft. high, 4-5 ft. wide. Medium green leaves are very narrow and linear, to 1/2 in. long. Flowers are white to pale blue and occur throughout the year in small, colorful clusters.

This species typically produces several upward growing branches and an open foliage character. Flowers provide good accent value, particularly when planted in areas of partial shade. It can be planted on slopes and for background screens, requiring only low amounts of supplemental water. This is a recent introduction that should prove equally adaptable to western regions as other species in the trade. Plate 1015.

Westringia 'Wynyabbie Gem'

A mounding shrub, 3-4 ft. high, 4-5 ft. across. Small linear leaves are distinctly pointed, grey-green above, pale below. Colorful light lavender to mauve flowers occur throughout the year.

This cultivar is a hybrid between *W. fruticosa* and *W. eremicola*. It maintains the dense habit and shape from the former and gets its richer flower color from the latter. This plant has been recently introduced into western gardens and should provide value and success similar to the coast rosemary. Plate 1016.

Xanthorrhoea

Grass Tree

Liliaceae

A unique group of long-lived woody perennials, including about 12 species that are native to Australia. These are slow growing plants that have long, grass-like leaves and eventually develop stout trunks several feet high. Tall flower spikes that can reach 4-6 ft. long, are covered with small, creamy white flowers on older plants in spring to summer. Most species are well adapted to heat, sun, and drought but are tender to temperatures below 25°F. They grow best in well drained soils with periodic deep irrigation. These plants work well in containers and rock gardens in coastal, inland, and frost free valley regions.

Xanthorrhoea preissii

This species develops long leaves, 3-4 ft. in length, and trunks that are 12-15 ft. high. It produces very long flower spikes on tall stalks that grow 6 ft. and longer. Plates 1017 - 1018.

Xanthorrhoea quadrangulata

A smaller growing species with trunks that eventually grow 2-3 ft. high. Leaves are square in cross section and reach 18-24 in. long. Flower spikes grow on tall stems that can reach 10-12 ft. high. This species comes from South Australia in inland foothill locations.

Xylosma congestum

(Xylosma senticosum)

Shiny Xylosma

Flacourtiaceae

A large evergreen shrub that is noted for its light, glossy green leaves and adaptable form. This plant naturally develops a mounding form, to 15 ft. tall and equal in spread. Older plants can be pruned into single or multiple trunk trees up to 25 ft. high. A cultivar, *X. c.* 'Compacta', grows 8-12 ft. high and is heavily armed with sharp, 1 in. long thorns on its trunk and mature branches. Inconspicuous yellow-green flowers occur in late fall and produce a pleasant honey-like fragrance that attracts bees.

Shiny xylosma comes from southern China, where it is adapted to moist climate regions that provide ample rainfall, warm summers, and cool winters. In western states, it has proven to be highly adaptable to coastal, inland, valley, and desert regions. It prefers full sun, good soils, and moderate amounts of water during the summer months. In desert regions, it does best in microclimates away from extreme sun and wind exposure, and where it can be provided with regular water.

Shiny xylosma is one of the most commonly used shrubs in commercial and residential landscapes. It is appreciated for its bright green foliage and easy cultural requirements. It is a large shrub that is often pruned or sheared to control its height to serve as a screen or hedge of varying sizes. It grows well on slopes and with age, it can become a handsome tree. It tolerates many soil types and moisture conditions and is virtually free of pests and diseases. In iron poor soils, chlorosis of leaves is sometimes observed. Plants become briefly deciduous in cool winter locations. Plates 1019 - 1021.

1017. Xanthorrhoea preissii

1018. Xanthorrhoea preissii

1019. Xylosma congestum

1020. Xylosma congestum

1021. Xylosma congestum, tree form

1022. Yucca aloifolia 'Variegata'

1023. Yucca aloifolia 'Variegata'

1024. Yucca baccata

1025. Yucca baccata

Yucca
Agavaceae

A varied group of perennials, shrubs, and trees that includes more than 40 species. These plants are native to North America with most types being found in arid climate regions of the Southwest and from the coastal regions of southeastern states. They are widely recognized by their long, pointed leaves that grow in distinctive rosettes and by their large spikes of creamy white flowers. Yuccas are often grouped with agaves and cacti when people think of plants that characterize the arid west. These plants are highly adapted to heat, aridity, and drought and have been successfully cultivated in ornamental landscapes for years. They grow best in full sun, on well drained soils, and with periodic deep watering. Many types are easily grown in containers, raised planters, and in rock gardens. Care should be taken to locate plants with sharp leaves away from areas where people walk or gather.

Yucca aloifolia
Spanish Bayonet

A large species with stout, tapered leaves, growing 8-10 ft. high, 4-5 ft. in dia. Leaves are dark green, sharply pointed, and arranged in tight rosettes on stems. Showy clusters of white, bell-shaped flowers occur on 2 ft. long stalks above the foliage in summer.

This is native to coastal dunes and limestone soils from Louisiana to Florida and north to Virginia. In contrast to its natural habitat, this species is very popular in desert regions where it is often used as a sculptural accent plant and for its bold silhouette character. It is well adapted to cold, heat, aridity, and drought and is also planted in coastal, inland, and valley regions. A cultivated species, *Y. a.* 'Variegata', has yellow margins on the leaves which brings greater emphasis to their blade-like form. Plates 1022 - 1023.

Yucca baccata
Datil Yucca, Blue Yucca

A clumping species that often develops several heads of foliage, growing 3-4 ft. high, spreading 8-10 ft. across. Large curved leaves grow 2-3 ft. long, are blue-green, and have a sharp point at the tip. Colorful clusters of flowers are creamy white inside, purplish brown outside, and occur on 2-3 ft. long stalks in early spring. Flowers are followed by large, fleshy fruits that grow to 7 in. long and are edible.

This species is native to all desert regions including California, Nevada, Utah, Arizona, and Texas, as well as Mexico. It is highly adapted to heat, drought, and aridity and is of greatest value as a member of the Joshua tree woodland plant community in natural landscape settings. It is seldom planted for ornamental purposes. Plates 1024 - 1025.

Yucca brevifolia
Joshua Tree

A tall tree species that develops many stout branches and slowly grows 20-30 ft. high and as wide. Foliage is comprised of sharply pointed leaves, 6-10 in. long, that persist on stems and trunks for many years. Clusters of creamy white flowers occur in early spring at the end of each stem on older trees.

The Joshua tree is one of the most characteristic plants of the high desert regions throughout California, Nevada, Utah, and Arizona. Mature specimens become quite massive and provide striking silhouette character in natural settings. This is a slow growing species that is often destroyed by expanding urban growth in desert areas. It provides the best landscape value when it can be preserved in combination with other desert natives including *Larrea tridentata*, *Artemisia tridentata*, *Yucca baccata*, and *Juniperus californica*. Smaller size plants can be transplanted and become established in courtyards, raised planters, and on gentle slopes. These trees can be seen planted as specimen and accent elements in all desert communities throughout the Southwest. The best success occurs in sandy, well drained soils with periodic deep watering. Plates 1026 - 1027.

Yucca elata
Soaptree Yucca

A tall tree-type species growing 10-20 ft. high and developing 2-3 or more short branches with age. Thin leaves grow 3-4 ft. long and are pale green; old leaves persist on the trunk and form a skirt for many years. Showy white flowers occur on tall, slender spikes, 3-7 ft. long, in early spring.

This species is native to intermediate and low desert regions in Arizona, Texas, and Mexico where it grows on exposed slopes, gravelly mesas, arid grassland plains, and along seasonal washes. It is highly adapted to heat, aridity, cold, and drought. Over the years, soaptree yucca has become widely cultivated as an ornamental plant within its natural range. Its upright habit enables it to be very effectively grouped for landscape use in medians, courtyards, and raised planters. It also has a fine textured appearance that is not as heavy in character as other species of *Yucca*. Plates 1028 - 1029. See also plate 376, page 150.

Yucca gloriosa
Spanish Dagger

A large multi-trunked species with a swollen base and numerous heavy trunks and stems, 10-15 ft. high. Deep green leaves are 1-2 ft. long and sharply pointed. Large clusters of showy white flowers occur on 2-3 ft. spikes in spring to summer.

Spanish dagger is one of the most commonly grown species for ornamental use. It is native from North Carolina to Florida, Mississippi, and Louisiana, where it grows on coastal dunes. It is adapted to sandy soils, salt spray, cold and wet winters, as well as warm and humid summers. Throughout its range, several forms have evolved that have both stiff and soft foliage character. In western gardens, this species has proven to be highly tolerant of Mediterranean and arid climate conditions and needs little or no supplemental water once established. It is often used in raised planters, around pools, and on slopes. With age, it becomes quite large and difficult to remove. Plates 1030 - 1031.

Yucca recurvifolia
(Yucca pendula)

A small species, developing short trunks that branch with age, growing 4-6 ft. high. Foliage is comprised of 2-3 ft. long leaves that are a distinct blue-green, soft, flexible, and pointed. Showy clusters of white flowers occur on 3-4 ft. long stalks in spring.

1026. Yucca brevifolia, Twentynine Palms, California

1027. Yucca brevifolia

1028. Yucca elata

1029. Yucca elata, Phoenix, Arizona

1030. Yucca gloriosa

1031. Yucca gloriosa

1032. Yucca recurvifolia

1033. Yucca recurvifolia

1034. Yucca rigida

1035. Yucca rostrata

This species is native to southeastern states from Louisiana to Florida and Georgia, where it often grows in sandy soils on low elevation plains. It is one of the most popular species of *Yucca* for landscape use due to its size, flowering character, and less hazardous foliage. It is planted in coastal, inland, valley, and desert regions as an accent plant, around pools, and in containers. It is well adapted to heat, sun, and drought and needs only periodic deep watering. Plates 1032 - 1033.

Yucca rigida

A tall tree-type species that develops single trunks and foliage to 12 ft. and higher. Leaves are blue-green, stiff, sharply pointed, and grow to 2 ft. long. Old leaves persist on the trunks for many years. Tight clusters of creamy white flowers occur on 2-3 ft. long stalks in early spring.

This species is native to the Chihuahuan desert regions of Mexico. It develops striking foliage character and colorful flower clusters that make it useful as an accent plant in arid gardens throughout the Southwest. Plate 1034.

Yucca rostrata
Beaked Yucca

A tall tree-type species, growing 8-12 ft. high, most often with unbranched, single trunks. Leaves grow in a dense, circular head, 3-4 ft. in dia., are pale green, and persist for many years on lower parts of the trunk. Showy spikes of creamy white flowers occur in spring.

This species is widespread throughout desert regions of Mexico, with small occurrences in southeastern Texas. It is considered by some to be the most attractive species of *Yucca* from arid climates. It develops a strongly symmetrical shape with a straight trunk. Old trees sometimes develop several short branches. As with other species, it prefers well drained soils, periodic deep watering, and is useful for accent character in residential and commercial gardens. Plate 1035.

Yucca schidigera
(Yucca mohavensis)
Mohave Yucca

A large clumping species developing stout trunks and reaching 6-12 ft. high. Large leaves grow 2-4 ft. long, are pale green, and sharply pointed. Tight clusters of creamy white flowers have purple to maroon markings and occur at the top of the foliage. Large, fleshy fruit matures in summer and is edible.

This species is native to dry gravelly slopes in high desert regions throughout California and into parts of Nevada and Arizona. It also grows within coastal and inland foothills within the chaparral plant community from southern California to Baja California. Within this range, this species is of greatest value within natural environments as a member of the natural flora. It is sometimes used in cultivation as a specimen or accent element in desert landscapes. Plates 1036 - 1037.

Yucca whipplei
Our Lord's Candle

A small mounding species growing 4-5 ft. in dia. Long, narrow leaves are grey-green and grow in a tight basal rosette. Flower stalks with numerous white flowers develop on mature plants in mid-spring into summer and can reach 6-12 ft. tall.

This species is native to many parts of California, principally in dry coastal and inland foothills where it is a member of the chaparral and coastal sage plant communities. It also establishes along washes and on gravelly plains, as well as within the edges of high and low deserts in southern California. Throughout this range, several distinctive subspecies have evolved that provide variations in foliage and growth habits.

Our Lord's candle is one of the most visible native plants in natural landscape areas when it is flowering during spring and summer. It is different from other species of *Yucca* because it will die after the flowering cycle is completed. However, both seeds and offsets from the parent plant will develop new plants. It takes many years of growth and the right combination of climate conditions to bring these plants to a flowering stage. In cultivation, these plants prefer well drained soils and can survive with the natural rainfall after they are established. They are used as accent plants in rock gardens and should be planted where their sharp leaves won't harm people. Plates 1036 - 1039.

1036. Yucca schidigera

1037. Yucca schidigera

1038. Yucca whipplei

1039. Yucca whipplei, San Gabriel Mountains, California

Bibliography

Allen, Barbara H. Ecological Type Classification for California: The Forest Service Approach. Berkeley: Pacific Southwest Forest and Range Experiment Station, 1987.

Attracting Birds to Your Garden, by the Editors of Sunset Books. Menlo Park, California: Lane Books, 1974.

Austin, Morris E. Land Resource Regions and Major Land Resource Areas of the United States. Agriculture Handbook 296. Soil Conservation Service, United States Department of Agriculture, 1972.

Australian National Botanic Gardens. Growing Native Plants. No. 2. Canberra: Australian Government Publishing Service, 1981.

_____. Growing Native Plants. No. 4. Canberra: Australian Government Publishing Service, 1984.

_____. Growing Native Plants. No. 9. Canberra: Australian Government Publishing Service, 1984.

_____. Growing Native Plants. No. 12. Canberra: Australian Government Publishing Service, 1983.

Bailey, L. H. The Standard Cyclopedia of Horticulture. New York: The MacMillan Company, 1947.

Barbour, Michael G., and Jack Major, ed. Terrestrial Vegetation of California. New York: John Wiley & Sons, 1977.

Barbour, Michael G., and William Dwight Billings. North American Terrestrial Vegetation. Cambridge: Cambridge University Press, 1988.

Beissinger, Steven R., and David R. Osborne. "Effects of Urbanization on Avian Community Organization." The Condor 84 (1982): 75-83.

Benson, Lyman, and Robert A. Darrow. Trees and Shrubs of the Southwestern Deserts. Tucson: The University of Arizona Press, 1981.

Berger, John J., ed. Environmental Restoration: Science and Strategies for Restoring the Earth. Washington, D.C.: Island Press, 1990.

Blombery, Alec, and Tony Rodd. Palms. London: Angus and Robertson Publishers, 1984.

Boland, D. J., M. I. H. Brooker, G. M. Chippendale, N. Hall, B.P.M. Hyland, R. D. Johnston, D. A. Kleinig, J. D. Turner. Forest Trees of Australia. Melbourne: Thomas Nelson Australia, 1985.

Bontrager, David. "Ecological Landscaping: Creating Bird Habitat in Suburban California Gardens and Public Landscapes." Endangered Wildlife and Habitats in Southern California: Memoirs of the Natural History Foundation of Orange County, vol. 3. Natural History Foundation of Orange County, 1990, 26-35.

Boomsma, C. D., and N. B. Lewis. The Native Forest and Woodland Vegetation of South Australia. Bulletin 25. South Australia: Woods and Forests Department.

Bowers, Wilbur O., Richard L Synder, Susan B. Southland, and Brenda J. Lanini. Water-Holding Characteristics of California Soils. Leaflet 21463. Cooperative Extension. Division of Agriculture and Natural Resources. University of California, 1989.

Brill, Winston J. "Biological Nitrogen Fixation." Scientific American 236 (March 1977): 68-81.

Brinkmann-Busi, Angelika, comp. Guidelines to Select Native Plants for Various Aesthetic and Ecological Considerations as Well as Garden Situations. California Native Plant Society, Santa Monica Mountains Chapter, 1989.

Brown, David E., ed. Desert Plants. Volume 4, Numbers 1-4. University of Arizona, 1982.

Canberra Botanic Gardens. Growing Native Plants. Vol. 6. Canberra: Australian Government Publishing Service, 1976.

_____. Growing Native Plants. Vol. 8. Canberra: Australian Government Publishing Service, 1978.

Clay, Horace F., and James C. Hubbard. The Hawai'i Garden: Tropical Shrubs. Honolulu: The University Press of Hawaii, 1977.

Coate, Barrie. Water-Conserving Plants & Landscapes for the Bay Area. East Bay Municipal Utility District, 1990.

Collinson, A. S. Introduction to World Vegetation. London: Unwin Hyman, 1988.

Conrad, C. Eugene. Common Shrubs of Chaparral and Associated Ecosystems of Southern California. Berkeley: Pacific Southwest Forest and Range Experiment Station, 1987.

Costello, L. R. and K. S. Jones. WUCOLS Project - Water Use Classification of Landscape Species. Cooperative Extension. University of California. Sacramento: Department of Water Resources, 1992.

Costello, L. R., N. Matheny, and J. Clark. Estimating Water Requirements of Landscape Plantings. Leaflet 21493. Cooperative Extension. University of California.

Costermans, Leon. Native Trees and Shrubs of Southeastern Australia. Dee Why West, NSW: Rigby Publishers, 1986.

Coyle, Jeanette, and Norman C. Roberts. A Field Guide to the Common and Interesting Plants of Baja California. La Jolla: Natural History Publishing Company, 1975.

Critchfield, William B. Profiles of California Vegetation. USDA Forest Service Research Paper psw-76. Forest Service. U.S. Department of Agriculture. Berkeley, 1971.

Daubenmire, R. F. Plants and Environment. New York: John Wiley & Sons, 1974.

de Noailles, Vicomte, and Roy Landcaster. Mediterranean Plants and Gardens. Calverton, United Kingdom: Floraprint Ltd., 1977.

Delwiche, C. C. "The Nitrogen Cycle." Scientific American 223 (September 1970): 136-146.

Dirr, Michael A. Manual of Woody Landscape Plants. Champaign, Illinois: Stipes Publishing Company, 1977.

Eliovson, Sima. Shrubs, Trees, and Climbers for Southern Africa. Johannesburg: MacMillan South Africa, 1981.

Elliot, W. Rodger, and David L. Jones. Encyclopaedia of Australian Plants. Melbourne: Lothian Publishing Company, 1982.

Emlen, John T. "An Urban Bird Community in Tucson, Arizona: Derivation, Structure, Regulation." The Condor 76 (1974): 184-197.

Everett, Percy C. A Summary of the Culture of California Plants at the Rancho Santa Ana Botanic Garden. Claremont, California: The Rancho Santa Ana Botanic Garden, 1957.

Fowells, H. A., ed. Silvics of Forest Trees of the United States. Agriculture Handbook No. 271. Washington, D.C.: United States Department of Agriculture, Forest Service, 1965.

Fremontia. Journal of the California Native Plant Society. (published quarterly) Sacramento: California Native Plant Society.

Gibeault, V. Turfgrass Water Conservation. Leaflet 21405. Cooperative Extension. University of California, 1985.

Gibeault, V., J. Meyer, A. Harivandi, M. Henry, and S. Cockerham. Managing Turfgrass During Drought. Leaflet 21499. Cooperative Extension. University of California, 1991.

Gibeault, V. A., J. L. Meyer, R. Strohman, R. Autio, M. Murphy, and D. Monson. Irrigation of Turfgrass for Water Conservation. University of California, Riverside and the Metropolitan Water District of Southern California, 1984.

Griffin, James R., Philip M. McDonald, Pamela C. Muick, comp. California Oaks: A Bibliography. General Technical Report Psw-96. Berkeley: Pacific Southwest Forest and Range Experiment Station, U.S. Department of Agriculture, Forest Service, 1987.

Harris, Richard W. and Raymond H. Coppock, ed. Saving Water in Landscape Irrigation. Leaflet 2976. Division of Agricultural Sciences, University of California, 1977.

Heritage Oaks Committee. Native Oaks—Our Valley Heritage. Sacramento: Sacramento County Office of Education, 1976.

Heywood, V. H., ed. Flowering Plants of the World. Oxford: Oxford University Press, 1978.

Hightshoe, Gary L. Native Trees for Urban and Rural America. Ames, Iowa: Iowa State University Research Foundation, 1978.

Hirschman, Joan. "Bird Habitat Design For People: A Landscape Ecological Approach." M.L.A. Thesis, University of Colorado at Denver, 1988.

Hogen, Elizabeth L., ed. Sunset Western Garden Book. Menlo Park, California: Lane Publishing Co., 1988.

Holland V. L., and David J. Keil. California Vegetation. San Luis Obispo, California: El Corral Publications, California Polytechnic State University, 1989.

Holliday, Ivan, and Noel Lothian. Growing Australian Plants. Adelaide: Rigby Publishers Limited, 1981.

Hora, Bayard, ed. The Oxford Encyclopedia of Trees of the World. Oxford: Oxford University Press, 1981.

Hosie, R. C. Native Trees of Canada. Ottawa: Canadian Forest Service, Department of the Environment, 1973.

Hudak, Joseph. Trees for Every Purpose. New York: McGraw-Hill Book Company, 1980.

Hughes, H. Glenn, and Thomas M. Bonnicksen, ed. The Society for Ecological Restoration; Restoration '89: the New Management Challenge: Proceedings of the 1st Annual Conference Held in Oakland, California 16-20 January 1989. Madison: Society for Ecological Restoration, 1990.

Johnson, Hugh. Encyclopedia of Trees. New York: Gallery Books, 1984.

Jones, David. Palms in Australia. NSW: Reed Books, 1987.

Jordan, William R. III, ed. Restoration & Management Notes. (published bi-annually) Madison: University of Wisconsin Press.

Kahrl, William L., ed. The California Water Atlas. Governor's Office of Planning and Research in cooperation with the California Department of Water Resources. Sacramento: the State of California, 1979.

Koss, Walter James, James R. Owenby, Peter M. Steurer, Devoyd S. Ezell. Freeze/Frost Data. Climatography of the U.S. No. 20, Supplement No. 1. National Oceanic and Atmospheric Administration. U.S. Department of Commerce, 1988.

Kuchler, A. W. The Map of the Natural Vegetation of California. Lawrence, Kansas: University of Kansas, 1977.

Labadie, Emile L. Native Plants for Use in the California Landscape. Sierra City: Sierra City Press, 1978.

Latting, June, ed. Plant Communities of Southern California. Special Publication No. 2. Berkeley: California Native Plant Society, 1976.

Latymer, Hugo. The Mediterranean Gardener. New York: Barron's, 1990.

Lenz, Lee W. Native Plants for California Gardens. Claremont, California: Rancho Santa Ana Botanic Garden, 1956.

Lenz, Lee W., and John Dourley. California Native Trees and Shrubs. Claremont, California: Rancho Santa Ana Botanic Garden, 1981.

Little, Elbert L., Jr., and Roger G. Skolmen. Common Forest Trees of Hawaii. Agriculture Handbook No. 679. Washington, D.C.: Forest Service, United States Department of Agriculture, 1989.

Lyle, John T. "A General Approach to Landscape Design for Wildlife Habitat." In Integrating Man and Nature in the Metropolitan Environment: Proceedings of the National Symposium on Urban Wildlife Held in Chevy Chase, Md. 4-7 November 1986, Adams, L.W., and D. L. Leedy, ed. Columbia, Maryland: National Institute for Urban Wildlife, 1987, 87-91.

McCurrach, James C. Palms of the World. New York: Harper and Brothers, 1980.

McGeachy, Beth. Handbook of Florida Palms. St. Petersburg: The Great Outdoors Publishing Co., 1960.

MacGillivray, Norman A. Vegetative Water Use in California, 1974. Bulletin No. 113-3. California Department of Water Resources, 1975.

McKell, Cyrus M., James P. Blaisdell, and Joe R. Goodin, ed. Wildland Shrubs—Their Biology and Utilization. General technical report INT-1. Intermountain Forest and Range Experiment Station, Forest Service, United States Department of Agriculture, August 1972.

McMinn, Howard E. An Illustrated Manual of California Shrubs. Berkeley: University of California Press, 1974.

McPherson, E. Gregory, ed. Energy-Conserving Site Design. Washington, D.C.: American Society of Landscape Architects, 1984.

Mattoni, Rudi. "Butterflies of Greater Los Angeles." Beverly Hills: the Center for the Conservation of Biodiversity/Lepidoptera Research Foundation, 1990.

Merilees, Bill. Attracting Backyard Wildlife: A Guide for Nature Lovers. Stillwater, Minneapolis: Voyageur Press, 1989.

Metcalf, L. J. The Cultivation of New Zealand Trees and Shrubs. Auckland: Reed Methuen Publishers, 1987.

Meyer, J. L., Janet Hartin, Donald Peck, and Ralph Strohman. Water Use of Landscape Trees in the South Coast Interior Valley of California. Metropolitan Water District Project 1602, 1989.

Mills, G. Scott, John B. Dunning, Jr., and John M. Bates. "Effects of Urbanization on Breeding Bird Community Structure in Southwestern Desert Habitats." The Condor 91 (1989): 416-428.

Mitchell, Alan. The Complete Guide to Trees of Britain and Northern Europe. Limpsfield: Dragon's World, 1985.

Mirov, Nicholas T., and Jean Hasbrouck. The Story of Pines. Bloomington: Indiana University Press, 1976.

Molyneux, Bill, Sue Forrester, Wendy Gammon, Roger Stone, and Alice Talbot. The Austraflora Handbook. Montrose, Victoria, Australia: Austraflora Nurseries, 1984.

Mozingo, Hugh. Shrubs of the Great Basin. Reno: University of Nevada Press, 1987.

Munz, Philip A. A Flora of Southern California. Berkeley: University of California Press, 1974.

National Oceanic and Atmospheric Administration. Arizona. Climatography of the United States No. 20. U.S. Department of Commerce, 1985.

_____. California. Climatography of the United States No. 20. U.S. Department of Commerce, 1985.

_____. Nevada. Climatography of the United States No. 20. U.S. Department of Commerce, 1985.

Nicholson, Nan, and Hugh Nicholson. Australian Rainforest Plants. Australia: Terania Rainforest Nursery, 1985.

Niering, William, ed. Restoration Ecology. (published quarterly) Cambridge, Massachusetts: Blackwell Scientific Publications, Inc.

Numata, M., ed. The Flora and Vegetation of Japan. Amsterdam: Elsevier Scientific Publishing Company, 1974.

Pacific Gas and Electric Company. Generalized Plant Climate Map of California. San Francisco: Pacific Gas and Electric Company, 1989.

Pacific Horticulture. Journal of the Pacific Horticultural Foundation. San Francisco: Pacific Horticultural Foundation.

Palgrave, Keith Coates. Trees of Southern Africa. Cape Town: Struik Publishers, 1988.

Pavlik, Bruce M., Pamela C. Muick, Sharon Johnson, Marjorie Popper. Oaks of California. Olivos, CA: Cachuma Press and the California Oak Foundation, 1991.

Perry, Bob. Trees and Shrubs for Dry California Landscapes. Claremont, California: Land Design Publishing, 1989.

Phillips, Roger, and Martyn Rix. Shrubs. New York: Random House, 1989.

Phillips, Judith. Southwestern Landscaping with Native Plants. Santa Fe, New Mexico: Museum of New Mexico Press, 1987.

Plumb, Timothy R., technical coordinator. Proceedings of the Symposium on the Ecology, Management, and Utilization of California Oaks. General Technical Report psw-44. Berkeley: Pacific Southwest Forest and Range Experiment Station, U.S. Department of Agriculture, Forest Service, 1979.

Polunin, Oleg. Flowers of Europe. London: Oxford University Press, 1969.

_____. Flowers of Greece and the Balkans. Oxford: Oxford University Press, 1987.

Polunin, Oleg, and Adam Stainton. Flowers of the Himalayas. Delhi: Oxford University Press, 1985.

Raven, Peter H., and Daniel L. Axelrod. Origin and Relationships of the California Flora. Berkeley: University of California Press, 1978.

Rosenthal, Murray, ed. Symposium On Living With the Chaparral. San Francisco: Sierra Club, 1974.

Salmon, J. T. The Native Trees of New Zealand. Auckland: Reed Methuen Publishers, 1980.

Sampson, Arthur W., and Beryl S. Jespersen. California Range Brushlands and Browse Plants. Publication no. 4010. University of California, Division of Agricultural Sciences, California Agricultural Experiment Station Extension Service, 1981.

Saratoga Horticultural Foundation. Success List of Water Conserving Plants. Saratoga, California: Saratoga Horticultural Foundation, 1983.

Schmidt, Marjorie G. Growing California Native Plants. Berkeley: University of California Press, 1980.

Schopmeyer, C. S., ed. Seeds of Woody Plants in the United States. Agriculture Handbook No. 450. Washington, D.C.: United States Department of Agriculture, Division of Timber Management Research, Forest Service, 1974.

Scientific American, Inc. The Biosphere. San Francisco, California: W. H. Freeman and Company, 1970.

Shantz, H. L. Water Economy of Plants. Leaflets of the Santa Barbara Botanic Garden, vol. 1, no. 6. Santa Barbara: Santa Barbara Botanic Garden, 1948.

Snyder, Richard L., Brenda J. Lanini, David A. Shaw, and William O. Pruitt. Using Reference Evapotranspiration (ETo) and Crop Coefficients to Estimate Crop Evapotranspiration (ETc) for Agronomic Crops, Grasses, and Vegetable Crops. Leaflet 21427. Cooperative Extension. University of California. Division of Agriculture and Natural Resources.

_____. Using Reference Evapotranspiration (ETo) and Crop Coefficients to Estimate Crop Evapotranspiration (ETc) for Tree and Vines. Leaflet 21428. Cooperative Extension. University of California. Division of Agriculture and Natural Resources.

Soil Conservation Society of America. Landscaping with Native Arizona Plants. Tucson, Arizona: The University of Arizona Press. 1973.

Soule, Michael E. "Land Use Planning and Wildlife Maintenance: Guidelines for Conserving Wildlife in an Urban Landscape." Journal of the American Planning Association 57 (Summer 1991): 313.

Stark, N. Review of Highway Planting Information Appropriate to Nevada. College of Agriculture No. B-7. Desert Research Institute. University of Nevada.

Stechman, John V. Common Western Range Plants. San Luis Obispo, California: Vocational Educational Productions, California Polytechnic State University, 1971.

Storie, R. Earl, and Walter W. Wier. Generalized Soil Map of California. Agricultural Experiment Station and Extension Service, Division of Agricultural Sciences, University of California, 1973.

Sutton, Ann, and Myron Sutton. Eastern Forests. New York: Alfred A. Knopf, 1987.

Thompson, H. Stuart. Flowering Plants of the Riviera. London: Longmans, Green and Co., 1914.

The Times Atlas of the World. London: Times Books Limited, 1988.

Tree of Life Nursery. Plants of el Camino Real: Catalog and Planting Guide, 1990-91. San Juan Capistrano, California, 1990.

University of California. Average Daily Air Temperatures and Precipitation in California. Special Publication 3285. Cooperative Extension. Division of Agricultural Sciences, 1983.

Van Zyl, Shelly, ed. Wild Flowers, South Africa in Colour. Cape Town: Centaur Ltd., 1984.

Vines, Robert A. Trees, Shrubs, and Woody Vines of the Southwest. Austin: University of Texas Press, 1986.

Walter, Heinrich. Vegetation of the Earth and Ecological Systems of the Geo-biosphere. Berlin: Springer-Verlag, 1985.

Walter, H., E. Harnickell, and D. Mueller-Dombois. "Climate-Diagram Maps of the Individual Continents and the Ecological Climate Regions of the Earth." New York: Springer-Verlag, 1975.

Wiggins, Ira L. Flora of Baja California. Stanford: Stanford University Press, 1980.

Williams, Keith A. W. Native Plants: Queensland. North Ipswich, Australia: Keith A. W. Williams, 1984.

Wrigley, John W., and Murray Fagg. Australian Native Plants. Sydney: William Collins Publishers, 1980.

Xerces Society. Butterfly Gardening. San Francisco: Sierra Club Books, 1990.

Index